ALSO BY DAVID YAFFE

Fascinating Rhythm: Reading Jazz in American Writing

Bob Dylan: Like a Complete Unknown

RECKLESS DAUGHTER

RECKLESS DAUGHTER

A PORTRAIT OF
JONI MITCHELL

DAVID YAFFE

HARPERCOLLINS PUBLISHERS LTD

Published by HarperCollins Publishers Ltd,
by arrangement with Farrar, Straus and Giroux, LLC.

First Canadian edition

HarperCollins books may be purchased for educational, business,
or sales promotional use through our Special Markets Department.

HarperCollins Publishers Ltd
2 Bloor Street East, 20th Floor
Toronto, Ontario, Canada
M4W 1A8

www.harpercollins.ca

Designed by Abby Kagan

Library and Archives Canada Cataloguing in Publication
information is available upon request.

ISBN 978-1-44344-481-1

Printed and bound in the United States
LSC/H 9 8 7 6 5 4 3 2 1

For my parents,
Martin and Connie Yaffe

CONTENTS

PREFACE: NOTHING LASTS FOR LONG   xi

1 ALL THINGS CONSIDERED, I'D RATHER BE DANCING   3

2 LET THE WIND CARRY ME: LESSONS IN WOMANHOOD   19

3 WILL YOU STILL LOVE ME TOMORROW?   28

4 A COMMON MODERN-DAY FAIRY TALE   34

5 DON'T GIVE YOURSELF AWAY   44

6 THE WORD MAN: LEONARD COHEN   52

7 EXPERIENCED   64

8 *CLOUDS*   86

9 OUR HOUSE   102

10 *LADIES OF THE CANYON*   114

11 SAND   122

12 *BLUE*   127

13 ▪ BETWEEN BREAKDOWN AND BREAKTHROUGH 140

14 ▪ THE SUNSHINE COAST 150

15 ▪ *FOR THE ROSES* 156

16 ▪ STAR-CROSSED 165

17 ▪ *COURT AND SPARK*: SOMETHING STRANGE HAPPENED 171

18 ▪ *MILES OF AISLES* 190

19 ▪ THE QUEEN OF QUEENS 194

20 ▪ *HEJIRA* AND THE ART OF LOSING 218

21 ▪ CRAZY WISDOM 225

22 ▪ MIRRORED BALL 243

23 ▪ *DON JUAN'S RECKLESS DAUGHTER* 253

24 ▪ *MINGUS* 261

25 ▪ NERVY BROAD 279

26 ▪ *WILD THINGS RUN FAST* 290

27 ▪ *DOG EAT DOG* 307

28 ▪ EMERGENCY ROOMS 318

29 ▪ SAVE THE BOMBS FOR LATER 321

30 ▪ TURBULENCE 336

31 ▪ SEE YOU AT THE MOVIES 348

32 ■ CURTAIN CALL   368

33 ■ JUST LIKE THIS TRAIN   374

Notes   377

Acknowledgments   393

Index   397

PREFACE: NOTHING LASTS FOR LONG

When I was fifteen, I had a high school girlfriend who was a couple of years older than me—dog years in those days. She had a piano and a stereo in her room, and very tolerant parents. We were both music students at an arts high school in Dallas; she sang, I played piano. We had a ritual of lying on her bed together in pitch-darkness, taking in what we were hearing with everything we had—the Velvet Underground, Miles Davis . . . One day, she played me Joni Mitchell's *Blue*. Years later Joni would tell me that when she made that album she was totally without defenses, as vulnerable as "a cellophane wrapper on a packet of cigarettes," as she once put it. When one is fifteen, everything is new and raw. I was falling in love with a girl and falling in love with this music. Neither came to you. You had to come to them. I held on tight in those tender, cellophane years.

In time, I would learn that while Joni was famous for being tender in public she also had to be tough in private. By the time *Blue* was released in 1971, she had survived polio and a bad first marriage, and recently fended off a marriage proposal from Graham Nash, whom she had loved. I didn't know about these things yet. But my need to know about this woman I heard on the record eventually brought me closer and closer.

Over the years, I would turn to Joni's music, sometimes when I needed to hear her tell me, as she does in "Trouble Child," that I really am inconsolably on my own: "So what are you going to do about it / You can't live life and you can't leave it." Ouch. And yet, in that voice, in those chords, there was nevertheless an implicit promise that life would go on, and would be full of surprises. And in her music, as again and again she sought someone who could understand her, who could offer a counterbalance to her ramblings and yearnings, she would tell us not to listen for her but to listen for ourselves. She wanted us to have some sort of transference. It was not a delusion to listen for yourself. It was an injunction.

That said, Joni's songs taunt listeners into biographical readings, and they also invite us to understand the mind creating them. That's what I wanted to understand, that's what I hoped to find out when I first met Joni Mitchell, in January 2007. She had just finished recording her first album of new songs in ten years, *Shine*, and the Alberta Ballet was in rehearsal with *The Fiddle and the Drum*, a collaboration between Joni and the choreographer Jean Grand-Maître. I had come to Los Angeles to interview her for *The New York Times*.

It was five p.m. at La Scala Presto, an Italian trattoria in Brentwood. Joni had picked the restaurant because it was among the local restaurants willing to incur fines just for the pleasure of having Joni Mitchell dine and smoke there. As urban centers all over America were banning smoking in public places, life for Joni Mitchell was still a noir film from the '40s, full of nicotine and screwball repartee. She kept smoking in public as long as she could, until she was eventually reduced to e-cigarettes.

I stood at the bar at the restaurant waiting for her, clenching my glass so tightly it broke into little pieces. That's when they figured out I was the one meeting Joni and told me to relax: she was really nice.

Really. I asked where she liked to sit. The outdoor table with the ash-tray, of course. It was unseasonably chilly for LA and I asked them to turn on the heating lamp. I took the seat she didn't prefer. I had brought a collection of Nietzsche's *Birth of Tragedy* and *Nietzsche Contra Wagner*, books I knew had inspired Joni's lyrics and weltanschauung, along with Kipling's "If," which I knew she had set to music. I looked to the final stanza, which I later learned Joni did not include in her adaptation, as a mantra to give me strength:

> *If you can fill the unforgiving minute*
> *With sixty seconds' worth of distance run,*
> *Yours is the Earth and everything that's in it,*
> *And—which is more—you'll be a Man, my son!*

I didn't want the earth or everything in it, and I didn't think Joni would want me to be the kind of man Kipling was telling me to be, but I thought, if this poem was important to Joni, then I would figure out why.

A half hour late, perfectly on time, a hand studded with more jew-elry than I could fully take in reached out to me. "I'm Joni," she said. "I know," I replied. *Be cool, just listen, and breathe. And listen some more.*

None of the wines at La Scala Presto pleased her. She tasted each one. None was smooth enough to suit. Much more to her liking was a 1998 Chateau Margaux she pulled out of a case, later, at home.

She was giddy about the album, and ready to unleash what she calls a verbal "cauldron." We talked about Miles Davis—about how she was introduced to him by Joni's drummer boyfriend Don Alias, who had played on *Bitches Brew*, and about how Miles once made a play for her, then passed out with a deathlike grasp on her ankles. She had always dreamed of collaborating with him, she said, and it was re-ported to her that he owned all her albums that had been released up to his death. She loved Duke Ellington; disliked Coltrane, but she so loved *Kind of Blue* that she even liked Coltrane on it. And Debussy, which she pronounced "De-Boosie." When she heard *La Mer*, she saw the sea.

Of course we talked about the ballet, and the new songs, which no civilian had heard yet. We talked about environmental apocalypse, about the Indian chiefs with their old beliefs, about the stupidity of Western medicine. "I'm mad at Socrates," she said at one point. We talked about our shared love of the films of the Serbian director Emir Kusturica; about how she missed the conversations in New York City; about how she loved Dylan's "Positively 4th Street" and "Mr. Tambourine Man," and *Blood on the Tracks* (the New York sessions, not the Minnesota), but that she thought *Desire* was just okay and that *Modern Times*, which had just been released and had hit number one, was a work of "plagiarism." "You can't rule Bob out, though," she said. "He and Leonard are the best pace runners I've got." Then she slammed Cohen's line from "Master Song," "Your thighs are ruined," as cruel to an older woman, and declared that even though he walked the walk and had become an ordained Buddhist monk, he was a "phony Buddhist."

And yet, as hostile as some of this might look in print, it was all delivered with a joie de vivre. She loved to be provocative. She loved to be what she called a "pot stirrer." She was trouble—and she was really good at it.

We closed the place down. The caravan continued to her house. There was a talking security system at the gate. I looked at her stack of books and noticed Simon Schama's *Rembrandt's Eyes*. Of course, I thought. She's the great Renaissance portrait artist in song. They go for every nuance, the chiaroscuro of human emotion, the overtones beneath the chords, the resonance of existence.

She was sleeping by day, chain-smoking and creating by night. It seemed like we could have talked forever (and by talking, I mean she did the talking and I did the listening). Even though she is known for her introspective brooding—comparing herself with Job in "The Sire of Sorrow," and singing lines like "Acid, booze, and ass / Needles, guns, and grass / Lots of laughs"—she actually *does* like to have lots of laughs. A devastating mimic and raconteur, she can serve up Dorothy Parker–like zingers with terrifying speed.

After twelve hours of Joni, up all night, my sense of reality had been permanently altered. On the flight home, I wanted to somehow keep the experience going, and I started listening to *Hejira*. The voice I heard was different. In the 1976 recording, I could hear her Saskatchewan cadences, her joys and her sorrows and everything in between.

During the week that followed, our conversation continued on the phone. And then my piece about her was published, and there were things about it that felt to her like an invasion, a betrayal.

I got bitched out by Joni Mitchell! She was a maestro, hurling one indignity at me after another. She loathed the picture the *Times* had chosen, and there was one phrase in particular that made her gorge rise: "middle-class." That was the adjective I had used to describe her home. It struck a chord—and not a chromatic one—through the heart of the author of "The Boho Dance," the art school dropout for whom there could be nothing worse than to be bourgeois.

"I don't know what *you* think of as middle-class, but I live in a mansion, my property has many rooms, I have Renaissance antiques."

"I meant that your home, at least what I saw of it, wasn't intimidating. It was inviting. It was earthy."

"Yes, that's true. You were in the earthy section of my property."

"Yes, earthy. I should have said *earthy*. If I could substitute the word now I would."

She was so disappointed in me. She had thought I was different, somehow better than the others. Now I was the *worst*.

Years passed. One night, I had a delightful time out with a friend of hers, a sculptor who inspired her song "Good Friends" from *Dog Eat Dog*. Without any prompting from me, he called Joni and told her she had to go back to talking to me, and she did.

I flew to LA to see her. Even under the fluorescent kitchen light, she looked more beautiful than she did in the ads for Yves Saint Laurent that were in all the magazines. She looked strong, resilient, defiant, head held high. Ready for battle.

"You have no attention span," she snapped.

"I've been sitting here for twelve hours," I said. "In what universe does that mean that I have no attention span?"

I got an idea of what that universe was. I had questions prepared about her music, about art, and we did talk about those things, but she would invariably shift to her emotions, her body, her desires, the desires of men, the impossibility of relationships. At one point, during a wrenching description of a miscarriage, she stopped.

"Why are we talking about this?"

"I don't know," I said. "I was prepared to talk about the music." But talking about the music meant talking about everything, because Joni Mitchell's songs go straight to the heart, to the marrow, to the stuff of life. We weren't going to sit there for half a day just talking about open tunings, though we did some of that, too.

And she played for me. She clipped her nails and began strumming a sequence of stunning chords. I recognized it as "Ladies' Man" from *Wild Things Run Fast* (1982), a song inspired by the notorious lothario David Naylor. I asked her why she'd chosen to play me that. "It was the first tuning I found," she said. I got up from the chair and watched her play from various angles. There is a picture from 1968 of Eric Clapton looking at her with similar wonder. His facial expression unmistakably said, "*How* does she do that?" This late in the game, she still had the power to confound. She delivered it once more, to an audience of one. When she was done, I applauded.

A couple of months after our encounter, Joni suffered a brain aneurysm. Joni would need to claw her way back yet again. Nothing lasts for long. All romantics meet the same fate. Albums are like novels or poems except that you can listen to them in the dark. You can always flip the record, put in another CD, reset the iPod. Close your eyes. Joni Mitchell will be there waiting for you.

RECKLESS DAUGHTER

1 ■ ALL THINGS CONSIDERED, I'D RATHER BE DANCING

One more time, she had to explain how she was born, and how the stage would be set for her to be the hero of her own life. The more unlikely, the more heroic. Things conspired—extraordinary things, things no one back home or anywhere else—could have ever imagined. She said she did not grow up playing air guitar in the mirror. But she painted, she danced, nearly died, came back, danced again, and began to unfold.

Roberta Joan Anderson was born on November 7, 1943, in Fort Macleod, Alberta. Her mother had been a teacher and her father was a military man who later became a grocery store executive. The world would come to know her as Joni Mitchell, winner of eight Grammy Awards (including one in 2002 for Lifetime Achievement), inductee into the Rock and Roll and Canadian Songwriters Halls of Fame. She wrote a song—"Woodstock"—that named a generation, and routinely makes critics' top ten lists of the greatest singer-songwriters of the twentieth century. "Big Yellow Taxi" and "Help Me" still play on classic rock radio every day, high school students still quote "The Circle Game" in yearbooks, and recordings of *Blue* are downloaded, Spotified, Pandora'd, and snapped up with mocha lattes at Starbucks around the world. "They paved paradise and put up a parking lot" has become so familiar it's almost a cliché. In 2017, "Free Man in Paris" played, in its entirety, on the HBO series *Girls*, and "Both Sides, Now" was sung at the Oscars in 2016, in tribute to a year in which the world lost a stunning array of creative luminaries ranging from Prince (who loved Joni) and Leonard Cohen (who was Joni's lover), to David Bowie, Gene Wilder, Mary Tyler Moore, and Carrie Fisher. In the contemporary imagination, Joni Mitchell is more than a 1970s icon or pop star. She is our eternal singer-songwriter of sorrows, traveling through our highs and lows, the twentieth-century master of the art song tradition that stretches to Franz Schubert. Joni is as introspective and eloquent as Bob Dylan or Leonard Cohen, but she went beyond them in melody and harmony, exploring chords only jazz virtuosi could play to her satisfaction. She has stopped performing, but her records keep playing, documents of beauty and imperfection. As long as people can listen to music, her story will be told in her voice, her weird chords, her inimitable way.

In her songs, big stories become gloriously condensed. And the story that began all the others—the story of her mother's life and marriage, and of her own birth—are all told, briefly, beautifully, and powerfully in an astonishing song, "The Tea Leaf Prophecy."

"It's a lot of history in a small space, shorthanded," Joni told me. "My mother, Myrtle McKee, had been a country schoolteacher and she came into the city. She was working in a bank next to the police station, and the windows of the cop shop looked down into the tellers' area, and they were always flirting from the windows. But the tellers found Mounties and cops distasteful. She and her girlfriend went to the fancy hotel, and they had a tea leaf reader, a palmist also. They wore white gloves and hats and it was very la-di-da, because it was the tail end of the Canadian Anglophile era. So it was a kind of poshy thing to do. And when he read her tea leaves, he told her three things: you'll be married in a month, you'll have a child within a year, and you'll live to an old age and die a long and agonizing death, which is a terrible thing, even if you see it, to say."

When Joni first recorded the song for her 1988 album, *Chalk Mark in a Rainstorm*, she used a pseudonym for her mother: Myrtle McKee became "Molly McGee." First she tells the story of her mother's visit with the tea leaf reader:

> *Newsreels rattle the Nazi dread*
> *The able-bodied have shipped away*
> *Molly McGee gets her tea leaves read*
> *You'll be married in a month they say*

"These leaves are crazy," says Molly McGee. It's a joke. Consulting the leaves isn't crazy; they're just not making sense. And Joni's musical mind emerges here figuratively. There are no men, just boys "talking to teacher in the treble clef." The next verse is a beautiful, lyrical telling of her parents' unlikely wartime romance. The man in this love story is, like Bill Anderson, a sergeant on a two-week leave. They meet and their fate is sealed. Joni imagines her young parents making love—a topic that would be awkward for most—with tenderness:

> *Oh these nights are strong and soft*
> *Private passions and secret storms*
> *Nothin' about him ticks her off*
> *And he looks so cute in his uniform*

This romance is immediately followed with the locked-in domesticity of long hard winters in the Canadian prairies that is her mother's life. There are endless chores, and the cycles are relentless, banal, with endless drudgery. And even her stated intention to flee becomes monotonous, too:

> *She says "I'm leavin' here" but she don't go*

The story of Joni's parents is one she attempted to unravel throughout her lifetime and in her music. Why had the stars aligned for Myrtle McKee, who had taught in a one-room school and was clerking at a bank in Regina, and William Anderson, on leave from the Royal Canadian Air Force? Anderson's family hailed from Scandinavia. When a grown-up Joni asked him why his name didn't have the usual Swedish spelling of "Andersen," he said the name was changed at Ellis Island from "Amberson." Joni suspected from her high cheekbones that she had Laplander blood. She also wondered if her father's family was hiding a Jewish name.

She came of age in the postwar baby boom, but she was an only child. Her mother's unhappiness with marriage and motherhood is threaded through "The Tea Leaf Prophecy": "She says 'I'm leavin' here' but she don't go." There is also, in the song, Myrtle's advice to her only daughter:

> *"Hiroshima cannot be pardoned!*
> *Don't have kids when you get grown."*

It was a line from real life that Joni found baffling. "She used to say it to me all the time: 'Don't have kids when you get grown.' I was an only child and I found it insulting. She meant that I was a pain in the ass. I was in conflict with her. She was a bigot, she was very cautious and conservative and wouldn't take any chances, no displays of emotionality or anything."

Joni sized up her parents and found them wanting. As a toddler, she had a recurring dream, more like a nightmare, of being in the car with her parents and her father losing control of the car. "I would wake up with the most horrible emotion," she told me. "And I would have never been able to figure that dream out, and I can usually interpret my own dreams easily, because I'm in touch with my own symbolism. This was a real incident that stored like film. I thought, 'Okay.' My dream was a stored photograph of what preceded his irrationality. The road ahead was flooded after we came on a bright, sunny day. The slough was overflowed, and you could see there was water lying across the road. We were in danger. And as an infant, I could see: What is he acting like that for? Turn the fuckin' car around. And I sucked my thumb and gave myself an overbite. My parents—their judgment was so sucky all the time. These people are not thinking and I'm small and in their care. Help! So I had to be my own person very young."

Many years later, she and her friend Tony Simon were with her father, talking about dreams; her father usually had an uncanny ability to interpret them. Joni, who was still unable to understand the dream, brought it up. Her father hung his head in shame.

"Well, that really happened," he said. "I behaved irrationally."

For Joni, it was a powerful affirmation of her childhood suspicion that she was being raised by adults who were not up to the task. She would veer back and forth between feeling contempt for them and the deep desire to protect them. "So, I was two and a half years old and I discovered that my parents were nuts—that they had really bad judgment. But that they were acting like they were in danger. After that incident, I perceived him as vulnerable, and I was kind of his champion. Because in school, people would say, 'If you talk about your dad one more time, I'm going to punch you.'"

She had similar memories of her mother's own shortcomings. Sharon Bell (who is now Sharon Veer) remembered, "Joni and I were hanging out at her house, and Myrt went to get groceries. She was buying liver for supper because Joni liked liver, which I could never understand at that age. Myrt went down to the basement, she tripped, she fell, and this liver splattered out and Myrt fell on the floor. We were all standing there looking down the stairs at her. [Our friend] Marilyn said, 'Is she dead?' And Joni said, 'I don't know, but I don't think we're having liver for supper.' For whatever reason, Joni thought that was just hilarious, and I bet she told that same story every time I saw her."

The near accident and Joni's traumatic recurring nightmares about it confirmed her feeling that her childhood was an ongoing car crash. She was alone in a house with her simple and conservative parents, in a countryside whose beauty she embraced and whose provincialism she abhorred. Nobody else could tell Joni how it felt when her parents' slights and shortcomings made impacts. No one knew how many times she felt the vehicle of family life flip and turn and crash.

Joni felt her parents lacked vision—figuratively and literally. As soon as Joni could identify her colors, she already had an advantage over Bill and Myrtle Anderson. "My parents are both color-blind and I'm color acute," Joni recalled. "I don't know how they got through traffic. My father wanted to fly and they grounded him, which broke his heart. But he wouldn't be able to see the color of the landing lights. They never tried to paint or anything. You could paint color-blind, but you'd be making green skies and blue water, which is okay. They'd think you were being very modern, daring."

Joni's mother was a housewife, and her father was the merchandising coordinator for Shelly Bros., owners of the OK Economy grocery chain. They led a modest life and never wanted to attract too much attention. And then they had Joni. In the words of Philip Roth: There is a God, and his name is Aristophanes.

"I knew her parents very well," said Tony Simon, her friend from Nutana Collegiate High School and the Y dances in Saskatoon. "They were friends with my parents. They were not friends with a lot of people. My parents were very social. The Andersons weren't. They were very nice. They didn't energetically mix with a lot of people, but they were always very receptive to anybody that Joni brought over. They paid attention. Her father especially, if you met him at any age from sixty-five up, you'd think, what a laid-back nice guy. But what you'd be missing was that he was an intensely competitive guy. Not many people have shot their age in golf. He has. He was a championship tennis player, and I think some of Joni's competitiveness came from that. He was quietly competitive. Saskatchewan during the war and right after was not a very competitive place. Being a grocery store owner in those days was a pretty prestigious job. They didn't have [a lot of] money, but in those days, people were careful with resources. Living was pretty goddamn good for Joni compared to what's going on today. Did she have to scrape along? Not really."

Growing up in the years after World War II made an impression on Joni. They made her a rebel, with a strain of Rosie the Riveter in her DNA. At the same time, she was a young woman of the 1950s; she came of age in the *Mad Men* era when happiness seemed just a purchase away. "There were only two stores in town," Joni explained. "My dad ran the grocery store and Marilyn McGee's dad ran the general store. She and I called the Simpsons-Sears catalogue 'The Book of Dreams.' It was so glamorous when I was a child . . . We'd be down on our bellies looking at every page, and she and I would . . . pick out our favorite matron's girdle and our favorite saw and our favorite hammer. 'I like that one best.' Every page, 'That's my favorite.' So in that way you learned to shop before you have money, you learn the addiction of the process of selection." The love of shopping stayed with Joni. So much so that even today, she says, "You could take me anywhere on any budget level and I'll go into 'That's a good thing for that much money. That's a beautiful thing.'"

She always loved music. "*The Hit Parade* was one hour a day—four o'clock to five o'clock," she recalled. "On the weekends they'd do the Top Twenty. But the rest of the radio was Mantovani, country and western, a lot of radio journalism. Mostly country and western, which I wasn't crazy about. To me it was simplistic. Even as a child I liked more complex melody. In my teens I loved to dance. That was my thing. I instigated a Wednesday night dance 'cause I could hardly make it to the weekends. For dancing, I loved Chuck Berry. Ray Charles. 'What'd I Say.' I liked Elvis Presley. I liked the Everly Brothers."

She called herself a "good-time Charlie" and her school friends still confirm it. The laughter at the end of "Big Yellow Taxi" was as familiar to them as a telephone call from an old friend. "I was anti-intellectual to the nth," she explained. "Basically, I liked to dance and paint and that was about it. As far as serious discussions went, at that time most of them were overtly pseudo-intellectual and boring. Like, to see teenagers sitting around solving the problems of the world, I thought, 'All things considered, I'd rather be dancing.'"

She was anti-intellectual, in part, because she had little faith or interest in rote learning. As a little girl she attended Parish Hall, which was associated with the Anglican Church. Canadian culture was deeply shaped by the English influence, and in the 1940s and '50s when Joni was growing up, nearly half of all the immigrants were British. Joni remembered, "Because of the Baby Boom population, I was there. It was grade three. We were marked and given grades. And this old lady that was brought out of retirement to teach this class was cheerful and well-meaning, but old-fashioned in her teaching methods. She examined us and broke down all the rows. She put the A students in one row and called them Bluebirds. She took the B students in a row and called them Robins. All the C students in a row and called them Wrens. Then the flunkies were lined up and she called them Crows. I looked at the A students with their hands clasped on the desks, looking like they'd won something important, and there wasn't a person in that line that I thought was smart. They were all looking so proud, and I remembered looking at them and thinking, 'All you did was she said something and you said it back.' So I broke with the school system at that moment and I had this thought, 'I'm not even gonna try from here on, until they ask a question that nobody knows the answer to.'"

This push and pull between not giving in to what she felt strongly were inferior metrics of success and the desire for other people to know and acknowledge her gifts would play out throughout Joni's career. She would later say, "I don't know how to sell out. If I tried to sell out I don't think I could. By that I mean, to make an attempt to make a commercial record. I just make them and I think, 'If I was a kid I would like this song' . . . You have to have a certain grab-ability initially and then something that wears well . . . for years to come. That's what anything fine is. It's recognized in painting [but] I'm just working in a toss-away industry. I'm a fine artist working in a commercial arena, so that's my cross to bear."

Just *how* she would bear the cross of being different was something that Joni wrestled with from her earliest days. She took solace in what she could. For example, when she began to explore astrology, she found what she considered a good reason for her interest in difficult questions. "I got into the zodiac and found out I'm born on Marie Curie's birthday [November 7], the day of the discoverer, the week of depth. So it's the deepest week in the year and I have an ability to discover. I have a scientific ability, really not just an artistic ability. The stars give me a scientific ability, too."

Just as she wasn't going to parrot back answers to a teacher, she had no interest in taking the Bible for gospel. "I broke with the church because I asked questions they found embarrassing," she told me. Then she proceeded to tell about the day she raised hell in her Sunday school class with all of her questioning.

"Adam and Eve were the first man and woman, right?"

"Right," said the teacher.

"They had two sons, right?"

"Right, Cain and Abel."

"And Cain killed Abel and then Cain got married. Who did he marry? Eve?"

The teacher "just went sour in the face from that," Joni recalled. "I only knew that there was only one woman. And then he got married. He had to marry the only woman. That shorted out my Sunday school teacher, so I didn't go back there. She made me feel so shabby that I just refused to go back."

She had so much courage and yet there's that telltale Joni vulnerability, too—she'd called the teacher out, but what she remembered was that in return the teacher made her feel *shabby*. It was a pattern that would be repeated with friends and lovers, music industry execs and a fickle fan base. Joni could roar, but many people had no idea how easily she could be wounded, how she would see and feel daggers that other people didn't even know they had thrown.

She had determined that she had the soul of a scientist and the heart of an artist; she was always trying to wrap her mind around what could be called the truth. She remembers telling her mother, "I like stories, but there's pages ripped out of them." Meaning, the stories seem somehow incomplete. Decades later, Joni stood by her younger self and that girl's view of the world. "That was a really good call," Joni told me. "Because there were literally pages ripped out of the Bible. At that point, you couldn't ridicule me or dunce cap me or anything to make me try. I drew clothes. I was going to be a fashion designer. I drew cartoons, I wrote funny things. I lived in my own world."

Joni wasn't the only girl growing up in the provinces of Canada rejecting the world around her and creating her own. When Margaret Atwood paid tribute to Joni Mitchell at the Canadian Songwriters Hall of Fame in 2007, she spoke about their parallel childhoods. "Don't worry, I'm not going to sing," Atwood quipped. Then she went on to say, "Joni Mitchell and I have some things in common. Though I'm older and she's blonder. For instance, we were both members of the Canadian Lunatic Generation. That was in the early sixties back when Canada was a blank spot on the map of global culture. If you said, 'Say, I'm a novelist.' Or you said, 'Hi, I'm Joni Mitchell and I'm going to be a world-famous singer-songwriter!' Other people said, 'You're a lunatic.'" Atwood added that you should "multiply that by ten for being from the prairies. But Joni did it anyway. And aren't we all glad that she did?"

Joni laughed hard at the lunatic joke, but you could also see in the way that she held Atwood in a loving, knowing gaze that she ached for her younger, isolated self. It would have made a world of difference if she had known that she wasn't really a lunatic when she picked up her first ukulele and wouldn't let it go although her friends begged her to stop. It would have been nice to know that she wasn't merely loony, but rather a high-flying loon, part of a far-flung flock that included brave, imaginative women like Margaret Atwood.

Joni did not know Margaret Atwood, but she found a kindred spirit in a girl named Sharon Bell, whom she met when her family moved to Maidstone, in 1946. The girls lived close to each other up until the age of five, then Joni's family moved again, to North Battleford. But Sharon came to North Battleford every year for musical competitions that lasted for ten whole days. Joni remembered, "You could go to the church and listen to choirs compete or you could go to school. I went to the church." She didn't consider herself a musician in those days. She hadn't yet picked up an instrument. Art was the gift she'd identified in herself.

"I could draw the best doghouse," she said. "We had to use perspective. Everyone else's was too skinny or cockeyed. They had their perspective warped. Mine was a good, solid little doghouse with a U-shaped door. It showed a cognizance of perspective, and a steady hand. So that moment, I did something well. I did it the best. So I said, 'I'm an artist.'" But her teachers (for the most part) solidly refused to give Joni her due. One sixth-grade teacher carped on her report card, "Joan should pay attention to other subjects than art."

Joni attended the musical competitions—but just as an audience member and as a supportive friend. But as was her style, she was interested in how excellence was construed in the competition. She had three friends who competed regularly. "Sharon was one, and Peter Armstrong—he went into an Italian opera company. And Frankie McKitrick—he was a precocious piano player. Frankie and Peter were my best friends in North Battleford. Sharon would come to town, and I'd go and watch them in competition and I'd see what the adjudicator was going to say—what was bad about it and what was good about it. I'd sit out there, listen closely, and the game was to see if I could figure out what the adjudicator was going to say. And a lot of the time we were on the same page, but a lot of the time she didn't pick up on things that I would pick up on, that I thought were flaws in the performance. So it was a kind of vicarious musical education."

Frankie, in particular, was a great influence on Joni's early consumption of music, and "He and I went to some pretty far-out movies together. My mother was horrified that the principal, his father, let us play hooky to go and see them." Among them was a movie called *The Story of Three Loves*, starring Kirk Douglas and James Mason, and its theme song was a "gorgeous nocturnal melody," which so moved Joni, she told me, that it made her "want to be a musician." It was Rachmaninoff's "Rhapsody on a Theme of Paganini." "The ballet in it looks dumb to me now, but I loved it as a child. It's so flitty.

"And that piece of music thrilled me to no end. It was the most beautiful piece of music that I ever heard. I had to hear the record of it. I asked my parents to buy it for me, but it wasn't in the budget. It would be seventy-five cents or something. So I would go down to

Grubman's department store, take it out of its brown sleeve, and go in the playback and play it maybe two or three times a week and just swoon."

At the age of eleven, Joni moved to Saskatoon, and there was more to be joyful about when she got to study with Arthur Kratzmann, who was developing quite a reputation at the Queen Elizabeth School. "He was a hero [to me] as a child, and . . . he sparked a lot of things in me. He read us Rudyard Kipling's *Kim*. He entered the room and said, 'This curriculum is a lot of crap. I'm gonna teach you what I know. I don't know much. I know my name. And I'm Australian, so we'll concentrate on Australia for part of the course and then you'll all pass with flying colors, but until then, I'm going to teach you about Australia.' He was kind of a creative character, and he swore, which I loved."

Joni would go on to dedicate *Song to a Seagull*, her first album, to him: "To Mr. Kratzman [*sic*], who taught me to love words." Joni walked into Arthur Kratzmann's class full of confidence, but then would receive Cs on her creative writing assignments. She remembered in particular one poem that she wrote and Kratzmann's reaction: "I wrote this ambitious epic poem for his class, and it went, 'Softly now the colors of the day fade and are replaced by silver grey as God prepares his world for night and high upon a silver-shadowed hill, a stallion white as newly fallen snow stands deathly still, an equine statue bathed in silver light . . .' I got this thing back, and it was circled all over with red. He had written, 'Cliché, cliché, cliché . . .' and gave me a B. I read the poem of the kid next to me who got an A+, and it was terrible, so I stayed after school and said, 'Excuse me, but how do you give an A+ to that when you give me a B?' He said, 'Because that's as good as he's ever going to write. You can write much better than this. You tell me more interesting things when you tell me what you did over the weekend.'"

"'By the way,' he added, 'how many times did you see *Black Beauty*?'"

Joni never forgot the lesson. In the '90s, Joni gave the guitarist Robben Ford some songwriting advice: "When you see a cliché, circle it and replace it with something that isn't a cliché."

Sharolyn Dickson was in that grade-seven class with Joni and Mr. Kratzmann, and she knew how much Joni looked up to him.

"I don't think she ever saw herself as an academic, but in truth, I felt like he brought that out in her, because he got us heavily into creative writing," recalled Dickson. "So when she says he taught her to love words, I really think that's where it came from. When he marked us, he was tougher on her than he was on the others. He marked according to our abilities, and his expectations of her were so high. If she didn't meet that expectation, he didn't mark her as well."

At the time, Joni understood this pedagogical method, but throughout the years, especially as she was fine-tuning her bitterness toward an increasingly large group of people from her past, she began to question whether that had been fair.

"But he would often use her work as an example to teach us," Dickson told me. "He'd put it on the board. We felt like she was a really outstanding writer even then. He was totally unconventional. We had caught wind of his class when we were in sixth grade, and we were all excited to get him. If our parents had known some of the things he was saying, they would have been on his doorstep. He was very outside the norm."

Kratzmann, alluding to Nietzsche, would tell Joni, "You have to learn to paint and to write in your own blood." "She picked up on that," said Kratzmann, "and started to write little things about her life and, of course, now you couldn't believe that Joni Mitchell was ever somebody who wasn't creative."

In Susan Lacy's *American Masters* documentary on Joni from 2003, Joni recalled Kratzmann telling her, "If you can paint with a brush, you can paint with words," which was the guiding principle of her televised concert *Painting with Words and Music*.

Kratzmann, who became the dean of education at the University of Regina and passed away in 2015, recalled Joni as someone at the very start of her creative exploration. "[Joni] wrote well . . . She used to copy a lot of stuff. She'd see a painting of a landscape and she'd duplicate it, and, when we'd be writing poetry, she'd have a tendency to sort of, like, pick Wordsworth's 'Daffodils' and write a poem about tulips but use the same rhyme scheme and style."

Copying was a big part of how Joni taught herself. She needed to write the words, draw the pictures, play the notes herself—or at least try. She saw her first Picassos and Matisses at the home of a classmate whose grandfather was a Canadian industrialist and art collector named Frederick S. Mendel. Mendel would go on to be the chief financial backer of Saskatoon's first major art gallery. Joni loved Picasso. She loved that he was a troublemaker, and admired, she said, "his constant creativity, his restlessness." Her relationship to music would also be personality-based. She loved Duke Ellington and had an intuitive relationship with the alto saxophonist Johnny Hodges. "So flirty," she would say. As a girl, Joan Anderson picked apart paintings, poems, literature, and songs the way some kids took apart toasters.

With the exception of Kratzmann, her classroom experience would be a series of disappointments, but she found a way to be an *engaged* troublemaker. "The way I saw the educational system from an early age was that it taught you what to think, not how to think. There was no liberty, really, for freethinking. You were being trained to fit into a society where freethinking was a nuisance. I liked some of my teachers very much, but I had no interest in their subjects. So I would appease them—I think they perceived that I was not a dummy, although my report card didn't look like it. I would line the math room with ink drawings and portraits of the mathematicians. I did a tree of life for my biology teacher. I was always staying late at the school, down on my knees painting something."

She did not write much poetry in those days, but one poem stands out: "The Fishbowl," written at age sixteen.

> *The fishbowl is a world diverse*
> *where fishermen with hooks that dangle*
> *from the bottom reel up their catch*
> *on gilded bait without a fight.*
> *Pike, pickerel, bass, the common fish*
> *ogle through distorting glass*
> *see only glitter, glamour, gaiety*

and weep for fortune lost.
Envy the goldfish? Why?
His bubbles are breaking 'round the rim
while silly fishes faint for him.

Joni remembers that she wrote the poem about the celebrities in the teen magazines she devoured at the time. "I felt sorry for celebrities with talent when I wrote that poem," she said. "Sandra Dee was breaking up with Bobby Darin and all the magazines had pictures of her with mascara running down her face, all paparazzied out." (Sandra Dee and Bobby Darin actually broke up in 1967, when Joni was twenty-four, but point taken.)

But it is also easy to see the poem as an allegory of how she is comparing and contrasting herself with the kids around her, wondering how far she might go or how stuck she might be in the rural world that surrounded her. Joni remembers that when she wrote the poem, "I never felt like I had any talent. I was a painter, but the musical and writing gift hadn't come in—even though that poem is pretty precocious."

The biggest gift of her Canadian childhood for Joni was the gift of nature: it was, in a way, its own religion and it would give her the truest compass she would ever know. "I lived in the tail end of a horse-drawn culture," Joni remembered. "We still had our water and the milk delivered by horses, and at Christmas a mound of packages would come on an open sleigh." Sharon Bell remembered that, as kids, she and Joni would go out and wander the prairie, with open sky as far as the eye could see. Simple pleasures like squishing mud between your toes—and then the simple scolding of having them washed by Joni's mother, the ever proper Myrtle—were priceless memories later on. "It was a simpler life and simpler times," said Bell. "We all go back to simpler times from time to time, but Joni more than others, because she had become separated from that."

In 1969, when she was just becoming famous, Joni told *The New York Times*, "My poetry is urbanized and Americanized, but my music is influenced by the prairies. When I was a kid, my mother used to take me out to the fields to teach me bird calls. There was a lot of space behind individual sounds. People in the city are so accustomed to hearing a jumble of different sounds that when they come to making music, they fill it up with all sorts of different things."

"I always thought I'd marry a farmer," Joni recalled. "I loved the country. But I don't think I would have been happy as a farmer's wife. It's a hard job and a lot of work. I'm naturally nocturnal, so farmers' hours would have been pretty tricky for me." She was a country girl who loved wide-open spaces, who loved to draw and to dance, but it was the 1950s and Canada was, as Margaret Atwood described it, still "a blank spot on the map of global culture." Joni found it hard to dream beyond a marriage that would let her live the way she wanted to. Was there another way to make a living that allowed you a big country house and a view of fields and prairies as far as your eyes could see? She didn't know, but she aimed to find out.

2 ▪ LET THE WIND CARRY ME: LESSONS IN WOMANHOOD

I n an interview with the CBC (Canadian Broadcasting Corporation), Joni recalled the day she fell ill with polio. "It was the day before I was paralyzed. And I remember what I wore that day. I dressed myself for school that day. I woke up and I went to get dressed, I looked in the mirror and said, 'You look like a woman today.' My face had filled out. Something had happened, or the impending disease . . . You ever see kids with cancer on TV? You see how mature they are? There's something about that, a maturity that happens that prepares you for the battle. I don't know what I saw. My face had changed shape. And there must have been something in my eyes."

It was November 1953. She had just turned ten.

"I walked to school with a chum. The third block before the school, I had to sit down and take a little rest because I was aching. And I said, 'Oh dear, I'm getting old. I must have rheumatism 'cause my grandmother had rheumatism.' The following day I couldn't get out of bed. I was paralyzed. When they diagnosed it they shipped me up to a polio colony, outside St. Paul's Hospital in Saskatoon."

The place was like a leper colony, designed to limit the spread of the harrowing disease.

"[We were in] annexed trailers, and they were kind of terrifying, in that the sound, not so much in the daytime because the halls were full of activity, but at night, the sound of the iron lungs—that wheezing breathing—it was a terrible sound and we all dreaded the possibility that we could end up in one of those cans. If the disease spread into your lungs you'd go into the iron lung because you'd have to have mechanical aid. And if you got into the iron lung, chances are you'd never get out. And there was a possibility that I would never walk. I was frozen and many of the muscles in my back were lost. As a result my spine was crooked, and arched up like a broken doll."

It was a powerful image for a young girl who felt alone in a home with a military father and a mother who longed to escape: she was a life-size, broken doll.

"Christmas was nearing and I said to the doctors, 'I want to go home for Christmas' . . . They hung their heads as if it wasn't really a possibility."

Jonas Salk's polio vaccine would not reach Canada until 1955. Joni and Neil Young are among the survivors of the 1953 epidemic.

"I remember visiting Joni in the ward when Joni had to lie flat on her back and couldn't move for quite a long period of time," recalled Sharon Bell. "She was told that if she moved, the polio would spread. That's a really scary thing for a young kid. We knew what polio was and wondered if she'd walk again."

The several months she spent in the hospital left a deep emotional scar and widened the fissure between Joni and her parents. Bill never visited her, and Myrtle visited only once—with a protective mask over her face. This was not unusual. Parents did not visit often—partly because of distance, partly because of hospital rules—but that was small consolation to a ten-year-old girl who was already deep in the throes of a struggle with loneliness.

"The loneliness that many polio patients experienced . . . was made worse by the very restrictive visiting policies of most rehabilitation hospitals in the 1940s and 1950s," writes Daniel J. Wilson, the author of *Polio*. "The Shrine hospital in San Francisco, for example, permitted the parents of patients to visit only on Sundays for a half an hour, and parents were not allowed to come together. Other hospitals took away patients' visiting privileges if they had misbehaved or if parents fell behind on paying the bills . . . By the time polio patients were in rehabilitation, they were no longer contagious. There was no medical reason for such limited visiting hours, except for the convenience of the hospital."

Joni did end up spending Christmas in the colony. Her mother brought her a small Christmas tree to cheer her up, which offered little consolation. Preternaturally willful, the child fought back: praying, or more accurately, demanding that she be healed.

"I said, 'Give me back my legs and I'll make it up to you.' I didn't know who I was praying to. It wasn't God or Jesus. I knew that there was a spirit of destiny or something. I just wouldn't believe that I'd be crippled in a wheelchair for the rest of my life. I just wouldn't buy into it. 'Give me that back and I'll make it up to you.' So I fought it like crazy and amazed them by standing up and walking."

This was the first of many willful, indeed creative, acts of defiance. Physically incapacitated, socially isolated, she marshaled her internal powers in order to maximize the effectiveness of the rudimentary therapies she was offered. It was not so much an overcoming as it was a rewriting of the odds.

"Somewhere all the cells said, 'Oh, she means no way!' So that in the weeks that followed, I took my treatments, which were hot, scalding rags, like a champ, and I allowed the therapist to bend me. I was very brave and very determined and I walked."

It is not hard to imagine why Joni, in her professional career, would time and time again defer to her own instincts. Her fortitude and endurance proved more reliable than her best advisers. Others would underestimate her, but she would not underestimate herself. "I came back a dancer," Joni said of the incident.

Literally, this is true. By fifteen, Joni would go dancing almost every Wednesday, Friday, and Saturday at the YMCA with her pal Tony Simon. Figuratively, in battling polio, Joni became an artist of her own expressive body. Shunted away in a polio colony in the provinces, she not only learned to fight like hell, but to sculpt her body and spirit in concert with each other. The origins of her *voice*—that inimitable voice of almost limitless range—can be located, figuratively and literally, in the polio year. The unique link between her inner life, her emotions, and her instrument—her whole body—was formed when she willed herself to stand up and walk.

Melancholy was not her stock-in-trade, resilience was. She would later say, "I celebrated my legs. I would have been an athlete. I lost my speed, you know, so that I was never gonna win a swimming contest. I was never gonna be the fastest again. But at least I was mobile. And so I turned to grace. I turned to things that didn't require such speed: water ballet, dance. And I think that it was a blessing in a way because it developed the artistic side." This artistic side, however, not unsurprisingly, produced an unintended side effect: rebelliousness. Schooled in her own strength, distrustful of the parents who seemed to abandon her to the medical authorities, Joni began to act out against the mores of her home and her small-town life.

In eleventh grade, Joni got caught shoplifting a pair of pants, having tried to slip them on under her own. The police drove her home. While no charges were pressed (Myrtle paid for the pants), the incident marked the next stage in the evolution not only of Joni's identity but of her relationship to her life at home. If the polio year produced an awareness of her own mental and physical strength, her brush with the law illuminated the divergent paths she had before her. The girl who could catch polio and then stand up and eventually walk out of the hospital was profoundly superior to a life of petty crime.

"There . . . came a stage when my friends who were juvenile delinquents suddenly became criminals," she told *Rolling Stone* in 1979. "They could go into very dull jobs or they could go into *crime*. Crime is very romantic in your youth. I suddenly thought, 'Here's where the romance ends. I don't see myself in jail.'"

Myrtle did not trust that her daughter would reach that conclusion. The standoff between mother and daughter would continue for all their days.

"I lied to her once in my teens. I told her I was going someplace and I went to a public dance, where I wasn't supposed to go. So I was always a liar after that. A liar, a quitter, and a lesbian. She's wrong on all three counts and would not stand corrected. She just got these things fixed and they wouldn't erase."

Myrtle was a cautious, conservative woman, who avoided major displays of emotion, and expressed her concerns about her daughter primarily through judgment and distrust.

Sharon Bell remembered her as an "exceedingly proper" woman who kept "everything" in the house "absolutely immaculate." The walls were painted in "neutral colors." The only exception to Myrtle's immutable law of cleanliness and order was a tree that Joni was allowed to paint on her bedroom wall.

One of the ways Joni thwarted Myrt's conservative country sensibilities was by exploring parts of Saskatoon that her parents would never visit. "My identity, since it wasn't through the grade system," she told *Rolling Stone* in 1979, "was that I was a good dancer and an artist. And also, I was very well dressed. I made a lot of my own clothes. I worked in ladies' wear and I modeled. I had access to sample clothes that were too fashionable for our community, and I could buy them cheaply. I would go hang out on the streets dressed to the T, even in hat and gloves. I hung out downtown with the Ukrainians and the Indians; they were more emotionally honest and they were better dancers . . . When I went back to my own neighborhood, I found that I had a provocative image. They thought I was loose because I always liked rowdies. I thought the way the kids danced at my school was kind of, you know, *funny*. I remember a recurring statement on my report card—'Joan does not relate well.' I know that I was aloof. Perhaps some people thought that I was a snob."

She indulged her more tomboy tendencies when she hung out with Tony Simon and his bowling club buddies. "There was a group of us— basically about a dozen guys," Simon recalled. "Somehow, she became one of the boys. She used to pal around with us and we would say anything in front of her that we would never say to any other girl. We used to go down to the riverbank in Saskatoon and have wiener roasts.

Usually, it was just drinking beer. Everybody would sing all these dirty songs. And nobody out of all of those people played a musical instrument—including her. She'd had a few piano lessons way back, but nobody could play. So she got a ukulele so that we could have some accompaniment for usually very dirty songs. We'd do classics like the limerick 'There once was a man from Nantucket / Whose cock was so long he could suck it / He said with a grin as he wiped off his chin / If my ear was a cunt I would fuck it.' We'd put it to music and have a highly intellectual time."

Joni remembered that it was around this time that "rock and roll went through a really *dumb* vanilla period. And during that period, folk music came in to fill the hole. At that point I had friends who'd have parties and sit around and sing Kingston Trio songs. That's when I started to sing. That's why I bought an instrument. To sing at those parties. It was no more ambitious than that. I was planning all the time to go to art school."

The decision to buy a ukulele was, not surprisingly, the product of a battle with Myrtle. "When I wanted a guitar, my mother said, 'Oh, no, no. You'll buy it and you'll just quit. You're a quitter,'" Joni recalled. "I couldn't afford to buy it on my own. So I saved up thirty-six dollars, and on the day when my wisdom teeth were pulled, with bloody sutures in my mouth, I went and plunked down the thirty-six dollars, bought this ukulele, and just hunkered over it everywhere to the point where my friends said to me, 'Anderson, if you don't put that goddamn thing down, I'm gonna break it in half.'"

Yet she didn't put the ukulele down; she didn't quit. According to Simon, "As soon as she got that ukulele, something went off inside her and she could not put that thing down. I distinctly remember standing in line to go into a movie and she wouldn't even talk. She was just playing this damn thing. She went through a lot of hard work to master the ukulele, and it set her off with some momentum that never stopped."

The tiny instrument filled a big gap in Joni's aesthetic education. There weren't many record albums in the Anderson household, and it wasn't until high school, when she began to pick up extra money modeling at the local department store, that she could have her own Miles

Davis, Duke Ellington, and Lambert, Hendricks, and Ross to feed her muse. Bill Anderson was an amateur trumpet player who also gave lessons; he was a Harry James man. "My father had *Flight of the Bumblebee* by Leroy Anderson, 'Ciribiribin' and 'Cherry Pink and Apple Blossom White' by Harry James. Those were his three records. My mother had 'Clair de Lune,' *Moonlight Sonata*, and they were all nocturnes. Those were all the records in our house. I had the *Alice in Wonderland* soundtrack and *Tubby the Tuba*. Later I had Jimmy Boyd, 'God Bless the Postman,' in his country child voice."

The music that she shared with her parents makes its way into "The Tea Leaf Prophecy." You can hear the hurt in it, when Joni sings about the three of them—her father, her mother, and herself—"laughing 'round the radio." While all the while, she knows that her mother is longing to leave Saskatoon and maybe she thinks that means her mother is also longing to leave *her*.

There is reason to believe, however, that the mother-daughter relationship also included friendship and even, at times, secret alliance. It is not difficult to imagine that Myrtle, a woman of a more conservative era, struggled to understand her daughter's libertine behavior: inclined, as a mother of the 1950s, to rein in her daughter's free spirit; tempted, as a woman herself, to nurture her daughter's spark.

Lorrie Wood, a co-conspirator in the shoplifting incident, remembers Myrtle taking pride in her daughter, betraying, perhaps, a deep sense of her daughter's unique charisma. "You never wanted to one-up Joan," Lorrie recalled. "We used to sew our own dresses. You could never outdo Joni in her mother's eyes. If you got compliments on your dress, her mother would say, 'Oh, but look at Joan's.' Joni never let you outdo her, and she got a lot of that from Myrtle."

In the late 1950s and early 1960s, the notion of womanhood was being challenged and reimagined. Joni clearly drew energy and conviction from the incipient radicalism of the times. A high school friend, Anne Logie, would recall Joni as "the most original person I knew."

Joni was always the leader. "I had a column in the school paper called 'Fads and Fashion.' I started fads and I stopped them. I knew the mechanics of hip. It's hip to wear your father's tie to school. Ugh, it's uncool, we did that last week. So by the time I was sixteen, I knew that hip was a herd mentality, certain people would do it, they'd follow you and you could embarrass them easily by saying, 'Ewww, that's not hip now.' And they would stop."

That ability to suss out what was hip was a quality that would hold Joni in good stead when she got into the music industry. She simply had an innate sensibility of what was commercial, which allowed her to anticipate and preempt the arguments of meddling record executives, and would make her impervious to the interventions of producers. (She would eventually demote her favorite producer to the status of "engineer.") Joni commandeered the sequencing and sound on her records, and what she picked was usually right: right for her and right for her audience.

It all began to swirl together, her rejection of the simple country life her parents led, her yearning for wide-open spaces, her desire to make art and how it differed from anything that had been held up as an example of a life she might lead. Years later, in the song "Let the Wind Carry Me," she would write about this time, about how her artistic ambitions collided with the lessons from childhood. In the song, she casts her father as her champion and her mother as the one who tries to hold her back:

> *She don't like my kick pleat skirt*
> *She don't like my eyelids painted green*
> *She don't like me staying up late*
> *In my high-heeled shoes*

Mama and Papa are arguing. Mama wants to hold Joni back, knowing what the rock and roll dancing scene can lead to. Papa wants to set Joni free. He wants her to follow her "star eyes." He has a feeling she'll be okay. Joni liked to say that her mother had the same birthday as Queen Victoria—the day of the extreme moralizer. And yet she taught Joni "the deeper meaning."

By the end of high school, Joni would begin barreling toward the creative life that she felt calling for her. Of the album on which the song appeared, *The New York Times* wrote, "Each of Mitchell's songs [on *For the Roses*] is a gem glistening with her elegant way with language, her pointed splashes of irony and her perfect shaping of images. Never does Mitchell voice a thought or feeling commonly. She's a songwriter and singer of genius who can't help but make us feel we are not alone."

Joni may have felt she was a misunderstood member of the Canadian lunatic generation, but it was her destiny to alchemize all that loneliness into music that made people feel they were not alone.

As Nietzsche, Joni's favorite philosopher, wrote, "I should only believe in a god who knew how to dance."

3 ■ WILL YOU STILL LOVE ME TOMORROW?

She had survived polio. Survived Saskatoon. She'd barely gradu-
ated high school, but that didn't bother her much. In twelfth
grade, she failed math, chemistry, and physics. "So I flunked and
had to take those subjects over, which was stupid because everything I was memorizing was fucking wrong," Joni told me. "If they
had told me, 'Light is an intermittent particle,' that would have been
intriguing. Light is matter? How intriguing."

She enrolled at the Alberta College of Art and Design in Calgary.
She didn't know it then, but doing time in art school was a rock and
roll tradition, particularly in Great Britain, where art schools were holding pens for dropouts and rejects. Like Joni, Keith Richards flunked
chemistry, physics, and math and wound up in art school. John Lennon,
Pete Townshend, and Jeff Beck went, too. (Lennon was thrown out).
And, later, in the United States, future musicians such as Michael Stipe
and members of Talking Heads found refuge in college art programs and
art schools like the Rhode Island School of Design (RISD).

Despite Joni's draftsmanship, no one offered her a scholarship. And so she found other ways to make ends meet. "I worked as a model, which was lucrative," Joni said. "It was wholesale modeling, so I was a quick-change artist, modeling a whole line. The buyers from the store would go to the hotel, travelers would come through the hotel, and you'd just model a line. You had to be poised in a size eight, and I did ramp modeling for the department stores, but small-town. It was a common way of presenting a line in those days. You wore a black modeling slip, a tight-fitting sheath dress, and you changed over it, so that you were never in your underwear. And it paid a lot of money."

Sometimes it's not the gig, it's the cover-up. Joni would learn the art of covering up soon enough. During her brief time as a matriculated art student in Calgary, her roommate was her fellow art student Lorrie Wood, whom she knew from back in Saskatoon, in the days of dancing, partying, and shoplifting. "When Joni and I lived together in Calgary, she started art school," recalled Wood. "It was at Seventeenth and Sixth. We didn't even have a bedroom. We had wall dividers and twin beds. When she came to Calgary, I'd been there for a while. She was interested in paintings and drawings and poetry."

It was 1964, the peak of the cult of the minimalist Barnett Newman, with his flat slabs of color, which Joni found about as soulful as graphic design. (Joni later devoured Tom Wolfe's harsh critique of the Abstract Expressionists and the Minimalists in *The Painted Word*, a book alluded to in her 1975 song "The Boho Dance.") If Newman was a minimalist, Joni was a maximalist. Her paintings, then her songs, were based on emotional premises, while his work, she felt, was meant to leave his viewers cold. It was a hard time for Joan Anderson the young artist. She had little patience for what she saw as the fads and fashions of the Abstract Expressionists and Minimalists. Jackson Pollock just seemed like surface splatter, and while Mark Rothko might have been impressive in his depth, she was in search of the human subject. Her theme would be relationships. Her biggest subject would be love, even in its absence.

She lasted at the school for only a year. But she would never abandon her artwork, which she would eventually show to acclaim. As she put it much, much later, "I sing my sorrow and paint my joy."

She began to teach herself to play guitar with a Pete Seeger instruction record. But in a very Joni way, she quickly grew tired of it and decided to teach herself. "I couldn't do what I first set out to do," she wrote in *Rolling Stone* in 1999. "I wanted to learn 'Cotten Picking,' which was kind of rudimentary. Elizabeth Cotten, who was Pete Seeger's housekeeper, a black woman, had a style of picking that every folkie could do. It was on this Pete Seeger record that started with how to tune the guitar. Most of it didn't interest me, but I did attempt to learn 'Cotten Picking.'" The song, with a simple I–V bass line, was too difficult for Joni's polio-weakened left hand. "I didn't have the patience to copy a style that was already known," she said. So she taught herself to play, just the same way she taught herself to sing. As she told *Rolling Stone* in 1969, "I used to be a breathy little soprano. Then one day I found that I could sing low. At first I thought I had lost my voice forever. I could sing either a breathy high part or a raspy low part. Then the two came together by themselves. It was uncomfortable for a while, but I worked on it, and now I've got this voice."

Once she had a voice, she was ready to put it out there and see what she could do with it. In Calgary, John Uren had just opened a club called the Depression. It was a dark and lonely walk down those steps to audition, but Joni was unfazed. She had a baritone ukulele around her neck, a vocal style that was equal parts Joan Baez and Judy Collins, and a repertoire of English and Scottish ballads known as the Child ballads, along with a handful of sea chanteys and other odds and ends.

Joni began playing three sets a night, starting on Friday, September 13, 1964. At twenty, she was a quick study, a natural mimic. The folk scene was about authenticity, not originality. She played songs like "Reuben James" and "When Johnny Comes Marching Home Again," which she sang with a Canadian "haroo-haroo" instead of "hurrah-hurrah." It was a fine way to earn fifteen dollars a week. That was enough to buy smokes and the occasional record.

"Joni was pretty good-looking and she was confident," Uren recalled. "There was no doubt about her voice. She had a smart mouth and was very engaging. Privately, I always thought she was shy." Uren wouldn't be the last person to find, even back then, that there was something complicated about what was then the Joni Anderson affect. It was serious yet playful, intimate yet withholding, outgoing yet taciturn.

It was in Calgary that Brad MacMath, tall, blond, and chiseled, came into Joni's life. "She went to the art school and she met Brad, brought him home, and we all became pals," recalled Wood. "We used to call Brad 'Moochic.' I think she thought he mooched. He'd come to our house and eat. But Brad was a really nice guy. I didn't think of them as being a couple. At the time, Joni was the only virgin left in art school and she was looking to lose it. So Moochie was the most available guy."

Joni got pregnant right away and Brad MacMath moved in, a first step toward doing the right thing. "I got pregnant right out of the chute with my friend," Joni told me. "It was my own stupid fault. That was not even a romance. It was just that I was the only virgin in art school, and I thought, 'What is this all about?' And I got caught out and that was bad."

Joni was young, pregnant, and far from home. But in a gesture that would both draw from her past and predict her future, she would alchemize her pain into music. Her first "real" song as a songwriter, "Day After Day," made poetry of a common situation. Recalling the stern admonitions of her beloved writing teacher, Mr. Kratzmann, she was careful not to fall into cliché. The melody sounded like a familiar ballad in F minor, haunting and almost familiar. Not all of the lines rhyme, but the melody compels the listener through a song of regret, where the movement eastward is to a terrifying and strange place, one where she will be truly on her own. The clock keeps ticking. The baby will come. The man will go. The only thing to keep time is to make music out of it:

> So this must be my fate
> To sit and weep and wait
> And pray my darlin' comes before too late

There is no turning back. The train is going forward. A new life of uncertainty awaits. It is a lonely ride. Joni was just another folkie singing songs of sorrow. But the song mattered, because it was the first time she discovered that, when her back was against the wall, she could create beauty. When she was hurt and trapped and scared, she could write and sing her way to a kind of freedom.

Anyone who was listening probably thought it was another Child ballad, another song about a young lass taken away by a rogue and tied to the tracks down by the river, waiting for her prince to save her. The song sounded like it had existed for centuries, yet it was about a predicament happening in the present tense.

In those days way before social media, it was easy for Joni to perform visibly pregnant, and not worry that word would get back to her parents that she was expecting. Joni would later try to explain the stigma and the burden of the pregnancy by stating, "That [pregnancy out of wedlock] was a terrible thing for a woman, nothing worse. You may have well killed somebody. You know, you were— It was losing face to the max." Joni and MacMath moved to Toronto, but soon after, he bailed, eventually to California. The parting gift was a drawing of a pregnant woman and a line by the Japanese Buddhist priest Ryokan: "The thief left it behind—the moon at the window."

Joni never shied away, in music or in life, from how much romantic love meant to her. She was a new kind of woman for the early 1960s: independent, irreverent, headstrong, but she was also deeply interested in love and how she could shape a married life that was modern and satisfying. In "Song for Sharon," which appeared on her 1976 album, *Hejira*, she sings:

> *When we were kids in Maidstone, Sharon*
> *I went to every wedding in that little town*
> *To see the tears and the kisses*
> *And the pretty lady in the white lace wedding gown*

She didn't know it when she was little, but all of this was what she would call, in "Both Sides, Now," "love's illusions." In childhood, they are very real, and as an adult artist, she could still be stimulated by them. Back when she was a little girl with Sharon Bell, she wanted it all: the white dress, the romantic love, the illusions. But in Toronto, things were getting real and adulthood was bleak. At that very moment—pregnant and alone—she concentrated on, quite literally, singing for her supper. She couldn't afford the local musician union dues of $149, so she supported herself at what she called "the best of the scab clubs," which included the Half Beat, the Place, the Village Corner, and especially the Purple Onion. She had already moved from the ukulele to the guitar. Now, her pregnancy increasingly visible, she moved on to the tiple, a mini-guitar that she could rest on her belly.

What would happen tomorrow? And the tomorrow after that? The more Joni's belly grew, the more uncertain her future would become. Will you still love me tomorrow? asked one of Joni's favorite songs from high school. And the song she loved would take on a different meaning once she became a mother. Because when it came to her baby, the answer would be a heartbreaking, resounding yes, after yes, after yes. Even after she gave her baby up, Joni would never stop thinking about her, writing about her, loving her.

4 ■ A COMMON MODERN-DAY FAIRY TALE

Joan Anderson was far from the only unmarried pregnant young woman looking for help and a safe harbor in 1964. She remembered that she tried to seek shelter in a home for unwed mothers and she "couldn't get in. They were flooded. I tried to." Protecting her parents from the truth, even though she was not close to them, was of the utmost importance. "I tried to spare my parents by going to the anonymity of a large city, under the ruse that I wanted to be a musician," she later recalled to her friend Malka Marom. "Because my mother already thought I was a quitter, so she'll believe it."

She arrived in Toronto with sixty dollars to her name. The cheapest room she could find cost fifteen dollars a week. She remembered that "it was the attic room and all the railings . . . there was one left out of every four because last winter, the people burnt them to keep the room warm . . . And I had six months ahead of me, no work."

Work at scab clubs kept her going, just barely. Martin Ornot, the organizer of the Mariposa Folk Festival, remembered Joni as beautiful, unassuming, and kind. "She wore long gowns or jeans, leather jackets, holding her guitar . . . She seemed quiet. If vulnerability can be translated into people wanting to do things for her, then she was vulnerable. You really wanted to be around her and help her, if you could. It wasn't that she was needy, it was that she was so nice."

Joni gave birth to a girl on a cold Canadian winter's day, February 19, 1965. She named the little girl, whose blond hair and pale features mirrored her own, Kelly Dale Anderson. She was alone, but she didn't want to give her baby up for adoption, so she left the baby in foster care and returned home to her attic room, unsure of how she was going to pay the next week's rent, unsure of whether she was going to be able to keep the child. Having felt so disconnected from her own parents, one can only imagine how holding the baby must have brought back memories of how abandoned she had felt years before in the polio ward.

It would be months before Joni signed the adoption papers. Lorrie Wood, Joni's high school pal and roommate from Calgary, saw Joni in Toronto after she had given birth. Wood was in a position to give advice. "I gave up a child, too, just prior to the time Joni gave up Kilauren [the name that the baby's adoptive parents gave her]," recalled Wood. "Adoptions don't come out of good things. It's a scary situation. You never know if you will meet again in later years. It's tenuous. You have to expect a lot of ups and downs out of it. I told Joan that life would go on, that she would get over it. I told her it was the best thing I ever did. She had her career and her music. Where was the place for a child? She'd be better off, especially since she didn't have a really committed mate. I said, 'You can't put yourself in it. It's selfish. You have to be beyond it.' Every time she looked at the child she was struck by how much the baby looked like her. That made it harder for her to give her up. I told her that she had to see it for the child and get over her own selfishness or self-centeredness. Plus, she was destitute and wasn't trained for anything. She had nothing but the music and she had no idea where that was going."

Enter Chuck Mitchell, then age twenty-nine. He was older and a more established folksinger than Joni. He had a BA in English from Principia College in Missouri, which, she says, he lorded over her. He was an upholder of traditions and Joni ended up loathing the kind of traditionalism he represented. She always prided herself on being forward-looking. Still, it was with Chuck that she became Joni Mitchell—and not only because she took his name in marriage.

Joni met Chuck at the Penny Farthing, where she corrected his rendition of "Mr. Tambourine Man." Chuck thought his revision of Dylan's classic wasn't so bad. "I tinkered with 'Tambourine Man,' changed a few words," Chuck Mitchell wrote to me. "I haven't sung 'Tambourine Man' in years and I don't recall the changes I made, but I'm sure they were worthy and improved the lyric to no end. After all, I'm an English major." One wouldn't know it from Joni's recollections, but Chuck Mitchell can be kind of funny.

Mitchell was tall, handsome, and in possession of a union card. He was also an American citizen, and represented Joni's best chance not only for a potential father for her child, but also for a visa. The idea was that Joni would move to Detroit and in with Mitchell, the couple would perform as a duo, and when they had saved enough money, they would, in Joni's words, "get the baby out of hock."

Chuck came from an educated family. His father had gone to Antioch. His mother had a degree from Mills. To him, Joni was a "prairie girl [from a] rube place . . . I mean, she liked to go bowling—talk about your kitsch!—and with those little balls, like they do in Canada!" When Joni later wrote about Chuck that he had "swept with the broom of contempt," she was still glowering with resentment about all his little digs.

But for a while, there was love. The couple moved into a walk-up, and as Joni remembered it, "We lived in the black neighborhood. It was cheap housing . . . It was big and low-rent, and people would stay with us, and when we traveled we'd stay with them. We couldn't afford hotel rooms at this point. We were making so little money. So people would take you in, and it was nice, the social aspect of it."

Today, Joni can be reluctant to revisit those painful times, but starting in 1973 she opened up to the Canadian broadcaster Malka Marom for a series of interviews, and the journalist Sheila Weller movingly captured Joni's conflict in her book *Girls Like Us*. Weller sets the scene: "By day, newlywed Joni, wearing jeans and chain-smoking dual-filter Tareytons, refinished the dark, ornate woodwork that Chuck had stripped, and filled the apartment with Indian quilts from J. L. Hudson's and thrift store antiques, eventually turning the heavy, depressing lair into a green-hued fantasyland straight out of the imagery of J.R.R. Tolkien." It was Joni's first time playing house and it would become one of her greatest gifts. To paraphrase the Graham Nash lyrics she inspired, Joni Mitchell could make almost anywhere into a "very, very, very fine house."

Chuck Mitchell told Weller that the backdrop to their early years was the fate of Joni's baby. "We have this issue, Chuck," Joni would say as the couple drove back and forth from Detroit to Canada, where Joni was still playing in clubs. "What should we do? What should I do?" Then finally, during one of those trips back to Canada, they visited the foster home where Joni's daughter was living. Joni held the baby. Chuck held the baby. And then Joni signed the surrender papers. There was a form in the baby's adoption files called "Non-Identifying Background Information." Without revealing either parent's name, there were details left for the baby: that her father had been above-average height, that her mother had once had polio and grew up in Saskatchewan, and then this telling line: "Mother left Canada for U.S. to pursue career as folksinger."

With the issue of the baby settled, Joni could turn her attention to music. She began performing at the Chessmate, Detroit's biggest folk club, and the couple began making friends on the scene: Tom Rush, Harvard-educated and fresh off the Cambridge folk scene; Bruce Langhorne, one of the few prominent African-American folk musicians. (Langhorne was the inspiration behind Dylan's "Mr. Tambourine Man.")

Chuck and Joni began performing together. Joni could certainly stand up for herself, but she needed a push to move from coffeehouse singer to a bigger spotlight. Chuck may have been traditional, but he was ambitious enough for both of them; he helped Joni start her publishing company. He told me by e-mail: "We were both talented, remember that, if in quite different ways. It was fun, and a lot of things were happening at once; songs getting written, tunings found, clothes sewn, curtains fashioned and hung, estate sales and auctions and roast beef and Yorkshire pudding and green beans and all-night card games and soirees with troubadours (a.k.a. hustling songs at the local clubs). It was. a. great. scene."

It is a portrait of a marriage in 1965 that had one foot in the '50s and one foot in all the creativity and chaos that was to come. Joni was writing songs and hanging curtains, cooking Yorkshire pudding and hustling songs at local clubs. She was not her mother. She was not stuck in old patterns of domesticity, but there was some of Myrt in her. She longed to roam and she craved home, all at once. That Mitchell feels the need to assert, decades later, that he, too, was talented, hints at what might have eventually driven the couple apart.

"Chuck Mitchell was my first major exploiter, a complete asshole," Joni told me. "We were a duo then. He was pandering all the time. His taste in music was so foreign. It was show tunes: Flanders and Swann— very quaint and clever—and *The Fantasticks*. To me, it was cornball stuff."

Chuck Mitchell insists that, at the time, Joni didn't think his music was all bad. He e-mailed: "She said she liked the Brecht/Weill tunes, 'The Bilbao Song.' She told me that was my metier and I should focus on that sort (cabaret) of music. I still think it was canny advice, but cabaret, that's New York City, or maybe Chicago, and as it turned out, I ended up a heartland kind of guy; not much call for 'The Sailor's Tango' in Des Moines, Iowa."

In June of 1966, fifteen months after they walked down the aisle, Chuck and Joni left Detroit for New York City. They played the legendary Gaslight, and Joan Baez was in the audience. Years later, the queen of folk recalled the moment: "I remember Joni with her bangs and long hair and she still had her partner singing with her, and I remember thinking, 'You've gotta drop this guy.'" The Detroit music scene and the urban "jazzers," as Joni called them, had put new sounds in her head, and she was blossoming out of her repertoire of folk favorites and beginning to make extraordinary music, getting better every day.

Chuck Mitchell still looks back on her musicianship with awe. "Joni's ability to tune was mystical, like her ability to beat me in gin rummy," he said. "I don't think she had it cold when she arrived, but it grew along with her songwriting. And, no matter what tuning she was in, we were always in a comfortable key for our duo songs. She did often play in standard tuning, too. I don't recall tuning as ever being a problem for Joni; there, it's done, let's sing. Listen to tapes of early live shows. You can hear it happen."

Standard tuning, also referred to as concert tuning, is most people's method of tuning a guitar in accord with the entire orchestra. The six strings of the guitar are tuned in the following manner: E A D G B E. And there are also alternate or open tunings to choose from: various forms of folk, Celtic, blues, and so on. These alternate and open tunings are notable for their resonant sound, as the open strings drone off one another. When Joni's songwriting started to take off in 1966, she took from various open tunings that already existed, then turned them into something that no one had heard before, and started writing songs primarily in open chords and dropped tunings. Some of her earliest compositions sounded like indicated orchestration—creating complex, almost orchestral melodies, using simple chord shapes across the fret board. Joni picked up open tuning from Eric Andersen and other coffee-house folk musicians, but quickly expanded the technique to create her idiosyncratic voicings. With these tunings, most listeners who knew nothing about the guitar were still hearing something utterly unlike anyone else's music.

The songwriting began flowing. "Born to Take the Highway" was a song about escape, an adventurous spirit that made her want to move on from Saskatoon, and somehow, bust out of the marriage. "Urge for Going" made the point even more explicitly. The birds know when to fly south for the winter. And humans know when a romance is over. The song was a hit on the country charts for George Hamilton IV and became a staple for Tom Rush. It was Joni's second song, a huge leap from "Day After Day." Even bigger leaps were soon to come.

On October 4, 1965, "Joni Anderson" went on *Let's Sing Out*, a popular folk television program hosted by Oscar Brand, joined by the legendary folkie Dave Van Ronk, known as the "Mayor of MacDougal Street." It was her debut as a folk artist, and she was entering and leaving at the same time. "I did that show twice," Joni told me. "That's when I was a folksinger. I was a folksinger as Joni Anderson. As soon as I became Joni Mitchell, I was no longer a folksinger. Once I started to write my music, that's not folk music."

Her new surname became for Joni a mark of independence, of disclosure, of sexual and emotional adventures. *Joni Mitchell* became the name of a Woman of Heart and Mind. It was not the name of someone's wife, even if, technically, it was. As the days unfolded and the songbook proliferated, Joni began to make a name for herself, and she and Chuck began to perform separately. The audiences were coming for *her* voice, *her* guitar, *her* stories, *her* idiosyncrasies, *her* songs. People began to fall in love. And in the dark clubs, it was still intimate enough to connect with the woman they were falling for.

Joni had taken Lorrie Wood's advice and signed the papers and given her Kelly Dale away. And in the process, she would find both the hope and the melancholy that would fuel her songwriting for decades. In 1966, Joni wrote a song called "Little Green," where she would tell all but reveal nothing. She didn't release it for five years—in another time, another moment, another level of fame, many lives later—but it became a staple of her gigs right away. On October 26, 1967, with the cameras rolling in full-bleed color, Joni Mitchell sat on the stage at a packed Cafe Au Go Go in the midst of folk fabulousness on Bleecker Street. She was wearing a shiny pink button-down shirt and purple form-fitting pants. She was still in the habit of smiling, or suppressing a smile, whenever she was performing, as if to say, *I know I am sitting on something extraordinary, and no matter how melancholy the contents, I am proud of this.* It was the same proud grin she wore when she was interviewed on the CBC and told the interviewers that "the general message of my songs is just happiness . . . Even the sad songs aren't depressing, they're just sort of wistful." As Joni got older, it became increasingly difficult for her to be so evasive. But she was giving her first televised interview, and it was showtime.

The song she was performing was "Little Green." The song had already been recorded at Philadelphia's Second Fret. She was still out to make people fall in love with her, and this packed and hushed crowd seemed to be doing just that. And yet she sang a song that revealed a secret hiding in plain sight. When the song eventually appeared on the album *Blue*, Timothy Crouse, reviewing it in *Rolling Stone*, complained that "the pretty, 'poetic' lyric is dressed up in such cryptic references that it passeth all understanding." But Crouse, like everyone else, had been duped.

There is nothing more honest than the lyrics:

> *Child with a child pretending*
> *Weary of lies you are sending home*

Or:

> *So you sign all the papers in the family name*
> *You're sad and you're sorry, but you're not ashamed*
> *Little Green, have a happy ending*

At the Cafe Au Go Go, the earnest crowd dutifully claps, and she flashes that big and generous smile, but beneath it all—way, way beneath—she is crumbling behind the poetic words and sonorous chords, different and even bluer than on *Blue*. It was the start, Joni would later explain, of her sending secret messages to her daughter in her songs. Even songs like "Big Yellow Taxi" were about the earth her daughter would inherit.

She had begun to chronicle the end of her short marriage in song, too. "I Had a King" was clearly the artist as memoirist. Joni, playing fairy princess, elevates her first husband to the role of king, but he's changed the locks anyway:

> *I can't go back there anymore*
> *You know my keys won't fit the door*
> *You know my thoughts don't fit the man*
> *They never can, they never can*

She sings the song as a solo performer who, not long earlier, was the reluctant half of a duo. Chuck Mitchell was the non-songwriting half of that duo, so her husband—but not, creatively, her king. After she moved out, he changed the lock. As she sang: "My keys won't fit the door." Joni Anderson gave her name up for him and a whole lot more. *Je ne regrette rien*, sang Edith Piaf, one of Joni's musical heroes, but this song brims with regret. It could not exist without it. When she was trying the song out in clubs, she called it a "common modern-day fairy tale."

The song has the sweep of a romantic art song, with repetitions on the first three lines, then a flourish at the end:

> *I had a king in a tenement castle*
> *Lately he's taken to painting the pastel walls brown*
> *He's taken the curtains down . . .*

> *I had a king dressed in drip-dry and paisley*
> *Lately he's taken to saying I'm crazy and blind*
> *He lives in another time . . .*

> *I had a king in a salt-rusted carriage*
> *Who carried me off to his country for marriage too soon*
> *Beware of the power of moons . . .*

The guitar repeats a pattern, develops, and resolves when the voice does the same. She had a king—in the past tense. She is who she is because she rejects what was; her guitar, her voice give her form and beauty as revenge. This is not the sneering rejection of Dylan's "It's All Over Now, Baby Blue" (a song she would record in rather altered form much later). This is much more delicate, much more elegiac. She never says why, except that the marriage, which happened because she'd had a baby, was simply "too soon," but any time would have been the wrong time. There is an undeniable regret in the song; it is not that things didn't work out, but that she had an unworthy partner. But she also shows some of the muscle she is developing, a hint at the steeliness that will drive her art and her life:

Ladies in gingham still blush
While he sings them of wars and wine
But I in my leather and lace
I can never become that kind

For a very long time, the world will see Joni Mitchell as a wispy blonde, a folkie with a guitar, a sweet smile, and a bell-like laugh. But there's another Joni emerging, one who knows her own mind, writes her own songs, and runs the show: a woman, not a girl, dressed defiantly in leather and lace. "My husband thought I was stupid because he had a BA in literature," Joni told me. "He took me on as a trophy wife. He liked my body, but he didn't like my mind. He was always insulting me, because he had the pride of the well-educated, which is frequently academic stupidity."

And while Chuck may have been the more formally educated of the pair, Joni's talent and intelligence were something astounding to behold. Echoing what Joni had told him, David Crosby would later put it this way: "She always had a very strong need for independence, but you know about Chuck Mitchell, right? That would give anybody a need for independence. There was a guy who was using her and keeping her down. The guy was a talentless nobody who hooked on to a tremendously talented girl and married her to keep her in line and used her to have an act and make a living. This guy was no more in her league than a sheep was the size of an elephant."

Joni would later say, "As my work began to mature, I began to long for my own growth. I felt that I couldn't grow with Chuck. That we would never grow together. That I had to separate myself from the duo, that I had to become an individual in order to grow. And as soon as the duo dissolved, the marriage dissolved."

Joni, even as a twenty-four-year-old divorcée who had secretly given up a child for adoption, was resolute. "Every bit of trouble I went through, I'm grateful for," she said. "Bad fortune changed the course of my destiny. I became a musician."

5 ■ DON'T GIVE YOURSELF AWAY

was reading Saul Bellow's *Henderson the Rain King* on a plane and early in the book Henderson the Rain King is also up in a plane. He's on his way to Africa and he looks down and sees these clouds. I put down the book, looked out the window and saw clouds too, and I immediately started writing the song. I had no idea that the song would become as popular as it did."

She'd been instructed to read the book by her soon-to-be-ex-husband. In it, Bellow writes about the mystery and majesty of traveling by plane. "We are the first generation to see clouds from both sides. What a privilege! First people dreamed upward. Now they dream both upward and downward." At the time, Chuck Mitchell ridiculed the song. What could his young wife possibly know about looking at both sides of life? Joni was indeed all of twenty-three when she wrote it, but she had seen more of life and love than most young adults. The description of Henderson's awe, filtered through experience, resonated for her: "And I dreamed down at the clouds, and thought that when I was a kid I had dreamed up at them, and having dreamed at the clouds from both sides as no other generation of men has done, one should be able to accept his death very easily."

After landing, when she picked up a guitar to match the music with the words, she followed the line "I've looked at life that way" with a blues riff that undercut any mawkishness from the words she had just sung, and even from the falsetto in which she sang them. That blues riff keeps coming back on every turnaround, a reminder that the images of childhood dissolve into a more complex mode, harmonically— in this case, the Mixolydian mode, with what bebop musicians called its flatted seventh—and thematically.

"Both Sides, Now" was an early instance of a method Joni would explore throughout her career: that of a repeated trope (or anaphora) that holds together a concept that widens throughout the song. First she sings:

I've looked at clouds from both sides now

Then she circles back and sings:

I've looked at love from both sides now

Each time, she returns to the phrase a little differently and a little deeper. Part of what makes her songwriting so powerful is that within the familiar four-minute melodic structure she consistently refuses to let a chorus be merely a catchy refrain. She chisels away at the rock of what is repeated until something more powerful is revealed. Finally, the third time around, she tells us:

I've looked at life from both sides now

But if she is a scientist, probing, studying, asking questions, exploring, ultimately she is dissatisfied enough with the data to pronounce that her findings are inconclusive:

It's life's illusions I recall
I really don't know life at all

Despite all she had gone through, Joni was, at heart, still a roman-tic. "I loved the beautiful melodies which belonged to the crooner era. But those melodies had very simple text. There wasn't much room for poetic description. They're beautiful, but they are very direct English. That's what suits that kind of melody. But I like the more storytelling quality of Dylan's work."

She followed Dylan's path from the coffeehouses to the concert stage, but she also followed the trail that he carved out as a songwriter, the opportunities that his particular, peculiar expression of music created for a young musician trying to find her voice. "Dylan inspired me with the idea of the personal narrative. He would speak as if to one person in a song. Like, 'You've got a lot of nerve to say you are my friend.' Nobody had ever written anything like that in song form. Such a per-sonal, strong statement. His influence was to personalize my work. I feel this for you, or from you or because of you. That was the key. This opens all the doors. Now we can write about anything."

Joni would have to find her own way: balancing the complexity of narrative that she aspired to and the music. "The thing I was reluctant to let go of was the melodic, harmonic sense. Whereas [with] Dylan, you could speak in paragraphs. But it was from the sacrifice of music. You get the plateaus upon which to speak. It was my job to distill a hybrid that allowed for a certain amount of melodic movement and harmonic movement. But with a certain amount of plateaus in order to make the longer statement, to be able to say more."

Al Kooper was sitting in Joni's New York apartment at 41 West Six-teenth Street when he heard her play "Both Sides, Now." It was his pas-sion for it, his instinct for what he had heard and what he had found in Joni that would change everything. Al Kooper was a master of seizing the moment. The most famous example involved him being in the re-cording studio when Bob Dylan was laying down the track for "Like a

Rolling Stone." When Kooper saw that the great blues guitarist Mike Bloomfield had showed up for the date, Kooper was ready to pack up. Then he saw no one was sitting at the organ and he saw an opportunity. Kooper kept insisting that the song needed an organ. When he started working out his part, the producer Tom Wilson turned to Dylan and said, "He's not an organ player." Dylan said, "Don't tell me who's an organ player and who's not an organ player." Wilson had a point: Kooper didn't know how to play organ, not really. But he hopped on the bench, started playing, and within seconds, created the simple yet iconic organ part that opens "Like a Rolling Stone." Dylan's instinct was correct, and Wilson was replaced with another producer the next day. It was the kind of luck that turned an obscure young studio musician into a music industry legend.

When Kooper heard Joni sing "Both Sides, Now" in her apartment, he leaped for the phone and despite the hour, three a.m., started to frantically dial a number. When Judy Collins picked up the phone, Kooper was blathering on about an amazing talent he'd discovered. He was convinced that he'd found the missing element for Collins's upcoming album *Wildflowers*, and that if she didn't snatch up the song right away, someone else would make it a hit.

Collins had, by that point, already made her way through a few musical transitions. She had been a classical piano prodigy, then a folkie siren whose only peer was Joan Baez. (Bob Dylan wrote "Daddy, You've Been on My Mind" for her to sing even as he was performing the "Mama" version with Baez.) Her recent role was that of popularizer, which began in the role of discoverer, something at which her blind disc jockey father excelled.

Although Judy was starting to write songs—Bob Dylan and Leonard Cohen encouraged her—her albums were essentially compilations of new rock and folk arranged with lush orchestrations that sounded destined for an Original Broadway Cast soundtrack. Covering the Beatles—even though she did it beautifully—meant competing with well-loved recordings. Discovering the optimal unsigned and unrecorded talent was priceless.

Kooper apologized for waking Collins up, but assured her it would be worth it. Without even saying hello, Joni, guitar tuned and ready, launched into "Both Sides, Now," an intimate song she was now sharing with someone she had never met.

"She did play me 'Both Sides, Now,' which is a miracle," Collins recalled. "Can you imagine? For that to happen to me? How extraordinary is that? Absolutely mind-boggling. I had an album that was being made right then and I wanted to record the song right away. That night, I went crazy and said, 'I must have this song.' So the next day, I said, 'Why don't I bring Jac Holzman to your place?' Which I did! I called Jac the next day and said, 'You won't believe what I just heard. We have to go see Joni.' So we went to see Joni. And there was some discussion about Dave Van Ronk wanting to record the song. Then she sang us the song and he said, 'Of course! It must be on this album!'"

The song as Joni played it was still too raw to be a hit—not without some studio tinkering—but Judy was immediately floored by hearing a young woman strumming and singing about illusions gained and lost, love seen from the heights of hope and wonder and the depths of disillusionment. Beneath the soaring soprano and cascading chords, there is a bluesy turnaround; admitting that one doesn't know life at all is when the fantasy crashes down to reality, and when one turns to the blues.

Judy remembered, "We went into the studio, we recorded 'Both Sides, Now' for *Wildflowers*, and, of course, the whole setup was right, it was right for the song at the moment, because we had Josh Rivkin, who was doing orchestration. I was mad about Joni's songs, mad about them. I went to her apartment and she played me 'That Song About the Midway' and 'Michael from Mountains,' which I recorded. It was all about getting those songs on this particular album, because it was a big, big deal. Everyone at Elektra was ready to make this happen. It took about nine months for it to go on the charts. We did it over and over. We remixed and remixed until they got it."

Collins was twenty-eight—four years older than Joni. She had known suicidal depression and the euphoria of romance, the disappointment of divorce, and the perils and pleasures of commercial success. Her perspective may not have been as vast as Joni's, but she could certainly hear herself in it, an experience Joni would strive for in her listeners as long as she made music.

"I was on the board of the Newport festival with all the boys—George Wein, Harold Leventhal, Pete Seeger, Peter Yarrow," Collins explained. "Ronnie Gilbert [of the Weavers] and I were the only women, and I started to campaign with the board to get a singer-songwriter afternoon, because I wanted Joni Mitchell on that show. And I wanted Leonard Cohen on that show. It was like coming up against a brick wall. They didn't want anything to do with this. They were in this odd retroactive phase. It was as if they forgot that Pete Seeger wrote all these songs. They wanted everything old. If it wasn't at least two centuries old, they didn't want it. And I had to bang their heads together to get them to understand that they had to have this afternoon concert with Joni and Leonard, and Tom Paxton was on it, also, and Janis Ian. It was a big, big, big deal. I wanted to do this for Joni, Leonard, and Janis."

Judy Collins could be a game changer for an up-and-coming singer-songwriter, and Joni knew it. Collins could call the shots at Newport and beyond, while Joni was just a musician's musician, not yet in a situation when she could afford to be dismissive of someone about to give her major exposure. Yes, she was being covered by Tom Rush, Ian and Sylvia, and Buffy Sainte-Marie, but she was living from gig to gig.

Those who had seen her were enthralled by this Aeolian harp, idiosyncratic tunings and all, and how she whispered back the secrets of their heart, with an honesty that could be terrifying. She developed a habit, which she would eventually take with her to the biggest venues, of locking eyes with someone in the front row. She would sing directly to that person the entire show, pouring out everything she had and sharing it with someone who was probably a total stranger. "Don't give yourself away," she sang, but give herself away was exactly what she was doing night after night.

And yet before most people could hear Joni perform "Both Sides, Now," they had to hear Judy Collins first. Joni was not impressed. She wasn't turning down the royalties or the glory of Judy Collins's Grammy, but she never did like what Collins did to her song. There are some people Joni can be very harsh about, and Collins is one of them. "Judy Collins sounds like the damsel in the greenroom," Joni said dismissively. "There's something la-di-da about her."

Joni has made no secret of her opinions about Judy Collins, a fact that Collins finds baffling. "Joni has never gotten over whatever it was that happened, which was that she got famous because I recorded the song," Collins told me. "It was amazing, and I am eternally grateful—Joni, I don't think so. I once asked David Crosby, 'Why is Joni so mad at me?' He said, 'Joni hates everybody.' There are other issues with what Joni's mind does for her when other people get around her, or when other people do something fantastic for her. I did something fantastic for her. And I was honored that I was a part of that. How could you think that that wasn't a blessing for the both of us? It was the beginning of her career! Why slam the person who did the biggest favor of her career? It's so insulting."

There exists a low-fidelity bootleg of Joni performing the song a few months after Judy heard it, and after Newport. It's from a date at the White Swan in Leicester, England, in September 1967. Joni would later describe the sound of her voice in this period as "a squeaky girl on helium," but her listeners are clearly enthralled. Back then, she had written some of her future hits—including "Urge for Going," "The Circle Game," and "Chelsea Morning"—but hadn't recorded them yet. Giggly and self-deprecating, Joni nervously chats up a storm between songs while adjusting her tunings for each one.

James Taylor would later say, with no small degree of admiration, "Joni invented everything about her music, including how to tune the guitar. From the beginning of the process of writing, she's building the canvas as well as she is putting the paint on it. No one's trained her, she trained herself. And even in these early compositions, she finds a harmony or a group of chords, and invariably, it's *never* straight on."

As she tunes to an open A chord (the *Clouds* version would be recorded in F-sharp—an open D with a capo on fret 7), she sounds deceptively rambling and timid, like an eager college student who hasn't finished her reading assignment. She explains to the crowd how she came to write a song that, by then, they knew well: "A short time ago, a friend of mine gave me a book called *Henderson the Rain King*, and I started to read it but I never got finished. I got halfway through and sort of left the whole plot up in the air—literally—and got inspired to write the next song . . . I liked the idea of clouds from both sides . . . and some other things from both sides." Then, as only Joni can, she starts to sing.

6 ■ THE WORD MAN: LEONARD COHEN

n 1954, the producer George Wein founded the Newport Jazz Festival. The first festival took place at the Newport Casino, where academic panels discussed the importance of elevating jazz, what would come to be known as America's classical music. Outside the casino, on the expansive lawns of that seaside town, were the performances. On Saturday, July 17, 1954, Ella Fitzgerald, Oscar Peterson, the Dizzy Gillespie Quintet, and more than half a dozen other notable jazz acts performed. On Sunday, July 18, Billie Holiday was the headliner. More than thirteen thousand people attended that first festival: a surprisingly young and racially mixed crowd. Although many of the white, upper-class residents of the Newport community protested against the festival, the event only grew in popularity.

Five years later, Wein launched a tandem festival: the Newport Folk Festival. Joan Baez was the surprise guest in 1959. Four years later, Baez made history when she introduced Bob Dylan as *her* surprise guest. Judy Collins knew well what she was doing when she brought a then unknown Joni Mitchell and fellow Canadian Leonard Cohen to the festival: she was introducing them to the world. What she didn't realize was that she was also introducing Mitchell and Cohen to each other, the beginning of a romantic and creative friendship that would deeply influence both of their careers.

In the photos from that day, Joni and Cohen don't look like they have just met. It could've been an album cover shoot. Cohen, thirty-three, in a blazer and crisply ironed shirt, holds his guitar. Joni is the picture of mod elegance in a chic minidress and T-strap shoes. The two brim with ebullience, youth, beauty, and artistic ambition. They look completely at ease together, as if they are already intimate. Joni is beaming, and Cohen shows no signs of the angst that had overtaken him, off and on, in the previous months. It was in that fragile state that Collins had brought Cohen to a performance at the Fillmore months earlier, and he fled mid-song in a fit of stage fright, only to be coaxed back by Collins, who held his hand until his performance of "Suzanne" was complete. The audience, impressed by this authentic neurosis, burst into approving applause.

Cohen had spent much of the previous year in the studio recording his debut album, *Songs of Leonard Cohen*—or trying to. "[The producer, John] Hammond created an extremely hospitable atmosphere and wasn't breathing over my shoulder," Cohen recalled. "He had a heart attack, and I went down to Costa Rica to cool out on a beach, because I was so anxious. Then I went to a hypnotist. And I said, 'I've forgotten what all my songs are about. Could you hypnotize me to remember what I meant when I wrote these songs?'" By Newport, Cohen was more confident. Or at least was having a better day.

Cohen was no match for Joni as a musician; he knew only a limited number of chords on guitar and his voice was a drone that could be hypnotic, but only to those persuaded by the material and the persona.

But Cohen had no vanity about his musicianship. He was a "word man," confident as a writer, a reader, a suitor, a lover. He passed whatever her jive detector was at that stage.

Cohen became the most significant man in Joni's life after Chuck Mitchell, and he was certainly more significant to her than Chuck Mitchell, even if her romance with Cohen, off and on, lasted only a few months. Joni would later call Cohen a "boudoir poet." Yet their boudoir wasn't just a place for seduction and consummation—even though, with Cohen, there was always plenty of that. It was also a place for poetry, for spiritual yearning, for a relentless, almost compulsive search for deeper and deeper meaning. When they met, he was nine years older than she was, and before recording *Songs of Leonard Cohen*, his first album (which would appear at the very end of 1967), he had already published four books of poetry and two novels.

The combination of her voice, her guitar, her words, and the way she looked—such beauty emanating from such beauty—made her irresistible. Yet with Cohen, even casual sex was never casual, but a pathway to souls, words, and inspiration. To inspire literally means "to breathe life into." The combination of lust and the life of the mind was essentially what the Cohen of this period was all about. He looked to the verse of Lorca, the philosophy of Camus, and the wisdom of Zen masters as part of the art of seduction. So here was this radiant woman who appeared before him at the Newport Folk Festival, not only offering her body, but also her mind. When Chuck Mitchell recommended books, it was with condescension. Cohen was a man who made Joni want to read more, to find more ways to be inspired.

Joni remembers, "I said, 'Leonard, I've got to read. I'm illiterate.' I said, 'I used to do my book reports from Classic Comic Books!' And he said, 'For someone who hasn't read anything, you're writing very well.' So I left that marriage with a chip and I said to Leonard, 'I need a reading list because my husband's given me a complex that I haven't read anything, except I did read the Tolkien books.'"

When she went on to read Lorca, Camus, and Rilke, she was disappointed to find that Cohen had taken lines from all of them. This was, she insisted, because she shared a birthday with "the discoverer"

Madame Curie. "It is in my stars to invent," she would say, and she was not impressed with T. S. Eliot's maxim "immature poets borrow, mature poets steal."

Leonard Cohen did not know at the time how much his literary influences rankled his new lover. He said, "I read somewhere that she felt that I had tricked her in some way because I hadn't told her that Camus had written a book called *The Stranger* and that I'd written a song called 'The Stranger.' The song had nothing to do with the book, nor was I the first person to call a song 'The Stranger.' She felt that I'd plagiarized Camus."

"I found a lot of Lorca and Camus in his lines," Joni recalled. "And he was living the life of Camus, even down to the way he dressed, and his house in Hydra. It was disappointing to me, because as far as I could see, he was an original. I have this perverse need for originality. I don't really care for copy, second-generation artists. I'm not a traditionalist. It's the discoverers that excite me. Not 'new' like a new face, the way 'new' is used to sell something. They're not new at all. They're a new person doing the old shit. 'Suzanne' is a beautiful song, though."

She (wrongly) believed that "Walk me to the corner / Our steps will always rhyme" was ripped off from Camus, but she could not deny the beauty of "Suzanne," a song about restraint. Just as Cohen's "Dress Rehearsal Rag" is a song about *not* killing yourself, "Suzanne" is a song about *not* seducing a beautiful woman. Many lifetimes later, Cohen looked back on it with wonder. "We were channeling some kind of reality that none of us was living," he recalled. "The songs were much better than we were. We didn't know how good they were. I didn't know that I'd be able to sing 'Suzanne' forty years later."

It was "Suzanne" that first made Cohen well known. Judy Collins recorded it on *In My Life*, the album preceding *Wildflowers*. The beautiful woman he elected not to seduce was inspired by the wife of a friend. Instead, he wrote a song, with the first and the third verse devoted to describing her beauty, and the second verse devoted to Jesus, a counterintuitive mood for a Jew who grew up in Montreal, a largely Catholic city. Cohen seemed like a man who knew just what to say, a man in possession of poetry, mysticism, and wisdom, and he used all of this in the art of seduction. *Songs of Leonard Cohen* is one elaborate pickup, and Joni, even as she knew that a relationship with such a man could never last long, could hardly resist Cohen's charms.

He would continue to influence her work. Traces of his line from "Suzanne," "The sun pours down like honey on our lady of the harbor," can be heard in Joni's line from "Chelsea Morning": "The sun poured in like butterscotch and stuck to all my senses." Joni also wrote a song, never released, called "The Wizard of Is," a dead ringer for "Suzanne," perhaps just as a private experiment, as if she wanted to inhabit it, albeit privately.

Back in 1967, when she and Leonard were still together, Joni changed the name of her publishing company from Gandalf (a nod to *The Lord of the Rings*) to Siquomb. "So," Joni told me, "based on the Tolkien books, I invented this kingdom: Queen SIQUOMB (She Is Queen Undisputedly of Mind Beauty), King HWIEFOB (He Who Is Especially Fond of Birds). They lived in Fanta on the border of Real (Ree-al). And I used to draw these fantasy birds that came from the border, sparrows with peacock tails, very naïve drawings. On the first album cover there's quite a bit of it."

Mind beauty was what Joni was trying to achieve while Leonard was admiring her beauty in many ways. "So Leonard thinks, like a lot of people, that it's about me. It's about the question: What is mind beauty? I very rarely see it. Most people think it's a conceit. They think everything is about me."

In a tribute written for the Luminato Festival honoring Joni on her seventieth birthday, Leonard still clearly thought that "mind beauty" was about Joni:

> *Master Poet. Master Painter. Most Subtle Technician of the Deep.*
> *You are indeed Queen Undisputed of Mind Beauty.*
> *Star-breasted, Disguised as a Ravishing Piece,*
> *You Changed the Way Women Sing, and the Way Men Listen.*
> *What an Astonishing Victory over the Unforgiving Years!*

Leonard found beauty in Joni's mind and in Joni herself. He may have ultimately disappointed her, but that feeling was far from mutual. "Her beauty was a very accurate manifestation of her whole being," Leonard remembered. "She was not just another pretty face, although that, too, of course, at my age, occurred to me, too. But there was something about her face that was carved."

It was coincidence that Joni and Leonard wrote songs called "Winter Lady" before they knew each other. But Joni's song "Marcie" displays a precise use of language, color, and repetition that seemed to demonstrate Cohen's influence, at least according to what she has said over the years.

"Marcie" is a sad and simple story of a girl waiting for a letter and hoping for love. Musically, it is beyond Cohen, scaling octaves and mixing and matching tone colors as dramatic as the colors of nature, emotion, tastes, and the city. The song was originally called either "Portrait in Red and Green" or "Ballad in Red and Green," and in it she reaches into her painter's palette: there's a yellow cab, green and red stoplights, red anger, green envy. Images pile up as a chromatic harmony, with chords as counterintuitive as they are inevitable, a shocking beauty.

"Marcie" is a reminder that there is so much going on in a Joni Mitchell song—tone colors, lyrics, that voice in its multi-octave crystalline splendor—sung by a woman so full of sadness and beauty and wonder, it's hard to know where to start. And watching Joni perform the song—as she does in the footage from the Cafe Au Go Go, in her shiny pink shirt and purple pants, her stunning features adding to the sensory overload—it is easy to see how she would inspire passion from Leonard, her teacher of sorts, and all the men who followed.

In 1968, she wasn't afraid to give Cohen credit for inspiring the poetic texture of "Marcie": "My lyrics are influenced by Leonard . . . My song 'Marcie' has a lot of him in it, and some of Leonard's religious imagery . . . seems to have rubbed off on me, too."

As in "Both Sides, Now," the repetition is in the melody and the use of the word *Marcie*, but the song has no chorus, no anaphora. First, she sings:

> *Reds are sweet and greens are sour*

Then she turns the colored candies into emotions:

> *Red is angry green is jealous*

Time passes and the colors of the heart become seasons:

> *Red is autumn green is summer*

Finally, we're in the city with the "yellow cab," and "Red is stop and green's for going."

B-flat major becomes A major, which becomes A minor and G major. "Marcie," which might have been a maudlin girl-group pop song about a lady in love waiting for a letter, becomes oh so much more in Joni's hands. Girl-group songs by Goffin/King or Bacharach/David are great, of course, but the storytelling here is richer and much more detailed, especially with the seasons and the colors. Daniel Levitin, a neuroscientist and musician who teaches at McGill University, Cohen's alma mater, later said, "Joni is incredibly innovative in terms of her song structure and harmonics. She broke from the standard Tin Pan Alley format of verse-verse-chorus very early in her career."

And yet despite Joni's claims from 1968 that the song was "Cohen influenced," there is a recording of it from Philadelphia's Second Fret from 1966, before she met Cohen or knew anything about him. Memory can be an unfaithful old lover, too. For some reason, she felt like saying that "Marcie" was Cohen influenced. Regardless, the song stands on its own. "Marcie" is a kind of skeleton key to Joni's pictorial brain. Another girl's sad story occasioned Joni's color-acute mind.

It was an imagination that still lingered for Cohen many years later. "She doesn't read music and it really is fully developed from the god's head," Cohen told me. "She just came out that way. When I saw her detune a guitar, for me, just tuning the guitar is an ordeal, worrying if I can tune the damn thing. I was so relieved when I finally had guitar techs. It was always an issue for me. To see Joni just twist those little knobs, tuning the guitar in about thirty seconds, into all different strings that nobody had ever heard, and nobody's ever played it. That indicated to me immediately that there was something very remarkable going on. Same with the piano. I was staying with her in Laurel Canyon when her piano arrived. She sat down and played the piano. Just to hold all those tunings in her mind indicates a superior intellect. I remember being overwhelmed by the fertility and the abundance of her artistic enterprise, because it was so much more vast and rich and varied and seemingly effortless than the way I looked at things. Naturally, I was very impressed and somewhat intimidated."

During their brief romance, from later summer 1967 (when she wasn't spending time with David Crosby) to early 1968, Noel Harrison, the son of Rex Harrison, who had recorded "Suzanne," asked Cohen, "How do you like living with Beethoven?" What a question! And yet, of course, what a compliment. For Harrison, Joni's genius somehow made her less feminine. Cohen didn't see it that way at all. "With all the obvious consequences, it was clear that her genius was already formed and just waiting to manifest," Cohen told me. "She was fully formed: uneducated, uninformed, uninstructed. Fully formed and unneeding of any kind of influences. So she was able to pick her influences, as I understand. I am happy to have been one in whatever capacity it was. It was clear that she could pick and choose, and that there was no learning curve. The songs were complete! 'Both Sides, Now,' 'The Circle Game,' complete. Her beauty was so compelling, she certainly existed as a figure in my heart. I think that Joni was in 'Joan of Arc.'"

Cohen's song "Joan of Arc" is, of course, about Joan of Arc. As a rich Jew growing up in Quebec, he was fascinated by the Sisters of Mercy around him. The song is a conversation between Joan of Arc and the fire that killed her. Some thought it was about Nico—a woman who Leonard felt, with great bitterness, was sleeping with everyone but him. Yet, according to Leonard, it was also about Joni—Joni of Arc. At one point, musing about her presence in Leonard's songs, she sang these lines to me:

> She said, "I'm tired of the war, I want the kind of work I had
>   before,
> A wedding dress or something white
> To wear upon my swollen appetite."

Joni, like Joan of Arc, is tough. She has a cause, and could even be a martyr to it, but that cause is her independence, along with a pack of smokes. (The song describes, morbidly, Joan of Arc's "long and smoky night.") As for that wedding dress, it made an appearance in many of Joni's songs—most notably in "Song for Sharon."

"Swollen appetite" is something else, something more like living with Beethoven—or someone living with a female version of Leonard Cohen, someone who could love her loving and her freedom. "I always thought 'Joan of Arc' was about me," Joni told me. "But what are my 'swollen appetites'? That's projection. See, those Don Juans all think I'm a Don Juan. I ran into Warren Beatty at a party and he gets fidgety around me. This is years since I'd seen him and he called me a Don Juan. I said, 'I'm not a Don Juan.' If a guy's undermining me, I'm not gonna stay there and let him squash me. It seems to be a masculine tendency."

And Joni was convinced that "Bird on the Wire" was inspired by a painting she showed Cohen, an eccentric statement about not fitting in with her husband's family. She thought Cohen would appreciate it. "I had this painting I did for the Mitchells. I was such a misfit in that family, and I did this painting, which I showed to Leonard. In this painting, there are these sparrows sitting on a wire. It's got a hot-pink background, and there are sparrows with peacock tails. There are all these fictitious birds. And there was one for each Mitchell, and one of them was hanging upside down. Guess who? I think that had some input on 'Bird on the Wire.' I showed it to Leonard. It was something I did on a Sunday about how I didn't fit in. They were the first Yuppies that I met. They were pedigreed consumers. They all had the same education. They were brand-name people. A suit had to be Brooks Brothers. No, you don't drink Canada Dry, you drink Vernors. Ice cream has to be Häagen-Dazs. Cars have to be a Chevy Corvair. Frank Lloyd Wright architecture and Danish modern furniture. They were so materialistic in such an unfamiliar way to me, and I didn't know what the fuck they were talking about."

"Bird on the Wire" became a hugely popular and widely covered song for Cohen, and Joni was certain that what spoke to the masses was the idiosyncratic self that Joni portrayed—an upside-down bird on a wire, one who does not fly well with others. The song was begun in Greece and finished in Hollywood in 1969, after Joni showed Cohen the painting. Kris Kristofferson said he planned to put the opening lines on his tombstone and Cohen, deadpan, said he would be disappointed if he didn't.

As for this bird hanging upside down, he was fascinated by her talent, but he was also strongly and passionately attracted to her, and his desires as a man were even stronger than his sensibilities as an aesthete. As far as he was concerned, he was, on that level, certainly not living with Beethoven. Other people could come to their own conclusions, but he was specific in the terms of their connection: "She existed as a presence for most people who met her," he told me. "For me, it was her physical beauty that touched me more than her music. The two are connected, but as a young man in the midst of the hormonal avalanche, she was a radiant presence. The music was part of that, but from my perspective, it was just Athena with the heart. It was just the heart was part of the beauty. I didn't feel competitive with Joni. I was on my own trip."

"I was a young man entranced by this radiant person," Cohen continued. "It was already current at that time that Joni was some kind of musical monster, that her gift somehow put her in another category from the other folksingers. There was a certain ferocity associated with her gift. She was like a storm. She was a beautiful young woman who had a remarkable talent. She was a great painter. I love her paintings. Her self-portraits are amazing. She turned several of her paintings into beautiful tapestries. She gave them to a weaver. She's a great spirit. She is a formidable presence. I wasn't vulnerable to her complications. Mostly, I saw her as a desirable woman, with whom I had a lot in common because of the musical connection."

Joni was taking in everything she could from Leonard as a lyricist, but she was already in her own stratosphere as a musician. As soon as they met, Cohen helped Joni build on what she already had, and discover that deeper place that gives a song its *duende*, a concept of poetic darkness imported from Lorca.

Songs are like tattoos, she would later sing, and the imprints came from deep, passionate, and even painful and potentially dangerous places. No lover gave her poetry like Leonard, and even after their affair ended, she continued to communicate with him in song; most memorably in "A Case of You." She recalled that Cohen told her, "I am as constant as the Northern Star." Shakespeare's Julius Caesar says this to Brutus, and it's not far from there to "Et tu, Brute." "I knew it was from *Julius Caesar*," Cohen recalled, "but I didn't say it with Shakespeare's irony. I think I actually meant it in relation to her."

"When I played 'A Case of You' for him, he said, 'I'm glad I wrote that,'" Joni recalled. The song begins:

> *Just before our love got lost you said,*
> *"I am as constant as a northern star."*
> *And I said, "Constantly in the darkness*
> *Where's that at?*
> *If you want me I'll be in the bar."*

It was a tension that spoke to a schism in their songwriting styles. "Leonard got mad at me actually, because I put a line of his, a line that he said, in one of my songs," Joni later said. "To me, that's not plagiarism. You either steal from life or you steal from books. Life is fair game, but books are not. That's my personal opinion. Don't steal from somebody else's art, that's cheating. Steal from life—it's up for grabs, right?"

Joni also recalls Cohen telling her, "Love is touching souls." That line came from Rainer Maria Rilke's "Love Song":

> *How can I keep my soul in me, so that*
> *it doesn't touch your soul?*

Joni's music and Cohen's music barnacled each other like lovers who would never truly separate, and her admiration for him was unending. When Bob Dylan's Rolling Thunder Revue came to Montreal in 1975, Joni gushed that she was a "stone Cohenite." When she came to his apartment, he picked her up and said, "My little Joni." As she did with most of her exes, she tried to maintain a friendship with Cohen. "We went out to dinner once in the late '70s or early '80s, and he was so quiet, and I tried to keep the conversation going, and he was distant and cold, and I said, 'Leonard, do you like me?' because he was so frosty. And he said, 'Well, what does one have to say to an old lover?'

"I said, 'Oh, my God. Surely there's some topic.'

"And he said, 'Well, you like ideas.'

"I said, 'Well, you can't open your mouth without an idea falling out.'"

Joni wondered, "What does that mean? I like ideas? I thought it must have been some Zen discipline he was going through. After that, every time I saw him, all he said was, 'They'll never get us, Joni.'"

When we met in 2015, Joni said something to me that spoke of the vulnerability and the longing that she believed so few people understood. "I'm so easy to win back," she said. "But if there's no meeting and no communication and the vibe is cold, what can you do?" Did Cohen ever know? Did anyone who ever loved Joni ever imagine that Joni Mitchell was, in her heart of hearts, so easy to win back?

7 ■ EXPERIENCED

Everything was changing for Joni and rapidly. "Both Sides, Now," as covered by Judy Collins, hit the Top 10 and won the 1968 Grammy for Best Folk Performance. Her own stardom was only a matter of time—especially considering that no one could play or sing her material better than she could. She could say no to an offer from Vanguard Records, Joan Baez's label, calling it "slave labor." And she did not jump at the chance to be managed by Bob Dylan's Svengali manager Albert Grossman (who would end up dying of a heart attack on a plane before resolving legal issues with his famous estranged client). After taking her out for sushi (her first time), they adjorned to her ornately and delicately decorated little room in Chelsea. He was so startled by her impeccable décor, he immediately took her to his place nearby in the Village, little more than a mattress on a floor. He was convinced that she was in the wrong business, and that she would be better off as someone's wife—maybe his. "I'm not going to manage you," Grossman said.

"Why not?" asked Joni.

"You should be managing me," Grossman retorted. She was too domestic, he said. She would hate the business. Years later, she conceded he'd had a point. "He was right," Joni recalled. "I am domestic and I do hate the business. But I had a responsibility to my gift because it kept growing, whether people noticed that or not."

After Grossman turned her down, Joni went to Arthur Gorson, whose stable included Phil Ochs and Tom Rush. He offered to manage her in exchange for fifty percent of her publishing company.

"Well," Joni replied, "give me fifty percent of your management company."

"Are you crazy?" asked Gorson.

"Back at you," Joni replied. "Are you crazy?" She walked out.

Joni just continued playing her gigs. She had already had success as a songwriter; she needed to seal the deal with everything else, and Elliot Roberts and others were sure it was only a matter of time.

Elliot Roberts had dropped out of high school and two colleges and given up on acting when he walked in the door of the famous William Morris talent agency. At William Morris, all of the aspiring agents started in the mailroom and Roberts was no exception. Sorting letters and delivering packages, he met another mailroom assistant who would prove instrumental to all of their careers, David Geffen. (Geffen attained the job with a faked degree from UCLA. When, at the appointed hour, the university wrote a letter to inform the William Morris Agency that Geffen, who dropped out of Brooklyn College, did not attend the school, he steamed open the envelope and replaced it with a fake letter.) Roberts was repping another Canadian singer-songwriter, Buffy Sainte-Marie, when she dragged him to hear Joni sing.

Sainte-Marie and Joni came out of the same Yorkville coffeehouse scene in Toronto. Born on the Piapot First Nation Reserve in Saskatchewan, Sainte-Marie had been raised by adoptive parents in Massachusetts. She'd written a hit song called "Cod'ine," about her addiction to the drug, that was and would be covered by artists from Donovan and Janis Joplin to Gram Parsons and Courtney Love. Sainte-Marie had just been named Best New Artist by *Billboard*. She was the star on the rise, but when Elliot Roberts heard Joni, to paraphrase the Carole King song, he felt the earth move under his feet.

It was the songwriting above all that blew Roberts away. "When she first came out," he remembers, "she had a backlog of twenty, twenty-five songs that were what most people would dream that they would do in their entire career . . . it was stunning."

But not stunning enough to get her signed. "Everything about Joni was unique and original, but we couldn't get a deal," Roberts remembers. He tried to shop her to every major label. "The folk period had died, so she was totally against the grain. Everyone wanted a copy of the tape for, like, their wives, but no one would sign her." Joni remembered that the timing of her music seemed to be against her. "I started at a time when folk clubs were folding all over the place. It was rock and roll everywhere, except for a small underground current of clubs."

"Elliot pitched being my manager," Joni remembered. "I said, 'I don't need a manager, I'm doing quite nicely.' But he was a funny man. I enjoyed his humor." So Roberts became her manager, following Joni on the road, paying his own way. On the road, in city after city, Roberts developed a game plan for Joni that would set the course of her career. "The role model was Bob Dylan, and it wasn't a matter of radio play or hits," he said. "It was a matter of people being guided by your music and using it for the soundtrack of their lives." It was a powerful new idea and one that would take some time to bring to fruition. But it spoke to all that Joni was: why men fell in love with her and women felt like she was singing their secrets out loud. It was 1967 and Joni was breaking the mold of what a girl singer could and should be, just as women were flipping the script on society's expectations and conventions on every level.

Joni was beautiful and she was gifted, but she worked her butt off. She remembers all of her naysayers—and vividly. Bernie Fiedler and his wife had a club in Toronto called the Mouse Hole. Joni was playing at a place called the Half Beat. Joni remembered that Bernie and his wife came to hear her play one night, "sort of snooping." Bernie had what Joni called a "great kind of dry wit. We're friends now, but at that time, I didn't really understand him."

Bernie approached Joni and said, "Trying to achieve the Baez sound, are you?"

Joni kept trying to get booked at his club, but Bernie wasn't having it. He rebuffed her every time, but with panache. Once he told her, "Darling, don't bother me, I don't like to associate with failures." Another time, he told her, "Yes, I'll call you when I need a good dishwasher."

It got under Joni's skin. "I was very angry with Bernie, those two times. I could remember really burning over those things. I was insulted. I really was . . . It was all like his sense of humor, but there was a certain amount of seriousness to it. He wasn't interested. I wasn't going to make him any money."

Joni became Joni through the ten-thousand-plus hours she put in on the road. Her mother may have called her a quitter, but it took an extraordinary amount of stamina and discipline to book herself all those gigs, to travel, mostly by car, all over the United States and Canada to play all those live shows. Joni realized pretty early on that there would be no shortcuts to the success that she craved. In particular, she would remember, with a little bashfulness, how she had once encountered Gordon Lightfoot, a folk-rock singer a few years her senior, who was becoming internationally known. Robbie Robertson of the Band called Lightfoot "a national treasure" and Bob Dylan famously said that when he heard a Lightfoot song, his only wish was that "it would last forever." Joni remembered approaching Lightfoot, eager for wisdom; he had the things she wanted—better bookings, a contract, and ownership of his publishing. "He really could do nothing for me, but I felt somehow or other let down by his attitude that he couldn't give me any advice."

Later, when people were turning to her for career advice, hoping that she might offer them a leg up in the music business, Joni thought back to Lightfoot and "the position that I had put him in." She would reflect: "The way I became successful between 1965 and 1973 . . . was the way that was available. It meant a lot of working in front of audiences. I continually performed, so that's something I say to people . . . I feel if you are great, you will be found out. I think it would be more difficult for people who are only good."

Joni knew that she was more than "only good." During a tour of Michigan clubs, with Elliot Roberts gamely in tow, Joni went to see her ex, Chuck Mitchell. Years later, he would recall that it was a "rainy fall night, with a moody golden light coming from the chandelier." Joni stood with her back to Chuck, her "tenement king," and peered out the window onto the street below. And what Chuck remembers her telling him is, "It's gonna happen, Charlie. I'm scared, but I'm gonna be a star."

David Crosby was not the most prepossessing of suitors. His round face, mustache, and fedora inspired Joni to compare him, not entirely kindly, to the Looney Tunes cartoon character Yosemite Sam. But this guy was a big deal. He was the arranger of the Byrds' harmonies—a crucial element of the band's sound that made a number one hit with Dylan's "Mr. Tambourine Man."

Crosby was in rock star limbo and had time on his hands. His exit from the Byrds was teased on the cover of the first issue of *Rolling Stone* ("Byrd Is Flipped"): In the end, the guitarist and vocalist Roger McGuinn just couldn't take Crosby's ego trips anymore—whether it was his acting like he was the first conspiracy theorist about the Kennedy assassination when introducing "He Was a Friend of Mine" in concerts or pushing a song, "Triad," about how much fun a guy could have with two girls.

Crosby was planning to follow the path of his cinematographer father and sail around the world. He had just borrowed $22,000 from Peter Tork of the Monkees to buy a boat that was docked in Florida— and he was in Miami, checking out the new talent, browsing the clubs where he had played when he was a fledgling folkie. He walked into the Gaslight South, in the Coconut Grove neighborhood, known among folk musicians as "The Grove." The rest would be a conversionary experience he would tell and retell for decades. Joni was seated on a stool, with her skirt just high enough to keep the crowd interested as she told anecdotes that would last just long enough for her to move from one open tuning to another. For a male heterosexual musicophile, there was so much to watch, so much to hear, and it was all coming from her. Unemployment did not make this ex-Byrd any less confident. And yet, even as he knew that he had the power to make her famous, he was also suddenly vulnerable in a new way. This beauty was a better musician than he was, and he knew it by the time the set was over.

"She was singing 'Michael from Mountains' or 'Both Sides, Now' or some other fucking wonderful song," Crosby told me. "And she just knocked me on my ass. I did not know there was anybody out there doing that. And I fell for her immediately. It was the highest quality of songwriting that I'd run into. I liked her better than Dylan or anybody. I thought she was the best girl songwriter that I had encountered. I was also very attracted to her. When she was done with that we hung out in Florida a little bit and then I took her back to Los Angeles and started introducing her to the Los Angeles record scene and I produced her first album. We went to Los Angeles, and there's a famous picture of her and I and Eric Clapton sitting on a lawn at Mama Cass's, and Clapton has this slightly stunned look on his face 'cause he had never heard her before. I did that regularly. I would say, 'Joni, could you sing a song?' and it was just a delight to watch their minds crumble out their noses when they heard this girl. They would tell me she was the best young girl singer-songwriter that they'd ever met, which was the truth. Nobody knew about the open tunings, and up till then, there were very few of us doing it. I was doing it, but I was nowhere near as sophisticated as Joni became. And the lyrics are deep, man. She is a truly magnificent writer."

If you go back to the photograph that Crosby referenced, there's something else, too. Besides Crosby lying back and looking blissful, besides Joni in a red-and-blue-striped shirt playing the guitar and singing, besides Clapton cross-legged and mesmerized, in the foreground of the photo, there's a baby, Mama Cass's daughter, chewing on a film canister. Joni is looking away from the little girl.

According to Joni, she and Crosby had a brief summer romance. It was never serious, but it was sweet. "I was kind of impressed," Joni recalled. "He was a star. He loved my music. And he was in a really good place, which he never got back to. He was relatively drug free. He wasn't doing cocaine. He was just smoking a lot of pot. I was so feminine then. I'm my own man now. I've had to fight so many battles. I had to get tough. He just was genuinely excited by the music, which was exciting for me that someone established thought it was good. I was young and I knew that it was good, but I didn't know if anyone else was going to think so. And he had just bought this boat, the *Mayan*. It was a beautiful boat. Coconut Grove was really sweet then. It was like Malibu when I first moved there. It was poor. A lot of artists, novelists, stuff like that. It was slow, and the air smelt of flowers, it was poignant, it was warm, and he was actually a joy. We used to ride our bikes and kid around and he had sparkly eyes and didn't show any signs of the problems to come. We had a summer affair. But there were no plans."

Riding on the *Mayan* was the peak of their seduction. By the time they arrived at her apartment on West Sixteenth Street (where Tony Simon was staying), the static was already beginning. "It was a summer affair, which did not translate to another city, or anywhere else," Joni said. "Chalk it up to a nice experience and move on. Because it's never gonna be nice again. When he came to see me in New York, he was just a whole other person. He was paranoid and grumpy. He was paranoid about his hair. He was unattractive in every way and overlording. He was not the same person. We broke up. It was a nice thing in Florida and this horrible thing in New York.

"Elliot and Geffen and I went to California."

Despite the static, Crosby welcomed Joni to the LA he knew so well. He drove her, and her friend Geffen, around town in a Mercedes, blasting *Sgt. Pepper*. Joni found a house in Laurel Canyon, though not the one on Lookout Mountain that she would later buy. But she had enough from her just-signed record contract to put up the money for a rental.

There is a photograph from *Record World* dated March 16, 1968. Joni is at a desk, ready to sign the contract. She looks lovely, but there is tension in her face. Three men hover over her: Reprise's VP and general manager, Mo Ostin; Elliot Roberts; and David Crosby, who is lending some of his fame by putting his name on the album, even though he has no idea how to live up to the title of "producer." Ostin looks directly into the camera and offers a professional ear-to-ear grin. Crosby and Roberts both look down, smiling serenely. Joni is pensive. Peggy Lee could have summed it up: Is that all there is?

The not-so-plush offer has come from a right-wing Englishman named Andy Wickham, who is living somewhat incongruously in Laurel Canyon. With the exception of Vanguard Records, he's the only person in the industry to make Joni an offer. Wickham's job at Reprise is unusual. Rumored about. No one seems to quite understand it. He's friends with Van Dyke Parks and Randy Newman, the industry oddballs. His favorite song is Merle Haggard's "Okie from Muskogee," which he plays for everyone he meets, and he's not being ironic. "Andy Wickham heard me somehow," Joni recalled. "He gave me the worst deal in the world. But it wasn't as bad as what Vanguard offered me. That was even worse."

By the time the papers were signed and Crosby and Joni were in the recording studio—his first attempt at production and her first at the console—their relationship had turned turbulent. But Crosby's genuine giddiness about Joni's gift would never fade. To his mind, they were embarking on a grand adventure: getting Joni's performances of her original material to the public. Crosby thought listeners should experience as closely as possible what first rocked his world in Coconut Grove, which meant pure Joni: guitar and vocal.

In 1963, this would have been a standard folk aesthetic. By 1968, this was way out of style. Dylan had gone electric in 1965. Psychedelia, LSD, Jimi Hendrix, and *Sgt. Pepper* had already happened. What Crosby was proposing was a throwback, and to industry insiders, it could sound like little more than a demo. The approach was cheaper, which was an upside on a deal of Joni's size, but it would also show off her orchestral approach to the guitar.

First albums are often made as an escape hatch to prevent them from being last albums, meaning that back then, for your debut, all you wanted to do was serve up appetizers. Back when the music business was plush, and deals were made for the long haul, you saved the good stuff for the second album, when your name was established and you had built up an audience. For his eponymous debut album, when he was being mocked as John Hammond's folly, twenty-year-old Bob Dylan went to the Columbia studios and recorded only one original song and a few folk standards, some of which he had never even tried in clubs. He was saving something for later, when he then quickly recorded his follow-up, *The Freewheelin' Bob Dylan* (1963), which would include "Blowin' in the Wind," "Masters of War," "A Hard Rain's A-Gonna Fall," and "Girl from the North Country." Life would never be the same. Simon and Garfunkel nearly blew their chances on *Wednesday Morning, 3 A.M.* (1964), an all-acoustic debut that contained "The Sounds of Silence," with some gospel and altar-boy songs that seemed like attempts to divert attention from their Jewish names. The album was initially a flop, and their careers were saved only when an electric "Sounds of Silence" hit number one the next year.

As a debut recording artist, Joni was in a place similar to Leonard Cohen's, except that she was much younger. At thirty-three, Leonard was slightly long in the tooth to make a pop debut. He had been sitting on lyrics for years, many of them poems, and held nothing back from *Songs of Leonard Cohen* (1967), a debut that laid everything on the table. It had been written and recorded before his encounter with Joni, but was released in the midst of their on-off transfiguration. That same year, another debut, *The Velvet Underground & Nico*, was released. As Brian Eno very famously observed, only about a hundred people initially bought the album—but each of them formed a band. It is now recognized as a classic. Also in 1967, Jimi Hendrix held nothing back for *Are You Experienced*, one of the most extraordinary debuts in the history of rock and roll, forever changing the depth, static, and attack of the electric guitar, loaded with hits that will continue to be played as long as classic rock is a format.

Song to a Seagull is an astonishing debut, but it did not give everything away. Joni already had enough excellent material for three albums, and she would sit on some of the greatest among her songs with the confidence that her career would unfold, and that whatever growth she would make along the way would accommodate some songs that, in the hands of others, had already proven to be successful. Her debut was, like Simon and Garfunkel's *Bookends* or *The Kinks Are the Village Green Preservation Society*, a concept album in the wake of *Sgt. Pepper*. Side A and Side B were titled Part 1 and Part 2, to call attention to its literary ambition. Part 1 was "I Came to the City," with some songs written when she lived in Toronto's Yorkville neighborhood (where you had to persuade someone to get out of the house already in "Night in the City"). Others were written when she was living on the edge of New York City's Chelsea district, at 41 West Sixteenth Street.

Part 2 was "Out of the City and Down to the Seaside," when David Crosby first spirited her away on a boat ride and then eventually on a plane to the other coast, to Laurel Canyon, all of which occurred just months before the album was recorded. Thematically, there was nowhere to put "Both Sides, Now" or "The Circle Game" or "Urge for Going." Everything had to fit the overriding narrative, and Joni also wanted the album to sound fresh, not like cover versions of her own songs. "Chelsea Morning," crackling with urban exuberance, could have fit on the city side, but would have been in danger of overwhelming it, sounding like too much of a good mood for an album that, apart from "Night in the City," was a story told by a fairy princess in an echo chamber resounding with her own melancholy. It is, of course, a gorgeous, compelling weariness, even an addictive one. It was the mood Joni would become best known for, even though, as her career unfolded, she would contain multitudes.

Perhaps she felt the need to make a Serious Statement, since she knew that it was hard to be taken seriously in the boys' club of American pop. The album was advertised on Sunset Strip billboards with slogans blaring, first, "Joni Mitchell Is 90% Virgin," then "Joni Mitchell Takes Forever," and concluding with "Joni Mitchell Finally Comes Across." Who knows what the good people at the label thought they were doing, but Joni needed to meet these attitudes with seriousness, what she felt she needed in order to be respected by a group of powerful men taking advantage of the sexual revolution without noticing the revolution part. She had to be even more serious than the competition.

Even *Bookends* had the whimsical "Punky's Dilemma" and "At the Zoo";
even *Bringing It All Back Home* had a couple of joke tunes ("Bob Dylan's
115th Dream," "Outlaw Blues"). And, of course, there were jokes all
over the Beatles' output, and the more revered they were, the cheekier
they got. She seemed to match the melancholia of Leonard Cohen, but
even his debut contained the exuberance of "So Long, Marianne," and
he would eventually sing a song (with a chorus including Allen Ginsberg and Bob Dylan) called "Don't Go Home with Your Hard-On."

"I'm starting to get my own vocal styling now," said Joni in 1968.
"It's sort of a law of averages. You don't bomb anymore."

It's telling of the era that when the *Rolling Stone* editors wrote their first
big profile of Joni, the article was accompanied by a portrait of her shot
for *Vogue* magazine the year before. The black-and-white photograph
shows Joni mid-song, holding her guitar and wearing a white embroi-
dered peasant-style top. The portrait is standard Woodstock-like fare,
but the words accompanying the picture are anything but. You can see
the editors struggle to explain why Joni is more than she seems on the
surface, how she may present like her girl-singer peers, but how it is
she stands apart. The writer is the legendary *RS* editor Ben Fong-Torres,
the date is May 17, 1969, and the questions raised are ones that will stay
with Joni for a very long time: "Just who—and what—is Joni Mitchell,
this girl who's so obviously perched on the verge?"

> The old names are back, but in more commercial regalia. Judy Collins,
> softened, orchestrated, countrified (and even, on national TV, mini-
> skirted), is a regular chart item now, after years of limited success. The
> music (someone called it "Art Rock," but that can be ignored) features a
> lighter, more lyrical style of writing, as exemplified by Leonard Cohen.
> As if an aural backlash to psy-ky-delick acid rock and to the all-hell-
> has-broken-loose styles of Aretha Franklin and Janis Joplin, the music
> is gentle, sensitive, and graceful. Nowadays it's the personal and the
> poetic, rather than a message, that dominates.

Into this newly re-ploughed field has stepped Joni Mitchell, composer, singer, guitarist, painter, and poetess from Alberta, Canada.

Miss Mitchell, a wispy twenty-five-year-old blonde, is best known
for her compositions, "Michael from Mountains" and "Both Sides,
Now," as recorded by Judy Collins, and "The Circle Game," cut by Tom
Rush. She has a first LP out (on Reprise). A second album—recorded
during successful concerts at UC Berkeley and at Carnegie Hall—is
ready for release, and another studio album has already been recorded.
She is editing a book of poetry and artwork; a volume of her compositions will follow shortly. And she has received a movie offer (to conceive, script, and score a film).

Not bad for a girl who had no voice training, hated to read in
school, and learned guitar from a Pete Seeger instruction record.

Just who—and what—is Joni Mitchell, this girl who's so obviously perched on the verge?

To those who don't spend hours in audio labs studying the shades,
tones, and nuances of the human voice, Miss Mitchell is just a singer
who sounds like Joan Baez or Judy Collins. She has that fluttery but
controlled kind of soprano, the kind that can slide effortlessly from
the middle register to piercing highs in mid-word.

Like Baez, Miss Mitchell plays a fluid acoustic guitar; like Collins,
she can switch to the piano once in a while. And her compositions
reflect the influences of Cohen.

On stage, however, she is her own woman. Where Joan Baez is
the embattled but still charming Joan of Arc of the non-violence cru-
sade, and where Judy Collins is the regal, long-time lady-in-waiting
of the folk-pop world, Joni Mitchell is a fresh, incredibly beautiful
innocent/experienced girl/woman.

She can charm the applause out of audience by breaking a guitar
string, then apologizing by singing her next number a capella,
wounded guitar at a limp parade rest. And when she talks, words
stumble out of her mouth to form candid little quasi-anecdotes that
are completely antithetical to her carefully constructed, contrived songs.
But they knock the audience out almost every time. In Berkeley, she

destroyed Dino Valente's beautiful "Get Together" by trying to turn it into a rousing sing-along. It was a lost cause, but the audience made a valiant try at following. For one night, for Joni Mitchell, they were glad to be sheep.

Joni would become an iconic singer-songwriter but she would never become a "star" in the biggest sense of the word. This was not for lack of talent. She had what it took: she had all the charm, the charisma, the poetry, the voice, the looks, and the chops. But the *Rolling Stone* analysis above hints at something that has never been fully explored: records were too limited a medium to capture all that Joni brought to her live performances. As an intensely visual artist, Joni would have thrived in this age when an artist like Beyoncé releases a concept album like *Lemonade*, with short films, more than music videos, to accompany every track.

Joni was sitting on a formidable songbook by the time she signed on to Reprise, and some of the songs, especially those that were never released, were at least as playful as "Big Yellow Taxi," a track that ends with laughter on her third album. She would save her stand-up for the clubs, where she would sing a song, "Mr. Blue," in response to hearing that Dylan had written "A Hard Rain's A-Gonna Fall" based on unused bits of other songs. (This would probably characterize much of Dylan's associative writing in his '65–'66 burst of brilliance.) Mr. Blue was blue because he was treating his old lady badly, Mitchell tells the coffeehouse crowd, so he deserved everything he got. "Oh, Mr. Blue, you blew your chances long ago," Joni seemed to relish singing. She was particularly proud of causing scandal with these lines: "Hang on one more day or two / Then I promise I'll be laying you." It sounds like Mr. Blue hadn't blown *all* his chances yet.

There was more whimsy—and some accidental self-revelation—in "Ballerina Valerie," inspired by a documentary about the dancer Vali Myers, so scandalous with her "redheaded fits" that she was even exiled from Paris. Just when she began receiving commercial offers after dancing alongside a Donovan performance of "Season of the Witch"—a deadly serious song for the Wiccan Vali—she was so bewildered, she hid in a cave. The ink on Joni's Reprise contract was barely dry when she was trying this song out in coffeehouses, and it wouldn't take long for her to have second thoughts and eventually plot her own escape. She announced her composition as a psychedelic song that would make a natural Coca-Cola advertisement—laughing as she spoke, pronouncing the word with her Canadian diction on the second syllable. Joni reveled in turning this wild gypsy into a Coke commercial, right down to the jingle melody:

> *Everything's bright as he draws on the pipe*
> *And the bowl glows redder*
> *And things go better with Coca-Cola*

That finale always got a big laugh in clubs where she would be on the same bill as stand-up comics like Mort Sahl. Her own dialogue was often peppered with screwball comedy timing. Before a woman could have political or economic power, she could be Lucille Ball or Elaine May. Joni had a big, generous laugh that welcomed everyone, even herself, from the introspection for which she is better known. The humor songs of that period have remained unrecorded, and the laugh lines stayed out of the music, at least for her debut. She had something serious to share.

There is an imperfection to this debut Serious Statement, and it was not the fault of the material. *Song to a Seagull*, sonically speaking, is not quite what it wanted to be, and this was largely because of a technical glitch, and the buck stops with David Crosby in the producer's chair. "I hadn't recorded it well enough," he recalled later. "I had allowed too much noise—too much signal-to-noise ratio—too much hiss." Removing this hiss also removed considerable resonance, and this was further marred by a failed experiment. Crosby, who had only previously experienced the studio as a performer, thought it would be a groovy idea to get the overtones and the resonance from the piano strings—Joni also was keen on this idea—but he had no idea how to get the levels right.

Compare the sound quality with her follow-up, *Clouds*, engineered by Henry Lewy, who would be Joni's cherished partner in the studio throughout her greatest experiments of the '70s. It is the audio equivalent of a blurry, opaque lens versus a sharp, lucid one. Almost immediately after the release, Joni said it sounded like it was recorded in a bell jar, which, given the emotional subject matter of the songs, was unintentionally appropriate. The Joni of her debut is trapped in the reverberation of her own voice, the echo chamber of her mind. Still, Crosby was enthralled with his lovely discovery, and also enthralled with himself for plucking her from the Gaslight South.

"He would take me around and show me off like he'd invented me," Joni said. "It was kind of embarrassing. You see the look on his face [referring to the famous photograph on Mama Cass's lawn]. Clapton couldn't figure out what I was doing. He was leaning on his fingers like a monkey. His mouth is gaping open. But Crosby is sitting there like a proud papa, as if I were his discovery. As much as I was young and wanted people to hear my music, I found it embarrassing. He'd trot me out and he'd call me down from upstairs and watch me blow their minds.

"But then we got into the studio, he kind of held court and he was incompetent," Joni recalled. "I don't know how he screwed up the sound the way he did. It's not on the masters. There was hiss on the tapes, but not on the masters. He was trying to get the sympathetic vibrations off of the strings. All they had to do was cut off that track and everything would have been fine. The masters weren't ruined. This was just voice and guitar with very few effects on it. So whatever it is that is making the sound suck could have been remixed in a night, the whole thing. Just balance the guitar and the voice, add a minimal amount of echo, a tiny touch, and remix it. But instead, he took it to David Adderley to remix it to try and get the hiss off, and in the process they took off the high end of the vocals. That was a really stupid call. I don't know what that cost me. You put it on with a stack of other records and you'll hear how bad the sound is. Judy Collins said it sounded like it was under a Jell-O bowl. The performance is strong, but it's scratched like an old silent movie negative."

Still, the sound quality couldn't bury such extraordinary material. Joni's ascension was unquestioned.

Joni's evenings are most people's mornings, and on "Night in the City," *Song to a Seagull*'s most ebullient track, she celebrates her nocturnal muse. She introduced the song in 1967 thus:

"It's about a night in any city where you go out and wander around listening to music. I wrote it about a place in Toronto, Ontario, called Yorkville Avenue. It's a little village there, and there are clubs all along for several blocks and you can . . . stand in what I think of as music puddles, where music sort of hangs from here to here, and if you step too far over into the other direction, then you're in . . . a new music puddle. And it's dedicated to all people who came tonight with someone who took much too long to get ready."

"Night in the City" is not harmonically adventurous by Joni's standards—it's straight-up blues with a lyrical melody—but it is set way past bedtime and, stepping into unknown "music puddles," anything could happen. It is the closest thing the album has to a group performance. On bass is Stephen Stills, who happened to be down the hall at Sunset Sound with Buffalo Springfield (whose other leader was Joni's old friend Neil Young). And Joni accompanies her guitar playing with some blues-based piano riffs.

"I got this piano idea for 'Night in the City,' and I hadn't played piano since I was eight years old," Joni recalled. "But I had to find the notes. It was about twenty minutes of groping, then I located the part, and now I had it. I had to bring it up to speed. It probably took about an hour, and I probably did it in an hour and a half, which isn't that long. I've seen people go for four days for a fucking drum sound. And David Crosby says, 'Shouldn't we get a real piano player, man?' So I thought, okay, I don't need a voice of discouragement here. I know I'll get it. I'm zeroing in on it, and just give me a little more time. He did a lot of things like that. Also, I'd do a performance and he'd go into raves when I knew I had a better one in me. I thought I'd be better off using my own judgment."

"Night in the City" ranges from rhythmic alto in her chest voice in the verses, to ethereal soprano work in the chorus, as if the pitch for the city has to have more of a rock and roll insistence—the only song on the album with this feeling—while in the chorus she sounds more like a fairy princess. But it is leaping into the forbidden puddle that is the song's most prophetic feature. "Music comes spilling out into the street / Colors go flashing in time," she sings, as if the demarcation of someone else's domain brought new colors to the canvas of evening. In an earlier cultural moment, Wallace Stevens wrote, "The night knows nothing of the chants of night. / It is what it is as I am what I am." In 1967, night was still a beautiful mystery, colored in the tones and timbres of psychedelia. Joni overdubs a bluesy piano part, her first recording on the instrument. If drums and an electric guitar had been added to the mix, Joni could have produced some acid rock herself.

Song to a Seagull ends with its most ambitious song, "Cactus Tree," a song Joni said she was inspired to write after seeing *Dont Look Back*, D. A. Pennebaker's documentary that followed a few weeks of Bob Dylan's UK tour in the spring of 1965. Throughout the film, which Joni said "made a big impression" on her, Dylan is rude, obnoxious, and particularly cavalier to Joan Baez. Joni clearly identified with Dylan and not Baez, and, inspired by "It's Alright, Ma (I'm Only Bleeding)" and "Gates of Eden," both performed in the film, piled image upon image, but with more euphony. She said she even lengthened her "a's," to sound like his, although her voice and guitar sound nothing like Dylan's. Even when she was influenced, she was still independent, which is what "Cactus Tree" is about. Experiences pile up, they make a huge impression, but she keeps moving. Joni's metaphor of the cactus tree is like the rolling stone gathering no moss, except it's even deeper. She keeps taking in experience, growing more resilient, storing up each storm to get her through each drought. It is about a strong woman who needs no gardener.

The song opens with how this album was made—and who was producing it—in the first place: David Crosby, the sailor who "takes her to a schooner / And he treats her like a queen / Bearing beads from California . . ." Joni is just getting started. The woman of "Cactus Tree" is collecting men and exfoliating in her own time. She fears that someone will "ask her for eternity."

"'Cactus Tree' is about a woman who has a lot of suitors and none of them are quite right," Joni recalled. "And it's ironic: She's so busy being free. It's dripping in irony. I was trying to maintain the freedom to be myself, and men always Svengali on you. They think it's their right. And they all have a different idea of what they want you to be." And she doesn't have to keep any of them. She doesn't even have to keep the person she was. On her first album, she lays out her many selves, from the city to the seaside, with chords that end on a question mark.

Before her first album hit the streets, Joni had an encounter with another innovator, Jimi Hendrix. It was the year everything changed, 1967, when the sound of electric guitars turned thick, fat, and gloriously clangorous. Very few musicians in any genre not only master an instrument but reconceive how the rest of us hear it. Hendrix's reinvention of the electric guitar belongs with what Louis Armstrong and Miles Davis did for trumpet, Charlie Parker for alto sax, Sonny Rollins and John Coltrane for tenor, Bud Powell and Thelonious Monk for piano. These are august names to invoke for a guitarist who never even learned to read music (much to Davis's surprise when he set up charts for Hendrix), but Hendrix lived up to them. He gave his audience feedback, distortion, and a huge attack that made earlier rock guitar seem spindly by comparison. There were great rock guitarists before Hendrix, but the very best who were around for the Hendrix revolution—Jeff Beck, Eric Clapton, Pete Townshend, Jimmy Page, Robbie Robertson, among others—quickly added the feedback and distortion just to compete.

Rock guitar, in other words, divides into pre-Hendrix and post-Hendrix. In addition, he wrote powerful and beautiful songs—"The Wind Cries Mary," "Castles Made of Sand," "Little Wing," "Voodoo Child," and "Angel," to name a few—and his covers were more like hijackings. He was, as Harold Bloom might have put it, a strong poet.

And so it happened that Joni and the Jimi Hendrix Experience were both playing Ottawa in March 1968. Hendrix left the following testimony in his diary:

March 19

Arrived in Ottawa. Beautiful hotel. Strange people . . . Beautiful dinner. Talks with Joni Mitchell on the phone. I think I'll record her tonight with my excellent tape recorder (knock on wood). Hmmm . . . can't find any wood . . . everything's plastic. Beautiful view.

Marvellous sound on first show. Good on second. Good recording. Went down to little club to see Joni, fantastic girl with heaven words. We all got to party. OK, millions of girls. Listen to tape and smoked up at hotel.

March 20

We left Ottawa City today. I kissed Joni goodbye, slept in the car awhile . . .

Hendrix's drummer, Mitch Mitchell, wrote about that night in his memoir, *Jimi Hendrix: Inside the Experience*:

We heard of this great girl singer in town, called Joni Mitchell. Hendrix and I had these portable Sony tape recorders, huge things that we dragged 'round the world. So we went to this little folk club, after our gig, with Hendrix's tape machine. We were amazed, she was wonderful. So we taped the show and then went back to the hotel.

Turns out, not only is she staying in the same hotel, but she's on the same floor. So we went back to the room, just the three of us, played the tape back, compared notes, that kind of thing. It's two in the morning, but we're keeping things low and we'd been there about an hour and the manager comes up. He went fucking berserk. "You can't have guests in your room."

What! We couldn't believe it. We were all staying on the same floor, for God's sake.

So we said, "We can't have any guests in this room, right?"
"Yes."

So we moved everything into my room. We got chased out of there and went to Joni's. This went on all night. Unfortunately, the tape recorder and the tape were stolen the next day, so end of story on that, but strange guy. Who knows what it was? Black man, white man, white girl, I don't know.

Nearly half a century later, Joni did know. "Back in those days, the music was segregated," Joni told me. "Rock and roll had not fully gotten into the arena scale where it was, mostly playing for dances, where it should have stayed. To me, rock and roll was dance music at its best." There was a theater in Ottawa that had been converted to stages. Rock and roll was performed to a seated audience, starting at 7:30 and ending at 10:30. Joni was used to the coffeehouses, which typically started at 8:30 with four sets until midnight, and the jazz musicians would play later. The rock promoter also owned the Libeau coffeehouse, where they had a party for Hendrix, attended by Mitch Mitchell and Joni. Hendrix, reel-to-reel in hand, came into the club and shyly introduced himself.

"My name is Jimi Hendrix and I was just signed to Reprise, the same label that you're on. Could I tape your show?"

"Sure," Joni said.

"So he put the reel-to-reel down," Joni recalled. "Here's the mic and here's me and he put it down on the side, on the left, facing the stage, and he spent the whole show leaning over it and watching levels all the time. He didn't put it there and back off. He engineered it all the way through. Once in a while, he'd glance up and smile and go back to this thing. After it was over we all went to a party that the promoter put on and I'm looking right and he's looking left. This guy came up to them and said, 'What sign is Joni?' And they said, 'Scorpio.' And he said, 'I've got all these songs. I've got one for every sign in the zodiac. I could pull any girl with these.' And Jimi said, 'Well, you won't be pulling her.' I don't have much memory of an asshole coming up to me and singing a Scorpio song, hoping to sweep me off my feet. We didn't stay there very long and we went back to the hotel. It's a stuffy old hotel that was part of the parliament buildings. And we went to my room first and we played back portions of his show, sitting on the floor like a campfire, really close to it. Not loud. And sitting cross-legged around it. Well, the hotel dick came up and told us to break it up. They didn't like the idea of three hippies sitting around, especially one black, alone in the room in this conservative hotel. So we left and we went to Mitch's room, and we had it down so low, we were huddled over it. And they broke it up again. We thought: 'Indian build him big fire, sit him far away, Indian build small fire, sit him close.' We built a small fire and sat him close. We were leaning over this thing. We went from my room to Jimi's room to Mitch's room, and the cop kept showing up and breaking us up, and we kept rotating around. In the course of the evening, it was a really sweet visit with both of them. Mitch had a very good memory, unlike everybody else's."

That night, Jimi confessed to Joni that he was already growing weary of playing guitar with his teeth, but he didn't want to disappoint his fans. He was envisioning a style more like Miles Davis's: an ensemble with no theatrics. Alas, Hendrix did not live long enough to evolve in this direction.

A month later, the outside world barged in on such innocent memories. Nineteen sixty-eight, after all, was a year not just of decadence and hedonism but of assassinations and riots. Dylan had stopped writing protest music after 1963. Joni hadn't yet developed the strident voice of protest that would alienate some of her fans in the '80s. The year *Song to a Seagull* was released, she had already expressed her misgivings about the fantasy world of much of the album. She was writing about emotional and erotic turmoil, but that didn't stop her from protesting in the press. In a 1968 interview with *Melody Maker*, she disclosed that she hadn't yet figured out a way to write about the violence inflicted on people her age: "I'm too hung up about what's going on in America politically. I keep thinking, how can I sing 'night in the city looks pretty to me,' when I know it's not pretty at all, with people living in slums and being beaten up by police? It was what happened in Chicago during the Democratic Convention that really got me thinking. All those kids being clubbed. If I'd been wearing these Levi's, they'd have clubbed me, not for doing anything, but this is the uniform of the enemy. That's what they are beginning to call the kids today, the enemy."

This does not sound like the giggly ingénue who was delighting audiences on the folk circuit, although it does foreshadow the deeply principled artist who was beginning to emerge. Creating beauty and truth was something Joni could always do on an intimate level. David Crosby believed that her maturity led to that early prodigal depth in her music. "I think she had more understanding than most people do of human beings. She had already been through some hard things. What makes human beings get wisdom is paying dues. Sort of like, you arrive as a boulder and you knock corners off yourself until you get smooth like a river stone. She was already starting to get smooth."

8 ▓ *CLOUDS*

oni thought of herself as a painter first, a musician second. But
Joni the painter went against all the trends in art school. Really,
the only twentieth-century painter she loved was Picasso. Her own
draftsmanship looked back further—to Van Gogh, to Rembrandt.
Yet her music looked forward, taking Dylan, Cohen, Ellington,
Piaf, Holiday, Miles, and so on and creating something new. Joni the
antiquated painter would be on display on many of her groundbreaking
albums, certainly offering something worlds beyond the imaginations
of the record labels' design departments. *Clouds* is filled with daring
emotions, open tunings, weird chords, enchantment, sorrow and ebullience, and everything in between. It offers no shortage of beauty, and
yet every song on *Clouds* sees beyond conventional ideas of beauty,
forcing listeners to rethink what they thought they knew or appreciated. Those chords, those feelings, for all their drowsy nights and
Chelsea mornings, could be dark, eccentric, brooding, difficult. And the
cover?

Joni is the girl on the cover. She is not smiling. She is in black, but offers a red flower with six petals. She is not going to pluck them to ask "How do I love thee?" Her gray-blue eyes aren't staring us down. They seem to be in a trance. They are certainly entrancing. But, for someone with such emotionally indeterminate songs, where is the chiaroscuro? Joni is posed before a Pacific sunset, filled with yellow, orange, and red. Wouldn't nightfall be a better moment for this album filled with such indeterminacy? *Song to a Seagull* didn't sell much. Would the pretty girl in the hills of Laurel Canyon—on an album featuring the tried-and-true successes of "Chelsea Morning" and "Both Sides, Now"—make the nickel go down the slot this time? Joni's artwork would become more daring pretty soon—the vivid and earthy paintings of *Mingus*, the takeoff of Rousseau on *The Hissing of Summer Lawns*—but on this record, a pretty girl could invite you into a dangerous and difficult brew. Fear is like a Wilderland, she tells us. Yet you are being led there by this stunning visage. It's hard to resist.

On April 4, 1968, Martin Luther King, Jr., was assassinated, and just hours later, Joni Mitchell climbed into her first limousine. She looked out the window at New York City and saw mounted police and fights breaking out everywhere. "We moved along slowly. People were beating on the limo." Joni had just been signed by Elliot Roberts and he had booked a concert on Philadelphia's Main Line, at Swarthmore College, where she was to be the opening act. The limo was not for Joni, but for the singer Laura Nyro, and they were on their way to pick her up, but once they did, it was hours before they could make it to the concert. "We rolled into Philadelphia and in the meantime, this guitar player had had to go on first, and such importance was placed on position billing. And he had to go on, and I got there, just as he finished his set, late. And I went on and he couldn't stand it. So he went on again, and everybody walked out on him. Talk about a stupid ego! I believe we stayed in Philly that night."

Riding in a limo while cities rioted, Joni felt history breathing down her neck. She had never been political before, but now politics would find her, and she would have to respond, in her way. Dylan—who had sung fiercely about the murder of Medgar Evers for Martin Luther King, Jr., at the March on Washington—was now out of the protest business, and it would be years before U2 ("Pride") and Paul Simon ("So Beautiful or So What") would eventually deliver their MLK eulogies.

Oscar Wilde famously quipped, "A map of the world that does not include Utopia is not worth even glancing at," but it was getting more difficult to believe it. Joni still had the fictional Sisotowbell Lane to cling to. "It was my dream of happiness. I didn't dream of being a rock star. My dream of happiness was Sisotowbell Lane—my place in Canada . . . Really rural . . ." The festival at Woodstock would keep the utopian ideal alive for a while. But not for long. These were turbulent times.

In his 1973 novel *Gravity's Rainbow*, Thomas Pynchon originally used a verse from "Cactus Tree" as the epigraph to section 4, "The Counterforce." After much anarchy and war, Pynchon's book ends with apocalypse, without the philosophical comfort of the counterculture. These lines are a kind of apolitical declaration of freedom:

> *"She has brought them to her senses,*
> *They have laughed inside her laughter,*
> *Now she rallies her defenses,*
> *For she fears someone will ask her*
> *For eternity—*
> *And she's so busy being free . . ."*
> —Joni Mitchell

Although this appeared in the reviewers' galleys for the novel, it was replaced in the finished book with

> *"What?"*
> —Richard M. Nixon

These were times when the demands on the artist loomed larger than personal experience, but Joni wasn't made for writing about collective movements. She was grateful to Buffy Sainte-Marie for singing her praises a few years earlier and for covering "Song to a Seagull," but she did not want to write a clone of Sainte-Marie's "Universal Solider." She needed the human element—character and narrative and humanity—which was all the more vital as her new adopted country was destroying itself: old vs. young, war vs. peace, silent majority vs. Weather Underground.

Joni was an exile—later, more of a roaming ambassador—from Canada, with a left-leaning prime minister, and where the biggest political controversy she could recall from growing up was when it was time to choose a flag. "It's good to be exposed to politics and what's going down here, but it does damage to me," she told a reporter in a cover story for the *Rolling Stone* issue dated May 17, 1969. "Too much of it can cripple me. And if I really let myself think about it—the violence, the sickness, all of it—I think I'd flip out."

A year later, on May 4, 1970, the Ohio National Guard shot four unarmed students at Kent State University during a protest against the Vietnam War. Neil Young, Joni's old friend from Canada, responded with the stomping, outraged anthem "Ohio." What could Joni do? She was the first to admit that hers was a naïve wisdom and that she was still trying to find her way in a world that was becoming increasingly difficult to comprehend. When she sang, "I really don't know life at all," she meant it.

Joni's and Neil's songs had sung to each other before. She told the story to an audience at a BBC taping in London in 1970. "In 1965 I was up in Canada, and there was a friend of mine up there who had just left a rock and roll band in Winnipeg, Manitoba, near where I come from on the prairies, to become a folksinger à la Bob Dylan, who was his hero at that time, and at the same time there were breaks in his life and he was going into new and exciting directions.

"He had just newly turned twenty-one, and that meant in Winnipeg he was no longer allowed into his favorite hangout, which is kind of a teeny-bopper club and once you're over twenty-one you couldn't get in there anymore, so he was really feeling terrible because his girlfriends and everybody that he wanted to hang out with, his band could still go there, you know, but one of the things that drove him to become a folksinger was that he couldn't play in this club anymore. He was over the hill.

"So he wrote this song that was called 'Oh to Live on Sugar Mountain,' which was a lament for his lost youth. And it went like this . . . [sings a few verses].

"And I thought, God, you know, if we get to twenty-one and there's nothing after that, that's a pretty bleak future, so I wrote a song for him, and for myself just to give me some hope. It's called 'The Circle Game.'"

Neil was a grumpy young man: he thought life would only go downhill the minute you became too old for the teen clubs and too young for the bars. The girl singing "The Circle Game" consoled the boy of "Sugar Mountain." Just you wait, Neil. Life will get *much* better. (Joni even made a rare use of standard tuning to perform "Sugar Mountain" on the radio in 1967 with Chuck Mitchell on second guitar.)

Joni and Neil would remain kindred spirits. He would add his harmonica to her later song "Furry Sings the Blues," and she would add her voice to his performance of "Helpless" in Martin Scorsese's concert film *The Last Waltz*.

The world around Joni was changing fast. But before her music could catch up, she had a backlog of songs from various incarnations, lovers come and gone, cities lived in and abandoned.

The songs on Joni's second album, *Clouds*, released in May 1969, emanated from Toronto to Detroit to New York, on the road in Fayetteville, North Carolina, and finally Los Angeles's Laurel Canyon. *Song to a Seagull* had peaked at a not-so-auspicious number 189 on the *Billboard* charts, yet Reprise was patient, especially since Joni, a vocals-and-guitar artist, was relatively cheap to record. She loaded her second album with songs—"Chelsea Morning," "Michael from Mountains," and especially "Both Sides, Now"—that had already been hits for Judy Collins. The *Clouds* songs were practically archival—the "new" album would be filled with "old" songs—but it was an opportunity for Joni to reclaim those songs for herself.

Before she could do that, however, there was a producer she had to get around.

His name was Paul Rothchild and he was best known as the producer of the Doors. In the three weeks in which Rothchild tried to whip one song, the lead track, "Tin Angel," into shape, it triggered a slew of painful memories. "When I was a child and took piano lessons, I composed a piece called 'Robin Walk' and I brought it in to my teacher to play, and she hit me with the ruler. I thought I was the only one, but it turned out that every piano player of my generation got a rap on the knuckles from their piano teacher. She said, 'Why would you want to play by ear'—smack!—'when you could have the masters at your fingertips?' Well, how did the masters come up with this music? By playing by ear, right?"

Even as an eight-year-old piano student, Joni was onto something. And she was self-possessed the next time an authority figure tried to squelch her muse. After an agonizing experience birthing "Tin Angel," the album's maudlin opening track, Joni—like a kid skipping school—asked the engineer Henry Lewy if he would help her finish the album over the next few weeks, before Rothchild came back from producing the Doors. Joni knew that Lewy was a busy man. She also knew she had to conscript him right away.

"Henry, I can't go through this," she said. "You know, this will kill my love for music, you know, I'll never want to record again if I have to go through this process. Could we get it done in two weeks before he gets back?"

Without missing a beat, Lewy said, "Sure." A relationship was born. Lewy, a soft-spoken German Jewish refugee, had already amassed an eclectic résumé, working with a range of artists from the Mamas and the Papas to the Chipmunks. Joni could have it both ways, utilizing the engineer's knowledge for all things technical without the imprimatur of a George Martin–Phil Spector model of producer as auteur.

"What happened with Henry is that he was a producer on her

records, without the title," said Larry Klein, a bass player and producer who would become Joni's second husband. She would eventually concede to this by calling Lewy, in the credits for *The Hissing of Summer Lawns* (1975), "more than an engineer."

"Rothchild and Crosby made her think of 'producers' with dread and anger. She came to simply hate the word. The idea that there are a lot of bad producers is absolutely true, but there are a lot of bad everything doing everything," said Klein. "There are a few people who are good at what they do, and there are a lot of people who are not good at what they do. But she had a real trigger when it came to the word *producer*."

She was a young woman dodging male authority in a man's world. "I found that all the producers were men, and if I stood in defiance of them, then someone would call me a 'ballbuster,'" Joni later remembered. She had a painter's ego; she did not welcome authoritarian intervention. Being told in the middle of a track that she had missed her mark was, to her, coitus interruptus. She knew her way around the studio better than Rothchild thought. But this was not really about music, it was about power, and Joni was going to seize it for herself.

Getting blown off by Rothchild for two weeks for the Doors was a gift. Joni liked the assistance, without the authority. "Henry's an engineer," Joni insisted later. "You don't need a producer. A producer is a babysitter if you don't know what you're doing. A producer is an interior decorator. I decorated my own house. I don't need a decorator . . . I never put 'producer' on the stuff that Henry and I did because there was no producer. My point was that you don't need one.

"But what happens if you have a vacuum? They started giving credit to the second engineer or anybody who was near." The second engineer, she would explain, got coffee for the engineer. "I'm the producer," Joni told me. "Henry was my assistant. My point was that I didn't need a producer. A producer is a leech. He's a babysitter and an interior decorator for people who are lazy or not full artists."

Joni now had a partner in Henry Lewy, someone who had exquisite ears and who knew how everything worked—and, most of all, what Joni wanted—all without vanity or authoritarian behavior. She didn't need Paul Rothchild or anyone else to step on her freedom. She and Rothchild would meet again: when *Clouds* won the 1970 Best Folk Performance Grammy and he was listed, just for "Tin Angel," as producer. With her golden hair, her joking, her miniskirts, and, of course, with the soprano end of her three-octave voice, Joni could seem so sweet, so girlish. But if she needed to bust balls, she would find a way to do it.

The songs on *Clouds* beautifully and elegantly meander toward enlightenment, sometimes reveling in fantasy, sometimes coming to terms with reality, when every new day can be greeted with ebullience or uncertainty. Lovers can light up the sky or disappoint. Euphoria or revenge or moping: pick your track, then pick the optimal part of the track, since the emotions, with their ambiguous chords, take unexpected journeys.

After the morbidity of the opener, "Tin Angel," with its foreboding minor progressions and "Roses dipped in sealing wax," ebullience bursts through with "Chelsea Morning." The song was written in 1967, and when Joni introduced it in clubs, she would blame Andy Warhol's film *Chelsea Girls* for giving girls in Joni's hood a bad reputation. (Leonard Cohen, who had become affiliated with Warhol's Factory crowd, coincidentally, was living a few blocks away at the Chelsea Hotel.) The song dances with the joy of the prairie girl from Saskatoon who, not even a morning person, still finds delight in wondering what excitement the day and the (not yet gentrified) neighborhood could bring. Notes that modulated down in club performances now veered upward.

Joni was spending a lot of time on Bleecker Street because of the folk clubs there. The golden era of Dylan and Baez had faded, but the audience, perhaps hoping to catch the next Dylan or Baez, was still filling the clubs, and Joni, with her homemade glamour, packed them in at the Cafe Au Go Go.

"I wrote ['Chelsea Morning'] in Philadelphia . . ." Joni recalled decades later. "Some girls who worked in this club where I was playing found all this colored slag glass in an alley . . . We collected a lot of it and built these glass mobiles with copper wire and coat hangers. I took mine back to New York and put them in my window on West Sixteenth Street in the Chelsea district. The sun would hit the mobile and send these moving colors all around the room. As a young girl, I found that to be a thing of beauty."

Joni had a small room, but its window and its reverberations brought the outside in. Joni was mugged three times while living on this block, but it did not dampen her hope. And even though she was cooped up in a little room, what happened outside of the room, including who she might bring into it, electrifies the song's buzz. (Chelsea Clinton would be named after this song, even though it was the Judy Collins cover that her parents loved.)

That buzz was stopping and starting in many directions on *Clouds*. Joni was changing so fast between 1966 and 1969, this collection sometimes suggested scattered selves, parts of which would be developed later and others that would be abandoned, stunted influences, innocence sometimes derailed on the way to experience. There are experiences, there are songs, and then there is the cultural "share," and *Clouds* is an instance of when these things did not all happen in order. "Chelsea Morning" and "Both Sides, Now" had already been popularized by Judy Collins. The Tolkien fixation of "I Think I Understand" was a phase. Joni was already living in Laurel Canyon by the time she recorded songs written in Detroit and New York. She was writing songs at a furious clip, and engaging in a cultural moment that was changing fast, too. Mother Nature, as Neil Young would put it in song, was on the run, and Joni was keeping up with her.

There were, of course, roads not taken and orphans left behind. In 1967, still an unsigned artist, she found herself playing a club in Fayetteville, North Carolina, and she asked a friend what she should see there.

"Well, there's Fort Bragg, you might as well go ahead and see that," he said. Unlike most of the members of the Woodstock generation,

Joni was not opposed to entertaining the troops. Her father was a flight lieutenant in the Canadian Air Force, and she believed that performing for soldiers was not the same as endorsing the policies of Secretary of Defense Robert McNamara. Still, Fort Bragg proved to be disappointing. She found the antics of the self-styled "Fayette-Cong" to be unpleasant, to say the least. Joni bought a guitar from an army captain, a little Martin classical. It had made it to Vietnam and back. The soldier who was carrying it was not so lucky. Just when she felt ready to give up on the charms of Fayetteville, inspiration came from the most unlikely place:

"The last day I was there, my friend said, 'I just remembered something you should do before you go away. You should go and see the dentist.' I didn't think that was a very exciting idea until we got out there and I found out that the dentist was not just a dentist, he was an amateur architect, and like a lot of rural North Carolina people, he had collected around his house lots of rusty junk, just discarded and abandoned things: wrecked cars and old decrepit tractors. Suddenly, he looked out and saw that he had three acres of rusty junk he'd collected and he hadn't done anything with it. It was just lying out all over the place. So he began to build a house, and he's still building it. I think he'll always be building it. It's made of portholes from ships and television screens and tractor wheels and Pepsi-Cola-crate paddle wheels, formal weed gardens, rusty palms with dead rubber mallard things at the bottom. Piped full of Muzak for the tourists, roof covered with spinning things, television antennas, those funny little air-conditioning units from the tops of buildings. It's really a wonderful place, so I wrote a little poem coming back, a silly little poem called 'Dr. Junk, the Dentist Man,' and I set it to this silly little Bo Diddley melody. It's a silly little song."

Joni followed a whimsical song about a hoarder with an achingly gorgeous love song that would become a standard in its time, a song about being kept in turmoil that could speak to anyone who ever felt that way. Some things are meant to be cast out—on the lawn, on the cutting-room floor, circled clichés from Mr. Kratzmann. But sometimes it takes a rumination on garbage before coming up with the flowers. Sometimes one has to produce a throwaway to come up with a perennial.

"The same day that I discovered crazy old Dr. Junk the Dentist Man, I sat up all night and wrote another song, on which I do a little trumpet solo. My daddy was a trumpet player. I always wanted to be a trumpet player." That song was "I Don't Know Where I Stand."

Even though "I Don't Know Where I Stand" is about ambiguity—an uncertain romantic status and an unresolved set of expectations from a lover—its delivery is as classic as Tin Pan Alley. The song starts minor, resolves major, and goes back to another minor chord, as if to say that happiness is brief and that loneliness has endless variations. Plus, she's writing from the road, a lonely room in Fayetteville, North Carolina. The nocturnal Joni probably didn't greet that many Chelsea mornings with such glee, and she probably didn't usually feel, as she did with "I Don't Know Where I Stand," "so drowsy now I'll take what sleep I can." The song's harmonic eccentricities were not obviously commercial, but its lyricism and emotional content would not have been out of place in the crooner era that she loved in her childhood. In the years since, the song has been covered more than thirty times, most notably by Barbra Streisand.

Did she want to know where she stood? Was she the doormat or the heartbreaker? No one wrote kiss-off songs quite like Bob Dylan, including "Don't Think Twice, It's All Right" and "It Ain't Me, Babe," and the song that turned Joni into a believer: "Positively 4th Street." But she never wanted the language to be at the expense of music. So her breakup song on *Clouds*, "That Song About the Midway," had a deceptive lyricism and melodic sweep. Judy Collins recalled in her memoir, "Joni wrote 'That Song About the Midway' about Leonard, or so she says. Sounds right: the festival, the guy, the jewel in the ear."

Although Cohen may have resonated in the song, David Crosby, four decades later, was sure the song was about him. "The 'David, hello, I love you' song was 'Dawntreader,'" Crosby said. "And the 'David, goodbye, we are done' was 'That Song About the Midway.' She came into a party that we were all at and sang it looking straight at me angrily and then sang it again. She didn't want there to be any misunderstanding."

Joni said of Crosby, "I guess people identify with songs that you write and think that you wrote them just for them." Joni's vocal performance of "The Dawntreader" is as intimate as her singing ever got. It is a breathtaking performance—as otherworldly as a mermaid, and as familiar as a lover. It's no wonder that Crosby, who produced the song on *Song to a Seagull*, would have wanted to be its source of influence. Joni's affair with Crosby overlapped with her affair with Cohen. Crosby was instrumental in her career; Cohen was essential for her art. And Joni's independence would ultimately be crucial for everything. "That Song About the Midway" does not sound, melodically, anything like a Dylan breakup song, but it is just as venomous in its delicate execution. Even if the song was addressed to a composite—Leonard Cohen from the 1967 Newport Folk Festival and Crosby from the Gaslight South in Coconut Grove, Miami—it wouldn't have stopped her from repeatedly singing it like a weapon to Crosby at a party, throwing his flamboyance in his face.

The song begins with attraction, although the man's dubiousness is obvious from the start, playing the horses as he was playing on a guitar string. And while Cohen influenced Joni's songwriting, it was Crosby who acted as Joni's talent scout, even if he was so confident in her gifts, he didn't see it as much of a gamble. The gambler becomes a devil, a man who stood out "like a ruby in a black man's ear." The passage evokes a line from *Romeo and Juliet*, I, v, 49: "It seems she hangs upon the cheek of night / Like a rich jewel in an Ethiop's ear / Beauty too rich for use, for earth too dear!"

This guy is a gambler, a pimp (of music anyway), an eagle taking unfair advantage of his prey from the sky. The usually indefatigable Joni—the one who could drink a case of her lover and still be on her feet—has had enough. At the end, the man is still gambling, and the singer is tired. "Slowin' down / I'm gettin' tired! Slowin' down / And I envy you the valley that you've found." Is the valley Laurel Canyon, so rich with musical and erotic possibility? Will the rambling gambler keep rolling the dice? The singer has had it and is ready to move on.

"The Gallery" has also been associated with Cohen, although it is clearly not straight-up memoir; it is about an artist who is a connoisseur of beauty, and who continually collects beauties while his old lady stays back. It is a doormat role Joni would never have created for herself in real life. If anything, she would identify more with the artist than the old lady, like the libidinously resilient singer of "Cactus Tree" from *Song to a Seagull*. The singer of "The Gallery" wonders what it would be like to devote so many years to such a cad: "I gave you all my pretty years / Then we began to weather / And I was left to winter here / While you went west for pleasure." This was as close to "Stand by Your Man" as Joni would ever get, and it ends with bitterness and regret.

A more eerie brew is cooked up in "Roses Blue." A curio in Joni's canon, one as eccentric as the unreleased "Dr. Junk," "Roses Blue" is a song that Joni introduced in a 1969 concert as a "song about a witch who lives in my nation's capital," referring to Ottawa and not Washington, D.C. "All you need to be a witch is the right amount of negativity and the belief that you have that power," she said. The combination of major and minor is not only appropriately creepy for her subject, but actually inspired a jazz cover by the eclectic trumpeter-composer Dave Douglas on his album *Moving Portrait* (1998), an up-tempo exploration of chromatic surprise, sounding an awful lot like Wayne Shorter writing for Miles Davis, chordal explorations for the future (Douglas even quotes Shorter's "Orbits" toward the end). "To me there was something incantatory and magical about 'Roses Blue,'" recalled Douglas. "I mean, obviously the lyric deals with the supernatural, the paranormal, and the dark side of where that can go. In addition, as with all Joni Mitchell songs, the musical content supports the lyrics in such a profound way that the entire effect is deepened. It's eerie. Joni has a deep, rich, elaborate, and finely tuned ear for harmony and its effects."

A version by the superb jazz pianist Brad Mehldau from *Live in Tokyo* (2004) shows how a virtuoso takes the song's spooky juxtaposition of major and minor keys, scrambles them up, and keeps the melody and the chords intact. There is no chorus, no bridge, just a refrain about thinking of roses blue; the musical trajectory is insistently grim, as if the rose's petals were wilting. The lyrics drift from a painterly image of roses blue—a still life with an ominous hue—and we learn, associatively, of a woman named Rose, who casts spells, mixes potions, and haunts. Among her dark arts are "zodiac and Zen." Even though Joni fit the '70s mold of a woman who believed, at least playfully, in astrology, and whose recent lover Leonard Cohen would eventually become an ordained Zen monk, and was already frequenting Zen monasteries and writing songs about them, lyrically, this song about the occult is an anomaly in Joni's songbook; musically, the sublime jazz covers—and their exploration of advanced harmonics way beyond the vocabulary of folk—speak for themselves.

On an album that includes songs of former neighborhoods, lost cities, ex-lovers, and the *Lord of the Rings*–inspired "I Think I Understand" ("Fear is like a Wilderland," goes the song's refrain, a chilling memory and wake-up call from her Tolkien period), Joni did not understand why America was killing civilians on a daily basis in Vietnam. Ever since the Tet Offensive of 1968, a consensus grew that America, strategically and morally, was losing the war, and televisions broadcast the evidence—a burning village, a crying Vietnamese child—seven days a week. Young men choosing between fighting an unjust war and risking prison looked to pop musicians for answers, even though none of them had backgrounds in foreign policy. Poets who wrote meaningfully on war—Tennyson, Yeats, Auden—weren't foreign policy experts, either, and didn't need to be. The best protest singer of the era, Bob Dylan (who was also no foreign policy expert), sat this war out, although songs from 1963—"Blowin' in the Wind," "Masters of War," and so on—could still apply to any war anywhere. John Lennon, proudly naïve, came up with "Give Peace a Chance," a song with a chorus anyone could understand, but with verses that needed an apparatus for anyone who wondered about most of the obscure figures name-checked in each verse. David Crosby's "Almost Cut My Hair," his reaction to the RFK assassination, turned the war into an aborted trip to the barbershop, and it was only slightly comforting to know that he decided to let his "freak flag fly." Jimmy Cliff's "Vietnam" was more like it: a simple story with a new groove—thought to be ska but actually what was then the new beat of reggae. Freda Payne's "Bring the Boys Home" was a soulful tearjerker. Amid the new antiwar anthems, Joni's first offering of peace sounded like the oldest ones, even older than "We Shall Overcome." The eerie acappella of "The Fiddle and the Drum" is, like "Blowin' in the Wind," a song that could have been written hundreds of years earlier, as long as there has been war, which has been forever, even longer than the guitar.

Here, as in Dylan's song, Joni uses eternal language for a topical issue, but with a twist. She sings the song to America, her "friend," but her friend is not her country. She had been living in the States on a visa for only a couple of years, and was singing as an exile, an outsider to America, as someone who left Saskatoon in the dust, but for what? She was starting to make it big in America, but what was America exactly? People in her age group had become increasingly enraged over Vietnam, and the young men were not only enraged, they were terrified. She looked at the soldiers as scared young men trained to kill. She looked at the same images everyone else was seeing night after night on Walter Cronkite. She looked at Nixon and saw the face of death. This was a long way from Pierre Trudeau. The mainstream had become so warped, a counterculture had to be assembled to register dissent. What is wrong with this place? Who are you people? Why must it cost so many lives on both sides to intervene in someone else's civil war?

The song is stark acappella, stripped of her usual chromatic harmony, as if to say: this is an outrage beyond ornament, or ornamentation. One didn't need to be against all wars to be against this one. There are neither fiddles nor drums in this song—just a voice, a melody, and words singing out against the beats of war. Joni would revive the song in 2007 for Jean Grand-Maître's ballet, for another war and another time. Much of the rock and roll around her sounded like the beats of war. She was singing for something more delicate. "How did you come / To trade the fiddle for the drum?" she sang. Marches never sounded good to Joni, not like Rachmaninoff, not like Debussy, Ellington, or Edith Piaf. "The Fiddle and the Drum" would have fit in perfectly at the New Generation

Club the previous year. And it provides an uncanny introduction to her finally recorded "Both Sides, Now." By the time that song appeared as the coda of *Clouds*, Joni would be three cities, many lovers, and an entirely new life beyond where she had written it two years earlier. Judy Collins won the Grammy for performing it, but Joni had been living it, and would continue to live it.

9 ■ OUR HOUSE

Joni moved out to California with her manager Elliot Roberts and David Geffen, who was just at the start of his own ascension. "I was their first racehorse, so to speak," Mitchell told the music critic Robert Hilburn. "We moved out together from the concrete jungle into the sun and the trees . . . and I'll never forget the smell of Laurel Canyon when we first moved in. Geffen didn't move there, but Elliot and the rest of us moved all the way up Lookout Mountain. It was an amazing time."

As Elliot Roberts described it many years later, "It was the time everyone was coming out to California, there was a camaraderie among all the artists . . . up and down the canyon . . . playing new songs for each other. There was so much happening. Electric music was starting to happen. Acid rock was happening. The Byrds and [Jefferson] Airplane and the Grateful Dead, all those groups were playing all the small clubs."

The house at 8217 Lookout Mountain Avenue in Laurel Canyon proved to be the escape Joni needed from the turbulence of 1969. It fit the elegant bohemian princess that Joni had become: a California bungalow with stone steps, Tiffany stained-glass windows, and a big picture window through which the late-afternoon sun streamed in. The house had a large stone fireplace, and a wildflower garden studded with azaleas, palm trees, and eucalyptus. Sunset Boulevard—all its traffic, clubs, and commotion—was just a five-minute drive away, but the Lookout Mountain house was protected by the foliage from all the noise. It wasn't the country roads and wild open prairie land of Joni's childhood, but it was the kind of retreat she craved. The house featured an intricate Balinese-style carved front door. When the house next door burned down and Joni's home was untouched, she ordered that the soot on her front door should never be cleaned: she considered it a talisman of good luck that had protected her home. Joni decorated the home with keepsakes from people and places she loved: a grandfather clock from Leonard Cohen, prints by Maxfield Parrish, Victorian shadow boxes, cloisonné boxes, and art nouveau lamps. There was a piano, and the house became a gathering place for the great musicians of the day.

She had come such a long way from such a different place, but Joni fit into the Laurel Canyon scene as one might imagine a Katharine Hepburn walking onto a movie set. Once she was in the room, you couldn't imagine anyone else playing the part. The music writer Bill Flanagan explained, "Joni took this really potent, popular image that had been building for seven or eight years anyway: the California girl, the Beach Boys girl, the beautiful golden girl with the long blond hair parted in the middle, and Joni not only *was* the girl, she was also the Bob Dylan, the Paul Simon, the Lennon-McCartney, writing it. She was the whole package. She was the subject and she was the painter and that was incredibly powerful for people."

The pull of Joni and the pull of Laurel Canyon was, and remains, one and the same for Graham Nash, who has said, "I can only liken it to Vienna at the turn of the century . . . Laurel Canyon was very similar, in that there was a freedom in the air, there was a sense that we could do anything. We were scruffy kids that were, in some small way, changing the world and changing the way people think about things.

There was a sharing of ideas and a true love for being in the right place at the right time."

Graham Nash came to visit Joni and found, in her living room, the next chapter of his career. He wrote in his memoir, "The sun had just left the western sky as the cab crawled up Laurel Canyon, bathing the Hollywood Hills in the golden flush of summer . . . It was a place where there were free-spirited people just like me doing the things that I wanted to do, being creative and making music . . . Man, it looked like home to me." On the run from his British rock star past, feeling very much like the "kid from Northern England" that he would always be inside, Nash had called Joni from the airport and she invited him over. He remembered that there was a green VW van parked in the driveway, and from inside the house he could hear "a jingle-jangle of voices." Then, he recalled, "Joni was at the door and nothing else mattered . . . our connection was instant. Joni Mitchell was the whole package: a lovely, sylphlike woman with a natural blush and an elusive quality that seemed lit from within. Her beauty was almost as big as her talent, and I'd been pulled into her orbit, captivated from the get-go."

David Crosby and Stephen Stills were in Joni's living room and David, calling Nash by his nickname, said to Stephen, "Play Willy that song." In two-part harmony, David and Stephen started to sing "You Don't Have to Cry." Nash remembered, "It's a brilliant song. They get to the end and I said, 'Wow, Stephen, that's an incredible song.'" Nash asked them to sing it again. Then he said, "'Bear with me, sing it one more time.' And on that third time, I heard the words, the melody and I knew what I was going to do." Crosby, Stills & Nash was formed in Joni's living room not just on that day, but in that moment. "Whatever sound that Crosby, Stills and Nash has was born in thirty seconds," Nash remembered incredulously. "That's how long it took us to harmonize that way. So much so that we burst out laughing. The [Buffalo] Springfields and the Hollies were good harmony bands, we knew what we were doing. We'd been making records in harmony for years. But this was different. Nobody has any claim on the notes that we sing.

But nobody can sing like David, Stephen, and I when we join our voices together."

And nobody saw music and lyrics the way that Joni did. "There really was an ethic of peace and love and art and poetry," said Elliot Roberts. "Amongst that crowd, poetry, even more than musicality, was revered, and Joan was the best poet of the time. It was the kind of period when she had a lot to say and everyone wanted to hear it."

Joni was the subject of her first major *New York Times* profile that year. When Susan Gordon Lydon, a reporter for the *Times*, came to visit in 1969, Joni played her the newly recorded cut of "Both Sides, Now." "She's the only one who can sing this song," Nash remarked. Lydon agreed, writing, "Her version, mellowed by the experience of having written it and having sung it many times, and by the meanings added to it by Dave Van Ronk and Judy Collins, sounded infinitely rich and definitive." Once the song was done playing, a lovestruck Nash jumped up and said, "That was magnificent, babe. I'm gonna kiss you for that." Elliot Roberts remarked, "You would've kissed her, man, if she would've spit . . . There sure is a lot of love in this house." Joni, for her part, was less mushy—at least in front of the reporter. "Just sit there and look groovy," she admonished Nash when he interrupted her guitar playing. Joni talked to Lydon about her songwriting process and how the songs evolved over time and with different interpretations: "I'm more prolific with melodies than with words, but quite often I write poems and then set them to music. I guess I'm primarily an artist; what I like best is making new music. It's like going into a trance; I sit down with a melody and reminisce. I find it easier to think about my feelings in retrospect. The way I'd like to work from now on is to go into a studio as soon as a song is finished, when the feeling of the song is most intense. You should record songs when you believe them the most . . . But it's funny—after a song's been written, it becomes a whole different thing; you don't own it anymore. I love to hear men sing my songs, because they're written from a feminine point of view, and men bring totally different things to them."

Nash marveled at how Joni wrote songs. "Watching her was the most interesting process," he said. "It's almost like she channels. She was gone for hours. I mean she was physically right there, but she wasn't there. She was gone. I'd say things to her and she wasn't even listening, she was gone. It was a great thing to see, to see someone taken away by vision." Joni was being taken away by vision on Lookout Mountain, but at twenty-five, she was also making the beginning of a domestic life with Graham. In his memoir, Graham remembered that the home he shared with Joni "was built in the 1930s by a black jazz musician, lots of knotty pine, creaky wooden floors, warped window sashes, mismatched carpentry. [It] cost about $40,000. She was not a rich girl at that point, so [Joni] used her artistic sensibility to dress that place in her inimitable style."

When the editors from *Rolling Stone* showed up to do their first major profile on Joni, Graham was "perched on an English church chair" and Joni was "making the crust for a rhubarb pie." She would have, as she ever did, one foot in the 1950s of her youth and one foot in the new counterculture. She told them, "Lately, life has been constantly filled with interruptions. I don't have five hours in a row to myself. I think I'm less prolific now, but I'm also more demanding of myself. I have many melodies in my mind at all times, but the words are different now. It's mainly because I rely on my own experiences for lyrics."

California was home, but New York was still calling. Joni performed her first solo concert at Carnegie Hall that year. There's black-and-white footage of her: she is wearing a long dress, holding her guitar, the microphone is so big it looks like a stage prop, and Joni's blond bangs are so long they nearly cover her eyebrows. She looks happy. By way of introduction, she says, playfully, "It's a long way from Saskatoon, Saskatchewan, to Carnegie Hall." She laughs at her own joke, a light and lilting, carefree laugh, and the audience bellows along with her. A man screams out, in a way that is quite undignified for the setting, "I LOVE YOU," and Joni laughs again.

Graham was with her, and he remembered that "the audience at Carnegie Hall was *ecstatic* that Joni was there and it was jammed to the rafters. It was Joan's coming out in a really big way . . . She had reached a place in her career that was indisputable." She sang, "When morning comes to Morgantown / The merchants roll their awnings down / The milk trucks make their morning rounds / In morning Morgantown." And in that moment, the audience was lifted away to brighter, simpler, more hopeful places.

Joni was proud of her Carnegie Hall debut. She'd flown her parents in from Canada, and the photos show them backstage. Myrtle's smile is wide and toothy as she sits back in her black dress and her double-stranded pearls. Beyond the optics, it was another story. Joni and Graham were wearing maxi coats before they were in style, and heads kept turning in their direction. Myrtle and Bill walked six feet behind them. As conservative prairie Canadians, they were embarrassed to stand out. When Joni took off her coat, she had Gypsy clothes underneath. Fifteen minutes before showtime, Myrtle scolded, "Oh, Joan, you're not going on in those rags."

"As if I was going to degrade them with my appearance," Joni recalled. "That was typical of my mother. And the people she was afraid of, the upper crusties, they would have that same reaction. So frightened and so nervous, poor thing."

There's a photograph from the end of the concert: Joni is holding a bouquet of flowers and a giant cutout heart that says, "Dear Joni, New York LOVES YOU."

A few months later, in August, Crosby, Stills, Nash & Young played at Woodstock. Joni was invited as well. David Geffen remembered that the group arrived at LaGuardia Airport and that, as he put it, he "picked up a copy of *The New York Times* and it said, *400,000 people sitting in mud*." He turned to Joni and said, "Let's not go." She was scheduled to make her national TV debut on the Dick Cavett show the next day. What if she got stuck up there? Joni wasn't pleased. She remembered, "The boys weren't going to miss out on it and they rented a helicopter. They got in and . . . they got out [and] they crashed the TV show the next day."

"The deprivation of not being able to go provided me with an intense angle on Woodstock," Joni recalled. "Woodstock, for some reason, impressed me as being a modern miracle, like a modern-day fishes-and-loaves story. For a herd of people that large to cooperate so well, it was pretty remarkable, and there was tremendous optimism. So I wrote the song 'Woodstock' out of these feelings, and the first three times I performed it in public, I burst into tears, because it brought back the intensity of the experience and was so moving."

On a personal level, though, hearing her boyfriend Graham Nash and her ex-boyfriend David Crosby waxing poetic about it was not easy to take. "They showed up raving about it," Joni said in an interview on *MTV News* in the 1990s, "which was really like salt in the wound . . . 'Cause to be young then and to have missed that, even though it was that close, that was everything to me. But I guess it was meant for a reason, and because I couldn't go, [Woodstock] dominated my mind. I watched everything on TV, I just sat in front of the TV and wrote most of the song in the first few days of the festival, and it was done by Sunday night."

Nearly four decades later, Joni saw the value in the song more than the event, and thought of it as a lost opportunity. She said to me:

"'Woodstock' wouldn't have been written if I had been there, because those events are full of the back room, full of sibling rivalries. There are pockets of cooperation, but everyone's desperate to win. It's not a sports event, but there is that element of it, and it accelerates up to opening night, and it translates to a lot of hideous effort. People will be playing beautiful at rehearsals, but by the time they get to opening night, their performances are grotesque with effort. It's like competitive children at those events. From the audience, they don't see it, but you see it backstage. I wouldn't have been able to write it if I had been there, because I would have been caught up in the backstage neuroses. I ended up in the position of the fan who couldn't go, so I could be more romantic about it than I could have been if I had been there and caught up in the reality of it. I saw it as the closing of a window of opportunity. It was the beginning of a potential, but it was also a funeral."

And so while a cultural moment was preparing itself in three days of peace, love, and music, with mud and mescaline and all the other now-legendary ingredients, Joni, holed up at the Sherry-Netherland, prepared to share music and quips with Dick Cavett, who, after the cancellation of the Smothers Brothers, had become TV's emissary between counterculture and mass culture. Cavett was a Yale grad in the showbiz tradition of Cole Porter, who could trade barbs with Groucho Marx or even sit as a mediator in the Norman Mailer–Gore Vidal feud (he sided with Vidal). He indulged past-their-primes Marlon Brando, Orson Welles, and Gloria Swanson, matched wits with Woody Allen, dished the dirt with Truman Capote, and had no idea how to talk to Stevie Wonder. He was sharp, a Nebraskan like Johnny Carson, but more erudite and proud of it. His Woodstock show would be like none other: a rap session where the most aggressive kids would get the most airtime.

Since the Cavett show was the entire reason Joni missed Wood-stock, it must have been unnerving, on her major American television debut, to be sharing the stage with people who had played Woodstock *and* made it back in time. Stephen Stills (who showed off genuine Woodstock mud on his jeans) and David Crosby (who compared the event to an "encampment of the Macedonian army") represented the flight (to and fro) that Joni could have taken. Jefferson Airplane was there as well, with plenty of ribbing between Grace Slick and Cavett (who, name-checking another rock icon who made a few appearances on his show, called Grace Slick "Miss Joplin" and teased her about her time at the Finch Academy, an Upper East Side finishing school). Joni managed to play four songs and chime in when she could about the virtues of Pierre Trudeau or share her views on astrology (she noted that Crosby, a Leo, looked like a lion), but mostly she had to sit back and hear war stories about the event she'd missed, and on the broadcast she'd missed it *for*. Cavett had no idea at the time that Joni had missed the festival for his show, and if he had known, he would have been a nervous wreck. "If I were to use this for a short story, I would have Joni say, 'I've gotta go to the festival. Everybody's gonna be there,'" Cavett ruminated more than four decades later. "And then I'd have the manager say, 'You want to play on somebody's farm for some pigs and a hundred people instead of being on the Cavett show?'"

All these years later, Cavett didn't see the downside for Joni:

"Where did anyone get the idea that the show was supposed to be about Joni? Never was the show conceived as a Joni Mitchell show. We were delighted to get her. Tony, my producer, said, 'We leapt at the opportunity to do a show on Woodstock because it was the kind of thing that Carson, et cetera, would never do.' We knew it would get a lot of attention. Airplane, Jimi Hendrix, and Joni Mitchell were to be the artists . . . On the morning we went on we learned that Hendrix could not be pried out of wherever he had gone to ground after closing Woodstock. That morning Stephen Stills and Crosby happened to drop into the studio and agreed to sub to fill in for Jimi. Because Neil Young is Canadian we had to get a special permit for them to perform and we could not get that out of the State Department on a moment's notice despite the best efforts of the ABC people in Washington. So, Stills and Crosby agreed to do a 'talk spot' to fill in the hole in our show. Joni was a dream. Airplane almost drove us into a mental hospital, and of course there was the 'Up against the wall, motherfuckers' line in the Airplane song that got broadcast after they promised to change it. In any event, it was *never* planned as a Joni Mitchell show. *Nobody* was told that it was. With just Mitchell, we could have stayed in our studio in our theater."

The set of the Dick Cavett show was as brightly colored as a *Brady Bunch* montage. He sat in a circle with Crosby, Stills, and the Airplane. Joni was wearing green and seated to his left, looking almost wistful as they regaled Cavett with tales of Woodstock. At one point, her hand is on her cheek and the regret and longing in her eyes is palpable.

About a year later, on the BBC, Joni still couldn't get over it. Sitting at the piano, she is golden and glowing in a peach-colored crocheted blouse and a turquoise necklace. Her blond hair is parted down the middle. Just as she smiled through the pain during the early performances of "Little Green," the girl who got left behind is still flashing her big toothy smile as she explains, "So I stayed home in New York and I watched it on television all day. I saw everyone playing and singing. It was really a nice festival, I guess, from the looks of everything." She then says, "I wrote a little song for my friends to sing." Then she pauses and taps her own heart. "For myself to sing as well, and it's called 'Woodstock.' It goes like this."

The new song is a powerhouse and Joni's voice has never been more magnificent.

> *I came upon a child of God*
> *He was walking along the road*
> *And I asked him, where are you going*
> *And this he told me*

Graham remembered, "By the time we got back to the hotel, having gone through that tremendous experience, the song 'Woodstock' had already been written." It's hard to imagine now that the historic event was not even twenty-four hours old, but Joni had encapsulated it all, beautifully, poetically, without cliché: "We are stardust. We are golden. And we've got to get ourselves back to the garden." David Crosby marveled, "She contributed more to people's understanding of that event than anyone who was there."

"Woodstock" became a classic rock staple in the hands of Crosby, Stills, Nash & Young, who turned it into an ebullient anthem. But Joni wasn't kidding when she compared the event to a funeral. Her version of the song is a modal dirge. It can be played on nothing but the black keys on the piano—a minor chord, a suspended chord, and moving down to a ninth chord. It is the product of listening to hours and hours of *Kind of Blue*, which is based on modal variations. "Woodstock" would have fit in as a brooding ballad. Joni lets out a wordless, tribal moan. This is not only "song and celebration." It is purgation. It is an omen that something very, very bad will happen when the mud dries and the hippies go home. That garden they had to get back to—it was an illusion. It must have been lonely for Joni. She was the only one who could see it.

––––––

After Woodstock, after the Dick Cavett show, Graham and Joni returned to California. They were back in the garden, but their time in Eden would not last. Years later, Joni would tell a twenty-two-year-old Cameron Crowe, "My relationship with Graham is a great, enduring one. We lived together for some time—we were married, you might say. The time Graham and I were together was a highly productive period for me as an artist. I painted a great deal, and the bulk of my best drawings were done in '69 and '70 when we were together. To contend with this hypercreative woman, Graham tried his hand at several things. Painting. Stained glass. And finally he came to the camera. I feel he's not just a good photographer, he's a great one. His work is so lyrical. Some of his pictures are worth a thousand words. Even after we broke up, Graham made a gift of a very fine camera and a book of Cartier-Bresson photographs. I became an avid photographer myself. He gave the gift back to me. Even though the romance ended, the creative aspect of our relationship has continued to branch out."

But before the romance fizzled, Nash would write the song "Our House." His version of the story began, "I don't know whether you know anything about Los Angeles, but on Ventura Boulevard in the Valley, there's a very famous deli called Art's Deli. And we'd been to breakfast there. We're going to get into Joan's car, and we pass an antique store. And we're looking in the window, and she saw a very beautiful vase that she wanted to buy . . . I persuaded her to buy this vase. It wasn't very expensive, and we took it home. It was a very grey, kind of sleety, drizzly L.A. morning. And we got to the house in Laurel Canyon, and I said—'You know what? I'll light a fire. Why don't you put some flowers in that vase that you just bought?' Well, she was in the garden getting flowers. That meant she was not at her piano, but I was . . . And an hour later 'Our House' was born, out of an incredibly ordinary moment that many, many people have experienced."

It was a lovely moment captured by a sweet song. But on a day-to-day basis, it would prove hard for two talented musicians, two bona fide pop stars, to share the idyllic space created within the three minutes of lyrics that make up "Our House." Nash recalled, "It was an intense time of who's going to get to the piano first, who's going to fill up the space with their music first." This wasn't a partnership of unequals, as her marriage to Chuck Mitchell had been. With Joni and Graham, it was different, harder. "It was an interesting clash of 'I want to get as close to you as possible' and 'leave me alone to create,'" Nash remembered. Joni for her part said, "Graham and I have been the source of many songs for one another. A lot of beautiful music came from it and a lot of beautiful times came from it."

The photographs of that era are like stills from a movie that we've never seen. There is Graham in a fur coat and Joni in velvet, in a photo-booth-like setting: Joni is on his lap and she is laughing, in frame after frame after frame. There are Joni and Graham walking in the woods, holding hands and swaying to music we can't hear. Look again and there they are in their house: Joni is wearing a silver bracelet and her golden hair is parted in the middle and she is both artist and muse. The window swings open and Joni is smiling, ever so lightly.

A fragment of the view was used for the cover Joni painted for *Ladies of the Canyon*, her next album. The house was such a keepsake of so many songs and so much love that, although Joni moved out a few years later, she never sold it. For years, she rented it to her road manager, Ron Stone. She could never quite let it go.

10 ■ *LADIES OF THE CANYON*

L*adies of the Canyon*, released in April 1970, would be an album of first and lasts. It was the first of Joni's albums to feature the piano; several songs (among them, the lyrical "For Free" and "Willy") were written when she was exploring the instrument with freedom for the first time. There was mad love for Graham Nash, and the prairie girl Joni would, with "Big Yellow Taxi," create what *The New York Times* called "perhaps the first entry in a new genre that might be called Ecology-folk." It would close with three giant hits—"Big Yellow Taxi," "Woodstock," and "The Circle Game"—and the album would be her first to be certified platinum. And it would mark the end of her folk princess days. Joni would emerge a genuine pop star.

The album opens with "Morning Morgantown," a burst of simple beauty that Joni wrote in 1967. She overdubbed piano and guitar, as she had on "Night in the City," but here it was with an almost baroque precision. And there was something new, too: the cowbell played by Milt Holland is the first percussion sound to appear on a Joni Mitchell album, and even the softest of brushes would alter her rhythmic landscape. From there, the album would move on to some of Joni's most memorable songs—and some of her least. It ends with a triple-header. Just when you've been grooving to the Bo Diddley beat and philosophical abyss of "Big Yellow Taxi," you're left reeling from "Woodstock" and taken over the top with "The Circle Game." After Judy Collins and the other hit makers, Joni finally became aware of her own stock. She was an album away from announcing that "songs are like tattoos," but she was leaving her listeners with something they would never forget. Between the splendors of the opening and closing, there are other high watermarks and a few curios only the initiated ever talk about. Who else talks about "The Arrangement" or "Blue Boy"?

"The Arrangement" is about a *Mad Men*–type character who "could have been more than a name on the door." It's a very '60s sentiment—you could have been so much more if you hadn't sold out. But then Joni was learning the distinction between selling herself and selling out, or selling *without* selling out. And this was Joni's first platinum album. It was twice "half a million strong," and what's wrong with that? She was spreading the word just the way she wanted to.

"Conversation" begins as a straightforward rock and roll song with a pulsating beat, on every two and four—the kind of meat-and-potatoes rock and roll Neil Young was ushering into perfection. But the presence of Holland, a pair of brushes, and a more subtle Latin beat intervenes, changing the feeling of the song. Milt Holland's musical credits were vast. He played drums with James Taylor and Randy Newman, bongos on the *West Side Story* soundtrack, marimba with the Beatles.

An early version of the song had more verses of frustration. When Joni introduced it at Philadelphia's Second Fret in October 1967, this was how she set it up: "Sometimes a best friend won't tell a best friend really anything near the truth, because they don't know it themselves. This is a song about a triangle."

The *Ladies of the Canyon* version sounded more like a party. This version would not be about brooding or complaining, but about being the girl the guy wants to cheat with, and eventually ditch his old lady for. "She only brings him out to show her friends," she sings. "I want to free him." Yes! And we are confident that she will. "Love is a story told to a friend / It's secondhand," she sings. We are all hearing it.

Back home in Canada, the *Toronto Star* raved that Joni's "old rambling folky lyrics are gone . . . replaced by a more sophisticated, compressed and direct poetry reminiscent of Leonard Cohen's. The words and melodies are oddly syncopated rather than obvious." In *The Guardian*, Geoffrey Cannon boldly declared, "Joni Mitchell is better able to describe and celebrate what it means, and should mean, to be alive today, than any other singer. She tells us what we already know, but have felt obliged, through life's circumstances, to forget; that we are free. That we have love. And she does this by scrupulous observation and thought only of what she herself has heard and seen and felt."

In real life, Joni may have been a scrapper, feuding in theory and in person with her colleagues, her critics, and her musical peers, but when it came to her music, she was unwavering in her commitment to truth as she saw it—even when the truth did not always flatter her. *Ladies of the Canyon* stands out among the early albums because she is growing in confidence as a vocalist and as a musician, but she has also become so much a part of her community that she can write about it, give a whole album a geographical sense of place. She's no longer the outsider, the girl from up north that she was when she first arrived on the New York folk scene. California in general, and Laurel Canyon in particular, had become, in ways big and small, home.

The title track hauntingly depicts a seemingly utopian community of women from the perspective of one who, as she has said repeatedly in interviews, prefers "the company of men." There is artistic Trina with her "wampum beads" and her coats "trimmed with antique luxury." And Annie, the free spirit mama who "always makes you feel welcome" and has "cats and babies 'round her feet." Then there's Estrella, "circus girl," who "comes wrapped in songs and gypsy shawls."

They were based on women Joni knew well: Trina Robbins, Annie Burden, and Estrella Berosini. Joni's portraiture of the women in song, as well as the iconic line drawing she created for the cover, would only add to the lore of Laurel Canyon as a countercultural paradise.

When Annie Burden and Joni met in 1968, Annie was twenty-two and pregnant with her second child. As Burden described it, the moment was full of uncertainty for women and the world. "In 1968 we all stood at a tipping point. Martin Luther King and Bobby Kennedy were assassinated. Andy Warhol was shot. Richard Nixon won the presidency. Peace and freedom protests and riots swept the world from New York to Paris to Prague to Mexico City to the Democratic Convention to the Miss America Pageant. Women gathered for the first National Women's Liberation Conference. The first humans orbited the moon. All the while I gave only passing thoughts to the headlines. With a blinding faith in the future, I simply made babies and brownies, encouraged by the fact that Joni Mitchell saw me as a sort of Martha Stewart of the '60s. Today, for me, 'Ladies of the Canyon' evokes a cherished snapshot of innocence but also a somewhat painful perspective on my own naïveté."

Annie's husband, Gary, designed album covers and was a pioneer in the field. His work graced the albums of such artists as Mama Cass; Crosby, Stills, Nash & Young; the Doors; and Jackson Browne. There's a photograph taken back then by Henry Diltz that shows Pic Dawson—Mama Cass's on-again, off-again boyfriend and drug dealer—Eric Clapton, Joni, David Crosby, Gary Burden, Mama Cass, and Annie's daughter, Amanda, tumbling on the grass in front of them. "My husband, Gary, worked from his studio off the back of the house," said Annie. "This brought a constant parade of artists and musicians flowing through. Many became friends, and nine days out of ten I set extra places around the dinner table. I never thought of myself as part of the scene—until Joni's song framed my role as a homemaker-hostess in the eye of the creative storm. I took it as a great honor to be included in the song, and I still do."

Trina Robbins was an underground comic book artist at a time when the art form was truly coming into its own. Like many artists of her era, Robbins started out as a science fiction fan in the 1950s. San Francisco was the heart of the alternative-comics world in the '60s, but

Robbins soon discovered it was a decidedly closed boys' club. She worked for a feminist newspaper called *It Ain't Me, Babe* and eventually helmed its all-female comic issue, "It Ain't Me, Babe, Comix." She would go on to become the first woman artist to draw Wonder Woman for DC Comics. Part of how Robbins made money was by sewing clothes, and she remembered that in 1970, after *Ladies of the Canyon* came out, "in gratitude I made her a little black minidress, very simple except for a patch pocket made from antique lace."

Of her part, Estrella Berosini has said, "That is the core of the beast, a.k.a. me. I was raised in the circus, the daughter of a Czech high-wire performer, Vaclav Veno Berosini. Before he legally changed his last name to Berosini, for theatrical purposes, it had been Holtzknecht (translation: Knight of the Forest). This means that, in the reality of my father being born in Bohemia, just as Bohemia was changed to Czechoslovakia, my true heritage name is Estrella Holtzknecht. It also means that I am, genetically, half Bohemian, and the circus life was nothing if not entirely what we come to think of as a Bohemian lifestyle; a life created by one's own imagination." With artistic wisdom, Joni boiled all that down to "Estrella circus girl."

Of course, in writing about all of those women, Joni was also writing about herself. Like Trina, she was a visual artist; she, too, filled her drawing book with line. She was a mother like Annie, even though very few people knew it, though they knew she was mothering—to her lovers, to her friends, to the circle of people who were part of the canyon. Her house was a very fine house because of the way Joni filled it with music and pies, friends and cats, flowers and love. And she was also a bit of a circus girl, producing and writing and performing: a one-woman three-ring circus.

Just as Laurel Canyon was exploding as a place to be in the 1960s, so was Hawaii. Its history with, and as part of, the United States was relatively recent. Imagine this: while the islands had been annexed by the United States in 1898, Hawaii had only become a state in 1959, less than a decade before Joni traveled there in 1968, riding a wave of American fascination with the nation's most exotic state. (Important cultural markers: 1961, Elvis in *Blue Hawaii* and the birth of Barack Hussein Obama on August 4, at Kapiolani Medical Center for Women and Children, Honolulu; and 1968–80, *Hawaii Five-O*.) And just as she had managed to encapsulate all the hope, energy, and magic of Woodstock in a single song, she would, within a matter of days, write a song that captured the conflict between our longing for beauty and the impact that we, as tourists and citizens, have on the places we flock to see.

Between 1960 and 1970, tourism in Hawaii grew from 296,000 visitors a year to 1.7 million. And even in 1960, a travel editor for the *Chicago Tribune* was bemoaning, "Hotels are rising on every hand. Apartment buildings are springing up like mushrooms. Stores and offices fill land that not so long ago was garden." When Joni got to Hawaii, she looked out her window and saw a magical landscape paved over for a parking lot and the kitschy Royal Hawaiian, which was, as the lyric says, actually pink. And she lamented. But with a beat you could dance to, and a peal of engaging laughter at the end.

When *Ladies of the Canyon* was released, "Big Yellow Taxi" became instantly popular—because its protest message was timely and right, and the song was completely infectious. Bob Dylan soon covered it, and replaced the line at the end about the big yellow taxi taking away "my old man" with a Woody Guthrie–like sentiment about a big yellow tractor pushing around his house and land. It was a line that Joni would add for live performances. Like "The Circle Game," "Big Yellow Taxi" was a song that became popular with children and families, reflecting both the innocence of young children and the parental hope that they will inherit a better world.

With "Big Yellow Taxi," Joni was not just riding the wave of American infatuation with Hawaii, she was also, more seriously, exploring the crest of a growing interest in environmentalism. In 1962, Rachel Carson had published *Silent Spring*, a damning condemnation of chemical companies and pesticides, a book that would be credited with launching the modern environmentalism movement and that inspired Joni's "Hey, farmer, farmer / Put away that DDT now." Just as Joni became a composer in her way, without any formal music training, Carson, too, despite her obvious and prodigious gifts, was a maverick without a Ph.D. who had to fight the sexism in her field to do her groundbreaking work. While it's unclear how much Joni knew of Carson's personal story, it seems certain she would have found the scientist to be a kindred spirit. "Put some time into ecology," Joni would muse on "Song for Sharon." She did it most memorably in this song. Marie Curie, Rachel Carson, these were scientists who took on the status quo. These were Joni Mitchell's kind of people.

From the alarm (albeit gentle and whimsical) of "Big Yellow Taxi," Joni ends the album on a more philosophical note. She sings:

> *Sixteen springs and sixteen summers gone now*
> *Cartwheels turn to car wheels thru the town*
> *And they tell him, "Take your time, it won't be long now*
> *Till you drag your feet to slow the circles down"*

By 1970, "The Circle Game" had already been a hit for Tom Rush and Buffy Sainte-Marie. It was a wistful song that singers loved to sing, and it changed with every singer—how they presented it. The carousel is a circle and a game. It may not move forward, but it's life, and even with all its shortcomings, it's a pretty good ride. Even if no one knows how it will turn out.

The critics praised *Ladies of the Canyon* and, as had become common in their approach to Joni's work, their appreciation of her beauty and the beauty of her music was often blurred. Writing in *The New York Times*, Don Heckman confessed, "I have been hopelessly in love with Joni Mitchell since the unheralded arrival of her first brilliant recording. This is her third collection, and she keeps getting better and better. Her crystal clear imagery is as shining bright as ever, and her melodies, if anything seem to be improving. She always has been a fine guitarist and now, surprisingly, she is becoming a growingly powerful singer, too. Unlike the sometimes delicate vocalizing on her first two recordings, Miss Mitchell's work here seems to revel in chance-taking." The stakes would soon be raised more than anyone could know.

11 ■ SAND

One of the loveliest songs on *Ladies of the Canyon* is the plaintive "Willy," about Graham Nash, but by the time the album was released in 1970, the relationship was over. "I had sworn my heart to Graham in a way that I didn't think was possible for myself and he wanted me to marry him," Joni later said. "I'd agreed to it and then just started thinking, 'My grandmother was a frustrated poet and musician. She kicked the kitchen door off the hinges.' And I thought maybe I'm the one that got the gene who has to make it happen . . . As much as I cared for Graham, I thought, 'I'll end up like my grandmother, kicking the door off the hinges.' It's like, 'I better not.' And it broke my heart."

The year was 1969, and she was twenty-six years old. Everything in the world was changing, and young men and women were rewriting, relationship by relationship, the rules of love, lust, marriage, and engagement. Joni took off for Greece and sent a telegram from Crete that said, "If you hold sand too tightly in your hand it will run through your fingers. Love Joan." For years, she would speak with great tenderness of Graham Nash. She could be maligning her contemporaries left and right, but Nash was a sacred subject. "I loved the man so I can't say a bad word about him."

That was before the publication of his 2013 memoir, *Wild Tales*. In the book, Nash describes sailing with David Crosby on his boat, the *Mayan*. They set sail on January 23, 1970, months after his breakup with Joni. Nash recalled, "Joni met us just outside of Panama, and that altered the dynamic. I knew she was coming and it was anything but pleasant. Some kind of argument broke out, with Joan yelling that I hated all women. Coming from somewhere else, I would have dismissed such an irrational remark, but from her I had to think about it and it hurt, for sure. In the end it was nothing more than a way to strike out at me. She had come to Panama to have a nice sail with David and me, but things had turned too ugly between us."

When we met, Joni countered all the important details of Graham's sailing story: "It was unbelievable what he left out—the drama, the real drama," Joni recalled in 2015. Because she is Joni, her first quibble is how the story of that boat ride is told. She agrees, the trip was monumental. But she finds Graham's *telling* of it to be lacking, "I think these people are not storytellers. They're sleeping through their lives." It bothers her that he is clearer about where they kept their stash than on the details of their relationship. She told me, "First of all, he remembers where the dope was hidden: that's the clue. Just before I got there, the cops raided the boat and they didn't find the dope. It was hidden in a jar in the refrigerator. He remembers that. He remembers where the dope was hidden. In the meantime, they're all beating me up for leaving Graham."

All of a sudden we are there: at the soft spot beneath the steely layers that Joni has become known for. In the rock and roll legend books, theirs is the fairy-tale romance of another era: Joni, the blond, blue-eyed girl who could both bake and play the hell out of a guitar, and Graham, the brown-haired British Prince Charming who wanted nothing more than to live in that little castle on the hill in Laurel Canyon with the girl/musical genius whom he adored. In the telling, Graham is guileless. Why? Because he does more press than Joni and wrote it down in a best-selling memoir. Even after all these years, Graham has never wavered from this narrative, so his version sticks. And there's even a score to it! "Our House" didn't just make it onto charts all over the world, it's become the ultimate paean to domestic bliss, a song to be played at weddings. In other words, Graham's version feels like truth because we can all hum along to it.

Not surprisingly, this gets under Joni's skin. Not just because she is competitive and prides herself on being more of a truth-teller than most of the Laurel Canyon crew, but because she loved him. She did not waltz away from the relationship without a second thought. She gave it a second thought, and a third, and by the time I interviewed her, she had thought it through thousands of times. "I was the great love of his life and I broke his heart," she says, a bit derisively. "Well, my heart was much more broken than his. He just jumped right back into dating, he had one after another after another. And I suffered because I really thought we had a very good relationship, but at a certain point I introduced him to David [Crosby]. Now I had to take Graham and David, and it was as if they were married and he chose David. I chose to leave."

Joni remembered the sailboat ride as torturous and ill planned. "Graham says I got on 'somewhere near Panama,'" she scoffed. "There was no 'somewhere near Panama.' We sailed from Jamaica to Panama. There's nowhere in between."

As Joni remembered it, Crosby and Nash were ill-equipped for the journey: there was no radio, no lifeboat. "David trained Graham, who had never sailed before, but who was a smart dog, as second mate," Joni told me. "But he doesn't mention that we hit seas that were completely abnormal, with ten-story swells, in good, sunny weather. And going up ten stories and down ten stories, I got what might have been my first Morgellons attack. I got a full-body rash. Every pore doughnuted up like chicken pox blisters. They wrapped me in a sheet and tied me to the railing because of these swells. And I spent three days throwing up over the side. I hit the shore and just ran, so glad to be on the ground."

When they arrived in Panama, Joni and Nash started fighting in earnest. Joni told me, "It got ugly. We had just broken up. I hadn't expected him to be on the boat. David invited me; there were quite a few people on board. I had enjoyed sailing with him, and he's a good sailor. Not so good that you don't have lifeboats and a radio when you're going to make a long sail like that, and then hit abnormalities. It was stupid. You'd think Graham would have the sense to be panicked, because we were in this extraordinary situation, improperly equipped. He says when we landed, it got ugly and I called him a woman hater. I racked my brain and thought, I wouldn't even call David Crosby a woman hater, and he's a human hater. He admires my talent, but not to my face. They admire my talent, but socially, it creates problems. They have to attack me. It's weird."

Graham has always professed his admiration and affection for Joni, and her reaction to his memoir reveals both her own deep feelings for him and how much she struggles with the notion that she alone is to blame for the breakup of their relationship, that if she'd only been a little less reckless with his heart, the two of them would still be playing piano and buying farm-stand flowers on Lookout Mountain.

Joni told me, hurt written across her face, "Graham says that I called him a woman hater. He said I was promiscuous."

In Nash's book he writes that he and Joni went to visit her parents in Saskatoon, and they wouldn't let the two of them sleep in the same room. "I can't describe what Joan's room looked like," he wrote, "because I wasn't allowed within twenty feet of it. Bill and Myrtle were a very straight, religious couple, and they weren't about to let a long-haired hippie sleep with their daughter under their roof . . . It wasn't like she was a virgin, not even close. But just to make sure, they put me in a downstairs bedroom, separating us by a floor, and made it clear I'd need an army behind me if I intended to sneak up there."

Joni found the line "not even close" to be deeply wounding.

"Now, does a man say that about the great love of his life?" she asked me. "No, he doesn't."

She grew even more heated. "It isn't even true. In the Summer of Love, I was one of the least promiscuous people around. I got pregnant right out of the chute with my friend. I called for that. Then I made a bad marriage trying to keep my child, then I had an affair with a drummer in New York whose girlfriend was away, and when she came back it was over. Four people! Is that 'not even close'?"

Looking back on the Summer of Love decades later, Joni said, "Free love—now we know there's no such thing. Pay later, always." She was joking, but not really. That sand ran through Graham's fingers long ago, yet the two old lovers were still telling competing versions of their story. Joni was convinced that it was her pictorial memory—stored up like film, she would say—that would matter in the end. She was right, she knew it, and she knew that he must have known it, too. Their accounts may differ, but the upshot is the same: you really don't know what you've got till it's gone.

12 ▨ *BLUE*

A s 1970 drew to a close, Joni did one more major benefit concert, Amchitka, supporting the launch of a fledgling environmental organization, Greenpeace, which was protesting nuclear weapons tests in Amchitka, Alaska. Joining her there, as a surprise guest, was a young James Taylor, who, for a brief but crucial time, would be Joni's old man (though not "My Old Man" of her song, a keepsake from her romance with Graham Nash). The two were both regulars at the Troubadour, a West Hollywood club on La Cienega that became famous as a launching pad for a generation of singer-songwriters. Taylor was twenty-two. Joni was twenty-six. She later said, "He wasn't very well known when I first met him, but the things I did hear were a bit conflicting. But I fell for him right away because he was very easygoing and free-spirited. We shared a lot of similar interests and common ground." Taylor fell hard for Joni, too, writing poems and love letters to her. He said, "She's so sensual and free with her body. She's like a goddess: a goddess of love."

At the Amchitka concert, they played together on "Mr. Tambourine

Man," and he jumped in when she forgot a verse. Later that month, they performed together again, this time at the Paris Theatre in London. Onstage, they harmonized—mellifluously—on "You Can Close Your Eyes," which he was said to have written for her. On the live recording, broadcast on the BBC, Joni can be heard giggling before their voices blend, as if they were meant to be together, as if closing their eyes meant entering a dream. "I don't know no love songs / And I can't sing the blues anymore / But I can sing this song, and you can sing this song when I'm gone." That was James Taylor's song, but it was about what both of them were experiencing and creating, something that's not quite a love song and not quite the blues. They can each sing this song—along with all the others, by both of them—when they're gone. When they sang together—on his album *Mud Slide Slim and the Blue Horizon*, or onstage—they each seemed to be in ecstasy, in harmony in more ways than one. But offstage, it was clear that they were each seriously disturbed. This euphony would not last for long. In one telling photo, Taylor is looking down, stoically enduring something that will turn dark very soon. Joni, one braid over her shoulder, has a look of distress in her eyes: her own Blue Horizon is coming soon. Given Taylor's history, it would be fair to say that he was self-medicating, and while it gave her material for a few songs, she knew that as his career was taking off, he was going down, and she wasn't going to go all the way down with him.

Taylor's "Fire and Rain," one of his best-loved songs, was a stark account of a friend's suicide and his own shock therapy; it is a beautiful distillation of end-of-the-rope mourning and melancholia, and if he had written more songs like it, he would have been closer to *Blue*'s level of astonishing vulnerability. The clinical depression he sang about so nakedly on that song had landed him in the famous McLean Hospital in Belmont, Massachusetts, which also treated Robert Lowell, Sylvia Plath, Ray Charles, and, later, David Foster Wallace. That depression led to a heroin addiction, and as he fell deeper into the pit, Joni stayed with him, long enough and deep enough that she emerged with a batch of new songs, some of them darker and more disturbing than ever. There is really no consolation for such misery, but if anything can come out of it, it can be not only surviving to tell the tale, but writing something greater than you have written before. Or composing songs as deep, honest, and achingly gorgeous, in their way, as anything anyone has ever done, which is what Joni would eventually do on *Blue*. All that suffering and turbulence was not in vain.

In 1962, Herb Alpert (then famous for Herb Alpert's Tijuana Brass band) and his business partner, Jerry Moss, formed a label they called Carnival Records in what was then Alpert's garage. When they discovered the name "Carnival" was taken, they used their initials and formed A&M Records, which would become one of the most important independent labels in the history of American music. They then purchased a complex of properties at 1416 North La Brea in Hollywood, the old Charlie Chaplin studios, which they transformed into a cutting-edge recording studio and a suite of executive offices. Through the 1960s and '70s, artists flocked to the Hollywood location to work with the finest mixers and sound engineers in the business. Burt Bacharach, Sergio Mendes & Brasil '66, Quincy Jones, Paul Williams, Joan Baez, Phil Ochs, Liza Minnelli, Cat Stevens, Joan Armatrading, and Peter Frampton all made music and magic in the buildings' four recording studios: A, B, C, and D.

Joni recorded *Blue* in Studio C. The Carpenters were recording in Studio A. Carole King was recording *Tapestry* in Studio B. King would write in her memoir, *A Natural Woman*: "A constant stream of singers, musicians, friends, and family flowed in and out of the recording studios along Sunset Boulevard. At A&M we commuted down the hall. Sometimes we commuted between A&M and Sunset Sound . . . When I wasn't working on my own album I drove to Sunset Sound to play as a sideman and sing background on James [Taylor's] songs . . . Periodically James came over to A&M to play acoustic guitar and sing background on my record. Physical proximity to me and romantic proximity to James brought Joni's beautiful voice to both James's and my albums. Sometimes it seemed as if James and I were recording one massive album in two different studios."

Joni's instinctual sense added to the lore that would surround Studio C. As Carole King recalled, "Studio C had a reddish wood Steinway piano that everyone said was really special. One morning I was able to slip in and try that piano out. I couldn't help but agree; there really was something extraordinary about it. It felt good to play, and its exceptional sound resonated with Lou [Adler] and [engineer] Hank [Cicalo], as well. Unfortunately, the red Steinway also resonated with Joni and Henry Lewy, which led to Joni and me vying for time in Studio C to record basic tracks. Unknown to me, Hank made several attempts to move the red Steinway into B, but Joni and Henry wouldn't allow it." One evening, King learned that Studio C was available—for three hours—before Joni was coming in. She rushed in with her team and in three takes recorded "I Feel the Earth Move."

In a departure from the covers of her first three albums, all featuring Joni's playful artwork, the cover of *Blue* was stark, graphic. The photographer Tim Considine shot her singing, possibly in ecstasy, possibly in sorrow, probably in both, and she is sinking into the color blue. In his 1976 study of black music, *Stomping the Blues*, Albert Murray wrote that the blues was like the catharsis of Greek tragedy, and that while one was singing or playing the blues, one was *stomping the blues away*. This kind of blue didn't seem like that.

"I like a look of agony," wrote Emily Dickinson. Joni liked the sound of it, even if it came out—with stacked chords, multi-octave vocal runs, and clanging open chords—euphoniously, but with an edge. But *Blue* is as much about an escape from blue feelings as it is about going deep inside and all that you discover as you make your way out. Aeschylus, the Greek dramatist known as the father of tragedy, wrote πάθει μάθος (pathei-mathos). Wisdom arises through suffering. So does one suffer, learn, mope, create, or, eventually, all of the above?

The final line of "All I Want" is "I want to make you feel free," repeated with vocal leaps that stretched the limits of what freedom could be. In a 1974 interview, one of the few she gave in the early '70s, Joni defined freedom as "the luxury of being able to follow the path of the heart," which is a long way from Kris Kristofferson's "just another word for nothing left to lose." In Joni's definition, in all its vulnerability, there is plenty to lose. It is a luxury, even when it lands on hate as often as it lands on love. With its polar extremes bouncing back and forth, "All I Want" is emotionally exhausting. It is the first of many demands. And the album is just getting started.

Joni recalled that the process of getting to the truth, the deeper wisdom, was very much a part of that time and place. "I took an overdose of acid. I only took one trip and I took way too much. I took one tab and it didn't work and then I took a second one. And I saw that it was all about electricity. I had hallucinations at the beginning of the trip. But then after that, it was definitely mind-expanding, and you're seeing things in a different way. I saw cutting-edge physics, things that mystics have talked about, natives have talked about. The luminous fibers that connect everything. My social conduct was disrupted, because I would weep at our society. And I'd weep at people. I could see right through them. If I passed a thief, I'd know he was a thief. In level-four Buddhism, your sixth sense comes in. The sixth sense is why the animals ran through the hills in the tsunami. All of your senses are incredibly sharpened. If you're an animal and you see that birds are not moving in their normal pattern and sound different, you can probably hear the wave coming in the wrong direction. It's a coordination of all your senses. I think that's what was happening that time. I wasn't reading anything at the time, but that was not a mental breakdown but the arrival of the sixth sense. But with no guide and nobody to recognize that there was a shamanic element, for lack of a better term. I know that sounds very witch-doctor-y. It is an increase in intelligence, but you have to learn how to handle it."

And yet Joni makes room for being the Good Time Charlie her friends from the Great White North so often said she was. The more she traveled, the more character studies she accumulated—colorful civilians who could not be subject to the kind of celebrity guessing game that she compares with *People* magazine. One of those specimens was

Cary Raditz, a cook in Matala on the island of Crete, where she slept in a cave and tried to get back to the garden, but didn't stay too long because she missed her clean white linen and fancy French cologne.

Decades later, Joni recalled "Carey" as one of the many "freaks and soldiers" she met along the way who found their way into her songs. "He blew out of a restaurant in Matala," she recalled. "That's how I met him. I was staring out towards Africa and the sun was setting and I heard this ka-boom and I saw this redhead, turbaned all in white, blowing out the door of a restaurant and I thought: Great person, I have to meet him. He just blew into my life. He was a character." They became lovers in a deliberately unserious way; even though she brought him to LA, she also knew that the circus could not last for long.

"By the time of my fourth album," Joni later told Cameron Crowe, in a cover story for *Rolling Stone*, "I came to another turning point— that terrible opportunity that people are given in their lives. The day that they discover to the tips of their toes that they're assholes [solemn moment, then a gale of laughter]. And you have to work on from there. And decide what your values are. Which parts of you are no longer really necessary. They belong to childhood's end. *Blue* really was a turning point in a lot of ways."

Joni was having strange dreams and even stranger waking hours. Years of bottled-up melancholy was pouring out—great for songwriting, unsustainable for living. "I lost my daughter," Joni later elaborated. "I made a bad marriage. I made a couple of bad relationships after that. And then I got this illness—crying all the time. My mother thought I was being a wimp, and she was giving me buck-up advice. Later in life, she was walking through the supermarket and started crying for no reason. She also had it, milder than this. She called me up and apologized. It also simultaneously appeared when my insights became keener, so I could see painfully—things about people I didn't want to know. I'd just look at a person and I'd know too much about them that I didn't want to know. And because everything was becoming transparent, I felt I must be transparent, and I cried. I dreamed I was a plastic bag sitting on an auditorium chair watching a big fat women's tuba band. Women with big horns and rolled-down nylons in house dresses playing tuba and big horn music, and I was a plastic bag with all my organs exposed, sobbing on an auditorium chair at that time. That's how I felt. Like my guts were on the outside. I wrote *Blue* in that condition."

That was a fleshy dream for such a thin girl. You don't have to be a Freudian to see the symbolism. This was an exposed woman's body. It was a form of emotional nudity. She was exposing herself in ways that made the men around her uncomfortable. Maybe they were genuinely concerned, but maybe it was such uncharted territory that they just couldn't hear it. Ingmar Bergman could reveal his emotions as a filmmaker, and Marlon Brando could do the same as an actor. Yet there was no Method for the singer-songwriter. Joni was on her own, and she was feeling it. In 2015, she wondered if the vocabulary of Western psychology even applied, or if she had been making a shamanistic breakthrough. "Was it a nervous breakdown?" Joni asked me. "People became transparent to me. People thought I had the evil eye. That's why we locked off the *Blue* sessions. Nobody could come in. If anybody came in, I'd burst into tears."

And on those locked-up *Blue* sessions, Joni was translating those emotions no one would want to have into music that everyone would want to hear—right in Studio C. The opening track, "All I Want," was among the final two songs to be written, and it plays high to the low of the closer, "The Last Time I Saw Richard." Joni had begun playing the dulcimer when she discovered one at the Big Sur festival in 1969. When she was in Greece the next year, she wrote most of the *Blue* songs on it. She could really slap it around and beat it like a conga. She realized at that point that her style had changed. She'd picked something up from watching Stephen Stills's aggressive style, but then she turned it into something that was inimitably hers. She found a sound to match her rawness of the moment, her new awakening. It felt and sounded like life and love itself.

The dulcimer is the first sound one hears on *Blue*. It's like the starting of an engine, an opening move. First the chords jangle and a riff begins and repeats. Then a fragment of the melody plays. This lasts for twelve bars and paves a way for that voice. It is a voice that has already changed from her first three albums. It is now freed from the Crosby, Stills & Nash influence—it feels darker and richer, even as it still has all its range and supple velocity. It is a voice that will tell stories of groovy Carey with his cane, and brooding Richard in some dark café, the romantic who meets the same fate as all the others. This album brings those recovering romantics together, but it's all her vision, her emotional reportage.

The sounds are acoustic and spare. Drums are brushed and muted. Guitars and other string instruments—including that coveted Studio C grand piano—are acoustic. The emotions are out on the surface, beating and exposed like Russ Kunkel's conga. With these songs, a cycle on the perils and pleasures of love and its discontents, Joni offers her own battered heart for anyone else who has dared to be vulnerable and survived the wreckage. Joni, on the edge of stardom, asks: Are you sure you want to know me? And so, with "All I Want," the story of *Blue* begins:

> *I am a lonely road and I am traveling*
> *Traveling, traveling, traveling*
> *Looking for something, what can it be?*
> *Oh, I hate you some, I hate you some, I love you some*
> *Oh, I love you when I forget about me*

The album's indeterminacy is announced with the first suspended chord. And its jangling introduces a song with mixed messages. No one wants a lover who says, "Oh, I hate you some, I hate you some, I love you some"—although many will put up with it—but Joni has said that her greatest curse is sincerity. Two hates and one love is not usually a promising starting point for the other person in a relationship, but then the song makes us wonder what yoked these emotions together. The title is deceptive. This is a woman who could never have what she wants, and this adds to the intrigue. We keep listening to wonder what this woman will seek out, and how she will still be unsatisfied, which keeps us listening some more. Like eros itself, "All I Want" sings of being perpetually incomplete, but searching for completion anyway. (Joni is two albums away from proposing, "You could complete me / I'd complete you" on the title track of *Court and Spark*.) After announcing that she wants a love to bring out the best of both of them, and she rhymes "talk to you" with "shampoo you," the playfulness dies down again when all of this lovin' and talkin' becomes obliterated in the saddest of colors:

> *Do you see—do you see—do you see how you hurt me, baby*
> *So I hurt you too*
> *Then we both get so blue*

The final verse restates the first one, except now she is traveling only once. The song is ending. And it is giving way to the opening chords of "My Old Man," a reminder of an earlier time, a sweetness of the past. Her listeners are feeling this with her. Their hearts have already capsized.

More than forty years after the recording of *Blue*, the drummer Russ Kunkel emphasized how important it was in the studio to be both emotional and unshakable at the same time. "Keeping time is like a heartbeat," Kunkel said, with an emphasis on *heart* and *heat*. "You have to be steady, but be able to fluctuate without being abrupt. There was always a rhythmic template to Joni's music, and she set it. She set it with what she played, or with the cadence of what she sang, or a combination of subdividing the tempo with what she was singing and the tempo of what she was playing, and they were always well matched. So, for me, what I had to do was find something that accentuated that template without being obtrusive. And that's all I ever tried to do— just support that without getting in the way."

"Joni's guitar playing and her dulcimer playing is incredibly rhythmic," he recalled. "It has a wonderful ebb and flow and a sway to it. All I tried to do was accompany that with a different sound. I didn't want to intrude, but I wanted to enhance."

Here's how Russ Kunkel came to meet Joni Mitchell. Cass Elliot (Mama Cass to everyone who knew her) was, as Graham Nash put it, the Gertrude Stein of Laurel Canyon. Cass's house was a meeting place for many of the neighborhood's famous musicians, and her younger sister, Leah, was married to Russ Kunkel. Russ met Crosby and Nash through Cass, and they introduced him to Joni. "Joni was there afternoons, on weekends at Cass's house, along with Eric Clapton and Jimi Hendrix," recalled Kunkel. He also recalled that, before the *Blue* sessions, Joni came to him at his loft and played the songs directly to him, and he responded, enthralled, playing quietly along on a conga. "Looking back on it, I was probably being auditioned," he said. He said that he played the uncredited conga part on "All I Want." "If you detune congas, they get really flat. I detuned them to the point where they were kind of human, like playing your chest."

He did, however, receive drum credits on three tracks—"California," "A Case of You," and "Carey."

In a studio with few people, Joni needed all the support she could get. Kunkel recalled that whatever instability Joni was experiencing went into writing the songs and not the performance of them. Joni recalled it differently. She later said, "My individual psychological descent coincided, ironically, with my ascent into the public eye. They were putting me on a pedestal and I was wobbling. I took it upon myself that since I was a public voice and was subject to this kind of weird worship that they should know who they were worshipping. I was demanding of myself a deeper and greater honesty, more and more revelation in my work."

"River" was one of Joni's solo performances, and it was as intimate as it could get. Thematically, it builds on the bicoastal theme of Irving Berlin's "White Christmas"—the biggest blockbuster in American song. A Christmas song, as Philip Roth put it, by a Jewish songwriter, who took the Christ out of Christmas and made it a holiday about snow. In Joni's version, she is nostalgic for ice and, when she wishes that she could just skate away after making her baby cry, she sounds ever so slightly like an ice queen. But she's not.

The song may sample "Jingle Bells" in the beginning, but this is not the kind of song of joy and peace that she refers to in the beginning. "River" is powerful because it encapsulates Joni's journey in a single song, much the same way "Woodstock" encapsulated an entire movement. It is Christmas and the girl from the Canadian prairies finds herself in a place without snow or ice, wishing for a river to skate away on. She's lost her lover, someone who loved her mightily and tried to help her—it sounds a lot like Graham Nash, but Joni has never said. What rings true is the sense of loss: loss, and self-awareness. "I'm so hard to handle / I'm selfish and I'm sad / Now I've gone and lost the best baby / That I ever had," she sings, rewriting the genre of love songs forever. She's not saying, "You broke my heart." She's not saying, "Baby come back." She's rejecting the image of the pining good girl wholesale. She's got issues and she knows it. Joni told NPR in 2014, "It's taking personal responsibility for the failure of a relationship." It was a big step, she added, for those who came of age in the Me Generation. But what makes the song rise above it all is that she's also got enough sense to know she's human and her heart needs a place and a way to ache before it can heal. There's hardly a person alive who hasn't, at some point, longed for such a river, a river to skate away on.

As a teenager, Janet Jackson recorded in the same studios where Joni had done some of her finest work. Twenty-five years later, Jackson wrote and recorded a song called "Got 'Til It's Gone," in which she would heavily, charmingly, and surprisingly sample "Big Yellow Taxi." And even more surprising was what the rapper Q-Tip intoned over and over in the background: "Joni Mitchell never lies . . . lies . . . lies . . ." Joni was clearly delighted, and more than that, honored by the respect paid, because to Joni, truth-telling has been her life's calling. And in "River," Joni's truth-telling soared from what some might have called a 1970s confessional to a universally beloved banner of truth. Joni has joked that she should write a song called "Have Yourself a Morbid Little Christmas." And as the song proliferates on holiday playlists every year, it is a song for those whose hearts don't swell when the holidays roll around, a song for those who find themselves far away from everything that feels like home, for those who find themselves mourning when others are decking the halls and making merry.

More than five hundred musicians have covered "River," and hundreds more have performed it. The British musician Beth Orton told *The Wall Street Journal*, "It is a song I've grieved to, cried along with, sung at the top of my voice to, because it feels so good to do so . . . I would dedicate this song to those who are grieving the loss of a sense of place, loved ones, family." James Taylor, who also recorded the song for his 2006 album, *James Taylor at Christmas*, told *The Washington Post*, "It's such a beautiful thing, to turn away from the commercial mayhem that Christmas becomes and just breathe in some pine needles. It's a really blue song."

When *Blue* was released in June 1971, its emotional intimacy shocked some of her peer group. Johnny Cash said, "You've got the weight of the world on you."

In the October 1971 issue of *Stereo Review*, Peter Reilly praised the "near perfection of her arrangements and accompaniment" and noted that Joni's "balanced dispassion makes her work truly womanly rather than merely girlish." He goes on to say that "the finest thing about *Blue*, however, is its message of survival." Then he quoted some of the title track's most hopeful lyrics: "Well, there's so many sinking now / You've got to keep thinking / You can make it through these waves." And while the early 1970s had a particularly grim lens on loss, a consistent theme of broken promises and heartbreaking despair, it would turn out that the era of *Blue* had no monopoly on the theme of youthful angst. In every decade, in every age, there would be those who were sinking, those who needed to be reminded by her "Joni Mitchell never lies" truth-telling that "you can make it through these waves."

Over time *Blue* has become Joni's biggest seller, eclipsing the commercial powerhouse *Court and Spark* (1974), and selling more than ten million copies in the United States alone. In its 500 Greatest Albums ranking on May 31, 2012, *Rolling Stone* placed *Blue* at number thirty.

But no one could have predicted this success initially. Don Heckman in *The New York Times* acknowledged its artistic success, but predicted commercial exile: "I suspect this will be the most disliked of Miss Mitchell's recordings," he wrote on August 8, 1971, "despite the fact that it attempts more and makes greater demands on her talent than any of the others. The audience for art songs is far smaller than that for folk ballads, and Joni Mitchell is on the verge of having to make a decision between the two." Joni Mitchell never had that decision to make. She was indeed moving toward art songs, and was, in fact, already making them, but her music would never be calculated. There was only one question, and it was a question, posed on "California," for all of us: "Will you take me as I am?"

13 ▪ BETWEEN BREAKDOWN AND BREAKTHROUGH

James Baldwin wrote, "Love does not begin and end the way we seem to think it does. Love is a battle. Love is a war. Love is a growing up." Before *Blue*, no one had ever written about the growing up of love the way Joni had. After *Blue*, the genre of the love song would be forever changed, haunted by Joni's hollowed-out hurt and her clear-eyed knowing. Sure, we would—as a culture— continue to write frothy, frilly love songs. But after *Blue*, that would always be a choice. We couldn't pretend that we hadn't heard the flip side and that, somewhere deep down, we didn't know better.

"I'm open," Joni told me in 2015. "I'm a living storybook." If this is true, then the deepest, truest chapter in the Joni Mitchell storybook might be *Blue*. It wasn't the way she wanted it to go, the life she dreamed for herself when she was a girl in Saskatchewan. In the late 1960s, there was a Sunday Canadian television news program called *The Way It Is*. Eager to capture a youthful, political audience, the show asked Joni to write its theme song. She declined. "I was totally politically green," Joni remembered. "I thought, 'How can I write the theme song for a news program?' My mother was always badgering me into keeping up with current events. All I wanted to do was dance. And kiss." A few years later, a few love affairs later, Joni was less starry-eyed about love. It is one of the hallmarks of *Blue*; it's about what you see when the façades of the fairy tales have faded away. Joni told me that the "whole concept that romance was suffering was really foreign to me, even though that's what a lot of my work was about. To me, romance should have been Hawaiian, if the church hadn't gotten involved. It should have been up and friendly and robust."

"*Blue* was very open and vulnerable, unprecedented in pop music," she said. "All the men around me were really nervous. They were cringing. They were embarrassed for me. Then people started calling me confessional, and then it was like a blood sport. I felt like people were coming to watch me fall off a tightrope or something."

On the Waterfront had come out in 1954, when Joni was still in elementary school, and decades later she marveled at Brando's performance in that movie and its influence on *Blue*. "Marlon Brando is touted by nearly every actor who came after him for his performance in *On the Waterfront*. No one had seen anything like it, and they all agreed that it changed the standard. It was unprecedented. It had nothing to do with the Method. It had everything to do with Marlon's personal genius. I'm a Method actor. The Method is that you deliver the lines like you never heard them before. So that every time you perform the song, it's gotta come up like you never heard it before. As a result, I will phrase it differently to keep it spontaneous. Marlon's take was that he couldn't watch the rushes. He was totally embarrassed by his performance. And when they started laying this confessional label on me, I felt really embarrassed . . . When *Blue* came out it was not popular and it was shocking to the men around me. Stunningly shocking. And upsetting. Kris Kristofferson said to me, 'Oh, Joni. Save something for yourself.' The vulnerability freaked them out."

So how did *Blue* rise beyond its initial reception to become Joni's best-selling and most canonized album? One powerful reason is that *Blue* fits into the Great Album theory of pop music. Like the Great American Novel benchmark in literature, the Great Album theory is about pop music's highest ambitions. If someone's music stash has only one Joni album, that album is likely to be *Blue*.

Great Albums are usually made in a period of crisis, or change, or transition, or all of the above. In the case of the Beach Boys' *Pet Sounds* (1966), Brian Wilson's incipient mental breakdown loomed over the material; with the Beatles' *Sgt. Pepper* (1967), it was Paul McCartney's competition with Wilson, with the band outgrowing the limitations of performing for screaming girls in stadiums, prolonged time in Abbey Road Studios, and generous tabs of LSD; just a few years later, they would outgrow one another, too. Van Morrison's *Astral Weeks* (1968) was driven by improvised Yeats-inspired lyrics sung against the grooves of jazz virtuosi (the guitarist Jay Berliner of Mingus fame, the bassist Richard Davis of Dolphy fame, and the drummer Connie Kay of Modern Jazz Quartet fame, anticipating Joni's scintillating collaborations with Jaco Pastorius, Herbie Hancock, and Wayne Shorter). Simon and Garfunkel's *Bookends* (1968) was superbly constructed, with beautifully crafted songs that fit together like book chapters—hence the title—and *The Kinks Are the Village Green Preservation Society* (also 1968) was similarly cohesive. On Marvin Gaye's *What's Going On* (1971, the same year as *Blue*), Gaye was breaking from the Motown hit factory to produce a major, harmonically adventurous artistic statement, one that would inspire his former Motown label mate Stevie Wonder to take the leap and create a masterpiece of his own with *Innervisions* (1973), on which Wonder played every instrument and sang every vocal track himself. And *Blood on the Tracks* (1975) was Bob Dylan's intimate and raw divorce album; Dylan said when he was writing the opening track, "Tangled Up in Blue," he was tangled up in Joni's *Blue*.

Even among these and other great albums, *Blue* still stands out. For sustained and beautifully wrought personal revelation—for sheer intimacy and soul baring—it is peerless. Often thought of as the ultimate depression album, it contains a great deal of joie de vivre, even if the more brooding songs left a bigger impact. The album, in fact, offers a cornucopia of moods and states: joy, sorrow, ennui, self-destruction, and getting loved so naughty, made weak in the knees. Joni has often criticized pop music for liking its sad songs in minor keys and its happy songs in major ones. But life is more nuanced than that. Joni described her approach—filled with suspended chords, mixing and matching chords with the roots of different chords, and with unconventional progressions—as "going along happy-sad." Even though the sad notes are generally the last lingering harmonies listeners take away from the album, *Blue* is not just about feeling blue. It is about feeling *generally*, with songs so intimate, Joni has described them as "private letters that were published."

Those letters are to California; to Cary Raditz, the Peace Corps volunteer she met as she was playing the role of cave hippie in Crete; to Graham Nash, her discarded "Old Man"; to Kilauren Gibb, her missing daughter, addressed as "Little Green"; to the composites (including Leonard Cohen and others) who inspired "A Case of You" and "This Flight Tonight"; to her own melancholy on "River" and "Blue" (where the "needles, guns, and grass" refer to James Taylor's addiction to "needles," and she wasn't done yet on the matter). But who the letters are *to* is less important than who they are *by*. Joni has often said that if you listen and are thinking of her, you're doing it wrong. You should listen, she insists, and find yourself. "Otherwise," she said in 2013, "you're just rubbernecking a car accident."

Of "Blue," Joni says, "I was demanding of myself a deeper and greater honesty, more and more revelation in my work in order to give it back to the people where it goes into their lives, and nourishes them, and changes their direction, and makes lightbulbs go off in their heads, and makes them *feel*. And it isn't vague. It strikes against the very nerves of their life, and in order to do that, you have to strike against the very nerves of your own."

Before the release of *Blue,* which the *Rolling Stone* reviewer Timothy Crouse praised in the August 5, 1971, issue as "some of the most beautiful moments in recent popular music," the same magazine, in an awards issue in February, anointed Joni "Old Lady of the Year." In a cruelly dismissive fashion, it presented an illustrated chart of how people in the music industry intersected and were connected. It was a familiar trope in magazines at the time. There were maps and constellations of writers and artists—who had worked with or inspired whom—and, of greater titillating interest, who had slept with whom. Joni was represented on the chart as a lipsticked kiss surrounded by a scattering of broken hearts, connecting her to David Crosby, Graham Nash, and James Taylor. They labeled her the "Queen of El Lay."

It was deeply unfair. Male rock stars were celebrated for their promiscuity, and no one parodied Stephen Stills for writing "Love the One You're With" (a song with a chorus dominated by Joni's soprano). *Blue* was all about being too much, excess love, excess pain, traveling through all those highs and lows. How low does she go? As far as blue can take her, as a mood, as a lifestyle, as a way of looking through a glass darkly. The Germans have a word for a poetic dwelling in misery: *Weltschmerz*, or world-weariness. Joni has a color, and she's not trying to brighten its hues but to dig as deep as she ever has, deeper than "Both Sides, Now," deeper than "The Circle Game." The cycle of life has stopped at a dark and dangerous place, and she takes us with her. This is a new place and it's not comfortable. A painter first, she dedicates the song to a color, and one can imagine, say, Picasso's 1902 masterpiece *Blue Nude*, in which there is a nude female figure turning away, one knee up on her elbows, where she is cradling her face. If it weren't for the shades of blue around it, the emotion would be indeterminate. With the use of this particular type of tumultuous blue, it looks like a study of a beautiful woman in agony, a recurring theme in Picasso's painting and life. And yet the viewer admires the stunning brushstrokes while feeling the figure's sadness. With Picasso in mind, she wraps her sad subject with haunting tones and dazzling vocal leaps. There are so many shades of blue, so many places to go. "Acid, booze, and ass / Needles, guns, and grass / Lots of laughs," she sings, and we know, as her voice is still pristine, that she's living it. Lots of laughs? Really? The song contains an allusion to the straightforward love song to Graham Nash, "My Old Man," as a brief reminder of those laughs before returning to the abyss.

As groundbreaking as it was to write, as many people have bought and listened to and treasured this album, *Blue* was as lonely to release as it was to write. It took a long time for Joni to hear the echo of approval and appreciation that the album created. "*Blue* is just human," she told me. "Everybody, if they've got a soul, is going to go through those changes, and yet the spotlight, nobody had ever written them in song, but I'm sure it's in cinema—certainly Bergman."

It's the feeling underneath the tears, before the tears, the surge and the power of heartbreak that Joni has captured so masterfully in her work.

We learn right away that songs can be like tattoos. If one is not a heroin addict but the lover of one, then tattoos can be the closest metaphor for what James Taylor was doing to himself, to feel high, get low, fall deeper, and, as an artist with indelible ink, leave a mark. "Ink on a pin" rhymes with "underneath the skin." Her dear old compatriot Neil Young sang hauntingly about "the needle and the damage done," but Joni went all the way inside. The right kind of song could be a fix, too. Outside the pit, the word is that "hell's the hippest way to go." She disagrees, but then she wants to "take a look around it though."

Joni has said that around this time she could cry if someone just looked at her. This was a problem for someone who had already played Carnegie Hall and would do it again the following year. "The club thing was kind of fun," Joni has said. And you can see it: in every taped performance in a smaller room, she is laughing to herself. She's a high school ham, just playing guitar with her friends. "The big stage, I hated it from the moment I went up there. I didn't like that lofty adoration. It seemed deluded. The idea of people at my knees is horrifying to me."

There's a contrast between Joni and her friend Leonard Cohen here. Cohen thrilled to the stage. As he once told *Rolling Stone*, "Tours are like bullfighting. They are a test of character every night. [That] is something I'm interested in examining."

A crowd is one thing. An ex-lover is another. At the end of the song, she makes an offering to Blue—the color, the mood, all of it. The song itself should be more than enough, but she ups the ante even more. It is a shell, and if Blue puts its ear to it, there is a foggy lullaby. Rest, rest, perturbed spirit. On Joni's next album, she would sing that "when you dig down deep, you lose good sleep." But even Blue needs a rest, and at the end of the song, Blue becomes an echoing soporific. It is the gift that keeps on giving.

This, from the vinyl era of its creation, was the end of side one. The movement to the next track, in its original format, meant getting up to flip the record, possibly right away, possibly later. Those suspended cadences at the end of "Blue" resound in the listener's mind even longer than they slowly fade out and finish side one's story. Side two starts with a remarkably different mood, one nostalgic for a Laurel Canyon home that she no longer shares with Graham Nash on Lookout Mountain. Despite her constant need for change—stylistically, chromatically, romantically—there is still a nostalgic part to Joni, one that recalls when it's "coming on Christmas," and wishes that she could transport herself from Laurel Canyon and its endless white noise of perfect weather to the Canadian prairie she couldn't escape fast enough.

And so, as side two starts, Joni gives us a portrait of where she is and where we might be, as her listeners, at the dawn of the 1970s. She tells us that she's sitting on a park bench in Paris, France, and there's a hint of the small-town girl that she once was—it's not just Paris, it's Paris, France—as if she still sees it through the lens of the girl who sat in a Saskatchewan schoolroom, looking at a map and memorizing all the capitals of the world. She mentions her trip to Greece; there's a reference to her former lover Cary, the rogue with the red hair; she goes to Spain but she's not one of the jet set. They invite her in, those "pretty people" reading *Rolling Stone* and *Vogue*, but while she likes the scenery, she knows she can't stay for long. All throughout the refrain is for California, the place that's not cold and old and settled in its ways. It's for California, the place that will take her as she is. She hasn't gotten love right yet. She's "strung out on another man" but she's going to come home, to the truest home she's ever known, and she's going to try again. The incredible thing about the song is that while there's some 1970s lingo here and there—"the folks I dig"—the song doesn't feel dated at all. There is this powerful sense of the eternal in Joni's best songs. It could be the 1970s, the '80s, the '90s, the 2000s, and unless something radically changes, you could be sitting in Paris, France, reading news from home that all seems bad and dreaming of California, that place that makes you feel good, like a rock and roll band.

The California of the song is more a collection of memories from afar than an actual space and place. "A Case of You" also patches together memories of love and loss, with the singer emerging rougher and tougher than any lover with a broken but still mighty and resilient heart, still big enough for the weight of the world. Cohen, quoting the Talmud, said that "there's good wine in every generation," but that "we have a special kind of feeling for the singers that we used to make love to." "A Case of You" shares that special feeling, and, like Cohen, she shares it in the past tense, lingering over the bouquet of a vintage bottle. Her open-tuned dulcimer bangs out percussive, rough-and-tumble chords while James Taylor's standard-tuning acoustic guitar tries to bring resolution but is drowned out. What makes "A Case of You" a masterpiece, lyrically, is the Leonard Cohen exchange, from "I am as constant as a northern star," from Cohen quoting *Julius Caesar*, to "constantly in the darkness, where's that at? If you want me, I'll be in the bar," what Joni *wished* she had said. And then, recalling the "Rainy Night House" trip with Cohen, recalls his mother with a painter's eye:

> *I met a woman*
> *She had a mouth like yours*
> *She knew your life*
> *She knew your devils and your deeds*
> *And she said*
> *"Go to him, stay with him if you can*
> *But be prepared to bleed"*

"That was about Leonard's mother. They have the same mouth. She warned me, 'Be prepared to bleed.' All the mothers warn me against their sons." In 2014, Cohen sang, "My father says I'm chosen, my mother says I'm not." (Cohen sang this, to comic effect, as an observant Jew and practicing Buddhist.) Marsha Klonitsky loved her son, but with a realist's eye. Then again, Cohen and Joni were never exclusive with each other. There were no promises to be broken. But the pattern of warning mothers, like a chorus of Cassandras, was what was so striking.

"The rest of 'A Case of You' is nothing," Joni said. "It's just a doormat song. Songs for women were always doormat songs. Songs like 'Stand by Your Man' were written by men. They're all male fantasy and my stuff is not male fantasy at all. It's instructed to make men a little more informed." Joni's vocal leaps are breathtaking, sounding like she's still the one at last call. If you want her, she'll be at the bar, and she could outdrink all her former lovers combined. This should not be taken literally. Her former lover David Crosby would set a new standard for substance abuse, and James Taylor, who played so sweetly, was hooked on the smack that Joni says she never tried. Sure, these guys have given her a hard time, and sure, she can take it, but the song itself is evidence of more beauty and truth. This is the Joni Mitchell that her listeners would want, frozen in vocal leaps, emotional depths, passionate, sultry, full of memories, but in absolute possession of them. This is a beautiful woman who is sensitive, sensuous, and fully attuned to experience, yet somehow beyond heartbreak. "Love is touching souls," says a Rilke-quoting lover, and she'll take it at face value, without asking the Carole King–Gerry Goffin question: Will you still love me tomorrow? Tomorrow, Joni will need to be emotionally independent enough to come up with this song. She's not demonizing her exes. The song is a tribute, not so much to them as to herself. She is the one who can drink a whole case and walk out upright. If the song is a love song to anyone or anything, it is to her resilience.

Eight years after its release, and for the first time since the nasty "Queen of El Lay" squib, Joni spoke to *Rolling Stone*. In the interview, she remembers the making of *Blue* as a time of thin skin and bare bones: "At that period of my life, I had no personal defenses. I felt like a cellophane wrapper on a pack of cigarettes. I felt like I had absolutely no secrets from the world, and I couldn't pretend in my life to be strong. Or to be happy." One gets a sense of what she means from the album's most morose moments. And it is those moments that have inspired the most intimate appreciation from her listeners, when she was between break-down and breakthrough.

At the end of 1999, the pop music critics of *The New York Times* selected twenty-five albums that were emblematic of the twentieth century. They chose albums, not singles, even though albums as a genre did not become popular until the late 1940s, because they wanted to choose artistic statements that were complete in their rendering. The works they chose ranged from Tito Puente's 1957 masterpiece *Dance Mania* to a very different album made the next year, *Frank Sinatra Sings for Only the Lonely*. Michael Jackson's *Thriller* made the list, as did albums by the Ramones, Nirvana, Public Enemy, the Beatles, and Bob Dylan. It surprised no one that Joni was one of only three female solo artists to be named. By the end of the twentieth century, the Joni Mitchell renaissance was in full swing. Of *Blue*, the critics wrote: "A restless woman travels, falls in love and longs for what she left behind as she moves on; in the background 1960s' ideals crumble. Joni Mitchell turned unsparing autobiography into sparse songs that quietly rejected symmetry and happy endings while they poured out her yearning. As she ushered in a confessional mode for pop songwriting, few of her emulators noticed that her seemingly unguarded revelations were so finely constructed." It was one of the few moments when Joni and her critics saw eye to eye. After all, it was Joni who had said, "You have to have a certain grab-ability initially and then something that wears well for years to come."

14 ■ THE SUNSHINE COAST

After *Blue*, the substitute for hope took the shape of not another lover, but a place: Canada, oh Canada. Although she had grown up in the central provinces, she went to the west, to British Columbia's Sunshine Coast: even the name seems like good medicine for someone struggling with depression. With unspoiled ocean views from every vista, old-growth forests, pebble beaches, and dozens of waterfalls, the region was the polar opposite of what Los Angeles was becoming in the booming 1970s. The First Nation communities of the coast, the Squamish and the Sechelt, kept their history alive through storytelling and environmental outposts in the region: something Joni would have also liked. "I know neighbors in B.C. and I go to town," Joni told me. "I'm not a recluse. I'd ride my bike in the country and smoke and watch the birds fly. And I'd come home feeling wonderful. I'm happy observing water, especially. So that was my shrink."

She bought property, put up her Canadian flag, and sequestered herself in what she called "a little stone house like a monastery where I could just go away and hide." There, she could live without electricity because she believed it was "so carcinogenic. I had a revelation about it. You'll never cure cancer until you go back to candlelight."

Tony Simon was very present in those days, a confidant from her Saskatoon days who had become, in a casual way, her lover during this period when she could trust very few people. "The place she originally built in 1971 was entirely designed by her," Simon recalled. "She made changes as the thing went along. She basically built the structure around herself, so it reflects her personality in a lot of ways. That little house, impractical now, was a jewel. There was a pet heron that stood out on a rock. There's a lot of things about that house that are so natural. It looked like it could have been there six hundred years—stone cottage, nothing fancy. I would think her memories about that place are all pretty positive. The original property she bought was around sixty acres. Because, arguably, the most beautiful sixty acres you could find in the world. The water is uncharacteristically warm for the area. You've got big trees and the place is so beautiful beyond description. She bought a couple of neighboring properties to give her more room and protect her from people building on the property. That area is unbelievably gorgeous. It was part of her artwork."

"I was at that place outside Vancouver," Leonard Cohen recalled. "It must have been soon after she got it. It was a beautiful house. It was very bare, like a stone cell. Very beautiful. Austere."

That was the plan—beauty, austerity, solitude. She had escaped to what seemed like paradise. She would call her B.C. retreat her Walden Woods, and like Henry David Thoreau, she wanted to live deliberately. She buried her electrical lines—this was standard—and avoided contact with the outside world, although if she really needed company, she could get it from Vancouver friends or invited guests. She had only one TV station and couldn't always tune in to *Midnight Special*, so there was even more time to turn inward. But the home was memorable because making a home was one of her great gifts. As Graham Nash once said, "She could transform a shack and make it look chic and gracious."

———

It may seem counterintuitive for an artist on the cusp of her greatest commercial success to be roughing it, but then what seemed necessary for Joni's life also became crucial for her art. She couldn't just keep writing relationship songs, when relationships, the further she went along, seemed to be mere folly.

She was more than a little battered after *Blue* and wanted to live up to her own words and get back to the garden for real. There must be more to life, Joni figured. "I bought every psychology book I could lay my hands on. Jung, Freud, theology, self-help, psychiatry," she said. She also said she threw all of them against the wall. And then she was introduced to Nietzsche, who came recommended by the singer Ronee Blakley—another singer on Geffen's new label, Asylum, who would eventually give an Oscar-nominated performance as a fictional country singer in Robert Altman's *Nashville*. Nietzsche would stick with Joni. He taught her that, among other things, "to live is to suffer, to survive is to find some meaning in the suffering." Nietzsche also wrote that "without music, life would be a mistake," and she would follow both of these ideas when she wrote the songs that would appear on *For the Roses* (1972), which would be Joni's first for Geffen's new label. The ironically named Sunshine Coast was a good place for a bad mood. Her view of the ocean was spectacular and the rain was relentless; Emily Carr, the nineteenth-century Canadian writer and painter, called it the wettest place on earth.

It was on this rainy, craggy coast that Joni would learn, as she would sing on the album's title track, "new lessons in survival." The girl who so famously sang "I'm selfish and I'm sad" wanted to not just sing the words, but do something about them. "Depression can be the sand that makes the pearl," she later said. "Most of my best work came out of it. If you get rid of the demons and the disturbing things, then the angels fly off, too. There is the possibility, in that mire, of an epiphany."

She came across a small study called *Beethoven: His Spiritual Development*. First published in 1927, it was a groundbreaking text because the author, J.W.N. Sullivan, argued, "I believe that in his greatest music Beethoven was primarily concerned to express his personal vision of life. This vision was, of course, the product of his character and his experience. Beethoven the man and Beethoven the composer are not two unconnected entities, and the known history of the man may be used to throw light upon the character of his music."

For Joni, the book was a valuable analysis of how a working musician struggles with the dual pressures of life and creativity. She told the *Toronto Star*, "It was all about his struggles, and self-doubts and his worries about how his work was being received and what it all meant on a deeper level and, of course, about his going deaf. At the time, that's just what I was thinking about too. How am I going to get back in the saddle? And what about the audience? Would you still love me if you knew what I was really like?"

Joni, seeking wisdom in solitude, away from the media circus described in "For the Roses," found a bona fide genius who, like her beloved Van Gogh, was too rough and coarse to be appreciated in his own time. Van Gogh famously cut off an ear, and Beethoven, also famously, lost the use of both of his, the ultimate betrayal. Joni, who had already survived polio, knew something about a rogue body. As the months on the Sunshine Coast went by, Joni began composing at the piano, a piece bigger and more ambitious than anything she had tried before. She could not come up with lyrics for a while, and, as a placeholder, called it "Roll Over Beethoven Revisited." Eventually, she called it "Ludwig's Tune," put in parentheses after settling on "Judgement of the Moon and Stars." This song presents Joni's biggest challenge yet: without classical training, she's going to give Beethoven a tribute from one of the roughs, whose piano had no smooth technique but was as open as the night sky. Even when ears have turned deaf, there is still the muse beyond the music. Joni preferred Beethoven to Mozart, who, when he wasn't at his darkest, sounded too perfect, too courtly, too much, she would say, like wallpaper for princes. Beethoven was the sound of what was rejected by the court. Joni identifies with a man too raw and wild for this world, whose ability to hear is denied him at the peak of his powers. On June 10, 1972, a few months before the release of *For the Roses*, Joni performed the song on the BBC, and while the network had its fill of programs on Beethoven, it had never heard anything like this:

This is a song about Beethoven. I was reading a book on his spiritual development and my heart really went out to him because here he was with all this genius, which wasn't really accepted in his own time. People thought he was really radical and crazy and you couldn't do parallel fifths. It just wasn't music, you know? Plus he was kind of an immalleable person and kind of coarse by the standards of the courts in those days, so though he had an eye for all of the women of the courts, they didn't really have much of an eye for him. So there was another frustration in his life, coupled with the idea that he couldn't even hear some of his final music.

Rock audiences can often be too rude, and jazz audiences can be too hip, but classical audiences can be the worst: so snooty, they have to repress all reactions. Schumann would have been too wild to sit still in the concert hall, and Beethoven didn't fit in, either. By the time he went deaf, even listening to his own great work was denied him. Manners could not have been less relevant.

For Joni, this was as pure as it could get. She first became an artist when polio stole her athletic ability. By the time she wrote this song, she learned there was so much more to lose: her daughter was lost and many relationships were in the dust. She still had her music—at the full range of her vocal powers—but she knew that one day she would lose those, too. When she read about Beethoven's *Geist*, she knew that, by the time of the Ninth Symphony and the late quartets, that's all he had left: his *Zeit* was not giving him his due. Just as Joni had the rustling arbutus tree for an audience, the only audience that mattered for Ludwig was the moon and stars. Their judgment was all he had left. "So you get to keep the pictures / That don't seem like much," she sang. Deafness was a raw deal for this raw spirit. The keys under his fingers were cold, just a touch and a memory of a sound. Beethoven was the first great composer for the piano forte, but he reached beyond the construction of any instrument: "Condemned to wires and hammers / Strike every chord that you feel / That broken trees / And elephant ivories conceal." Musical instruments, even when they are made from nature, are still artificial. The deaf genius just needs to pound the hell out of that piano, the wilder, the better.

As Joni's legend grew, she was known to compare herself to Van Gogh, Picasso, Miles Davis, and Beethoven. Modesty was not her thing, but "Judgement of the Moon and Stars" proves that her identification with such hallowed figures was more legit than most people could know.

15 ▪ *FOR THE ROSES*

t was up there, north of Vancouver, shrinking herself with the ocean
air and musing on Beethoven, that she began writing the songs that
would become her fifth studio album, *For the Roses*. She presented
many of the album's new songs at a concert at Carnegie Hall on
February 23, 1972, about eight months before its release. There was
thunderous applause for each one. The audience was getting to know
the many sides of Joni Mitchell: the dark and the light—and yes, they
still loved her. But "For the Roses" is about the complexity of applause,
and after the clapping died down, she explained the meaning of the
title to her rapturous fans:

> It comes from the expression "to run for the roses" . . . That's when
> you take this horse and he comes charging into the finish line and
> they throw a wreath of flowers around his neck and then one day
> they take him out and shoot him. It's kind of a macabre thing to say,
> I guess.

She concluded this "macabre thing" with a giggle, but she was deadly serious. She knew she had been groomed to be a prize horse, but that she would eventually be put out to pasture, and so would James Taylor, and so would the next poet who would tremble and make up tunes for love and sing sorrow into the sound hole. When she first began to get mainstream success and reporters asked about her management team, Elliot Roberts and David Geffen, she would tell them, "I was their first racehorse, so to speak." She was always aware that her ambition and her success did not come without a price. But she had made a decision a long time ago to run for the roses, aware of what would happen once that wreath was hung around her neck.

Before she moved to the Sunshine Coast, Joni had said, "I'm a little in awe of cities, being raised in a prairie town in Saskatchewan. I thought then that cities were beautiful. I judged them by their neon. Then in New York I found that cities are really vulgar. I saw their dirt, found they were plastic and in a rush for the dollar. Now I'm ruralizing myself again. I owe it to myself to live where there's greenery." She had taken her own advice and gotten back to the garden, but she had become more of a city person than she realized. In a year, she found herself back in California again. With no place to stay, she "came to stay with David Geffen as a guest. And I was kind of the Woman Who Came to Dinner. I ended up staying on for a while." Geffen for his part remembers the period fondly. "We were roommates. For me, it was a very heady time. I had just signed Bob Dylan and I was dating Cher. You know, it was very tumultuous and a lot of fun and seventies."

It was 1972 and confusion was the order of the day, as Marvin Gaye continued to sing in his prophetic masterpiece, "What's Going On?" There was an atmosphere of immense struggle and a lingering through-line of possibility from the '60s. The inner cities of America were flooded with drugs, and the groundwork for the incarceration nation was building. Angela Davis was released from prison and Shirley Chisholm made her historic bid for the presidency. We were still at war with Vietnam, and the Watergate scandal was breaking. Loretta Lynn made music history with "Coal Miner's Daughter," *Ms.* magazine had just been launched, and the first female FBI agents were hired. Joni, the traditional girl who was raised in the 1950s and came of age in the '60s, created an album that spoke to the duality of that moment in a way few musicians could have. The *Los Angeles Times* wrote, "At a time when so many of our most successful and respected songwriters—from Carole King to Gordon Lightfoot to James Taylor—are having difficulty coming up with something fresh in their music, Joni Mitchell, as literate a writer as we have, continues to produce works of richness and value."

Vocally, *For the Roses* would be the first time Joni explored a sultry quality in her voice, one she didn't have before, a quality that would continue to deepen and ripen over time. This was partly her continuing emancipation from the influence of Crosby, Stills & Nash, partly from aging, but, most dramatically, from cigarettes, which she had been smoking since she was nine years old. Accelerating the maturation process, something that was, at this stage, like a fine wine.

It is not just her voice that has deepened, but the range of her concerns. "For the Roses" is as elegantly crafted a song as Joni would ever write, but behind its lovely hooks, turns, and resolutions is a cynicism stewed over a summer of solitude. In an insistent soprano, she announces that life in the wilds of the Sunshine Coast has led her to reflect on subject matter broader than *Blue*'s cycle of love, romance, and inconsolable melancholy. And she isn't the only pilgrim on this album. There are questers everywhere, looking up for divinity and down for junk. "Some turn to Jesus / And some turn to heroin," she sings, leaving no room for anything in between. Joni nods to the daughter she gave up when she adds, "Some watch their kids grow up." And yet, even in the midst of all the very Joni imagery, there's the clarion song of a revolutionary:

> *Who let the greedy in*
> *And who left the needy out*
> *Who made this salty soup*
> *Tell him we're very hungry now*

The title song would inaugurate a series of what Joni called "I Hate Show Business" songs that would include "The Boho Dance" (1975) all the way up to "Taming the Tiger" (1998), in which she declared herself "a runaway from the record biz." But she never hated on showbiz any better than she did in this song's deceptively dulcet tones.

The song begins with a sound that resembles applause. It concludes with the sound returning, but it's just the arbutus trees rustling. The arbutus was a species of tree that fascinated Joni. They spring up in the least likely environments, even bare land. Yet when Vancouver tried to import several of them for a street named after the tree, they couldn't survive. They would bloom and thrive only where they wanted to be, even when there didn't seem to be any soil. But they could not be transplanted. Joni knew the feeling. She would not go anywhere she wasn't thriving, and she would live as she chose, from the country to the city, and from perpetual retirement to going back to the grind one more time. She said that when she first heard the arbutus rustle, she felt the impulse to go out and take a bow. She was joking, of course, but she also knew that even as she remained in the public eye, a kind of songwriting wood nymph, a lady of the canyon, even she could never get entirely back to the garden.

Dickens wrote about sending off his novels to the shadowy world, comparing them, as Joni did with her songs, to his children. "For the Roses" was her petulant child, but also a beautiful and brilliant one. The song is a warning, first, she has said, to her ex-lover James Taylor, beginning in the second person but then ending up in the first. Like a poem in the tradition of pastoral elegy, in which the poet is mourning the dead but really self-mourning, Joni is really talking to herself, and also imagining the applause that she will face when she next performs.

Decades before music videos allowed artists, particularly female artists, from Annie Lennox to Madonna to Björk and Beyoncé, to use film to shape and reshape their public image, Joni was playing an elaborate game of show-and-tell with pictures. It started with the self-portraits that she painted for her album covers. With *For the Roses*, she took it up a notch. For the gatefold of the album Joni ventured out onto a rocky promontory in the tranquil water by her home in British Columbia. She was nude, ravishing, buck wild, untamable. "Joel Bernstein took the picture on *For the Roses* under my guidance," Joni recalled. "That was going to be the front cover. It was going to be like a Magritte or a *Starry Night*. And it's a very innocent nude. It's like Botticelli's Aphrodite. I've had a few bum comments. It's a nice bum. It's no big deal. The cock of the leg is Aphrodite rising from the clamshell. It's an art posture borrowed from paintings."

Her manager Elliot Roberts argued against it. "Joan, how would you like to see $5.98 plastered across your ass?" he asked, convincingly. The stunning image was moved inside the cover, and for the front, Joni posed, a sort of wood nymph overlooking the sea, in green velvet and brown suede boots, and with the tan of one who went indoors only to sleep. It was a sign that the music world was beginning to really get Joni, and the stance she was taking in her work, when *Rolling Stone* said of the cover that it underscored the "unique feeling that one gets about the person who made this record, who can emerge from the hazy watercolor of life and say, 'I am the best person it is within my power to be. Here I am.'"

On *For the Roses*, Joni was just an album away from a commercial breakthrough that would change everything. Goodbye folk clubs, goodbye privacy. The mixed blessing of goddess fame was on its way, and it would hit hard. Would it make her happy? Anyone could be happy. The bigger Joni got, the more prophetic the words of Nietzsche would sound: "There is a musician who, more than any other musician, is a master at finding the tones in the realm of suffering, depressed, and tortured souls, at giving language even to mute misery . . . He draws most happily of all out of the profoundest depth of human happiness, and, as it were, out of its drained goblet, where the bitterest and most repulsive drops have finally and evilly run together with the sweetest." It is almost as if Nietzsche is talking about the holy wine that Mitchell immortalized in "A Case of You." It is that mixture of the bitter and the sweet, along with the desire to fulfill her own definition of creative mastery, that continues to intrigue her on *For the Roses*, and that will lead her eventually off the trails of the pop charts forever.

It is easy to get lost in those chords, that voice, the melody, the naked Joni in the gatefold and the clothed, pensive, and fascinating woman sitting in nature on the cover. She is looking right through us. "You turn me on," she will sing, but be careful. She will also be serenading us with devastating songs about the One Percent at their fancy banquet, a junkie getting his fix, a musical genius trapped in his deafness, the electrical currents that will ruin us as a species, a prize horse about to get shot. The songs on the album follow nature's cycles. Several are as perfectly formed as any she had ever created. Others are angrier, more confrontational, and more meandering than those on *Blue*, yet they dig even deeper.

She was never more confrontational than she was on "Woman of Heart and Mind":

> *Drive your bargains*
> *Push your papers*
> *Win your medals*
> *Fuck your strangers*
> *Don't it leave you on the empty side*

You might be trying to impress Joni, says the song, but she is far from impressed with you. *For the Roses* has not achieved the canonical status of *Blue*, perhaps because it was even more emotionally exhausting than its predecessor. It was also tougher, which tested those for whom defenselessness was a virtue. Yet in 2007, it became one of twenty-five albums selected by the Library of Congress to add to its National Recording Registry. It's the only one of Mitchell's albums to earn that exalted place, one for the ages.

In a review of her 1972 Carnegie Hall performance, Don Hackman in *The New York Times* raved, "Her voice has a far greater range of timbre and articulation, especially in its ability to resonate with warm, dark chest tones. But what makes Joni Mitchell really special is the great esthetic density of her music. Starting from a base that is rooted deeply in her own psyche, she builds metaphoric excursions-through-life trips that are common to us all. And she does it with a brilliant harmonic sense, lyrical melodies and almost effortless poetry. I suspect that in her own way Joni Mitchell may be one of the most genuinely gifted composers North America has yet developed. That she chooses to express her art in small forms and personal sentiments in no way reduces either its impact or its importance."

This last line was important because the knock on Joni, from the beginning, had been that she was an eloquent troubadour of heart matters, but not a true genius like her male peers, including Dylan. In 1969, *Newsweek* had heralded Joni and her generation of female singer-songwriters in an article titled "The Girls—Letting Go." The writers began by stating, "For all its individuality, the rock-music scene has lacked the personal touch. Largely, it has been a world of male groups, of pounding, thunderous music that drowns out the words, which are rarely of the moment." They praised Joni for her "love of words, her delight in imagery [and] complex inner rhymes." But in the same paragraph, they criticized the songs of *Clouds* for being "thin in subject, nebulous in form" and "self-conscious in their poetic effects."

The *Newsweek* article echoed the still-new idea that the personal is political. That sentiment was becoming a slogan of the modern women's rights movement around the time that Joni released *Clouds*, and it explains why her music was beloved by so many women who came of age in that era. In her landmark essay "The Personal Is Political," published in 1969, Carol Hanisch wrote, about the consciousness-raising groups she attended, "the reason I participate in these meetings is not to solve any personal problem. One of the first things we discover in these groups is that personal problems are political problems. There are no personal solutions at this time . . . I've been forced to take off the rose-colored glasses and face the awful truth about how grim my life really is as a woman." It was a sentiment that Joni might have echoed had she not been isolated by fame and profession from the average young woman of her age.

Hanisch goes on to ask a very Joni question: "Can you imagine what would happen if women . . . stop blaming ourselves for our sad situations? We are thinking for ourselves for the first time in our lives. As the cartoon in *Lilith* put it, 'I'm changing. My mind is growing muscles.'"

For the Roses is a watershed album for Joni, not only because it's a bridge between two masterpieces. In it, you can hear that she is changing, you can sense her mind growing muscles. And by the time *For the Roses* was released, even the establishment journalists were getting it: just because Joni's music was personal did not mean it wasn't powerful. Joni's work was much, much more than the sophomoric musings of a long-haired girl, which it might have seemed to be at first glance. Even when she was writing about her own particular sadness, struggle, and depression, her lyrics and her tunings were filled with a generous sense of grandeur, as if the doors of her heart had been flung open and she was inviting the world in. *Rolling Stone* raved, "Love's tension is Joni Mitchell's medium—she molds and casts it like a sculptress, lubricating this tense clay with powerful emotive imagery and swaying hypnotic music that sets her listener up for another of her great strengths, a bitter facility with irony and incongruity. As the tiny muscles in your spine begin to relax as they are massaged by a gorgeous piano line or a simple guitar or choral introduction, you might get quietly but bluntly slammed with a large dose of Woman Truth."

The praise that *For the Roses* garnered must have been bolstering after her monastery year on the Sunshine Coast. The critics and her still-growing legions of fans were admitting that, yes, she was unconventional. Yes, she was not always commercial. But she was, without argument, extraordinarily gifted, and by all means, she should keep going.

Blue had been the last album on Joni's contract with Reprise, and David Geffen and Elliot Roberts had moved quickly to sign Joni to the newly formed Asylum Records. Geffen and Joni were friends, but despite her tremendous critical success, he urged her to record at least one song that would be what his new label desperately needed: a Top 40 hit. "I kept on telling Joni I wanted her to write a hit," Geffen said. "She was always making fun of me about the idea that she should have a hit. But I wanted her to sell a lot of records." He still remembers the first time she sang it to him: "I'm a radio / I'm a country station / I'm a little bit corny / I'm a wildwood flower." He said, "When she sang it to me, it was almost her making fun of me for trying to get her to write a hit record."

"To write a hit song because David Geffen wants you to have a hit is like saying, 'Go take a paper route so that you can do public service,' when she had already worked as a candy striper," said Russ Kunkel.

Joni was up to the challenge. She had a direct marketing campaign to charm the DJs, using their argot: "Dial in the number," "Broadcasting tower," "Who needs the static?" The playfully tongue-in-cheek "You Turn Me On, I'm a Radio," which used what Joni called her "own peculiar warped sense of humor," hit number twenty-five on *Billboard*. Maybe she'd do better the next time without trying.

16 ▨ STAR-CROSSED

Nineteen seventy-three opened with Carly Simon's "You're So Vain" at the top of the charts. It was rumored to be about Warren Beatty. In recent years, Simon has insisted it was (mostly) about someone else, but no one actually seems to believe her. Even Beatty, who called Simon to thank her for it.

If the year opened with accusations of vanity, it unfolded, for Joni, with every stripe of narcissism.

Joni did not experience anything like culture shock; she was thriving on fluidity, grooving to the extremes. Either do it all the way or not at all: be at the center of the star-maker machinery or secluded in the woods. "Look at my chord changes," she told me. "There *are* abrupt changes of key. I'm equipped to ride big changes. I had no trouble making the transition." But she was hardly starry-eyed. "These are not fun people," she said. "Stars are hardly ever fun. They're neurotic, they're self-centered, they're nervous, they're insecure, especially movie stars. I'm more comfortable with farm people."

And yet even if Joni was uncomfortable, she was still brimming with inspiration. A photograph shows her standing in front of Geffen's grand piano, with a bowl ashtray on one side and pen to paper. Her anticipation is palpable; she could not wait to pounce. This material was just too good to waste. Celebrity, psychoanalysis, decadence: Hollywood in 1973 was filled with actors and directors embracing the new freedoms that came with the collapse of the studio system and the end, just five years earlier, of the prudish Hays production code. Now you could get away with almost anything in a film, and Joni felt that, in her songs, she was making movies of her own; she, too, could go for broke.

The melancholy of the Sunshine Coast did not magically disappear in Hollywood. Warren Beatty suggested she do what he and most of his friends did: turn for help to the renowned German psychoanalyst Martin Grotjahn. Dr. Grotjahn had established Southern California's first psychoanalytic training center, the Los Angeles Psychoanalytic Institute, while at the same time maintaining a private practice in Beverly Hills, with a massive clientele that included Beatty, Geffen, and many of their celebrity friends. Dr. Grotjahn, Joni recalled, was "Freudian, proud, happy to be a narcissist."

Joni, still reeling from one failed relationship after another, certainly had a lot to talk about. From the couch, she answered the same kinds of questions the journalists would have asked her. But she was barely speaking to journalists, and when she did, these were precisely the topics she wanted to avoid. "James [Taylor] was in a bad place and it just didn't work," she told the doctor. "He had gotten off heroin and was on methadone. He was broody and moody and I was trying to be cheerful, which was really the wrong thing. You can't be self-destructive without destroying everything around you." Joni could not handle being on this path of destruction for long.

And Taylor was not simply morose, he was bitter. "He said, 'You think you're hot shit.' He was incapable of a relationship . . . There were some very likable things about James, but for the most part, he was incapable of affection. He was just a mess. If somebody's dark and brooding, you're better off brood[ing] beside them. Don't go acting cheerful. You're just a reminder of what they're not. They'll hate you for it. The last thing you want is a cheerful person when you're down like that. That's when I learned that lesson. And then I bought the property and spent a year up there and sealed myself from that."

After she wrote much of *For the Roses* with the memory of Taylor in the periphery, she was then thrown on the road with Jackson Browne, another brooding singer-songwriter who was even more harmful to Joni's already fragile emotional state. "I did love, to the best of my ability, and sometimes, for a while, it was reciprocated, and sometimes the person was too far gone on drugs or whatever, that they were incapable. James numbed on drugs and Jackson Browne was never attracted to me. We got thrown out on the road together and traveled all around. We were companions, because we were playing in Amsterdam and playing from London to New Orleans. But when he spoke about old lovers, he leered. He was a leering narcissist."

The relationship was temporary, and the breakup less eventful than has been reported elsewhere. But Jackson Browne committed the unpardonable sin of instigating the breakup. Larry Klein, Joni's husband from 1982 to 1994, was sure that this was why Browne was vilified by Joni. "Joni had a great deal of anger towards Jackson," Klein said. "I don't know all their history. I certainly know some of it from her perspective. Maybe it stems from the fact that he was the one to end the relationship between them. I think that's a pattern in her life. She would do things that would lead to the end of the relationship. She would force the hand of the person and then feel unjustly abandoned."

"Jackson's mother warned me against him," Joni recalled. She was not the first mother whose warnings Joni recalls. She would come to see the mothers as a sort of "women's union," sharing collective knowledge, raising collective concerns. Chuck Mitchell was, according to his mother, the firstborn and "first waffle" that should have been thrown out. As for Leonard Cohen, his mother was the one who said, "Be prepared to bleed." One evening Joni was having dinner at Browne's family's house. Beatrice, his schoolteacher mother, turned to Joni and said, "I wondered what form your perversion would take." Was Mrs. Browne calling her perverse? Joni eventually came to feel she was being given a heads-up. Maybe there was something off about Jackson's relationships. And he did seem to be more giddy with his male friends than he could ever be with a woman . . . And why was he so obsessed with women having holes in their clothes? He would run her sweaters through the Laundromat a dozen times just to fray them. This guy had issues.

James Taylor and Jackson Browne would both move on, although they would not entirely leave Joni's life (about which everybody seemed to have an opinion). Once, in Joni's telling, Carole King came up to her and said, "You don't like yourself. I can tell. I like myself." Then she walked away. *What a little brat*, thought Joni. *So much*, she thought, *for the women's union.*

There was a lot to unravel on Dr. Grotjahn's Beverly Hills couch. Joni was not only there to talk about her recent romantic disappointments, but also her current life, which included Warren Beatty, another of his patients.

By 1973, Beatty and his friend Jack Nicholson were the two biggest male sex symbols in Hollywood—and both were after Joni. Beginning with the success in 1967 of *Bonnie and Clyde*, Beatty was being seen as a combination of Cary Grant and Orson Welles—equal parts sex symbol, writer-director-actor triple threat, and control freak. This guy could dominate Hollywood. He was having a hard time understanding why he couldn't dominate Joni. Nicholson was also a legendary smooth operator, but he could have an easier time living with not being able to sleep with every beautiful and fascinating woman on earth. He would be a fixture at Joni's parties in Bel-Air; he would be a fan and a friend.

Beatty and Nicholson each made moves on her—their games were among the best honed in town—but Joni thought, *No way.* The three of them had a ritual of going to dinner together, but Joni would always take her own car. She thought they had a bet going on who would get her into bed first. (In *Reds*, Warren Beatty, as John Reed, and Jack Nicholson, as Eugene O'Neill, were comrades fighting over Diane Keaton.)

This chase was certainly entertaining, but Joni had no intention of taking it all the way, which was very disturbing to Warren Beatty, who was used to having his pleasure served to him from any woman

whose stock was high, and Joni's was. Beatty thought this was irrational behavior, and told Dr. Grotjahn so.

Said Joni: "Most women would have been flattered [by the atten-
tion]. It was flattering, but there was no way that I would have . . . My
problem was that I was sad. I wasn't mentally ill. I was sad, trying to
get something going in impossible situations. When someone's undermining your self-worth, it's not a healthy situation. Well, it's not
James's fault, he's fucked-up. And Jackson's just a nasty bit of business.
So to go from one to the other kind of scared me against going into
another relationship. I knew the game [Beatty] was playing. He told
Grotjahn that I was the only woman that beat him at his own game,
and I said at that point, 'I don't know what the game is, but I don't feel
like a victor. If I won something, what did I win?'"

Spurning the advances of Jack Nicholson and Warren Beatty was
less competitive sport than self-preservation. Joni would tease Beatty
and call him "Pussycat." Joni was referring to Beatty's famous pickup
line, "What's new, Pussycat?"—a line that inspired Woody Allen's first
screenplay. This might not have penetrated the cultural barrier for the
German Dr. Grotjahn. (He and his family had fled Berlin when he
realized that "there was no room for Hitler and me in the same town.")

"You call him the pussycat?" asked Dr. Grotjahn in his thick
German accent.

"Yeah, for obvious reasons," she replied, perhaps not realizing that
they were not obvious to the good doctor.

"What does a pussycat do?" he asked. "He's cute and fluffy and
then one day, you get scratched: *Meow!*"

At this point, Joni threw up her hands.

"Warren is not my problem."

"But you are his!"

"That's indiscreet. Believe me, Warren is not my problem, nor will
he be my problem. If he has a problem that I won't let him be my problem, then he's got a problem."

Joni might as well have continued throwing psychology books
against the wall. The sessions became increasingly absurd. If Joni had
a dream, then Dr. Grotjahn was sure he was in it. "You're just like John

Lennon!" he would say. Lennon was having a Hollywood crisis of his own at that time. Was he part of this, too?

"You're just like Marilyn Monroe!" he would then say.

She loved Monroe's line from *The Misfits*: "If I have to feel lonely, I'd rather be alone." Figuring out the difference between alone and lonely would be a lifelong project for Joni. "I've covered a lot of [loneliness] on my records. I mean, I have expressed it almost like open letters . . . I need a lot of time, solitary time. Ideally, I would like to be able to withdraw into a corner in a room full of people and work. I love the bustle of a room of people interacting where perhaps I am apart but busy on my own project." She knew when she could be alone and not feel lonely. "Sometimes I go up to my land in British Columbia and spend time alone in the country, surrounded by the beauty of natural things. There's a romance which accompanies it, so you generally don't feel self-pity." But back in Los Angeles, she too often felt "surrounded by people who are continually interacting, the loneliness makes you feel like you've sinned, as Leonard Cohen said."

Joni wasn't afraid of exploring the complex caverns of her heart and mind. But Dr. Grotjahn was putting dark thoughts in Joni's head. She didn't trust him. She didn't bond with him. Finally, he told her, "You have come to the wrong psychiatrist."

He then put Joni in a group he was running with eight psychiatrists as patients. Now she really saw what was going on in the kitchen.

This therapy for therapists would later surface in some of "Trouble Child," but first there were songs to write, music to record, boundaries to break. Joni's love affairs tended to be with fellow musicians, and not with men with more power than she had. The movie star world would be a different kind of power. If she made herself vulnerable, she would feel the same terror many of her own lovers would feel. Even if people around her assumed that there had been, at some point, some sort of encounter between Joni and Warren Beatty—he was, some have speculated, the man "weighing the beauty and the imperfection" in "Same Situation"—she would not let her guard down. Maybe she liked herself more than Carole King could know.

17 ■ *COURT AND SPARK*: SOMETHING STRANGE HAPPENED

f, looking from the outside, you wanted to be Joni Mitchell, this was the moment you would want to be her. If she were a stock, this would be the time to short it.

She had been summoned back to the City of the Fallen Angels by David Geffen when he heard through the grapevine that she was suicidal after a breakup with Jackson Browne. (For the record, she insists she wasn't.) She moved into Geffen's Hollywood mansion on Copley Drive, which he was renting from the director Blake Edwards and his wife, Julie Andrews. (The hills were alive with the sound of music! Oh, and Geffen was living with Cher.)

Joni was back in the crowd, although not the same crowd of her earlier life. Here was a new set of characters to inspire a new set of songs, each of which would be realized with a band, including, on some tracks, a full orchestra. The escape from society that produced the brooding introspection of *For the Roses* was followed by an embrace of civilization and its discontents: flawed people, lust masquerading as love, parties that could get awkward, and the search for meaning that was as unquenchable as ever. The spectacle beckoned and she beckoned back; the album would be the result.

Many things in the '70s seemed like a good idea at the time, and the drummer John Guerin was one of them. "I'm frightened by the devil," Joni sang in "A Case of You." "And I'm drawn to those ones that ain't afraid." Guerin was one of those. With his feathered dark hair and chiseled features, he had just enough of the derelict in him. (In "Just Like This Train," Joni playfully imagined her vain darling's hairline receding.)

Joni and Guerin would spend hours in bed listening to Miles (whom she adored and revered) and John Coltrane (who she decided, based on tone and note choice and his "corny-ass adjacent-valve doodeloos," was overrated and a "midget" compared with the Ellington altoist Johnny Hodges, a "giant" who made her "melt"). Guerin made her melt, too. He played the rogue and the virtuoso. They did indeed court and spark, and the spark lasted long enough for a record and a tour, which by the standards of the decade was pretty impressive.

Guerin was crucial in raising the bar for musicianship, taking it to places Joni wanted to go before she quite knew the route. Folk musicians are used to looking at one another's left hands to follow the chords by what is on the frets. Bob Dylan, for example, recorded *Desire* (1976) with no rehearsals, no charts. The bassist Rob Stoner got through the sessions following Dylan's frets. But playing this way with Joni is a waste of time. Her left hand, weakened by polio, is just a single finger running up and down her guitar's neck. Joni leaves all the work to her right hand, which builds polychords with her open tunings. She can't name them, but they are the basis of her chromatic harmony—the quality that gives her chords color and fluidity. Imagine songs filled with a few chords on top of each other—that still make complex harmonic sense—and you will get the idea of what it's like to play with her. It's not necessary to learn open tunings. All you need, as George Martin said, is ears.

Guerin was the drummer for the jazz-pop ensemble L.A. Express, which would build on Joni's musical eccentricities in new ways that would be as exciting to her as they would be to her listeners, who were accumulating along with her musical expansion. In jazz, as with many other cultural entities, many of the things that were going on in New York were also going on in Los Angeles, sort of. In the 1950s, there was an identifiable West Coast Jazz sound. It all came out of appropriations, adaptations, or outright imitations of the great swing era and Count Basie alum tenor saxophonist Lester Young, whose latter-day mellowed-out style came from his running out of steam and everything else. (He and his musical twin, Billie Holiday, sounded like they were, sublimely, running out of steam together, and died in the same year.) Gerry Mulligan, Chet Baker, and Stan Getz—all superb musicians—popularized this conception and made it sound, to use a word associated with Miles Davis, "cool," and it was Miles Davis who was being riffed on again in the '70s when his hugely popular album *Bitches Brew* spawned an entire generation of bands that combined the sounds and rhythms of James Brown, Jimi Hendrix, and Sly and the Family Stone with extended improv. Some of this music was powerful and innovative. Some of it sounded like expertly played soundtrack work. Some of it dated like a pet rock. Many jazz purists never accepted this music as real jazz, but Joni was not one of them.

The '70s was a golden age of session musicians, in New York and LA. Many musicians, including Joni's future collaborators and friends Herbie Hancock and Wayne Shorter, moved from New York to LA and stayed there. Top call players could get way more than scale and never have to leave their SoCal homes if they didn't want to. (Victor Feldman, who became an L.A. Express keyboardist and toured with Joni, turned down an invitation to tour with Miles Davis because he was making too much bread on LA studio gigs.) The top ones could all play "real jazz" and the new style. None of them were purists if they wanted to work. And Joni was the least purist of all. She loved the styles of her teenage years, but prided herself on looking forward. Artistic conviction went hand in hand with something that became, almost accidentally, hugely popular.

Joni had worked extensively with Tom Scott on *For the Roses*; he'd overdubbed his parts on woodwinds and reeds the way she overdubbed her parts. After seeing his band, the L.A. Express, at a Studio City club called the Baked Potato, she invited them to join her at the studio, and what was left of her ties to the folk era would be severed, mostly, for good. The music they were playing then was definitely more like the jazz-rock crossover in the shadow of *Bitches Brew*. It sounded nothing like the genuinely weird and avant-garde music Davis was making by 1973, or the compositional innovations of Wayne Shorter and Joe Zawinul's Weather Report. It was basic meat-and-potatoes rock and roll and funk with killer solos and excellent rhythm. It is easy to hear, when listening to the 1974 album *Tom Scott and the L.A. Express*, why drummers fawned over Guerin. He sounded like he could do just about anything. And now these stellar musicians could take their chops and put them in the service of Joni's music. They passed the audition, and she was soon joined in the studio by Scott, the bassist Max Bennett, the keyboardist Joe Sample, and of course, Guerin.

When Joni began looking for musicians to work with her on what would become *Court and Spark*, Russ Kunkel, the drummer on *Blue* and *For the Roses*, gave her some advice. "You need to work with jazz musicians," he told her, begging off the drummer's seat she had offered him again. "I thought that the direction she was going in would be conducive to playing with an established rhythm section," Kunkel recalled. Kunkel managed to stay out of Joni's way on the two albums he recorded with her, but he opted to pass on this one. "I guess in my mind, if it had been taken to the nth degree, it would have been: How great would it have been for her to play with Bill Evans or Miles Davis or Philly Joe Jones? But what was available were amazing musicians in LA. As history would say, it worked out."

It turned out Kunkel was right. These guys were very quick on the uptake. The bass player, Max Bennett, was the oldest member of the band. He had played with Charlie Parker, Dizzy Gillespie, Ella Fitzgerald, Billie Holiday, and Stan Getz; Bennett had famously advised a young singer named Peggy Lee that she should record a song called "Fever," which included his memorable syncopated bass line. Even with all this experience among musical royalty, playing with Joni was still remarkable to him. "I felt like everything she did was about something or somebody and very honest," Bennett recalled. "She never sang anything for a special effect or to impress someone. It was always, 'This is the way I feel about it.' I worked with many great singers, but she was different. She was a great player. She was a great musician. She had great time, rhythmically. She was right on the money. With real professionals, she really held her own. We were all jazz musicians, and jazz musicians are more flexible than any other type of player, in every aspect of music."

Larry Carlton, the lead guitarist for the Crusaders ("Street Life") and an extremely prolific session player who had just joined the L.A. Express, was not at all flummoxed by this unorthodox method the day he walked into the studio: "Humbly, I could hear the chord changes. I didn't have to watch her fingers. None of us were struggling harmonically to figure out what to do against her great chords." These were musicians with superlative jazz technique, who were also content to engage with aspects of jazz harmony and rhythm without playing jazz. And none of them held on to jazz-sized conceptions about how long their solos would be, or if there would be anything other than riffing behind a vocal line.

"When we went into the studio with Joni," said Carlton, "my job was to help her make her music. It wasn't about me. My job was to help make those songs as great as I thought I could help make them. Our job was to help arrange behind her so that she could present those great chords on her songs. Let's take a C major seventh chord and you put a G major chord on top of it. Now you have a C major ninth sharp eleventh chord. Joni would instinctively hear those kinds of sounds. I would just hear it and write down the chord chart. I remember her putting a cassette on and Tom Scott and I would grab pencils and pieces of paper, writing down chords."

Carlton also found the best way to complement Joni's rhythm playing, a method that would later be used by Robben Ford (on the Miles of Aisles tour of 1974) and Pat Metheny (on the Shadows and Light tour of 1979). "In 1971, I got my first volume pedal and I used it on the first Crusader records, and that became an identifiable Larry Carlton sound, so that was a way to play where I wasn't just chucking rhythm or playing licks," he recalled. "In the right hands, that can really enhance a track without it being so typical guitar."

What Carlton is describing could also be captured by the Italian musical marking *una corda*: drama, but with the mute. With this group, there was no lack of drama—it was in high supply in the soap opera between Joni and Guerin as the show went on—but there was no lack of precision, either. The volume pedal sustained single notes or chords, so that it would complement any rhythm playing Joni would do, and it would provide the kind of sonic atmosphere that Joni would often request. Joni now had a contrapuntal voice. She would still write alone— and she was still the maestro—but in the studio, she wasn't all by herself anymore.

The results were extraordinary. Jon Landau, who would go on to manage and produce Bruce Springsteen, raved in *Rolling Stone*, "On first listening, Joni Mitchell's *Court and Spark*, the first truly great pop album of 1974, sounds surprisingly light; by the third or fourth listening, it reveals its underlying tensions."

It's the lightness that draws the listener in so seductively and powerfully. Joni may have missed performing at Woodstock, but with *Court and Spark*, she orchestrates, on wax, a festival of epic proportions.

If you close your eyes, you can almost picture yourself in a wide-open field on a bright sunny day. There's Joni and her band on the stage. When the album starts it's sunset, you might be alone listening to the album, but it feels like you're surrounded by thousands of music lovers, all swaying to the beat, all ready to fall in love, to tune in and be turned on. "Court and Spark," the opening song, evokes both the Delta blues of the American South and the palm-tree-studded skyline of Los Angeles. There is dirt and wildflowers underneath her feet as Joni sings, but there is also glamour-tinged stardust overhead. She is at once the boho queen of the festival world and the gowned A-lister of the red carpet, dualities that Joni has been able to hold throughout her career in a way that makes her deeply engaging and unique. And yet, while many people are grooving to it, the music is also intimate, personal, challenging, complex, taking each listener into their own darkened bedroom. It is a festival for one, and every *Court and Spark* encounter is a little different every time, and for each person who hears it. Open your eyes, and you are just looking at yourself, or the person lying next to you. Close them again. It is a festival for your mind.

The title track opens up the album with an E major chord that turns into a suspended chord, and finally to a minor chord, when we learn that infatuation can turn into rejection in just a night—and it is the singer who is in control. Whether intentionally or not, that chord, and the places it moves to—D major, back to E major, then to G major, then to the E suspended chord (D major with E in the bass, a favorite chord of hers)—evokes one of Joni's favorite pieces of music from her childhood, Claude Debussy's "Clair de Lune," the third movement of Debussy's *Suite bergamasque*, with its dramatic D-flat major that transports listeners into one of the most well-loved progressions of late Romantic music.

Court and Spark is romantic, too, in the musical sense and in the sense that these songs will be about the seductions, follies, and illusions of eros. "Love came to my door," she sings, and we hear courtship in the timbre and register of her voice, as it floats along stacked and suspended chords. Her musical idea of courting and sparking—with cadences and chords that flirt with the listener—is far more enthralling than this fanatic who shows up at her door. Sure, he seems to be reading her mind, and sure, he even makes a compelling proposition: "You could complete me / I'd complete you." But this album is narrated by a sinner, one of the "guilty people" the madman is ranting against. Later, in "Same Situation," Joni sends up a prayer wondering who will hear it with "Heaven full of astronauts / And the Lord on death row," and it sounds like she's preaching to herself. But this album is not about salvation, it's about seduction, even if the seduction feels empty without a search for love that "don't seem to cease."

The corrupted, guilty, and deeply flawed human comedy of LA will dominate this landscape. That madman at the door, in "Court and Spark," whoever he is, inspired a sultry, hot mess of a masterpiece that clocks in at under three minutes. But he cannot hang around for this album. As she shows him to the door, she is reminded that just as LA is filled with people with no soul but coke to spare, it is also filled with sanctimonious types who think they have the answers. Joni doesn't pretend to have the answers herself, but she's going to go looking for deeper meanings where she can. And she will take us along for the ride.

At the end of the track, you can hear bells. It's not a wedding, and it's not a funeral. It's something in between—amorous limbo, with partners keeping their options way, way open.

"Help Me" comes next, and it comes to the listener through the sun-drenched lens of a 1970s Polaroid camera. The song begins with an escalating guitar rhythm and it is almost like Joni is driving a car full of dreamers idling outside your house. She's at the wheel of a 1974 baby-blue Mustang convertible that matches her eyes. Where are they going? Anywhere and everywhere you might ever want to go. Joni has described herself as a frustrated filmmaker and nowhere is this more evident than on "Help Me," in which she constructs a three-minute-and-twenty-four-second movie with music and lyrics. There's the heroine, who has met either the love of her life or, as Sheryl Crow so deftly described it, her "favorite mistake." The love interest is "a rambler and a gambler and a sweet-talking ladies' man." They will talk and dance and lie there, "not talking," and it all feels so good. But it isn't built to last. Not because he's a rogue. Yes, he loves his freedom more than he loves the loving. But she does, too. It is *Love, American Style* as only Joni could have written it.

"Help Me" would become Joni's only Top 10 single as a recording artist, and within two months of its release, *Court and Spark* would peak on the *Billboard* charts at number two, an amazing feat. It would sell more than two million copies in its first year, and eventually attain double-platinum status.

In his 33⅓ series monograph on the album, the music writer Sean Nelson keenly puts this accomplishment into perspective: "The significance of such a quantifiably huge success is difficult to distill given that Joni Mitchell was already unquestionably a big star with a couple of gold records under her belt and also given that rock music was still the key cultural influence on young America, such that grown-up America had to take it seriously. The difference between the Top 20—where her previous hit records had peaked—and number two, however, is more than just a few numbers. It's the difference between being well known in your field and being a household name. It's the difference between having fans devoted to following your work and reaching people who buy whatever's on the radio hit parade in a given week . . . In 1974, before cable TV, before the internet, before the heroic expansion of leisure possibilities that represents the past thirty years' most obvious form of progress, a number one record meant pretty much everyone was listening."

> *Mind if I turn on the radio?*
> *Oh, my favorite song, she said*
> *And it was Joni singing,*
> *Help me, I think I'm falling . . .*

That's Prince, an avid Joni Mitchell fan, echoing the power and reach of her music in his sultry love-and-lust song "The Ballad of Dorothy Parker."

In a June 1974 cover story for the Canadian magazine *Maclean's*, Joni spoke to her friend Malka Marom about what the runaway success of *Court and Spark* meant to her. In the interview, Joni admits that she never expected to hit it so big. She says, "I always kept my goals very short, like I would like to play in a coffeehouse, so I did. I would like to play in the United States, you know, the States, the magic of crossing the border. So I did. I would like to make a certain amount of money a year, which I thought would give me the freedom to buy the clothes that I wanted and the antiques and just some women trips, a nice apartment in New York that I wouldn't have to be working continually to support. But I had no idea that I would be this successful, especially since I came to folk music when it was already dying."

One of Joni's defining qualities has come to be the way that her prodigious musicality and her powers of observation put her consistently ahead of the curve. If pop culture was a winding road from Sunset Boulevard up into the Hollywood Hills, one might imagine that Joni was driving the pace car, leading us through each zigzag. "People's Parties," for example, had the incredible timing of debuting within weeks of the premiere issue of *People* magazine. After a $40 million investment and with great hoo-hah, Time, Inc., published the first issue on March 4, 1974, with Mia Farrow on the cover. Three thousand miles away, Joni had been hanging out at all those Hollywood parties—intrigued, attracted, and sometimes disgusted—and her song functions like a reporter's dispatch from the front lines of the entertainment industry.

> *Some are friendly, some are cutting*
> *Some are watching it from the wings*
> *Some are standing in the center*
> *Giving to get something*

Joni is our emissary into the world of glitterati. She sees vanity, success and failure, outer beauty and inner emptiness. What does she have? Is she that special? She says she's not the sharpest tool, wandering around with "a weak and a lazy mind." Trevor Horn, the British music producer who some have dubbed "the man who invented the eighties," once told BBC's Radio 4 that "People's Parties" was the song he'd most like to pass down to his children. He said he'd considered "citing Bob Dylan as an example of lyrical excellence, and Debussy as a master of melody, but then realized Joni Mitchell did both at once. *Court and Spark*," Horn declared, "will stand up in two hundred years' time, in my opinion."

She has one foot planted in the 1970s, and another in a timeless realm. Here we find every subtle and glaring aspect of love—the chase, the quest, falling in, falling out, falling again, being dizzy, disappointed, and everything in between. And we don't just feel, we *hear* it. "Car on a Hill" is an elaborate expression of what it means to be stood up. You are alone, you are waiting for a lover, and the hills of Hollywood represent the thing that's on its way, maybe. The car could be caught in traffic, you tell yourself. But that car could be picking up another girl, one who has already been picked up. You plot your next move, you contemplate revenge, you are furious, but you still aren't sure.

Joe Sample's keyboard climbs up and down the keyboard, Larry Carlton's guitar evokes traffic, John Guerin's sticks hit the skins like pacing feet, and the horn section signals the next car. Cars were never bigger or flashier than they were in 1974. Those gas-guzzlers were boats. It would be hard to miss one coming. The singer knows that men are like cars—there really will be another one. Still, it's a lonely wait up there. This is a movie scene with no resolution, losing hope with every added line. "There's still no buzzer, they roll on," she sings, "and I'm waiting for his car on the hill." The action of this song is where things don't happen.

The same could be said, in a sense, of "Free Man in Paris," in which our man feels "unfettered and alive" with "nobody calling me up for favors / And no one's future to decide." David Geffen begged Joni not to include the song on her album. It had been inspired by a vacance taken by Joni, Geffen, and Robbie Robertson of the Band, and Geffen was that momentarily free spirit.

"But why?" she asked. "It's not an unflattering portrait."

And it wasn't—but the liberation expressed in the song wasn't just about escaping dreamers and telephone screamers. It's about trawling the Champs Élysées, going from café to cabaret, thinking how he'll feel when he finds "that very good friend of mine." It was about the freedom to express your true sexual self.

Geffen is gay, and was terrified the song would out him. This was less than five years after the Stonewall uprising of 1969, a response to the treatment of men caught in gay bars in New York City, men whose names would be punitively published in *The New York Times* whether they were schoolteachers or surgeons at Mount Sinai. Gay liberation was still a fringe movement, and for someone as ambitious as Geffen, exposure felt downright dangerous. The inspired and unstable singer-songwriter Judee Sill blew her Asylum deal when she began outing Geffen in a radio interview. (She was furious that Geffen was paying too much attention to Joni.) Geffen was at heart a businessman, as savvy an operator as the industry has ever seen, with a knack for knowing who to sign, then a knack for knowing who to hire to do the signing when he got too old to know what the young people would want. And when he sensed the traditional music business was about to go belly-up, he sold his company at its peak market value. It would take Geffen twenty years to come out of the closet, when the times really had changed—and when he was too rich and too powerful to take down.

It is beyond ironic that such a stubbornly independent artist as Joni would also move in with her label boss and even write an affectionate song inspired by him. The Stones loved Ahmet Ertegun, but was he really expecting Mick and Keith to write a song about a Turkish music mogul taking a vacation? "Free Man in Istanbul"? Bob Dylan and Leonard Cohen never wrote songs for John Hammond, and wouldn't have moved in with him, either. (Dylan and Hammond as roommates? Seriously?) Joni ended up hating the music business as much as anyone who had thrived in it, but she was also in way deep with the Man. (For a song about what was really wrong with David Geffen, one would have to listen to Aimee Mann's "Nothing Is Good Enough" many years later.) Joni is philosophical about her old friend. "The music business has always been operated by crooks . . . but at least the crooks loved music," Joni would say.

What is striking to recall is that back in the 1970s, privacy was something you could travel for. Parisians didn't know who, say, David Geffen was, and they were less likely to care if they did. You could walk into a club as one thing, and walk out something else. Straight-gay, rich-poor-Jew-gentile: these distinctions could collapse in the stunning scenery of a Paris night.

As of 2017, Geffen is the hundred-ninetieth richest man in the world, with a fortune of $7.35 billion. Joni did not blow his cover—and in truth, few people hearing the song when it was released would have understood what it was about. It did make one thing clear, though: No one is immune to loneliness.

"Same Situation" is not about loneliness ipso facto. It is more of a rumination on what happens on one's way to intimacy, or at least an attempt at it. It is about artifice, about a phone that stops ringing, and about a room full of mirrors that turn a simple ritual of primping into a fun house of desperation. The song begins with Joni, who, like the rest of us, is preparing a face for the faces she will meet. She is not the resilient woman of "Cactus Tree," who collects men but doesn't need to be watered. Nor is she the precocious sage who has looked at life from both sides, now. She is looking at her reflection in "a room full of mirrors." Those mirrors are meant to catch her least flattering angle, and, as the title has it, she has been here before. The singer of "Same Situation" wonders how she can measure up to another girl gazing in another mirror. This is not narcissism, but reflection as blood sport. In El Lay, there's always another pretty girl looking at another mirror, and that girl could be having the same doubts, too. But this song is not about the competition. In 1974, the rules were changing fast. The man has told her he loved her, but she wonders if it can be real. The piano climbs up and down, the bass and the cymbals come in right in time. The L.A. Express is there, but she is inconsolably alone. There is a man, but it's complicated.

Joni was said to be involved with Warren Beatty when she was writing these songs, at least according to gossip rags and a tabloid photo in which they are walking together, looking down and in cahoots about something. Whatever their history, Beatty was clearly on Joni's mind in those heady days of 1973–74. Writer, actor, director, lothario, major pain in the ass, Beatty was as discerning about his paramours as he was with his work. This was the guy who, when working with Robert Altman in *McCabe & Mrs. Miller*, would reshoot Altman's scenes after the day's shooting had wrapped. Beatty, who was romantically linked to Julie Christie in this period, was always looking for perfection, and the songs on *Court and Spark*, meticulously wrought, take dead-center aim at a man who is "Weighing the beauty and the imperfection, to see if I'm worthy."

David Crosby said that Joni was "about as modest as Mussolini." Yet in "Same Situation," the singer is uneasy about what this man, who has known lots of women, will find. The imperfection is never defined. Is it physical? Is it emotional? Is it the same thing that makes her vulnerable, and is it vulnerability that made her an artist? Can the beauty of the art be bracketed from the imperfect woman who made it? Beauty and imperfection are big categories for a song that doesn't quite reach three minutes. The air gets pretty thin up there, where the search for love sticks around in the highest of stratospheres. It's quite a swirl of neuroses, a perfect storm for a Joni Mitchell song.

The singer is expected to measure up to every standard of beauty while also expected to be a moral exemplar, "like the church, like a cop, like a mother." Larry Carlton's slide guitar cries in the distance, and the strings, arranged by Tom Scott, swell. This same situation is not something that can last for too long. Heaven is full of astronauts. The Lord is on death row. The weight of the world is even heavier than the judgmental gaze of any heartthrob. She wants this man's approval, but she can also see to the other side. The search for love will go on.

"What came first? The music or the misery? Did I listen to pop music because I was miserable? Or was I miserable because I listened to pop music?" wonders the protagonist of *High Fidelity*, Nick Hornby's landmark novel about love and music. *Court and Spark* was fabulously popular in 1974, maybe because all the lonely people were listening to it, too. "What are you gonna do now? / You got no one to give your love to." This question, placed in the bridge of "Just Like This Train," is a variation of the second-person interrogation of "Down to You," even as it is in the context of a more playful song, about accumulating lovers ("I used to count lovers like railroad cars") and coming late to all occasions, a sure sign of success. Joni doesn't count on anything anymore, so why should anyone count on her? The sculptor Nathan Slate Joseph, who rented a SoHo loft to her from 1978 to 1987, recalled that making a Sunday brunch plan with Joni was always dicey: she would often get lost in a song or a painting and shrug plans away. What is the price of independence? A brunch plan is with a companion; a song could be for the world. But these emotions could be annoying! "Jealous lovin'll make you crazy / If you can't find your goodness / 'Cause you lost your heart."

The singer of "Down to You," a rumination about looking for love and walking away with lust, hasn't lost her heart, and that is where the trouble begins. The casual hookup inspires her to take a cold, hard look at solitude. "Blue" is sung to a color, a mood, a spectrum of melancholy. "Down to You" is addressed to all that, plus everything else, all in second person. She is singing to the listener, or to anyone else looking for warmth and beauty, settling for less than fascination, and having a morning-after regret. "Everything comes and goes" is the opening line and opening move of the song. Most things are ephemeral: fashion, relationships, pop songs, and dance crazes that disappear among the flotsam.

"Down to You" is about the bigger picture. The "You" is a "constant stranger," both kind and cold. You, Joni says, have a choice. Even though, on the Top 10 single on this album, Joni sings about loving one's freedom even more than one's loving, the woman *Rolling Stone* crowned Queen of El Lay is actually morally unrelenting with this second-person interlocutor. "You" could live a life that means something. "You" are better than the zipless fuck. "You" are more than a hedonist, and Joni said that she never met a self-described hedonist who wasn't a total asshole.

The "You" of the song is probably not a total asshole, but does have a moment of hedonism so acute, "You" become less discerning with every drink, craving "warmth and beauty," settling with less than fascination, and waking up with an emotional hangover. True to the song's inarguable observation that "Pleasure moves on too early / And trouble leaves too slow," the craving for warmth and beauty is immediately followed by shame, with the darkness of night covering a body like a fig leaf. It is impossible to go lower than "Blue," but "Down to You" makes the abyss more expansive, opening up the melancholy into a narrative. "You" is a projection: brutish and angelic, on all fours and soaring in the air. "Down to You" makes no attempt for resolution. "You" are the one to figure it out.

Joni performed the song only once, on her Miles of Aisles tour of 1974, backed by the London Symphony Orchestra. She caused a stir when, improvising the passage between the third and fourth verse, she lost her place and gave up. It was as if she had become her own inter-locutor, and even music couldn't rescue her. The London Symphony Orchestra, in the Royal Albert Hall no less, was scandalized. She never tried to play the song live again. Although she and the London Symphony would meet again, "Down to You" is forever unresolved.

The album closes with Joni's cover of Annie Ross and Wardell Gray's gem, "Twisted." Leave 'em laughing, the entertainment-savvy Geffen would have told her, but she knew that already. After so much soul baring, the placement of "Twisted" at the end of this emotionally exhausting and rewarding album was a mark of showbiz genius. Laugh away. To everything, there is a season. And like a trailer for the albums to come, the jazzy rendition of "Twisted" lets Joni's listeners know the direction she is heading in musically.

Joni has said that when she was in high school, Lambert, Hen-dricks, and Ross were her Beatles. Dave Lambert, Jon Hendricks, and Annie Ross took scat singing—wordless jazz vocalizing, invented by Louis Armstrong, perfected by Ella Fitzgerald, Sarah Vaughan, and Betty Carter—did the difficult yet somehow whimsical work of put-ting it into words that rhymed, told stories, and swung. Putting enter-taining lyrics to, say, a Charlie Parker solo is sort of like running the ten-yard dash with a wrestler on your back while composing witty sonnets. This feat is known as vocalese, putting wacky lyrics not just to jazz melodies, but to jazz solos. For a teenage listener in Saskatoon, it was the sound of liberation, the idea that anything with words and music was possible—that something difficult and complex could also be lighthearted and fun as hell.

In 1952, when Annie Ross was in her early twenties, the owner of Prestige Records, Bob Weinstock, challenged the young singer (who had already appeared on *Our Gang* at the age of six) to put lyrics to one of the label's bebop numbers. She chose Wardell Gray's "Twisted" for the title, and, before the word *vocalese* even existed, she took Gray's melody and solo and wrote words overnight. The lyrics have become canonized, and the opener, "My analyst told me that I was right out of my head," became a "Call me Ishmael" of jazz libretto. Looking back on it, Annie Ross remembers, "I was telling a story, and that's what I do when I sing. I wanted to get it done quickly because I was broke." It was a story that gave just the right humor to an album that had its share of the blues, and even some madness, too. "I had a brain, it was insane," went the rhythmically supple lyric.

"Twisted" rounded out the dark emotions of the album with a clever punch line—"Instead of one head / I got two / And you know two heads are better than one." But this would be an album that, however popular it was, punched in many ways. *Court and Spark* would be a turning point. Joni would soon be demanding even more from her listeners.

The success of the album would bear fruit on the road, and the success of the tour would be documented on another hit album, *Miles of Aisles*. On the road, Joni debuted two new songs. One of them, the biblical, erotic, emotive ballad "Jericho," where walls tumble down everywhere, and gloriously, was given a second and even greater pass, in another phase, on *Don Juan's Reckless Daughter* three years later. Another track, "Love or Money," was placed at the end of the album, never rerecorded or revisited and, oddly for such a popular album, seldom talked about. It is about that precarious perch Joni has found herself on. And it makes her think of the unappreciated artist in the "firmament of Tinsel Town," asking, "Where's my own shining hour?" It is such a hard-driving rock song, it's easy to miss that this is a tender story about a "well-kept secret of the underground / . . . in debt to the company store," someone who might have recorded an album or two for Asylum that never made it, someone who would never be Geffen's houseguest. He writes songs about loss—"stacks and stacks of words that rhyme / Describing what it is to lose." He wants success, he wants that girl. He doesn't get anything. He can't get anything down for love or money. He's that close to playing real good for free. At the end of the song, recorded live, there is roaring applause.

Just as Dylan's storytelling had opened the door for Joni to write music in a different way, Joni was beginning to influence a wide range of musicians. Led Zeppelin, reportedly, wrote "Going to California" as a love song to Joni:

> *To find a queen without a king;*
> *They say she plays guitars and cries and sings*

In performances, Robert Plant would utter the name "Joni" after these lines; it was a reference to "I Had a King," the opening track on her debut album, *Song to a Seagull*. Jimmy Page would tell a reporter, "That's the music that I play at home all the time, Joni Mitchell. *Court and Spark* I love because I'd always hoped that she'd work with a band. But the main thing with Joni is that she's able to look at something that's happened to her, draw back and crystallize the whole situation, then write about it. She brings tears to my eyes, what more can I say? It's bloody eerie."

In *Hammer of the Gods: The Led Zeppelin Saga*, Stephen Davis writes, "Later Jimmy was aglow because he had been introduced to Joni Mitchell at a restaurant called the Greenhouse. It was just small talk, but Jimmy had at last met one of his true idols. Later Robert passed up an opportunity to meet La Mitchell at a party, saying he was too shy to talk to her."

Prince Rogers Nelson was a high school student living in Minneapolis when *Court and Spark* exploded onto the airwaves of radio stations around the country. In an interview with *New York* magazine, Joni remembered, "Prince attended one of my concerts in Minnesota. I remember seeing him sitting in the front row when he was very young. He must have been about fifteen. He was in an aisle seat and he had unusually big eyes. He watched the whole show with his collar up, looking side to side. You couldn't miss him—he was a little Princeling." She laughed as she recalled, "Prince used to write me fan mail with all of the U's and hearts that way that he writes. And the office took it as mail from the lunatic fringe and just tossed it."

Decades before artists like Lady Gaga would encourage their fans to, in a paraphrase of David Crosby, "let their freak flag fly," Joni

Mitchell songs permeated the cities and the suburbs of North America, assuring her fans that whatever they were going through, they were not alone and they weren't certifiable. One of the best compliments Joni said she ever received was when she was approached, in the 1990s, by two teenage girls who told her, "Before Prozac, there was you."

18 ■ MILES OF AISLES

Joni's first album with a band would be followed by her first tour with a band. It would be too soon when the tour began to know just how big it would be. It turned out to be quite big indeed, so big that the live album from the tour, *Miles of Aisles*, charted at number two. The tour began on January 18, 1974, the month *Court and Spark* was released. Early dates included college campuses (Yale, Cornell) and prestigious halls (Massey in Toronto, Avery Fisher in New York, Constitution in D.C.) that were still intimate for a big rock show. *Miles of Aisles* was recorded during a two-night run at the Berkeley Community Theatre (where she name-checked San Francisco's Fairmont Hotel in "For Free"), a night at the LA Music Center, and a whopping five-night run at Universal Amphitheatre in Universal City, California, which had recently opened for the new generation of rock concerts. The venue filled at 5,200, which, for five nights of a packed house at a hometown venue (and performances for a hit live record), is more than 25,000 tickets, about one-sixteenth of the mostly nonpaying audience of the Woodstock festival she'd so memorably missed. The hall's very existence—it was the venue for Andrew Lloyd Webber's blockbuster musical *Jesus Christ Superstar*—was evidence that the utopia of Woodstock had quickly moved on to capitalism. Guys with long hair could play nasty, loud rock and roll, and quickly co-opted by the system. There was big money in being stardust and golden, and Joni was getting a taste herself. "I felt like having come through," she told *Circus* magazine in the June 1974 issue, "having had a small taste of success, and having seen the consequences of what it gives you and what it takes away in terms of what you *think* it's going to give you."

Joni, as usual, had figured out the implications of her success even as it was unfolding. And yet all her decisions, even if they were not exactly avant-garde (she would get there soon) were entirely musical. Even though she had David Geffen in her back pocket, she took industry advice from no one. She just wanted to take the band that had been so magical on *Court and Spark* and show them off on the road. John Guerin, her partner in music and all the love and lust she sang about (in songs about earlier paramours), was there on drums, along with Max Bennett on bass and Tom Scott on reeds. Joe Sample and Larry Carlton both had commitments with studio work and would have lost money on the road, but Robben Ford, a twenty-two-year-old guitar player, joined up. He had just quit a gig with the blues shouter Jimmy Witherspoon. Joni was no shouter, certainly not onstage, but she would be demanding in other ways, all of them stimulating. Like Larry Carlton, he had no trouble translating the language of her open chords.

"I didn't use the open tunings," Ford recalled forty years later. "It wasn't necessary for me to use them. It wasn't an issue. The way she tunes the instrument, it's like a chord on top of a chord. It's very natural—it's like the white keys at the piano. It's still just the key of C, but you'd have a G triad on top of a C triad. That's why her music sounds so different, because she's superimposing chords. Instead of playing a C triad, you'd be playing a G triad with a C in the root. And it was a different way of approaching being an accompanist. I had never heard music like that before. We certainly allowed her to have a more expansive presentation . . . I just felt like I had the greatest opportunity in the world. To be happy to be an accompanist is a chop. I learned it there. To me, I take great pleasure in accompanying." To be twenty-two and a musically deft guitar player in a Joni Mitchell band in 1974 was, to use Wordsworth's formulation, very heaven.

Joni's 1974 tour would run for seventy-five dates, between January 19 in St. Louis and September 2 in Boulder. In the midst of it, on August 9, 1974, Richard Milhous Nixon became the first president to resign from office. That night, Joni's band played the Pine Knob Music Theatre in Clarkson, Michigan. "I was so apolitical," Joni recalled. "I don't find politicians that interesting. I'm with Lincoln, who said, when he left Congress, that it was better to not have any intelligence to be a politician. I followed Watergate. I felt no need to comment on it. Neil Young would have. But the politics of rock and roll was so junior, so baby anarchist."

The L.A. Express was the opening act and the backing band. Some disaffected keyboard players came and went. Roger Kellaway complained about playing pop triads and went back to leading a jazz trio after a few months. Larry Nash suddenly insisted on being paid in cash. They needed him for three nights, paid him his cash, and kicked him out. Victor Feldman, who played on half of Miles Davis's *Seven Steps to Heaven* (1963), cowrote the title track, and turned down Davis's offer to join the band—because he was making a fortune as a session player and even the top small-group jazz gig would have been a financial downgrade—finished the gig, and made the same complaints as Kellaway, but then, he was known as a misanthrope anyway, and the rest of the band were honored to have him finish the tour.

Even for these pros, Joni's music wasn't easy, and they would need to reconvene after any time off the road. "Her harmonic structures for her tunes were so elusive that when we came back after a two-week vacation, we'd have to go back to the studios and rehearse," recalled Max Bennett. "If you analyze some of the tunes, the chord changes don't go where you think they're going to go. The whole attitude was elusive, but great."

Bennett and Guerin were running the band, and they would get bonuses for ticket sales that went above 15,000, which was happening more and more. Joni and Guerin were inseparable. They would always share hotel rooms and, after Joni left David Geffen's house and before she bought her home in Bel-Air, Joni and Guerin lived in Burbank with Max Bennett, who had a spacious house, a pool, and no wife. These sidemen were making $5,000 a week.

And so the shows went on. Joni was playing to the biggest crowds of her life. Her reviews were love letters, *Court and Spark* kept selling, and the two-record live album *Miles of Aisles* hit number two on *Billboard*, something live albums (outside of industry cash cows like *Frampton Comes Alive*, which hadn't come out yet) don't usually do. At Temple University in Ambler, Pennsylvania, on August 22, she introduced "Barangrill" talking about her impassioned reading of Nietzsche, but then added that such things lack a certain warmth "when you like somebody." Joni liked somebody indeed, and the world decided that they liked Joni Mitchell very much. What could possibly go wrong?

19 ■ THE QUEEN OF QUEENS

Joni wants to step outside the Boho Dance. It's tired, it's clichéd, and it's really based on a myth. Noble poverty doesn't make you better; it actually is an impediment to greatness. It's life and life only—not to mention innate talent and vision—that makes the perfect storm of art. Low wages and slums are what they are. Joni grew up having to rent albums rather than buy them. She sewed her own wedding dress and performed at her own wedding. It was a big deal when, right before "Both Sides, Now" changed her life forever, she could be the proud owner of a checking account with a few hundred dollars in it. She struggled before she made it, even gave up her daughter in the bargain. So if she feels like having a house with a pool, she will have a house with a pool. And if she feels like taking a dip in her Bel-Air pool, and showing off her athletic, toned body to anyone putting down their $5.98 for her new album, she will do so. She was nude, at a distance, in the gatefold of *For the Roses*. Three years later, back in the gatefold, she's not exactly wearing a fig leaf (she's in a bikini), but the garden has become a different place indeed.

Joni is at a crossroads with label bosses—well, one label boss in particular, David Geffen—wondering how many more *Court and Spark*s she can churn out before she's put out to pasture. In this allegory, Joni is the doomed Edith Piaf and the Free Man in Paris is her pimp. No one asked Van Gogh to paint *A Starry Night* again, because no one bought it in the first place. Many people bought *Court and Spark*, and now she's given the luxury to express contempt for the people who made her popular. "You're still fucking peasants as far as I can see," sang John Lennon, who visited Joni while she was recording *Court and Spark* and suggested she put some fiddles on it if she wanted a hit. He was a mean drunk, telling Joni, "It's all a product of overeducation," when they had the same educational background: art school dropouts.

The Hissing of Summer Lawns is not quite what the label bosses had in mind. It is obsessed with the wildness beneath the suburban surface, and it is directed straight at the haute bourgeoisie, and Joni wants to confront them, not love them. Listen to the slave ships making your clothes, look at the pimps and hos who toil while you sleep, look at the Boho Dance, where artists are frauds and critics are sophists. See the world like I see it, she's saying, in all its gradations and degradations. To the people with paper wives and paper kids—people who might have spent good money on concert tickets for her—she responds with social critique, and *they* are the ones she's critiquing.

The title track—a collaboration with John Guerin, a first—was an ironic response to a visit to José Feliciano's house in the Valley shortly after his marriage. The new Mrs. Feliciano apparently "patrol[ed] that fence of his / To a Latin drum"—or Feliciano's Latin guitar. These were the people, as opposed to a wacky Peace Corps volunteer in Matala, Greece, who were now part of her social circle. Joni still wanted to get back to the garden, in a way, but her garden was now manicured by professionals. The streets she wrote of were now those of exclusive gated communities. Everywhere, she heard the sound of sprinklers; everything seemed utterly fake.

"Paper wives / And paper kids / Paper the walls to keep their gut reactions hid," she sang, gloriously, in the cinematic sweep of "Harry's

House." But while Joni was singing about an unsatisfying marriage, making the music with her boyfriend Guerin was still a thrill. "You listen to 'Harry's House,' and we're falling in love during that performance," Joni told me. "And what he said about that piece of music was so astute and smart. And I said to Henry [Lewy], 'Set me up in front of the drummer,' and Henry said, 'Oh you little flirt.' I just fell in love with him on that piece of music."

Joni was falling in love making music that would cause some listeners to fall out of love. On the delectable "Don't Interrupt the Sorrow," the chords, the rhythm, the trance are so musically right, the listener doesn't want to interrupt the song. But what does it *mean*? The song began as a lark with Bob Neuwirth, a pop artist most famous for being the ultra-cool guy hanging out with Dylan in *Dont Look Back* and playing guitar and kicking in harmonies on the Rolling Thunder Revue tour, which Joni would soon join. One night, the two were pretty blasted on alcohol and they decided to write a "drunk song." "What do we call it?" Joni asked. "Don't Interrupt the Sorrow," he offered. "Darn right," she replied. The rest was drivel. Joni trashed everything but the title and the rejoinder. "Anima rising, queen of queens," she realized later, was taking the Jungian archetypes and reversing them. A man has an anima, a woman an animus. If this had been intended or a Freudian slip, it would not have devalued the song one iota. Since the song, error included, is perfect the way it is, it was a fortunate mistake. "God goes up the chimney / Like childhood Santa Claus" dresses religion down pretty dramatically for someone who, in her Laurel Canyon/ Graham Nash era, could be seen in photographs with a cross necklace and who wrote a song—deleted from *Blue*—about a Good Samaritan.

Joni had been expected to be a singer-songwriter martyr, suffering for her public, but she was getting tougher, and more of an observer than a subject. In the absence of heartbreak songs, for which *Blue* had raised expectations, she set new standards for third-person portraits, more ambitious and sprawling than anything she had done before. The album inspired both a young Elvis Costello and Prince to write their own third-person songs. Those songs were not for everybody, but they were a gift for the musically sophisticated.

"Edith and the Kingpin" must have startled some listeners. This is not a satire of bohemia or a send-up of suburbia. And it is not a love song, either. Unlike, say, a painter, a fiction writer, or a director, a pop songwriter of 1975 was expected to deliver a more limited type of goods. Doing so as a flagrant sellout could be derided as a kind of prostitution, which is, peripherally, what this song is about. "In 'Edith and the Kingpin,' part of it is from a Vancouver pimp I met and part of it is Edith Piaf," Joni told me. "It's a hybrid, but all together it makes a whole truth." Edith the self-destructive singer—a French Billie Holiday—is also a prostitute waiting for her kingpin, or big daddy badass pimp. The greatest of French chanteuses still needs someone to pimp her out. This is not a heartbroken song of waiting for her "sugar to show" like "Car on a Hill" just an album ago. This is an anesthetized world where all that lovin' is reduced to commerce. "Women he has taken grow old too soon / He tilts their tired faces / Gently to the spoon." This is pretty close to Joni's take on the music biz, as soon as it went sour for her. A label takes on a pretty young girl, takes her out on the road, feeds her drugs, and then puts her in the recording studio, billing her for every dollar she hasn't earned out. Eventually, it will lose interest, stop promoting the work, guaranteeing commercial failure, and find a younger model and stamp "New and Improved" on it. The kingpin cynically watches his whore and wonders, as if she's a prize horse (a metaphor in "For the Roses"), just how many good tricks she has in her.

Among all the social commentary, third-person narratives, reverse-gender mythological references, and '50s rock and roll madeleines, Joni, the personal figure who was followed so avidly on *Blue* and *Court and Spark*, returns on one song. With her heart on her sleeve, Joni sings on "Sweet Bird" about a beauty that hasn't faded yet, but would be inevitable if she were fortunate enough to fade away and not burn out. That piece of reflection, so personal it's as close as her own skin, is palpable throughout "Sweet Bird," the album's penultimate track. On the level of orchestration, it's the most pared down on the album: Joni on piano and acoustic guitar, Larry Carlton on electric. On the level of theme, it continues the inquiry of her earliest, wise-beyond-her-years fledgling work. If "Both Sides, Now" is prophecy, "Sweet Bird" is fate. Joni was twenty-one when she dared to announce that she had looked at life from both sides, now. She was thirty-one when she imagined herself on some borderline lying down "golden in time" and waking up "vanishing."

The song's title makes a passing reference to Tennessee Williams's *Sweet Bird of Youth*; its contents refer to every human ever on earth, alive or dead, certainly every female. The Sweet Bird of time and change laughs at this woman in possession of beauty in her voice, her words, her music, and that lovely physique she sprawled in the gatefold of her album. She was the singer, the guitarist, the pianist, the writer, the painter, and the subject. No wonder she scared people. The promises made by "beauty jars" are all in vain. Joni scrutinizes her still young and beautiful face.

> *Behind our eyes*
> *Calendars of our lives*
> *Circled with compromise*
> *Sweet bird of time and change*
> *You must be laughing*

Joni could see all the way around the circle game when she was all of twenty-two. The album flaunted it all: the pool, the house, the body, the genius, the voice. It seemed immortal, but it was very mortal, and, at thirty-one, she felt it every minute.

Joni would tour in support of *The Hissing of Summer Lawns* just as she had for *Court and Spark*. Before heading out, though, she found herself on a diversion, catching Bob Dylan's Rolling Thunder Revue tour and then, as she put it later, joining the circus. Her ride with Rolling Thunder lasted not quite a month. She began on November 13 in New Haven and ended on December 8 at Madison Square Garden, a fund-raiser for a legal defense for Rubin "Hurricane" Carter, a boxer whom Dylan was convinced had been wrongly convicted, which he sang about in his song "Hurricane" every night of the tour.

With their compatriots Joan Baez, Ramblin' Jack Elliott, and Roger McGuinn by his side, Dylan and his crew would show up for unplanned small gigs around the country. Dylan still missed the Bleecker Street of 1961 and tried to re-create it, sort of. His wife, Sara, was on the verge of leaving him, but she came along anyway, and he sang "Sara" to her every night. If that didn't bring her back, nothing would. (As it turned out, nothing would.)

Joni was there partly because Dylan essentially invented the singer-songwriter game, and because she considered Dylan and Leonard Cohen to be her best "pace runners." There was a part of Joni that constantly weighed decisions and revisions. And then there was the part of her that would go on a road trip on the spur of the moment. How could she say no to Bob Dylan? The competitive analogy of being anyone's pace runner was far from Dylan's mind when, in a 1978 interview, he said he was inspired to write his much celebrated "Tangled Up in Blue" after spending a weekend listening to *Blue*—not just the title track, but the whole album. Joni didn't know this at the time, but she loved *Blood on the Tracks*, welcoming it as a return to the greatness of the astonishing three-album run of *Bringing It All Back Home* (1965), *Highway 61 Revisited* (1965), and *Blonde on Blonde* (1966), which besotted her and set new standards for what a pop songwriter could do, raising the stakes of her game, allowing her to bring something new to the table. *Blood on the Tracks* offered a new intimacy, a new vulnerability, a Dylan inspired by Joni. She could take that influence and raise the level of musicianship substantially.

For Joni, ambitious lyrics didn't have to be at the expense of music; they could be matched with ambitious music. Lyrically, Dylan, at what she considered to be his best, was an influence—and Leonard Cohen was even more—but musically, she came from Debussy, Rachmaninoff, Piaf, Holiday, Ellington, and Miles. But there was still an aura around Dylan, and this was a chance to hold her own in its presence; no one checked their ego at the door.

The Rolling Thunder Revue kicked off in Plymouth, Massachusetts, on October 30, 1975. Joni joined in New Haven two weeks later. Although she would find herself in close quarters with fellow artists and be inspired (Sam Shepard) and infuriated (Joan Baez), it was really the power of an early acetate of *Blood on the Tracks* that drew her to the combination of robust, cocaine-fed egos that made the experience a dream, a nightmare, and a refuge from reality. There was already trouble in paradise with John Guerin, who had been an intuitive musical collaborator and passionate lover. Joni found herself drawn in—really kidnapped by the tour. A jealous Joan Baez, in an opening move, shoved Joni to the top of the bill. Allen Ginsberg told Joni she was a masochist. (Who did he think he was? Carole King?) Meanwhile, Elliot Roberts told Joni that, in fact, she *was* being a masochist.

"Why would you make yourself subordinate to them? Those old has-beens?"

"Well, I wouldn't call them that. Bob is still worth looking at."

She thought that Dylan hadn't really been fully present in his records since *Blonde on Blonde*. She thought they were just a "collage of other people's thinking." This was different. This early version of *Blood on the Tracks* was a fully present and vulnerable Dylan, too vulnerable, finally, for prime time. More than forty years later, she remembered greeting the original recording with excitement, only to be disappointed later:

"Joel Bernstein gave me a tape of it, and it was really good, it was really good. But people said, 'Oh, it's like a Joni Mitchell album,' so he went and recut it with his brother in Minnesota. They butchered it all up. They stomped all over it. But originally, the writing was different, it was more vulnerable, and the orchestration was subtle, very like when I was using just a little of that stuff to my performances. It had Al Kooper on it, but he was mixed kind of under, you know, like some of his early players. It was beautiful. And one night, I had a party here, and it was so star-studded, you wouldn't believe it. It made the newspaper. It said, 'If a bomb hit Joni Mitchell's house, it would have wiped out the music industry and the acting industry.' And you wouldn't believe the crashers. Robert De Niro crashed it, David Bowie crashed it, Robin Williams crashed it, and Bob crashed it. And the bootleg of that first *Blood on the Tracks* was playing. They were out in the garden, and somebody said that Bob wanted to see me. And the bootleg was still playing and I said, 'Why didn't you put that out?' And he said, 'Somebody stole the tape.' Which was not true. He chickened out. People said it was like a Joni Mitchell album. There was some stylistic production to it, but not the material. It was more honest. He'd already cracked by the next one. He took the vulnerability out of it, and in the process he took the depth out. The New York sessions were touching. The Minnesota sessions were not touching at all. He asserted himself again as a man."

That night, when all of Joni's guests walked out, the recording walked out with them. "When they left, it disappeared," she recalled. But those New York sessions of *Blood on the Tracks* are not hard to find. Some tracks were issued on Dylan's first *Bootleg Series* release (1991) and the rest are widely available as bootlegs, and will eventually be commercially issued as part of the ongoing *Bootleg Series*.

Joni would be disappointed by the new songs on the tour that would end up on *Desire* (1976), but she had already joined the circus by then. She had missed Woodstock. This time, she would not be the girl who got left behind. Joni did not allow herself to be filmed for *Renaldo and Clara*, the experimental film made during the tour with a skeleton of a screenplay by Sam Shepard. The mostly improvised film would be a failure, spending only a couple of weeks in theaters. It is not, in any sense, a good movie, but the musical performances are excellent and a scene with Dylan and Allen Ginsberg at Jack Kerouac's grave is a keeper. Joni would later recall that almost everyone on the tour—not Joan Baez—was on coke, which was fine with her, no stranger to what Gilda Radner called "the devil's dandruff." Fighting a flu for the entire tour, she would stay up all night on the tour bus writing songs, which she would premiere in every place they landed. Allen Ginsberg was house poet, Joan Baez was Queen of Folk, and Joni was Queen of Rock. A busload of egos, coke to spare, and everything decided on the whim of Bob Dylan, in a great creative moment of his own but not necessarily someone meant to be master of ceremonies.

Dylan, who had been dissatisfied with his much-anticipated tour with the Band in 1974—his first in eight years—had an idea. Why not just make the music without being rock stars? He wanted to go back to the clubs, the kind of intimate venue that Joni missed, too. The irony is that the whole enterprise, while shrinking the performance spaces, seemed to only enlarge the egos. And the concerts ended up getting bigger anyway—the War Memorial Coliseum in Rochester, the Quebec City Coliseum, and so on. But they were still traveling and sleeping in vans, like circus performers. How could so many illustrious people share space without sibling rivalry or competition? Dylan's marriage was doomed, but he would try to bring himself back to his version of the garden, which had nothing to do with Joni's Woodstock, but with his memories of 1961 New York and its "music in the cafés at night and revolution in the air." With so much crisis and so many drugs, it's not hard to imagine that the next stop would be Jesus. He was on his journey, and Joni was on hers. Before his religious conversion, he told her, "God is just a word." When just a few years later, in 1979, he became a born-again Christian and started preaching to her, she told him, "Bobby, don't you know the Bible was written by poets like you and me?"

This tour was in between the encounters about God. One of the motivations for joining the Revue—where she later said she must have lost an octave singing in the rain and getting sick—was getting closer to Bobby. At last, a peer, someone who would understand greatness as only a great person could. But she found that between Joan Baez and Sara Dylan, there was little room for her. (Baez and Sara Dylan also felt frustrated. Dylan was very difficult to be around, and was an ever-present conversation topic when he wasn't, when they would say, "Here we are—just the three of us.") In fact, Joni recalled only two conversations with Dylan in total for the whole tour. If you're Joni Mitchell and you can't have the conversation you thought you'd get, what can you do but write a song? In this case, the song was "Talk to Me," which she would perform on her Hissing of Summer Lawns tour the following year.

> Please just talk to me
> Any old theme you choose

Just come and talk to me
Mr. Mystery, talk to me

While Joni was trying, with great difficulty, to have a meaningful conversation with Dylan, the journalist Larry "Ratso" Sloman, covering the tour for *Rolling Stone*, was meeting great resistance in trying to talk to her. "I'm much jiver than my work and I'd rather have people think my work is me," she told him in what could be a coherent manifesto. She was using the word in a very 1975 way, the way the Bee Gees used it that year in "Jive Talkin.'" She could have also sung him "Talk to Me": "You could talk like a fool (I'd listen) / You could talk like a sage / Anyway the best of my mind / All goes down on the strings and the page." Dylan could have told her the same thing. Here we are: two poets who could have written the Bible, and instead we're getting back to the garden by joining the circus, when either of us could have filled these places up alone.

What pulled Joni in? She couldn't stand Joan Baez, was disappointed in Dylan, and she had her own tour to do. Why join this particular circus? More than forty years later, the Revue had a force of its own, even as it came with flawed people and mounds of cocaine:

"On Rolling Thunder, I went out to see the show, and it was so bizarre and everybody was so insane, I mean insane, that I decided to stay for another one, then they coerced me into playing, and I did in two cities, and in Boston I was kind of sucked into it. In Boston, Joan Baez spoke to me for the one and only time. She came to my door, and she said, 'You got the biggest applause tonight,' and I said, 'Oh.' And she said, 'Oh, come on. You knew that.' And I said, 'How would I know? I didn't see the whole show.' First of all, I had seen it before I was in it, and Baez got the biggest applause in the show, and for a cheap trick. She'd hit a high note and put her arm in the air. If you want to get your applause that badly that way, you've got it. I've been moved when the audience was so spellbound, they forgot to applaud. I said to her, 'I don't know. I just use the applause to tune up in,' which was true. If it runs out and I'm not in tune, I have to start storytelling to get through it."

Baez has no memory of measuring who got the louder applause. "If I told her she got louder applause than me, I was saying it to be accommodating," said Baez. "I knew that I was queen of that outfit. It sounds like something I would have said to make somebody feel okay. Apparently, it didn't."

Joni kept awake and kept writing. Everyone but Baez was on coke, and everyone included Joni. "John Guerin's grandfather owned a circus and the clowns used to be paid in booze," Joni recalled. "So, I said, 'Pay me in cocaine,' because everybody was out of their minds. I was the only straight person. Try being the only straight person. So I thought: I might as well bite the bullet and see what this thing is about. Well, it had an incredible effect. It made me so aggressive, the next thing I knew, I was ripping off cops. And I couldn't sleep. I read Freud's *Cocaine Papers*. It was the only thing of his I could recall because Freud was such an idiot and a narcissist. He was a cocaine addict himself, so he was proselytizing it. He thought it was a cure for the inferiority complex. And I kept thinking, this is a warrior's drug. You'd be like Scarface. You could have ten bullet holes in you and you'd still be shooting. Initially, what it does is it's a new head and by tracing the dragon it creates epic thought, so much thought. I think too much anyway."

Joni really *was* stealing badges from policemen and keeping them as treasures. Most cops were happy to have their badges stolen by Joni Mitchell—a luxury only a noncivilian could enjoy.

"Coyote," which Joni was performing on the tour while she was still writing it, was written under the influence of cocaine and Sam Shepard, who had a wife (O-Lan Jones) at home, as if that mattered. Shepard had chiseled movie star looks with movie star acting chops and a Pulitzer Prize–winning literary talent. Shepard wanted to get back to the desert of the American west—a place he loved and revered as an uncorrupted land, a long way from Bel-Air. In his play *True West* (1980), part of the "family trilogy" of plays (with *Curse of the Starving Class* and *Buried Child*), two brothers nearly kill each other trying to write an authentic western for Hollywood. Austin, the screenwriter, yearns for a real American west he never had:

There's nothin' down here for me. There never was. When we were kids here it was different. There was a life here then. But now—I keep comin' down here thinkin' it's the fifties or somethin'. I keep finding myself getting off the freeway at familiar landmarks that turn out to be unfamiliar. On the way to appointments. Wandering down streets I thought I recognized that turn out to be replicas of streets I remember. Streets I misremember. Streets I can't tell if I lived on or saw in a postcard. Fields that don't even exist anymore.

In Shepard's *Rolling Thunder Logbook*, the bard of the American west marvels at the siren of the Canadian prairie, with her guitar, beret, and "history of word collage." It is also not lost on him that the audience hangs on all of those words. He's hanging on, too. He quotes from "Don't Interrupt the Sorrow," and he is in transport:

Her word maneuverings tend to verge on the uncanny. "I got a head full of quandary and a mighty, mighty, mighty thirst." She seems to have merged into a unique jazz structure with lyrics and rhythmic construction and even managed to bite the masses in the ear with it.

Shepard and Patti Smith had been romantically entangled when they were both downtown obscurities. For one night, Patti starred in their cowritten off-off-Broadway rock and roll play with the Dylan-inspired title *Cowboy Mouth*. Dylan, who was photographed with Smith for the cover of *The Village Voice*, begged her to join Rolling Thunder, but she refused. *Horses* was eliciting critical raves; she was now the doyenne of the CBGB scene. Why lose herself among bigger stars from a completely different crowd? Joni and Joan were struggling to share the limelight as it was. And so Shepard could instead concentrate on Joni.

It didn't take long for the news to spread across the revue that Joni and Sam were having a casual romance, even though there was nothing casual about their artistic commitments (and what would inspire them). In Chris O'Dell's memoir about her life as a tour manager, she recalled the odd feeling of finding out that the married man she was sleeping with was keeping company with Joni Mitchell. "How could I compete with her?" How indeed? In "Coyote," Joni writes of such a juggling act: "He's got a woman at home / He's got another woman down the hall / He seems to want me anyway." This song became a mantra throughout Rolling Thunder; it followed the rhythms of the bus, the sights of white lines along the freeway. The melody gave way to however many syllables it needed to accommodate, as wild and as feral a beast as the coyote it brings alive in song. It was understood that what happened on the road ended on the road—except, of course, in the music:

> *No regrets, Coyote*
> *We just come from such different sets of circumstance*
> *I'm up all night in the studios*
> *And you're up early on your ranch . . .*

Joni and Sam both celebrated their thirty-second birthdays shortly before the tour, his on November 5, hers two days later. "Don Juan's Reckless Daughter," a response to Carlos Castaneda, makes an overt reference to the closeness of their birthdays: "I'm Don Juan's reckless daughter / I came out two days on your tail / Those two bald-headed days in November / Before the first snowflakes sail." Back in Saskatoon, this was pretty much the weather pattern, but this is a song about the meeting of two geniuses, both reckless, "twins of spirit," but also as ill-suited as feathers and steel. He has a wife to go home to. She has a tour to get on with. The circus will end soon.

"The aim is to balance the terror of being alive with the wonder of being alive," wrote Carlos Castaneda in his *Teachings of Don Juan*, a trendy read in the '70s. It was a mantra Joni took seriously. In those hazy, crazy final months of 1975, wonder would drown out the balance of terror, even as a little bit of danger made things interesting.

"Sam and I had a flirtation," Joni remembered forty years later. "He got scared of me. What panicked him was we were sitting in a bar and we were talking and all of a sudden he said, 'You're really smart.' Often when people would say that, they would lean away from me like I had a disease. He made a Sicilian gesture across the eye or something like that. And then we talked a little bit more, and I was saying things and he'd go, 'How do you know that?' It was like we were twins. The stars were really funny. He was born November 9 and I was born November 7. I was born beneath a really powerful sky, and I think he was, too. He's multi-expressive. He's a playwright and a singer and an actor and he's good at all of them. What I think was happening was that I was forming sentences like he would've. Everything was creating an aversion. But for me, on coke, I found him very attractive. He reminded me of the people that I come from, from the region that I come from. He ran off the tour."

December 7, 1975, a day before the "Night of the Hurricane" benefit concert for Rubin Carter's defense fund, the last concert of the tour, the Revue played a concert at the prison where Carter was being held. Because of the media attention swarming around Hurricane, including a staged photo op with Dylan for *People* magazine, Carter was moved to the Clinton Correctional Facility for Women in Clinton, New Jersey. At Rahway, Joni was practically booed offstage, causing her to respond, "We came here to give you love; if you can't handle it, that's your problem." The rejection from a room full of mostly black women—where the subtleties of "Coyote" or "Don't Interrupt the Sorrow" might have been lost on that particular population—must have hurt, especially when they showered Baez with approval for hitting the highest note on "Amazing Grace."

Baez felt sympathy for Joni that day. "I can tell you that she didn't know how to deal with black prison inmates," Baez recalled. "She was very white, and her choice of songs were very white. And I was just praying she'd get off the stage. I thought it was more difficult for her, because I think she didn't get why they weren't responding."

Baez never got to know Joni well. Before Rolling Thunder, Joni, recording *Court and Spark* just down the hall at A&M studios, added vocals to Baez's track "Dida," on her 1974 album *Gracias a la Vida*, a record produced by Henry Lewy. "I got shoved into this 'Doo-dah' record and I went in for Henry's sake, and for David Blue," Joni recalled, somewhat viciously. "And the song was so dumb. I'm searching and trying to find a way to blend with her vibrato, in order to musically contribute to this stupid piece of music. I'm looking for a blend. I'm not trying to flash off my range. I'm just trying to be harmonious."

The harmony was strictly musical. "*Aloof* was hardly the word for her," Baez recalled. "She was beyond aloof. It didn't matter. We did the song. And then we did it again. It was good working with her. Her voice is a wonderful voice. I didn't know if it was shyness or what." "Or what" was probably the more likely explanation. The lack of warmth between the two women intensified when they shared a sleeping van on the Rolling Thunder tour. Baez was often socially isolated as the only '60s pop music figure who never smoked or did drugs. (She smoked a total of four joints in her life. Reaction: paranoia.) She was obsessively protective of her voice and avoided smoke at all costs. Joni, of course, avoided *avoiding* smoke at all costs. This led to a very bad night for Joan Baez:

"One night, as I remember it, the carnival was moving out from one town to another. I didn't see Joni getting into any vehicle, and I didn't know whether she had been assigned to anything, so we stopped, and I said, 'Pick her up,' and she got on in our van and she nearly smoked me out. It was awful. She couldn't stop smoking and then she went up front with my two road managers. I'm not sure what they did all night, but it was not a happy experience. I asked her if she could stop. She was on cocaine and weed, I think. I was in the upper bunk, so there was no way to sleep."

Baez now looks back at Joni with admiration: "She has such a qualified and earned 'fuck you.' I really admire her. She's a really strong woman who doesn't give a fuck about what anybody thinks, and we all wish we could be that way, but we can't."

Rolling Thunder culminated in a benefit concert at Madison Square Garden a day after the prison concert, and it was the perfect moment for Joni and the Revue—which would continue without her while she went on a tour of her own—to part ways. Around this time, Joni began to have her doubts about the cause anyway. "I had talked to Hurricane on the phone several times, and I was alone in perceiving that he was a violent person and an opportunist," Joni said. She thought of the irony of Dylan and Baez painting their faces white, commedia dell'arte style. "I thought, Oh my God, we're a bunch of white patsy liberals. This is a bad person. He's fakin' it."

As Joni got ready to break ranks on the Night of the Hurricane, Muhammad Ali made an appearance at the event, and Joan Baez asked Joni to introduce him. "Fine," Joni recalled telling her, "what I'll say is—and I never would've—I'll say, 'We're here tonight on behalf of one jive-ass n—— who could have been champion of the world and I'd like to introduce you to another one who is.' She stared at me, and immediately removed me from this introductory role . . . Anyway, Hurricane was released and the next day he brutally beat up this woman . . ." Joni knew she was pushing buttons with the patron saint of the left with her use of the most offensive racial epithet in English. (Baez had no memory of this exchange years later.)

What made this blonde from Saskatoon believe she had the right to use it? Joni believed she had an inner black person, and she would bring him out more over time, making even more extravagant provocations, all in an attempt, however foolhardy, to break barriers. It was no doubt more jive than her music, but she said as much already when she begged off the interview for *Rolling Stone*. This night would be it for the Revue. One friend she picked up on Rolling Thunder was Kinky Friedman, who went pretty far for a novelty act, with ersatz country songs like "They Ain't Makin' Jews Like Jesus Anymore" and "Proud to Be an Asshole from El Paso," which Joni sang onstage with him, decked with a sombrero. In March, Joni came to a Friedman party in his Hollywood apartment that was said by Dennis Quaid and others to be the party of the decade. Joni and Dylan disappeared into a room for hours. When Dylan fell asleep, people just watched him. Joni and Dylan were the last to leave. They stayed all night and then hitchhiked to Malibu together.

Dylan inspired Joni, but she would never follow him for any extended period of time. She was her own woman. And, besides, it was time for her to start planning her next gig. The Hissing of Summer Lawns tour would be starting up soon. Tom Scott would be replaced with David Luell ("a kind of yakety-sax player," Joni recalled. "He didn't make much of an impression on me as a player, frankly. But he was good enough"). New songs would have to be rehearsed, some of which were written on Rolling Thunder.

Joni began her tour in mid-January, a little over a month after her departure from Rolling Thunder. Sales of *The Hissing of Summer Lawns* had tapered off from the blockbuster success of *Court and Spark*, but people were still filling halls to see her, many of them no doubt eager to hear material from the earlier albums, while others must have realized that they had the privilege to capture a brilliant artist in motion, in the process of creating some of her most important work, at the summit of her powers. The band was not only reconfiguring material from *The Hissing of Summer Lawns* into band performances—replacing studio effects with group cadences—but they were also giving birth to the first live performances of "Talk to Me" and "Don Juan's Reckless Daughter" played as a medley with "Coyote." Still, she hit Houston for a Rolling Thunder reunion and a solo set, a second night of the Hurricane, even though she was quite clear in her reservations about the first. Dylan returned the favor a couple of nights later, on January 28.

There are photographs of them performing "Both Sides, Now" that night, but Joni remembers it differently, perhaps because it was a particularly charged night. "Dylan showed up at the Austin concert, and he was acting really weird. He showed up onstage like a crazy person. He wandered around through the amps. He made it very apparent to the audience that he was there, but he never came forward. He just got on the stage and wandered around. We didn't sing anything together. That made John nervous."

John Guerin thought he had some reason to be nervous. "We were invited to a party and John decided not to go," Joni recalled. "So, I entered in fighter mode, because he was all jealous about Bob Dylan. *Nothing was going on.* Dylan was acting like a maniac and there was nothing between us. But I'd been out on Rolling Thunder and he's imagining all kinds of stuff. So I go to this party and Bob is there and my friend Boyd Elder is there and Bob and I ended up in this bedroom." Boyd Elder was a Texan friend of Kinky Friedman's, whose friendship with Joni went back to her Laurel Canyon days with Graham Nash. He was a graphic artist best known for his Eagles covers, to his great regret.

Joni and Bob were talking about God like college kids in a dorm room. "It was dark, with Bob and Boyd and I, and Boyd was sitting up in a chair right behind the door, and Bob was looking out the window, and I was sitting on the foot of the bed." This was when Joni and Dylan had their exchange about what he meant when he used the word *God.* Was it the Old Testament God? Joni never got an answer. "And just then, the door flew open, and there's John Guerin, and he doesn't see Boyd because the door covers him up. And he looked at me like I was a monster, and he leaves and goes back to the hotel."

When Guerin thought, incorrectly, that there was something between Joni and Dylan, he brought in the first woman he could find. He imagined that Joni was unfaithful, so, for such a ladies' man, the only response was to bring in another lady. And, right on schedule, Joni left Dylan's party without getting his answer to what he meant by God. (The answer would come a few years later during his born-again Christian phase.) Joni went up to her room. They had two doors, a sitting room, and a bedroom, all close together. As she goes by the door she could hear what she described as "a feminine sniff."

"Oh, he's got a girl in there," she thought. Joni knocked on one door and stood behind the other, and, sure enough, the girl came out. Then Joni and Guerin got into a tussle. She was really mad at him, and he usually behaved like a gentleman.

"My shoulder on my coat got torn in the scuffle, but he deflected like a gent," Joni recalled decades later. "He had a good mother and a good grandmother. He had wonderful women behind him. And he just deflected my assaults as I was saying, 'How dare you bring this girl into our room?' It came out that he was suspicious about Bob and there was nothing to be suspicious about. Anyway, I had an interesting experience that night because of the emotions it stirred up. I'm lying in the room and I'd done some yoga, and I did these exercises with chakras. My throat chakra opened up like a lotus, so much so that the petals touched along my throat and it was hard to breathe. I ran to the window and I did these breathing exercises and it was kind of like a big flower opening up in there, but like petals. It was delicate, but suffocating. So I opened the window and took some deep breaths and it went back into place. And then we continued to tour a few cities, but we stayed in separate rooms."

Shortly after the news had spread among the band that Joni and John were sleeping in separate rooms, John pushed the limits of his freedom further. Joni played the Spectrum in Philadelphia, and, while she should have been excited to share "Furry Sings the Blues," a new song with a colorful story, she did so in a voice utterly flat and expressionless, making it all the more odd when she said, in a drone, "I love a good story." But Joni was unable to love a good story when she was in the midst of one that was getting rougher and rougher. Max Bennett recalled that Joni was palpably pissed off at this point. In her performance of "Harry's House," instead of moving from the chord sequence of the song to the Lambert, Hendricks, and Ross vocalese take on Harry Edison's "Centerpiece," she sang the Jon Hendricks lyric, which, on Lambert, Hendricks, and Ross's *Everybody's Boppin'* and on *The Hissing of Summer Lawns*, is the hippest of love letters, set to a twelve-bar blues: "The more I'm with you, pretty baby / The more I feel my love increase / I'm building all my dreams around you / My happiness will never cease / But nothing's any good without you / 'Cause baby, you're my centerpiece." Amid the Sturm und Drang with John Guerin, at the Spectrum, Joni sang the lyrics not as a twelve-bar blues but in the "Harry's House" changes, strummed forlornly. Suddenly, the lyrics were even more ironic than they were on the record, where Joni, as Harry's henpecking wife, repeats, "Nothing's any good." Nothing was any good, indeed.

Joni was navigating new territory as a woman: as bandleader. She wanted to keep working with John, and she didn't want to stop him from pursuing other relationships, but she needed to protect both her heart and her leadership position with the other musicians. As the saying goes, it was complicated. "John was a lover and a Scorpio. [Scorpios], we are kind of loyal to a fault, so if we loved someone, we wanted to keep the relationship going, we tried to flow with the changes. So, anyway, even after we broke up, he was very bonded to me in a funny way, and he ended up marrying one girl four behind me, but the girl before me was named Judy, so he said, 'I want to send for Judy. I can't pick up women on the road.' And he was a very sexual man, and I said, 'I can't have tyranny in that department anymore. I relinquish it. But, if you're going to do that, don't embarrass me. Don't make me uncomfortable. You will have to take commercial flights, because we had a private plane, and you can't come on the plane with her, and she will have to stay in the hotel. You can't bring her to the gig, because everybody will feel sorry for me and it will be a mess. You have to keep her as a secret, and you have to make it clear to her that those are the terms of the situation. I'm fine with that, but you have to have some respect for me.' So he agreed to that, and then in the next town, I got sick. I got the flu from the stress."

Judy was not just a young lady, and not just one who had been a girlfriend of John's in the past, but, according to members of the band, she was a dead ringer for Joni. And so it must have been a surreal visual gag to see this Joni double, sitting with both of them in Joni's limo, and having fans scream Joni's name when they spotted her doppelgänger.

Joni didn't think Judy was her double. "Judy was a lot skinnier that me," Joni recalled. "She was very fashionably skinny. I'm more zaftig. There was one encounter in a limo, but one only. So I call for the plane to take off at night. I have to have a sick day in New York because I'm going to have to play sick. I want to rest there rather than resting in Boston. So, we leave for New York late at night—ten thirty or eleven.

We go to the plane and the horn player—horn players are like plumbers for the most part. They're really like beer-drinking plumbers. They were playing cards and the cards had red backgrounds, and they had these naked pink girls posing against a curtain. And their eyes are intense, in mild horror. And I thought, 'What's up?' Their mouths are covered up by these pink nudes. And I walk in, and I went where the jump seats were for the stewardess. The roadies are there playing poker. I walk in and the room just freezes. So I go into the next part of the cabin, and I go to my seat. John has brought Judy and he has sat down where he always sits. Judy is sitting in my seat, and there's no place for me to sit. It's unbelievably stupid on his part, especially in the face of what I said to him, which is more than generous. It made me sick, it was so generous. I tend to be ridiculously fair sometimes, so there's a case of it."

Since the Miles of Aisles tour, Joni had always enjoyed the camaraderie of being one of the guys. Now the vibes were getting exceedingly worse. After the new girl rode in Joni's limo, she then flew in Joni's private plane from Boston to New York. At this point, Joni was telling Elliot Roberts that she really couldn't work under these conditions, but he urged her to carry on. Meanwhile, limo politics kept getting worse when Joni collided with Gayle Ford, the wife of the guitarist Robben Ford.

"Gayle Ford was nothing but trouble. Gayle Ford was a queen bee. She was in our limo, and I get in and light up a cigarette and she says, 'Put that out. I don't like smoke.' I said, 'I'm going to put *you* out. This is my car. You get on the bus.' I could give you twenty examples of that kind of queen bee behavior. Really out of line. Insensitive. And I tolerated it. Usually, I didn't flinch. She told me she was coming on the road with Robben. They were newly married. And I said, 'Women on the road are not good. They disturb the husbands, they disturb the music generally. There's a rule: no women on the road. And it's a good rule.'"

Gayle Ford was determined to not be thrown off the tour. She appealed to Joni's industrious side by asking not for leniency as a wife, but for a job. Joni remembered that Gayle came to her and said, "'Oh, I won't get in the way. I'll help you. Give me a job. Give me something to do.' So I said, 'Oh, okay.'" Wardrobe was more complicated for Joni than for most of her male counterparts. The roadies had put John Guerin's blue suede jacket, which was wet, in with Joni's beautiful gowns. By the time they arrived in Memphis, the dresses were ruined: covered with big blue ink stains. Joni thought it might be worth it to hire Ford to be the tour's wardrobe mistress. But as Joni tells it, Ford's competitive nature and unmasked lust for Joni's clothing got in the way of her doing even a halfway decent job. "She's a clothes freak," Joni told me. "I left some stuff in my trunk and she says, 'There are still things in your trunk. Name everything you can't remember and everything else is mine.' So I said, 'Okay, wardrobe mistress is not right. I'm gonna put you in charge of food.'"

Ahead of her time as a bandleader, Joni wanted the band to be able to eat well on the road. "When we get there, we're going to have a room and we need fresh carrot sticks and healthy snack stuff, because everything's closed in a lot of these towns," Joni told Gayle. "You can be in charge of that. So right before we checked out, she brought in a plastic cooler of nuts and stuff like that. And we were rehearsing still. So I went down and picked up a bag of almonds and it was that kind of crunchy cellophane that you can roll over but it pops back up. So I took some almonds out and I rolled it over and it popped back up and I set it back in with everything upright. All of a sudden, she starts screaming, 'Who did this?' And somebody reached in there and the almonds had gotten inside the container. And she's freaking out and I thought, 'This girl is too much. She's disruptive and megalomaniacal. She's a nightmare.'"

In New York, Joni met up with Emmett Grogan, a founding member of an anarchist street theater group who distributed free food in Haight-Ashbury. Grogan, who by all accounts was a charmer, had grown up in Bay Ridge, Brooklyn, had kicked a teenage drug addiction, gained admission to a fancy prep school, and parlayed his access to New York's elite into a lucrative sideline as a Park Avenue cat burglar. Joni was more than intrigued. She had met Grogan in Paris and remembered,

"He spoke French with a Brooklyn accent." Eager to have a nice evening with Grogan, she put Ford on notice. "I said to Gayle, 'Lookee here, we'll have none of that funny business tonight.' It was the first time I had ever stood up to her, except for the one time in the car, when I said, 'This is my car and I'll smoke if I want to.' So Emmett said I was like De Gaulle. He said if anybody had pulled a gun on me that night it would have bounced off of me and they would have missed. But I was very strong because I was very sick and very fed up."

Joni could be like De Gaulle for only so long. She made it through a gig at Nassau Coliseum on February 20. By the time they got to Cole Fieldhouse at the University of Maryland, College Park, on February 22, she had clearly had enough. She saw a near replica of herself—only visually, of course—flaunted before her by her ex-lover, who was also keeping time behind her, an act that Russ Kunkel compared with the intimacy of a heartbeat.

That night in Maryland, the L.A. Express played their opening set as always. The resentment had been building since the airport in Boston. This woman would be dangled before Joni for the rest of the gig, and by a guy who was not only her ex, but *working for her*, and being paid nicely, too. Joni had had to tolerate this for days, and it was getting tougher and tougher. She wasn't kidding when she told Elliot Roberts she could take it no more, and now she was supposed to get up there and entertain a stadium of eighteen thousand on a college campus and sing about drinking a case of her lover or courting and sparking or even going twisted? Joni could be tough, Joni could be sensitive. And she also knew when to take off.

The sound check was foreboding. "The sound was bouncing off the walls and between being sick and the sound being horrible, I thought, 'I can't play under these circumstances.' I was just hearing echoes of myself. It's like when you're talking on the phone and you get slap-back and you can't really talk to the person." Joni was in her own echo chamber that night. When it was time to sing her opening number, the band played the familiar groove, and Joni took to the mic and sang, "Help me . . ." before bolting from the stage. She really *did* need help. Eighteen thousand tickets were returned. Five more domestic gigs were canceled. A European leg was scrapped. Max Bennett estimated that he personally lost $60,000—in 1976 dollars. Joni would play a few gigs after that—the Band's Last Waltz concert on Thanksgiving, a Save the Whales benefit, a Bread and Roses festival in 1978—but she took off because she felt like her well-being was more valuable than any deals that the men who managed her had made for her to perform. It didn't feel like it was about letting down the fans. It felt like it was about saving her own soul. Emmett Grogan died in 1978, on the F train to Coney Island, of what appeared to be a heart attack but others believed to be a heroin overdose. Bob Dylan dedicated his 1978 album, *Street Legal*, to Grogan's memory.

A road trip to Maine ended up being a circuitous solo trip back home. She wrote many songs, enough, with some that she had already accumulated, to make another album. One song was tentatively called "Traveling," but she flipped through the dictionary to find a better word. She finally came upon it—*Hejira*: escape with honor.

20 ■ *HEJIRA* AND THE ART OF LOSING

The art of losing isn't hard to master; so many things seem filled with the intent to be lost that their loss is no disaster," wrote Elizabeth Bishop in the poet's final volume, published in 1976. Joni's music seemed, from the very beginning, to capture this uneasy truth, how quickly life teaches us to get good at the art of losing, how many things—places, and people, as well as beloved possessions— seem filled with the *intent* to be lost. For Joni, 1976 was a year to master the art of losing more and more. She had already given up her daughter, left lovers in the dust, and abandoned a two-month tour that was supposed to go much longer. One thing she was certain she needed to lose was her ego—that beast fed and inflated by cocaine.

You don't know what you've got till it's gone, she'd already told us, yet she wasn't done losing. There was so much yet to be lost in the future: her entire soprano range, much of her audience, her critical grace. Starting with *The Hissing of Summer Lawns*, some of the reviews were becoming increasingly obtuse, the more adventurous she became. Joni was in the sweepstakes to lose big; the higher the art, the greater the loss. Indeed, for Joni, loss often is where the creativity starts. It had been this way ever since polio robbed her of her dreams of being an athlete. In her childhood, when Joni returned from the ward and found she was no longer picked first for the teams, she turned inward and eventually found that she was an artist. A Joni Mitchell without polio might well have been a Joni Mitchell who could never reach the depths and darkness of *Blue*.

Running out on her Hissing of Summer Lawns tour was a loss of a different kind, certainly a financial loss for the members of the L.A. Express (and for her, of course). And yet those months of free time—first with fellow travelers, then on her own—led to discoveries that might have never happened if life went on as planned. And they certainly would not have led to the perfect storm of *Hejira* (1976), an album that is as loved by her most ardent fans as *Blue*, and sometimes makes it to the very top of various lists of favorite Joni Mitchell albums. Perry Meisel, an NYU English professor, slammed *Hejira* in the pages of *The Village Voice* for failing to live up to Freud and literary theory. Meisel becomes worked up about her look, reminds everyone about the *Rolling Stone* smear, and disses her clothes before ripping apart her language:

> *Hejira* presents the Queen of El Lay more explicitly in the guise of a poet than ever before, festooned with cape, beret, slanted pinky, and the backdrop of a resolutely abstract landscape. Well, that's the way poets are supposed to look, I guess, and Mitchell's (self-)portrait here seems to be a little too aware of that. Mitchell, of course, has always tried to pass herself off as a poet by printing out her lyrics on the covers of her recordings. No mere listening aids, the printouts constitute a tacit commitment to the perils of scrutiny and rereading. Mixing your metaphors in ignorance is one thing, but flaunting your pretensions in black and white is quite another.

Because Joni had the chance to look back on her time in what she called, in the title track, the "petty wars" with John Guerin (who still played drums on the album), and have some minor flings along the way, she could open up the arsenal of heartbreak and love-'em-and-leave-'em songs that fans of *Blue* and *Court and Spark* had been yearning for, even if coming back to the old subject always meant coming back in a new way. *Hejira* is no sequel to anything. It's about being high on coke and getting drunk on love, and finally about a moment of sober clarity. It is the late-night party and the morning after. Her listeners had already learned, from "Down to You," that everything comes and goes; this time, life's ebb and flow would return, but in the first person. Things were now down to *her*. Whether she was ruminating on Amelia Earhart's brave, independent, but doomed journey, or on the philosophical implications of turning thirty, the music seems to break free of its own confines, making as much room as it would take. It had been five years since *Blue*, but it sounded like a lifetime.

During that time, much had changed. She was maturing, her life was progressing, and this was captured on her recordings in real time. She claimed to have lost an octave at Rolling Thunder (her soprano was still there, floating above Neil Young at the Last Waltz). Her voice certainly sounded heavier, both literally and figuratively. In 1971, it was still shocking to her that life fell short. In 1976, it was a grim reality, even as her passion was as deep as ever. *Blue* may have been private letters that weren't published. *Hejira* is filled with personal revelations blurted out to anyone who would listen. And it would find God (or the devil) in the details: Coyote picking up a woman's scent on his fingers, mama's nylons underneath her cowgirl jeans, a man and a woman sitting on a rock that will either thaw or freeze. Joni's mind picked up pictures and put them into words. It wasn't poetry she was after; it was more like movies for your mind. "Girl, you make me see pictures in my head," said a woman to Joni backstage at the Grammys. Joni has received many compliments, but this, she told me, was among her favorites.

In March 1976, shortly after Joni went home following the aborted Hissing of Summer Lawns tour, she left LA on a road trip with two male companions—an Australian ex-lover and a young flight attendant who would inspire "A Strange Boy." The idea was cooked up on the beach at Neil Young's house. The destination was to be Damariscotta, Maine, to save her ex-boyfriend's daughter from his in-laws. Surely, the way to forget her ex-boyfriend troubles was to travel with *another* ex-boyfriend and another man destined to be a romance with a built-in expiration date. She was still on coke when she called Robben Ford, her guitarist from both tours and *The Hissing of Summer Lawns*, who must have still been reeling from the canceled tour. "Hey, Robben, I'm gonna be in Boulder," she told him. "Great, come on by," he said. Why the hell not? He had crashed with her before in LA when she had recently moved into her Bel-Air sanctuary. When she wasn't having a breakdown, Joni was a blast. Besides, he had something to share with her that he knew she would dig—an advance copy of the bass player Jaco Pastorius's eponymous debut album, released by Epic in 1976.

This was anything but a casual recommendation, in a cultural moment when a recording couldn't be shared just anywhere, and when certain releases, even on major labels, could remain unknown. At the time of release, most people in the music world hadn't heard of Pastorius, but they had heard of the other musicians playing with him, including Herbie Hancock, Wayne Shorter, Michael Brecker, and even a reunited Sam and Dave on one track. And once they did hear it, word spread fast. Most electric bassists in 1976 were just keeping time or slapping in the funk style of that moment. Pastorius seemed to come out of nowhere to make every electric bass player rethink their game—really, rethink their lives. "If Charlie Parker Was a Gunslinger, There'd Be a Whole Lot of Dead Copycats," went the provocative title of a composition by the great Charles Mingus, who would enter Joni's orbit a couple of years later. Pastorius would leave a lot of copycats in his wake, too. Pastorius made the electric bass sing, and in a range never imagined by other players, playing the notes, using the rhythms, and leaving the spaces that Joni was yearning for and demanding of other players without success.

For Joni, Robben Ford played Pastorius's solo bass ballad "Portrait of Tracy," which is played with an extravagant and idiosyncratic use of harmonics, the high end of the instrument no bass player of record had explored in that sort of depth at all. The song sounds like a duo with a single player, with bass notes bringing in just enough support for the acrobatics on the high end. Never had such sublime treble emanated from a bass guitar. It was as if a baritone began singing soprano. Pastorius ripped the frets off a bass guitar in an attempt to combine the volume of an electric instrument with the freedom of an upright. He wasn't the first fretless bass player—Bill Wyman of the Stones, Jack Bruce of Cream, Rick Danko of the Band, and John Paul Jones of Led Zeppelin all preceded him—but he was its first virtuoso. Pastorius compared frets to speed bumps. He had to vandalize the instrument to isolate these notes. The sound that resulted was something entirely new, as if he had found hidden beauty in an instrument that was not made for this range at all. And he kept time with such precision, he could do all these other inventive flourishes while never forgetting the pulse.

Some of the most audacious innovators look outside of what an instrument is even built to do. Charlie Parker was known to have practiced from a violin book. John Coltrane played out of a harp book, trying to make a tenor saxophone play in a single note what the most ornately chordal instrument would play in cascading notes; attempting to make a tenor saxophone play harp chords—to play fast enough, the chords would somehow congeal—Coltrane brought the instrument beyond its intended function. "Portrait of Tracy" was a track that made many players rack their brains and wonder how Pastorius did what he did, especially on a ballad, as emotionally deep as it was innovative. It took live performances to prove to skeptics that there was no studio trickery involved. He really was making those sounds all by himself—a bass way out of range and then back again. It would be an understatement to say that Pastorius—who proclaimed "I'm the baddest" so often it should have been on his tombstone—was not a humble man; these Promethean adventures on the instrument showed the reasons.

Joni said that he sounded like she had dreamed him up. She had always yearned for a bass player who approached the instrument as someone who could go all the way up to her soprano range. Max Bennett, who was a superb accompanist, bristled at some of the audacious things

Joni was asking for. Even if, years later, Joni listened back to her work with Max Bennett, from *Court and Spark* ("Trouble Child") to *Hejira*, and realized that he was right to put his foot down, with Pastorius, she heard a kindred spirit, someone who took an instrument—the bass guitar—and remade it, as radically as Charlie Parker remade the alto sax or as Jimi Hendrix remade the electric guitar. Joni learned that this guy was in Miami, playing gigs with Bob Hope and Phyllis Diller. The next time she was in a studio, she'd have to bring him out.

But she hadn't written all the songs for the next album yet, and in those peripatetic months, she would clock as much time on the road as she would have on the tour she'd escaped, except without limos, private jets, an entourage, and paying customers lined up to see her. She'd be in the company of whoever she felt like being around—certainly not John Guerin, at least not until things had cooled down and she would be back in the studio, where she trusted him to play drums as only he could.

Her itinerary was exhausting. She had escaped her tour, and she would keep escaping. Cocaine kept the energy and confidence brimming, and would be part of what kept some songs going—the proliferating verses of "Song for Sharon," in particular. That song had ten verses with no chorus or bridge, an act of audacity, perhaps, except that one could not imagine the song any other way. Joni took chances when she was on cocaine, but then again, she had been taking chances all along. The giddy song-speak was written on coke; so was the associative "Don Juan's Reckless Daughter" and the loquacious "Talk to Me." Joni had been giddy, associative, and loquacious before, but her ambition was now even more magnified. The romantic sweep of so many of her songs, from "Both Sides, Now" to "Sweet Bird" (and, later, on "Amelia"), gave way to lines that accommodated conversational syllables from a woman, already a big talker, becoming a flagrantly *bigger* talker, "always talkin'," as she put it, "chicken squawkin'."

The breathy folksinger of the past was shoved aside, although not quite for good. She later often said that cocaine destroys the heart and that it was the greatest source of what's wrong with pop music. This period of coke was, if not *the* essence, then certainly *an* essence of her work at this stage, but so was the sobriety that followed it. Indeed, when she needed to kick, that would be part of the journey, too. She took a drive to Maine, went solo, landed in New York City, got diverted to Florida, traveled incognito in the Deep South, then through the desert. When she got home, *Hejira* was ready to be recorded.

21 ■ CRAZY WISDOM

R obben Ford not only turned Joni on to Jaco Pastorius, but his wife, Gayle Ford, who had caused Joni such grief on the Hissing of Summer Lawns tour earlier that year, took one look at Joni and "said I was in bad shape and took me to this guru." This was not just your run-of-the-mill Colorado 1970s guru. This was Vidyadhara Chögyam Trungpa Rinpoche, founder of the global Shambhala network of Tibetan Buddhist communities and of Naropa University, located right there in Boulder. Trungpa was considered a reincarnate lama, or "tulku," the eleventh such lama in the Trungpa line; a figure of monastic authority in Tibet while he was still in his teens, before the Chinese invasion and his subsequent exile.

"I was introduced to Buddhism at art school when that infatuation with the East was floating around," Joni told Malka Marom years later. "I wasn't drawn to the mystical East at that particular time. They all seemed kind of like mystical gobbledygook to me."

But in Trungpa, Joni would meet her spiritual match.

Sometimes, it takes a thief to catch one. The Tibetan Buddhist master and Joni met just before Easter. "He asked me, 'Do you believe in God?'" Joni told me. "I said, 'Yes, here's my god and here is my prayer,' and I took out the cocaine and took a hit in front of him. So I was very, very rude in the presence of a spiritual master."

It is more than likely that he had seen worse. In fact, it was even likely that he had *done* worse. Best known in popular culture for his association with Allen Ginsberg, the Beat Eminence of the Rolling Thunder Revue crew with whom Joni spent that unforgettable month in late 1975, Trungpa was an unusually charismatic teacher, and he did not play by the rules. He was a hard drinker—heavy use of alcohol certainly violates a Buddhist precept against intoxicants—and it was counterintuitive (to say the least) to think that a self-styled "healer," even such a celebrated one, would be able to help someone kick one substance, cocaine, while going heavy on the booze himself (indeed, Trungpa eventually *died* of alcoholism).

Trungpa never tried to hide his heavy drinking—he often gave public lectures quite soused—or his tendency to have affairs with his female students. Such contradictions are like an old joke. "Make me one with everything," says the Buddhist to the hot-dog vendor, handing him a fifty-dollar bill. When the hot dog with all the fixings is delivered, no cash is returned. The punch line? "Change comes only from within." Getting clean with a drunken healer sounds like another joke, too, except that Joni did find her own way to become one with everything and to change from within. Crazy wisdom—Trungpa's phrase—was a metaphysical conceit that had a way of working.

Pema Chödrön, who became Trungpa's student a couple of years before Joni's encounter, had this to say about her experience of having him as her teacher:

> When I asked Trungpa Rinpoche if I could be his student in 1974, I was not ready to enter into an unconditional relationship. But for the first time in my life I had met a person who was not caught up—a person whose mind was never swept away—and I realized that was also possible for me. And I was incredibly drawn to him because I saw

that I couldn't manipulate him. You felt seen by him? It wasn't as personal as that. It was more like: This is a man who knows how to cut through people's trips . . . [W]hen we work closely with a teacher, all the ways that we hold back and shut down, all the ways that we cling and grasp, all our habitual ways of limiting and solidifying our world become very clear to us, and it's unnerving. At that painful point, we usually want to make the teacher wrong or make ourselves wrong or do anything that is habitual and comforting to get ground back under our feet. But when we make an unconditional commitment to hang in there, we do not run away from the pain of seeing ourselves—and this is a revolutionary thing to do and it transforms us. But how many of us are ready for this? One has to gradually develop the trust that it is ultimately liberating to let go of strongly held assumptions about reality.

Most of Trungpa's students tried to impress him, but Joni figured out that this was not the right way to experience him. "I came in looking down on him because I thought the girl who dragged me there [Gayle Ford] was a jerk and then I saw he had some shit, so I looked up at him and flattered him and I busted myself for flattering him." What Pema Chödrön said of Trungpa was true for Joni, too: "This is a man who knows how to cut through people's trips."

All it took was fifteen minutes: they were meeting, barriers were breaking down. She was suddenly genuflecting to something even more powerful than cocaine. Trungpa began to do a breathing technique that, for Joni, emanated grace waves. Joni lost her "I." An ego that had been so extravagantly fed by fame, cocaine, and adoring, handsome men competing for her affection had been extinguished. In Tibet, they call it the "fast way." It certainly felt like a quick escape. She left there in what she called "the awakened state." In "Refuge of the Roads," she paid tribute to him as a "friend of spirit" who "drank and womanized." When she rerecorded the song for *Travelogue* in 2002, she changed it to "a drunk with sage's eyes." He was all of those things. Joni was also always convinced that he was the real thing.

So in other words, this was an ongoing teacher-student relationship. Once she got to what she considered to be level-four Buddhism—otherwise known as the fourth of the four stages of attainment—she thought she could ask what she called an "arbitrary stupid novice question: 'What is the meaning of life?'" Trungpa responded with the cynicism she knew she deserved. "When he finished, he made me laugh and I felt like an insider," she told me. "I felt like he was talking to me, not like a novice. We had one of those shared laughs that went on and on. It got better and better. It was delicious. My comment was cynical, but it was realistic. There was no beguiling to it. 'Life's shit and then you die.'"

Maybe so. But Joni wasn't ready to die yet. She still had to live up to the muse and deliver songs on one of her creative peaks. When the ego returned, she had perspective on it. It was finely tuned, nuanced, and decanted. And the album she was about to record benefited from all kinds of inspiration. It would be executed in the cold light of day, with her painter's ego back with her, like an old friend.

Even if cocaine fueled some of *Hejira*'s powerful songs, the clarity of going off coke produced other songs that came from a different and equally compelling kind of power. She had to let go of the ego she already name-checked in "Coyote"—"I tried to run away myself / To run away and wrestle with my ego."

It is a painter's cap she wears so memorably on Norman Seeff's beautiful album cover. And inside, Joel Bernstein would capture her in the wild, as he had in his photo for *For the Roses*. Joni knew precisely what she wanted and she micromanaged the shoot so that there could be no room for error. After she ran away from the debacle at the University of Maryland, the band played one more gig at the Dane County Coliseum in Madison, Wisconsin, on February 29. It was near there, on a frozen pond by the Edgewater Inn, that the skating pictures on the gatefold were shot. Joni dressed in funereal black; a sable stole, a crepe skirt, and a woolly hat. All she needed to complete her look were black ice skates. But this was the 1970s, and women wore white, or pink, or "nude" skates. Men wore black or forest green. It was like wanting to play Roy Rogers on the playground all over again. It was harder than one might think for a woman to convince a salesman to sell her non-female skates.

"Look. Just fit me for a man's skates."

"But they're for men."

Joni argued with the skate salesman. Finally, she demanded, "Just fit me for black skates."

She knew they looked weird. But she also knew that these black clothes against the snowy background would produce the contrast she was looking for, no matter what. She told Bernstein: "I just said, you know, just shoot a lot. And those are the best pictures that were taken, other than the bare bum shot, which I think is also a striking landscape and figure."

Whether it was black boots or a bare bum, Joni's cover was going to look exactly as she wished, almost as if she were shooting her photos herself. As for the record the jacket contained, there was a reason she was so specific about what happened on the outside. What happened on the inside was yet another breakthrough.

That was some trip to Boulder. Robben Ford played her "Portrait of Tracy." Gayle Ford introduced her to Trungpa. Then Joni kept driving, coast to coast, back and forth. And on that trip, in motel rooms, sometimes in disguise, checking into motels as "Charlene Latimer," Joni wrote the rest of the *Hejira* songs. At Rolling Thunder, she wrote "Coyote" and, saved for later, "Don Juan's Reckless Daughter" and "Talk to Me." On her Hissing of Summer Lawns tour, she wrote "Furry Sings the Blues." Those songs were driven by cocaine. The rest were driven by something else. Trungpa helped her find clarity. And Jaco helped her find a new harmonic world. These two enlightened derelicts were crucial in making the eccentric, inspired masterpiece that is *Hejira*. And, as soon as Joni, inspired by Trungpa, might have figured out how to lose her ego, that ego was on extravagant display, especially when it was unveiled from the wild, untamed genius of Jaco Pastorius. Although he plays on only four of the album's nine songs—"Coyote," "Hejira," "Black Crow," and "Refuge of the Roads"—his presence is so expansive, it seems to go even beyond the boundaries of these songs. You can hear him bubbling over everywhere. He is crucial in making "Coyote" sound like what it feels to be driving on the highway: the alternating strummed chords with the contrapuntal bass accompaniment is the aural equivalent of driving under highway lights, alternating light and darkness.

Max Bennett played bass on "Furry Sings the Blues" and "Song for Sharon," as sturdy, precise, and empathetic as ever. He and Pastorius never saw each other in the studio at all, and Bennett was feeling so alienated from Joni, he never even owned the album. Larry Carlton played guitar on five songs—"Coyote," "Amelia," "A Strange Boy," "Blue Motel Room," and "Black Crow"—and he overdubbed his parts, with Joni just telling him, "Play what you feel." The same year, Carlton played on Steely Dan's *The Royal Scam*—including a legendary solo on "Kid Charlemagne"—where he showed off rock theatrics and sophisticated understanding of jazz chord changes at the same time. Carlton's parts are memorable: lyrical on "Amelia," aggressive on "A Strange Boy," sophisticated and harsh on "Black Crow." He saw neither Bennett nor Pastorius. He played by day, they played by night. Joni was sufficiently self-possessed, her sidemen could each work independently on overdubs.

"*Hejira* was more separate," Joni told me. "With the great players, all I had to say was 'Play what you feel.' They'd make a chart, so they knew what the harmonic structure was. I had only one battle with Carlton. I yanked the guitar around and played it quite boldly, especially for a girl. Carlton's got many chops that I don't have, but he's not a yanker. He's a graceful arcer. And I wanted him to yank this note, and he wouldn't do it. It's the only instruction I ever gave him. And he wouldn't do it. So I cued him in on four instead of one, and raised the volume on it in the mix. And that's how I got that note on it."

In 2013, many, many years and cultural moments later, Joni gave her last public interview, a couple of days before her last public performance, both for the Luminato Festival in Toronto, which was presenting a two-day celebration of Joni's music at Massey Hall. At the interview, the *New York Times* pop music critic Jon Pareles cautiously asked her a question about what most excited her in her own work. Her memory went to the second verse of the *Hejira* track "Furry Sings the Blues," a lament for a nearly destroyed Beale Street in Memphis, Tennessee, with a moribund Furry Lewis, broken down but still singing till last call. Lewis was a minor blues figure who spent forty years as a street sweeper and was said to have played with W. C. Handy himself. Handy had famously wondered, in song, what would happen if Beale Street could talk. Now, in its death rattle, Joni was singing for it. That was in 1976, with blaxploitation, disco, and drugs springing up in the land where the blues began. In Toronto, Joni remembered the decay of Beale Street and all the gleaming details it inspired:

> I don't know if it's the best, but the [verse] that excited me [the most] when I wrote it . . . was in "Furry Sings the Blues," the second verse, the second part. I'm trying to describe this trip I took into this ghost town of the old black music neighborhood with wrecking cranes standing around while the city fathers decided whether to keep it for historic reasons or not. And there were three new businesses there aimed at black exploitation. There were two black exploitation films at the New Daisy Theatre and two pawnshops . . . [The song] poured out almost in blank verse . . . I thought, "Oh, girl, the blarney's with you now."

That verse described the demise of a once proud cultural landmark, but made poetry out of its final throes. If *The Great Gatsby*, which name-checked Handy's "Beale Street Blues," had been written in the era of *Shaft* and urban renewal, some of Fitzgerald's images might have sounded like this.

> *Pawnshops glitter like gold tooth caps*
> *In the grey decay*
> *They chew the last few dollars off*
> *Old Beale Street's carcass*

With the wrecking ball just waiting to strike down what little is left of Beale Street—a run-down movie theater, and the sad little joint where Furry croaked out what he had left—Joni is there as a designated mourner. The pawnshops are gleaming, where final trades are like a last call for the final barters. The music—and Old Furry himself—is dying, paved paradise all over again.

In the footage of Joni singing this song in her thirties, as an outtake from *The Last Waltz* and as a song from a video of a 1979 performance broadcast and released as *Shadows and Light*, she is a stunning and vital woman, in full voice and full bloom. Take notes and the pain goes away, said Virginia Woolf. Joni could take notes in her head, and someone else's pain, too. When she performed the song a couple of days after her 2013 interview, she riffed on her memory of attempting to find common ground with Lewis because they both played in open tunings: "I can play in Spanish tunin's, I don't just play in toonin's!" And she quoted him, as she quotes him in the song: "I don't like you!"

This material alone would have already made *Hejira* superb; if Bennett had played bass on every track that needed a bass player, it would still be a classic. But what takes things up several notches further is Jaco Pastorius. Keeping time and lending support is a given for any professional bass player. Pastorius was confident enough about already taking care of this aspect of his role that he could then hit harmonics for maximum drama, and make the tricky seem easy, as if playing a fast-fingered riff—with the melodic sweep of a solo, yet still with the rhythmic and harmonic support of the accompanist—were as natural as breathing, eating, drinking, making love. And so, suddenly, the animal-like lover of "Coyote" shifts from Sam Shepard, who inspired the song, to Pastorius, who takes it over in the studio. The lyrics celebrate a certain wildness. Its alliteration—"privately probing the public rooms" and "pills and powders to get them through this passion play"—teases the listener, and Pastorius's harmonic response teases back. Pastorius, who, like Shepard, had a wife at home, would become Joni's lover. He was, she said, the bass player of her dreams.

"He had this wide, fat swath of a sound," she recalled later. At the time, Pastorius was truly high on life, and high on the high end of his bipolar disorder, a phenomenon difficult to separate from his ego, his genius, and what seemed like an expansive, and overwhelming, joie de vivre. He was a moving target in those days, jumping, diving, running amok, and breaking all the rules. He ripped the frets out of his bass to get a sound that became imitated everywhere, even when he was sleeping in parks in his final years. When Joni met him, in 1976, he introduced himself by saying, "My name is John Francis Pastorius the Fourth and I am the greatest bass player in the world." Once people heard him, they were converted, convinced that this guy was the Muhammad Ali of the fretless. His face on his debut record reminded Joni of a Tibetan sage. Like Trungpa, he was utterly unconventional, a bad boy, a derelict. Yet he was somehow in the possession of the divine. He showed her a new way. Trungpa was her "friend of spirit." Jaco was her guide to the lower frequencies. He was getting high on the low end, which sounded like bliss. He broke the rules. He let her open up in ways she had been yearning for as long as she had been making music. She didn't know what to call it, because there was no name.

They became lovers in a noncommittal way. The Tracy who inspired "Portrait of Tracy" was his wife and the mother of his children. Joni, feeling the biological clock, wanted to have his baby, convinced that they would produce a musical genius. Fucking around with Joni was one thing—hey, he was working for her—but he was still a husband and a father, at least in his mind. Tracy knew what was going on. She even called Joni's house late at night and Jaco answered. "I always knew you were a witch," he told her. But that witch was still Mrs. Pastorius.

When it came to music, though, no one could get in their way. He pushed her to go further and she let him do all he wanted. Pastorius had a way of making a place for himself even when he wasn't invited. When *Down Beat* named him the greatest bass player of the year, he crashed an Oscar Peterson gig and bounded in front of Ray Brown, the great upright bassist, who had no idea what was going on. Pastorius violated boundaries everywhere he went. In music, it was genius. In life, it was trespassing, which he got away with for a while, too.

The first track that Pastorius recorded for *Hejira* also turned out to be the most radical: its moody, searching, and splendidly ruminative title track, too unfixed for typical bass support. In the liner notes to *The Hissing of Summer Lawns*, Joni thanks John Guerin for showing her "the root of the chord and where 1 was." If a chord is a C chord, then if a bass player plays a C, the player is stating where 1—or the tonic—is. By the time Joni made *Hejira*, she no longer needed to be shown where 1 was, because if you're working with virtuosi, it should be obvious. Pastorius ran amok and took 1 with him. Joni didn't miss it. The Greatest Bass Player in the World claimed to have absolutely no prior knowledge of Joni's music. He was so busy as a working musician, he claimed he didn't have time to listen to records. But he did know the Beatles and James Brown, and he knew Stravinsky well enough to quote from *The Rite of Spring* on "Hejira" (an allusion he would make again on "Talk to Me").

"Hejira" celebrates flight itself. Pastorius's tone is muted, but the effect is like Miles Davis's muted trumpet. Subduing the instrument's natural tones kept the lyrical expression while lowering the curtains on anything too cloyingly bright. It was also closer to the sound Joni initially heard in the rhapsodic harmonics of "Portrait of Tracy." As his tone is dampened down, it is also overdubbed, so that he can hit more than one eccentric note at a time, even riffing on Joni's melodic flourishes. Joni seems to want it all—freedom and companionship, human contact and solitude, recognition and anonymity. She wants to know where 1 is, and then have a bass player blissfully disregard it. Does she contradict herself? "I'm porous with travel fever / But you know I'm so glad to be on my own / Still somehow the slightest touch of a stranger / Can set up trembling in my bones."

Albert Camus, from Leonard Cohen's reading list, makes an appearance here, from *Notebooks, 1935–1951*: "What gives value to travel is fear. It is the fact that, at a certain moment, when we are so far from our own country . . . we are seized by a vague fear, and an instinctive desire to go back to the protection of old habits. This is the most obvious benefit of travel. At that moment we are *feverish* but also *porous*, so that the *slightest touch* makes us quiver to the depths of our being." (emphasis added)

Camus describes the alienation from one's self when one is in an unfamiliar place. For the existentialist, the self is all. Joni wanted to go further: beyond the self, then back again with greater perspective. Joni picks up the idea of porousness and also the idea of the "slightest touch," except, crucially, she adds the stranger to it (certainly not Camus's Stranger), which is what makes the whole image most distinctly hers. Alienation is alienation, passed around between poets and philosophers. The trembling from a stranger—that's pure Joni Mitchell. She needs to be alone to have these insights. She's a "defector from the petty wars" with Guerin and others. But she knows that love will suck her back in.

Joni has said that she often begins a song with many verses and then chisels it down, since most people don't like overly long songs. One song that was spared this editing process was "Song for Sharon," which has ten verses and no chorus and clocks in at 8:40. There is no center, perhaps because it describes a life with no center. "Sharon" is Sharon Bell, a childhood friend from Maidstone of whom Joni had seen very little since her Saskatoon debut in 1963. Bell later said that most of their conversations were "Remember when . . . ?" and so she could be a figure that is, on the surface, one of nostalgia, someone who can still evoke the uncanny, or the return of the repressed. Joni, always looking forward, even as she looks back, digs deeper, to reflect on what she had gained and lost. She looks to her friend from the distant past to help her make sense of her present. As the song describes, Joni really did take the Staten Island Ferry to Staten Island's North Shore to Mandolin Brothers, where she bought a 1915 Gibson Mandocello and a Martin herringbone guitar. While this purchase opens the song, it is already addressed to Sharon, the recipient of this open letter, where Joni reflects on a long-gone childhood of the Canadian prairie, back when she went to every wedding in the town, chasing white lace. More recently, she had been chasing white powder, and was trying to escape from it—one of this album's many attempted hejiras. Joni has said that she has been cursed with sincerity. Unlike Dylan or Cohen, she has no character to hide behind. It's part of what makes her work so human, so intimate, but it also leaves her more vulnerable.

In "Song for Sharon," her coked-up shout-out to her childhood friend, Joni devotes a verse to the suicide of Phyllis Major, which occurred in March 1976. It was around the same time that Trungpa roused Joni to a new level of reconciling who she was and who she was becoming. "When Chögyam zapped me, I spent three days in the awakened state," she told me. "The awakened state is glamorized by charlatans—bliss, nirvana. It's not a glamorous state. It's a wonderful state. But it is ultra-mundane. Your 'I' thing is gone. You could say 'ego,' but that's misleading. Your whole 'I' thing is gone. The thing you think you are is not there. But your full nature is there. Your soul is there. I know what a soul is from that experience. Whatever your full nature is—that's your soul. So if you're mischievous, you'll be mischievous even without an 'I' thing. There's nothing to report back to. Our whole head is filled with insane entertainment of our thoughts and our assumptions. Then you're just a living, viewing machine." Joni could see herself seeing her past, where she was trying to go, who she was, all while taking a sabbatical from the first person. And it was when she was still in the midst of this process of figuring out how to live, she was commemorating the dead, in her way: Phyllis Major, the wife of Jackson Browne, had committed suicide. Joni's relationship with Browne had been four years earlier. So much had happened! That was way before she had—for three days, but still—let go of herself. And yet these feelings were coming back, to be commemorated in some new writing, that had to be done, had to be transformed into music. The "I" thing was gone, but then it wasn't. But when it did go, she had gone to a new level of perspective. She could see herself as particles of change orbiting the sun, but she still felt a trembling in her bones from the slightest touch of a stranger. A woman, who had been married to an ex-lover, commits suicide. She feels bad. And she can't let go her bitterness toward the man who surely drove her to it, which makes her feel even more sympathy, more anger. The Korean word *han*, a mixture of melancholy and rancor and anger, covers the emotional spectrum here. She is

On the prairie at recess, determined to be Roy Rogers and not Dale Evans
(Photograph by Myrtle Anderson)

(Left to right) Garry Korven, Len Lang, Joan Anderson, and Tony Simon lounging around on a lazy afternoon at Waskesiu, a lake near Saskatoon
(Courtesy of Tony Simon)

Joni (right) at the Provincial Institute of Technology and Art, with pep and a hairdo at the height of fads and fashions
(Courtesy of SAIT Archives)

Back in the fledgling days when Joni told the CBC that her songs were about "happiness" (Frank Lennon / Toronto Star Collection / Getty Images)

THE CHESS MATE
(COFFEE HOUSE)
NO AGE LIMIT

JONI AND CHUCK
MITCHELL
DETROIT'S FAVORITE FOLK SINGERS
Appearing Nitely Thru Sun., Jan. 30
17126 LIVERNOIS
at McNichols
PHONE 862-1554
Jazz Every Fri. & Sat.
2 A.M. 'til 6 A.M.

Joni and Chuck Mitchell, when his union membership got her into the better clubs in Yorkville—from the Clef Club to the Riverboat (Copyright © Detroit Free Press / ZUMAPRESS.com)

The Penny Farthing, where Joni corrected Chuck Mitchell's rendition of "Mr. Tambourine Man," and that's where the trouble began (Courtesy of Lesley [Dalrymple] O'Neil)

Joni and Leonard Cohen on the day they met, Newport Folk Festival, 1967. "Part of you pours out of me / In these lines from time to time." (David Gahr / Premium Archive / Getty Images)

to right) the three Js, Joni, Judy, and Joan, at the Big Sur festival, 1968 (with John Byrne ke and Nancy Carlen) Robert Altman / Michael Ochs Archives / Getty Images)

ABOVE: At the piano on Lookout Mountain in Laurel Canyon, 1969, in the halcyon days when she and Graham Nash, a.k.a. Willy, were fighting over it
(Copyright © Jim Marshall Photography LLC)

BELOW: Joni and Graham Nash, in the midst. "I loved the man, so I can't say anything bad about him." (Copyright © Jim Marshall Photography LLC)

ABOVE: With James Taylor, recording backup vocals for Carole King's "Will You Still Love Me Tomorrow," when King was recording *Tapestry* down the hall from the *Blue* sessions (Photograph by Jim McCrary)

BELOW: Joni with her label boss, host, and "Free Man in Paris," David Geffen, now the two-hundredth-richest man in the world. (Julian Wasser / The LIFE Images Collection / Getty Images)

ABOVE: Exchanging a look with Jaco Pastorius, the bass player of her dreams, at the Berkeley Jazz Festival, 1979 (Photograph by Ed Perlstein / MusicImages.com)

BELOW: The Last Waltz: Thanksgiving 1976, belting out "I Shall Be Released." (Left to right, front row) Dr. John, Joni, Rick Danko, Bob Dylan, and Robbie Robertson; (behind them) Ringo Starr, Neil Young (head), Van Morrison (eyes), Ronnie Hawkins, and Levon Helm (Photograph by Ed Perlstein / MusicImages.com)

TOP: "I love to play with Herbie." Joni and Herbie Hancock at the Bread and Roses Festival, Berkeley, in the fall of 1978, when she premiered some of her collaborations with the still-living Charles Mingus (Photograph by Ed Perlstein / MusicImages.com)

ABOVE: Joni and Larry Klein, her "magnificent ex-husband," accepting a Grammy, amazed that they pulled it off for an album made "in a state of divorce" (AP Photo / Eric Draper © 2017 The Associated Press)

ABOVE: Generations: Joni in public with her parents, Bill, who is beaming, and Myrtle, who is pensive . . . (Photograph by Anne Bayin)

BELOW: . . . and her found family—daughter Kilauren and grandson Marlin, the inspiration for "Bad Dreams Are Good" from *Shine* (Photograph by Mark Lipson)

sad, she is angry, she takes umbrage. She would like to be above settling scores, yet she is compelled to do so.

It all came rushing back. Jackson had the nerve to dump her. Then she had such a vivid sense of what was wrong with him, and she could see what he was doing to the women who came after. Poor Phyllis, Joni thought. She was reaching a new sense of being present while being confronted with her past. And so she reaches back further— way, way back to her friend from Maidstone, from between the ages of three and five. Without naming names, Joni, in this rambling conversation with Sharon Bell, thinks about what happens when the dream of the white lace turns into a nightmare:

> *A woman I knew just drowned herself*
> *The well was deep and muddy*
> *She was just shaking off futility*
> *Or punishing somebody*

Over the years, accounts have surfaced that Joni, too, became self-destructive after her breakup with Jackson Browne. Not so, said Joni in 2015. "I read a page in one of these books. It said, when Jackson Browne dumped me, I attempted suicide and I became a cutter. A cutter! A self-mutilator! I thought, Where do they get this garbage from? I'm not that crazy. I'm crazy, but not that kind of crazy."

Phyllis Major apparently was that kind of desperate. She had already been with Joni's friend Eric Andersen—who showed Joni the open G tuning back in the early folk days of '65. It hadn't started, or ended, well. "My friend Eric Andersen was married to Debbie Green. He ran off right after their baby was born. He ran off with Phyllis. Phyllis was a gorgeous girl and he had taken her at a young age to the [Roger] Vadim scene. That's a woman-hating scene. Phyllis was a sensitive, artistic, beautiful girl, who was passed from guy to guy to guy. Her brother committed suicide, too."

Joni described Major as a "poetic, beautiful girl, looking, with that stupid 'Someday My Prince Will Come' dream that so many of my generation inherited. Especially if you were beautiful, you'd figure that your prince would choose you. You were even more susceptible to being conned."

Joni remembered Eric Andersen calling her and going on about the beautiful girl he'd just met. He was, Joni said, "the kind that would seem to be a prince: he's sensitive, he's romantic, he's poetic." A week later Eric called, distraught. Major had gotten the flu and Joni could hear her throwing up in the background. Joni was incredulous that Andersen "called for sympathy from me. Like, 'Oh, God, she's sick. *My toy is broken!*' And that's basically the mentality of all the men of my generation that I met, just narcissistic, fair-weather types. So I felt really sorry for her."

Later, when Major ended up with Jackson Browne, Joni was even more concerned. "So, here comes another one—the worst one of all. *The very worst one.* And all of the shit that she's gone through to fall into his clutches." The funeral would be revisited in a later song, "Not to Blame," when finger-pointing against Jackson Browne escalated. "Song for Sharon" spends only a stanza on Phyllis Major's funeral. The song is dominated by disappointments and frustrations, not tragedy. But what is clear from the song is that, with the wrong people, white lace can turn into a funeral shroud.

When Joni was a child, there was no such thing as a singer-songwriter, and she knew she didn't have the classical chops to play the Rachmaninoff theme from "The Story of Three Loves" that had already besotted her. She did not envision herself as a performer, but dreamed of the path to love, which, as she put it, stimulated her illusions more than anything. The childhood dreams of white lace were dashed quickly enough, and she became the twenty-one-year-old who could look at life from both sides now. Fast-forward a decade, and after she had stretched herself as an artist and as an independent woman, she looked at the life of Sharon Bell as the road not taken. "I've got the apple of temptation," she sings, "and a diamond snake around my arm." Joni's description of her jewelry reminds her of the Garden of Eden—a snake waiting to tempt, an apple waiting to be eaten. After all the sex, drugs, and rock and roll, Joni ends the song with a reference to Psalm 23: "The Lord is my shepherd, I shall not want. He makes me lie down in green pastures; He leads me beside quiet waters. He restores my soul; He guides me in the paths of righteousness." Joni, an awakened sinner, tells us she'll walk green pastures by and by.

So many nights in hotel rooms made a Gideon reader out of Joni. But could anyone really imagine a Joni who shall not want? The Joni of "All I Want" wants her lover to feel free, and she wants to feel free even *more*. Joni hardly sounds contented at the end of "Song for Sharon," eight and a half minutes of reverie that surely could have gone on even longer. The psalm allusion is the last word of the song, but those green pastures are not the last word of the album. There will be crazy wisdom to spare before the hejira of *Hejira* reaches its destination.

There is no Lord's Prayer in "Amelia," even though one can imagine, at the moment of doom, its subject making a desperate one. Amelia Earhart was, of course, the famed aviatrix who made record-breaking flights before getting lost in the Pacific, while trying to break her own record. Her disappearance is the coldest of cold cases. Watching six jet planes soar off in the desert made Joni think of the strings of her guitar, which is what put the song in motion. Earhart was a precursor woman who also subverted, ignored, and reinvented the idea of what a woman could be four decades earlier, pushing herself to greater and greater heights, ultimately to mystery. She had been lost for nearly forty years when Joni wrote "Amelia," and yet Joni addressed her as intimately—maybe even *more* intimately—than she addressed Sharon Bell. While on her hejira from John Guerin (and all those who preceded and succeeded him), Joni is making a solo drive across the country. She's not comparing herself with Earhart, not really. She's just thinking about her, and even having imaginary conversations with her.

> *Oh, Amelia, it was just a false alarm*

Joni was getting off drugs, and her newly cleared brain was giving her an insight into what could make someone self-destruct so spectacularly. Getting off cocaine is no joke, and yet she never spoke of going through withdrawal, one of the miracles she attributed to Trungpa. Amelia surely had her share of false alarms before the big one finally hit. And Joni, chronicling her own brush with disaster, knows she will live to tell her tale and sing her sorrow, all in a sultry alto, without, in this song, a single soprano leap. Joni pulls into an imaginary lodge named for her own song—the Cactus Tree Motel—evoking a song celebrating her own resilience. She dreams of 747s, of "geometric farms," of "dreams and false alarms." Joni may have spent some of her life in clouds at icy altitudes. "Maybe I've never really loved," she said, riffing on Marianne's line from Ingmar Bergman's *Scenes from a Marriage*. But she is not really like the Nordic Liv Ullmann. She was just feeling that way at that moment on her road trip. She *has* really loved and will really love again. It's her great subject, even in its absence. She knows that Amelia will eventually get a real alarm.

Even when Joni lands, the subject of travel—persistent since the yearning to escape winter in "Urge for Going"—proliferates, and not just about where she went, but the pain in the ass of getting there. Many associate travel with pleasure, excitement, material for Sunday newspaper sections and glossy magazines. Joni's songs about travel are more dark and brooding—about escape, restlessness, dissatisfaction, running away, nameless yearning. Just hearing her check off her itinerary—a ferry to a pontoon plane to a taxi to a train—is exhausting. "Black Crow" is about a hejira of sorts, but it is not about the journey that inspired much of the album; it is instead mused upon from a terminus in British Columbia. Musically, it is a funk tune without drums, so Pastorius can have more room to keep a pulse, but hit some eccentric harmonics and leave plenty of space for Larry Carlton to rip through it with as much distortion as he ever used with Joni. When Joni was a C student in third grade, her reading group was Wren Row. The D students behind her were the Crows. Those D students seemed deficient at the time, but now the crow is picking up a prize, something much more appealing than polishing a teacher's apple. On her Sunshine Coast property, she saw a black crow diving down for something shiny, and she could relate. The Joni of "Black

Crow" was not the little girl of "Song for Sharon" chasing white lace. This was the artist in search of love and music, an exhausting quest, reflected by her "haggard face in the bathroom light." She was also a road-weary soul, marveling at how the black crow is always on the hunt, diving down for something shiny, while we human beings get jet-lagged, carsick, lovesick, homesick, or, for this wild seed, roadsick.

And the road is where Joni ends *Hejira*, to keep us in transit forever. The finale's title, "Refuge of the Roads," says it all; the oxymoron—like Trungpa's "crazy wisdom"—resolves itself like a metaphysical conceit. In her encounter with Trungpa, his crazy wisdom was meant for Joni to find her own. She explained to him that, as an artist, she couldn't take his advice to stop analyzing, but that didn't mean she didn't think twice about it. Joni was enjoying meeting regular folks during her travels, especially in the Deep South, where she was not so well known. "It was a relief," she told the *Ottawa Citizen* on the thirty-year anniversary of *Hejira*'s release. "I was able, like the Prince and the Pauper, to escape my fame under a false name and fall in with people and enjoy ordinary civilian status." In the midst of this road party, Joni catches herself thinking too much: "Till I started analyzing / And I brought on my old ways / A thunderhead of judgment was / Gathering in my gaze." It was in Joni's nature to analyze; if she had truly taken the healer's advice, this song would not exist. Letting go was a process, not a destination. One of Trungpa's greatest achievements was his English translation of *The Tibetan Book of the Dead*, the same version that John Lennon riffed on in the lyrics to "Tomorrow Never Knows." "Turn off your mind," begins the Beatles song, essentially intoning the same advice. Yet Joni accepts her own tendency to do precisely the thing she was advised not to do. *Hejira* is not a how-to album.

And yet "Refuge of the Roads" is about an awakening of sorts. Joni was in fight-or-flight mode. She needed to know how to keep moving, but with clarity. Sometimes she needed an overdecorated house, sometimes she needed something austere. Sometimes she was in search of love and music. Sometimes she needed painting and solitude. This was a crop rotation of the mind. When Buddha, according to Huston Smith, was asked not "Who are you?" but "What are you?" he is said to have replied, "I am awake." When Joni was "zapped"—her word—by Trungpa, she was jolted to a state of being present, not distracted by the fantasies or story lines in her head of the past and future—taking in every moment of the present with an alert and awakened mind. She was, in effect, looking at clouds from every side, now. They were illuminated, vibrant. She could see around them, above them, and below them. She felt like she could see anything:

> *These are the clouds of Michelangelo*
> *Muscular with gods and sungold*
> *Shine on your witness in the refuge of the roads*

Those were not really clouds of Michelangelo, but in Joni's mind and music, they seemed that way. And they were in that moment a beatitude, a vision, as is the rest of the song, getting lost with drifters, passing through random towns, meeting random people, buying Winn-Dixie cold cuts, making a strange journey that was somehow illuminated. They were present in the moment, real, vivid. "Refuge of the Roads" brims with the vibrancy of the awakened state. How do you kick cocaine with an alcoholic? Hire a bass player who never shows you where the 1 is? And how do you take refuge in the roads? The car is moving. Those white lines on the freeway are zooming by. Try looking for safety in the middle of the freeway and see what happens. Only a lunatic would think of something like that. Only someone who sounded like they had nothing left to lose.

22 ■ MIRRORED BALL

Throughout her career, Joni often spent the time between albums in painting periods. She called this "crop rotation." She simply couldn't go on a version of Dylan's Never Ending Tour. Even though *Hejira* made it seem like the drive would go on forever, there was only so much she could take of the grind. That's why "Black Crow" sounded so world-weary. She had been traveling so long, how would she even know her home? She had recently started renting a loft in Manhattan from the sculptor Nathan Joseph. It was in SoHo, on Varick Street, just south of Houston, near the Film Forum, where she would binge on foreign films. When she became involved with the percussionist Don Alias, it would also become a rehearsal space for his bands and whoever was sitting in with them. She made the most of both coasts, reveling in the conversation and culture of New York City, while retreating to the private space of Bel-Air. "Home" could mean B.C.'s Sunshine Coast, SoHo, or Bel-Air. In each space, there was room for her to sleep to the afternoon, and create as long as the blarney would run.

But Joni was not at any of these spaces on Thanksgiving, the most homeward bound of holidays. She had a good reason. Robbie Robertson was breaking up the Band, and they were staging at San Francisco's Winterland what was being touted as the greatest group rock concert since Woodstock or the Isle of Wight, to bid farewell to rock and roll's Class of '76. If the rock critics were to be believed, the Clash, Patti Smith, the Ramones, and Talking Heads were putting the old guard, if not out of business, then at least on notice.

The artists of what was being called the Last Waltz—including Van Morrison, Eric Clapton, Neil Young, Bob Dylan, and Joni— represented an older sensibility; they were adults, and they did not share this new generation's angry and blasé spirit, although Neil Young would be embraced as a trailblazer from punk to grunge. (Muddy Waters would be there as sixty-one-year-old elder statesman. Neil Diamond was allegedly there to represent Tin Pan Alley, but really, because Robbie was convinced they had made a monster record together.)

No one yet knew that the classic rock radio format would keep the airplay of many of Joni's contemporaries alive—while she would mostly live on in CSNY's "Woodstock" cover. The Band's farewell seemed like a fork in the road. Martin Scorsese would make a film out of it, showcasing eccentric interviews with the members of the Band— including a heartbreaking story of Sonny Boy Williamson coughing up blood, and some wink-wink, nudge-nudge remarks about how the "women of the road" kept them going more than the music. And this was the segment that introduced Joni, the only woman on the bill.

Except for the drummer and Arkansan Levon Helm—who sang lead on many of the best-known songs Robertson wrote for the group— the Band were from Canada, and had released their debut, *Music from Big Pink*, in 1968, the same year as *Song to a Seagull*. Decades later, the Band's keyboard eminence, Garth Hudson, was still marveling over that album. "We all fell in love with Joni. There are certain Canadian-isms that sneak across the border, and she was very careful in creating her vignettes," Hudson recalled. "I wondered how she came up with those melodies—so analytically creative."

The Band had a studio in Malibu called Shangri-la, built in a house—with swimming pool intact—that had been owned by Sammy Davis, Jr. Before the Last Waltz, Joni once paid Hudson a visit to look at the Yamaha CS80, the first fully polyphonic synthesizer. She wasn't a woman on the road at that point. She was another musician in the studio, someone with whom to talk shop. It was in that spirit that she was the token female at the festivities. She was one of them. At the Last Waltz, there was no female dressing room; Joni shared a trailer with her friend Neil Young. While she was honored to be the only female artist there, she also felt a little lonely. Scorsese clearly realized this deficiency and added Emmylou Harris and Mavis Staples (along with two of her sisters) in a sequence shot later for the film.

Scorsese had been an assistant director on *Woodstock*, and by the time he got to Winterland in '76, he had made his reputation on *Mean Streets* (1973) and *Taxi Driver*, which had stunned audiences when it was released in February. His intent was to make the greatest rock concert film ever, and there is a critical consensus that he did exactly that.

Somehow, the Band leaving the road was an occasion for an entire generation of rock stars, in the middle of the 1970s, to consider what they were doing to themselves. Robertson said that they had been on the road for sixteen years—and he couldn't even begin to think about making it to twenty. The road meant drugs, regrettable hookups, exhaustion, alienation, despair. Rock and roll was supposed to be an escape, yet it seemed like a trap. "The road has taken a lot of the great ones: Hank Williams, Buddy Holly, Otis Redding, Janis, Jimi Hendrix, Elvis," rasped Robbie Robertson at the end of the film. "It's a goddamn impossible way of life." (To which Levon Helm, who opposed the breakup, replied, "I ain't in this for my health!")

It happened that the Last Waltz concert was performed the month *Hejira* was released. Joni would harmonize on Neil Young's "Helpless," and would present—bolstered by Levon Helm's brush work, Garth Hudson's organ adventures, and especially Robbie Robertson's subtle and elegant guitar accompaniment—"Coyote" (which made it to the film), "Shadows and Light" (strummed, like the Rolling Thunder version), and "Furry Sings the Blues" (with Neil Young doing the shambolic harmonica part he performed on the record).

Much has been made of the lengths the filmmakers went to cover up Neil Young's notorious "cocaine booger," doctored to disappear against his nose. What is less known is the degree to which the sound had to be modified. "When Neil and Robbie asked me to sing on the Last Waltz, they were so high, and they were so out of tune, I thought, 'How am I gonna do this?'" Joni told me.

The story has often been told that Joni sang on "Helpless" from behind a curtain, so as not to detract from making a grand entrance before it was time for her set. But Joni remembers it somewhat differently. "I said, 'I'll do it offstage,' because it was going to take such concentration." Neil and Robbie wanted her to "lock up with them in three-part harmony. No way I could do that," she recalled. "Their pitch was all over the place. And Neil calls out to me, 'Sing with me somehow,' not realizing why I can't. He was just unaware. CSN was always out of tune. They were never aware of how out of tune they were, partially because of drugs, I guess. When Neil played on 'Furry Sings the Blues' he had to play on four harmonicas. It was kind of adventuresome. It was very unusual harmonica."

The first shot of Scorsese's film is of the bass player Rick Danko setting up a pool table, explaining the terms of a game called "cutthroat." These were very competitive guys. It is sad to see Danko in the film, after the concert is over, listening to playbacks and unable to imagine the future. When the Band ended up going on the road without Robbie Robertson, the venues got smaller and sadder. Richard Manuel, who seemed to be crying for help in songs like "The Shape I'm In" and "Tears of Rage"—the latter cowritten with Bob Dylan and ending with the refrain "And life is brief"—hanged himself in a hotel room between gigs in 1986.

Joni didn't want to be a road hog or a road casualty. She sought refuge in it, and didn't want to see the concert mark the end of an era while she was still making new discoveries. Still, she didn't tour for another three years. Nor did she feel the desire to record, until one day, in 1977, at home in Bel-Air, she suddenly hobbled to the piano and began improvising chords. On guitar, she would do this by finding new tunings. But she was too weak for guitar. She had been sick for some time, in and out of the hospital. She hadn't really played piano since her tour was aborted early in 1976, so those eighty-eight keys had some novelty. In her weakened state, she felt a sense of the uncanny. It was somehow impossible for her to hit a wrong note. The more she explored, the more fascinating it became, so complex, and yet the combination of dissonance and euphony hit her sweet spot. Even in recovery, her jive detector was never wrong. She knew she had to commit this to record as soon as possible. A call to Henry Lewy was in order.

"Henry, I don't know what's happening, but I'm an idiot savant," Joni told him. "I haven't played it in three years, and all of a sudden I'm playing. You got to go into the studio and capture it. I can't hit a wrong chord. We've got to go into the studio."

"I'm sick," he replied.

"So am I. What's wrong with you?"

"I've got bursitis."

"Well, I'm just getting over abscessed ovaries," she said. "I'm coming back to life and gimping along. Let's go in."

And so they made their way back to A&M studios, far from hale and hearty, but with Joni's muse to spur them along. Joni, in increments (with cigarette breaks scheduled in), recorded a series of the same chords that had her feeling like a savant propped up from her sickbed. These improvisations added up to two hours of music, cut and spliced with tape, the old-fashioned, predigital way. If Joni knows anything about the piano, it is where middle C is, and that was the focal point; wherever she wandered, middle C was home. Joni then returned with lyrics that spilled over in what became "Paprika Plains," a song that would end up running more than sixteen minutes, with more than seventy lines that didn't make the final cut, but were included on the printed lyrics in parentheses.

Unlike "Both Sides, Now," where she would take huge themes—innocence and experience—and distill them to just three verses, "Paprika

Plains" is twice as long as "Song for Sharon," with more diffuse subject matter, all inspired by a cocaine-fueled dream she had had on the Rolling Thunder tour.

Childhood memories scatter. Fragments of her life as a young adult filter in. Then comes a memory from a 1965 concert with Chuck Mitchell in Winnipeg—the night she met Neil Young, as if she were free-associating an anthropological study of the ways of central Canadians: "Back in my hometown / They would have cleared the floor / Just to watch the rain come down / They're such sky-oriented people / Geared to changing weather." This actually happened at the concert. A storm broke out and the whole audience ran to the windows. Joni is remembering an agrarian prairie town where a rainfall could mean feast or famine. She and Neil would be destined for other things, but they hardly knew it then. From her perch in Bel-Air, she could look back on the people she grew up around, preoccupied with their crops. At that point, this was the only reality Joni of Saskatoon knew. A dozen years later, she would have lived many more lifetimes. She came to feel that people of warmer climes were warmer themselves, more open, more affectionate. Still, she never forgot the season cycle from the Great White North. It haunted her dreams, and it haunts this song. That prairie girl was in there, and reconciling where she came from with where she had arrived would take a very long song.

People were shocked when Bob Dylan had a hit with the six-minute "Like a Rolling Stone," and even more shocked when the Beatles had one with the eight-minute "Hey, Jude." But no one really thought that any song that ran over sixteen minutes, the way "Paprika Plains" did, was going to be a hit. Joni wasn't really thinking about hits at this point anyway. It was all about art, in the spirit of Beethoven scandalizing his audience with the *Eroica* Symphony, with its demanding length of more than fifty minutes, and responding with something even longer—the Ninth Symphony, which usually clocks in at more than *seventy* minutes.

"Paprika Plains" begins as a childhood dream, an earliest memory. It's about the clash between creativity and—in the worst and best sense—civilization, or as Huck Finn called it, "sivilization." Civilization has its discontents, of course, in this case, native people who "cut off their braids and lost some link with nature." "Paprika Plains" is about getting that link back, even if it's filtered through the memory of a little blond girl paired with Joni's untamed piano. This is the girl who fell in love with Rachmaninoff, then Debussy. And it was this inspired wild child who was capturing something primal, tribal, and improvised, and translating it into an orchestral suite. Through an arranger, Michael Gibbs, a professor at the Berklee School of Music, she got it all out—imperfectly, but soulfully.

Gibbs had been recommended by Jaco Pastorius, and Pastorius had told Gibbs that he'd showed Joni some piano exercises that had put the wind to her sails. "When I listened to it, I already knew that Jaco had shown her something at the piano that gave her a freedom, which is why the piece happened," Gibbs told me. "She was suddenly released from something, and this music poured out. She recorded nearly half an hour and edited to the version I got. It was a backwards kind of approach to then do the orchestra afterwards, but it seemed like a natural challenge to take on."

Jaco had the right guy with the right chops and the right eclecticism. They recorded in Columbia's 30th Street Studio, a former Greek Orthodox church known as the greatest studio in the world, where Glenn Gould recorded both his 1955 and his 1982 versions of Bach's *Goldberg Variations* and Miles Davis had recorded *Kind of Blue.*

Joni was nervous, daunted perhaps, by the challenge of keeping an improvised piano piece from getting lost in translation. She had to drag Henry Lewy to New York, with the incentive that Dizzy Gillespie was playing that week at Birdland. In his weakened state, he could not stop what was happening, and he wouldn't have been able to stop it even if he'd been stronger. His hands were trembling on the console, but that was preferable to leaving the recording in the hands of the second engineer they both deemed incompetent. "Paprika Plains" was too long to be a song, but did not have the multiple movements that would have made it a symphony. If one were to give it a name, it would be a Rhapsody in C.

Gibbs was enthralled with the material. "The roughness of her playing is part of its charm. The purpose was to give the piano part something to lie in. It was just exposed and it didn't have anything to hold it up, not only structurally, but to envelop it, like putting on a robe. When I met her to talk about it, I remember seeing the Grand Canyon as I flew, and it gave me the idea of plains, which is wide-open flat spaces, and paprika, which is hot. That had boiled one idea to an essence. What I ended up with sounded ice-cold to me, but it didn't matter. When I started talking to Henry and Joni like that, Joni looked really happy, because I wasn't talking about quarter notes and eighth notes. I wasn't talking about technical music, but poetic ideas. We got along very easily from the start and she never did give me any instruction. She never told me what she wanted me to do."

Gibbs brought first-call players, virtuosi as well versed in classical as they were in jazz, all handpicked by the violinist David Nadien. The jazz violinist Harry Lookofsky was on the date, as was Ron Carter, one of the greatest upright bass players in the history of jazz.

Given the stellar musicianship in the room, how, one might wonder, did the orchestra notoriously go out of tune? Most people can't hear it. And, as Gibbs points out, "It's not constantly out of tune, there's just a moment when it was out of tune," though that moment seems to last through much of the eighth minute. According to Joni, when she tried to point it out, Gibbs couldn't hear it, Henry couldn't hear it, and the assistant engineer couldn't hear it. But Jaco Pastorius noticed it right away: "There's out-of-tuneness there," he said. And when Joni met Charles Mingus the following year, the first thing he said to her was "The strings on 'Paprika Plains' are out of tune." She was impressed that he'd noticed, and replied, "Yeah! Did you hear that?" Mingus was taken aback. He thought he was telling her something she didn't already know.

So what happened? The problem was the improvisations, those Joni and Lewy had hastened into A&M studios to record, to capture the magic before it disappeared. There had been four of them, around half an hour each: one was thirty-one, one was twenty-nine, and two were thirty minutes long. (She would play until she needed a cigarette.) And then Joni and Lewy edited them down, and put the pieces together. The problem, said Gibbs, was this: "They were done on different days, and the tuning on the piano changed. So when we put it to-gether, we tuned to the piano at the beginning. When the piano's tuning shifted, the orchestra became out of tune. Usually, a piece for piano and orchestra has a fixed piano part, and then the pianist will work with the orchestra. What Joni did was not normally done. I never knew of anyone who worked this way."

Says Joni, "With Pro Tools, I could have gotten the middle part more accurate, but we had to cut tape, so it was pretty clumsy—the timing and the spaces between edits—because I cut that from two hours of improvisation down to ten minutes." But the sour notes were only part of the story of this ambitious and fecund piece of music. What soared above it were the most ambitious and expansive lyrics she would ever write, as open with possibility as the prairie sky.

A few years earlier, miles from the prairie, Joni found herself at a party thrown by Paul McCartney and Wings on the *Queen Mary*. She was seated with Bob Dylan, who, unlike Joni, doesn't dance. They talked about painting; Dylan was a neophyte student of Norman Raeben, the Russian-born painter who taught on the eleventh floor of Carnegie Hall. Dylan later said, "Five days a week I used to go up there, and I'd just think about it the other two days of the week. I used to be up there from eight o'clock to four. That's all I did for two months . . . It changed me. I went home after that and my wife never did understand me ever since that day. That's when our marriage started breaking up. She never knew what I was talking about, what I was thinking about. And I couldn't possibly explain it."

At the party, Joni asked him, if he could paint anything in the room, what would he paint?

"I'd paint this cup of coffee," he said.

Looking up, Joni said, "I'd paint that mirrored ball."

It was emblematic of their friendship that what felt like idle chit-chat would soon be captured in song. Soon after, Dylan wrote "One More Cup of Coffee." And Joni wrote these lines in the final section of "Paprika Plains":

You see that mirrored ball begin to sputter lights
And spin
Dizzy on the dancers
Geared to changing rhythms

Changing weather becomes changing rhythms. Now the disco ball is shining on the dancers, illuminated by an artificial globe. It's a continuum. She's still as "wide-eyed open to it all" as she was when she was "three feet tall." Everywhere she looks, she sees patterns and makes poetic images out of them. Like a medicine ball, the mirrored ball is moving, yet it is also a center, like coming back to middle C. That mirrored ball shines on everyone. Jaco Pastorius, John Guerin, and, for the first time, the great jazz saxophonist Wayne Shorter are all there to give her support, and to give the song a big summation, as harmonically rich as jazz and as rhythmically direct as rock and roll. They give a big and powerful resolution for a song that digs deep into the earth she sings about. Running away, coming back, running away again: it's a cycle that needs an entire side of an album to get it across. It could have gone for even longer if she had found a place for the additional seventy-plus lines on the jacket. Joni's cup runneth over, and it was as grand and sweeping as anything she would ever do. The dancers, the players, the dreams, all of it: she demanded much of herself, so it seemed only fair that she make demands of the listeners, too. "I'm floating back to you!" she sings at the end. To Don Alias? To her listeners? To reconcile her prairie girl self with her urban pop sophisticate self? "Paprika Plains" is Joni's most ambitious challenge yet—too big and sprawling to be a pop song, but too wild and untamed to be a concerto. *You think you can keep up with me? I dare you.*

23 ■ DON JUAN'S RECKLESS DAUGHTER

There are only three saxophone players Joni truly loves: Johnny Hodges of the Ellington band; Charlie Parker, pioneer of bebop; and Wayne Shorter.

She met Shorter at the Roxy in 1974, when they were walking in to see Miles Davis at the same time. Jaco Pastorius and Shorter were bandmates in the jazz-fusion group Weather Report, a collective that was, largely because of the Cult of Jaco, filling stadiums and playing to rock and roll–sized audiences. The more Pastorius took center stage, the more Shorter seemed to vanish in the distance, so much that a Weather Report album would be called *Mr. Gone*. But Pastorius was there to make a listener rethink the lower end. Shorter was there to make listeners marvel at how he could fill space with perfect and inspired impressionistic splashes.

When she reeled him in three years later to work on the album that would come to be called *Don Juan's Reckless Daughter*, she heard him talking to the rhythm section for "Paprika Plains," telling them to imagine a woman with her baby in a boat on a pond. *Whoosh!* Weather

Report might have called him Mr. Gone, and he may have painted "Mr. Weird" on his saxophone case, but he also called one of his own albums *The All Seeing Eye*. It described the vision that would make Shorter Joni's first-call sax player. He understood her weird chords, and a whole lot more. Mr. Gone was, for Joni, exactly where he needed to be.

Shorter first emerged as a tenor player who was the dominant composer for Art Blakey, then Miles Davis in what Davis called his second great quartet (1964–68). Davis, who was used to getting his way, had to wait for four years while Shorter was under contract with Blakey. It was worth the wait. Davis was resistant to the free jazz that had become so au courant with critics and younger, more progressive musicians. He hired a group of younger virtuosi, including a fledgling Herbie Hancock, who were stretching out (if also fearful of their leader, who was known, accurately, as the Prince of Darkness). During that period, Shorter would write compositions that would become part of the jazz canon: "Speak No Evil," "Footprints," "Wild Flower," "Masqualero," "Night Dreamer," "The All Seeing Eye," among many others. Some of these songs would appear on Shorter's Blue Note albums, some would become Davis staples.

When jazz fusion became the music's next, stadium-sized step, Shorter was on the vanguard of that, too, as a member of Weather Report, trading his tenor for a soprano so that he could be better heard above the electric instruments. And his conception on soprano was completely different from his tenor playing. Suddenly, he was no longer in the Sonny Rollins–John Coltrane school, but in a school of his own. He was suddenly using more space, like Miles. This suited Joni perfectly. Pastorius was the wild man, the maximalist, the baddest. Shorter was the visionary, holding back, taking the long view, assessing the broad expanse and putting in the right notes at the right time. Like Miles Davis, what he *didn't* play was as important as what he did.

In her years out of the studio, Joni had amassed enough material to fill another two-LP album. "Paprika Plains" would take up a whole side.

There was "Jericho." It had originally been recorded with the L.A. Express for *Miles of Aisles*, but now she had a chance to record it with Pastorius and Wayne Shorter. "Talk to Me" and "Don Juan's Reckless Daughter" had been written on the Rolling Thunder Revue in 1975 and played on her brief Hissing of Summer Lawns tour in the first two months of 1976. And "Dreamland" began as a demo dating to *The Hissing of Summer Lawns* in 1975.

Joni had Pastorius for all of those, and there was quite a percussion circle assembled for "Dreamland": Airto on surdo (bass drum), Jaco on cowbells, Manolo Badrena on congas, Alejandro (Alex) Acuña on shakers, and her lover Don Alias on snare drum and sandpaper blocks. Still, she felt something was missing. And so, as one does, she called her friend the R&B singer Chaka Khan in the middle of the night. Khan was the lead singer of the funk collective Rufus, who had won a Grammy for the funk classic "Tell Me Something Good," written and produced for them by Stevie Wonder. Joni and Chaka had made a connection. Khan worshipped Joni's music, and had come to a place of mutual admiration and emotional intimacy with her as a friend—a rarity for both of them, who tend to prefer the company of men.

"She called me at three in the morning and she wanted me to come to the studio," Khan recalled years later. "And I got my shit on and went down there. We were partying. That track was like a drum circle song. Joni added her vocals later. She told me to sing some stuff. She already had the bass vocal part—'Dreamland, Dreamland, Dreamland . . .' So I had a key. And she wanted me to sing some chanty stuff . . . I was glad to work with her, of course, but that wasn't the song I wanted to work with her on. I wanted to work with her on a real song. 'Dreamland' was kind of a chant. I wanted to sing with Joni, you know, *sing* together."

Chaka Khan, who has made deep and soulful covers of "Don't Interrupt the Sorrow," "The Hissing of Summer Lawns," and "Two Grey Rooms" (from 1991's *Night Ride Home*), had a particular Joni Mitchell song in mind. Still, she added the kind of voice that had not been heard on a Joni track before. Years later, in 2000, Khan was scheduled to cover "Dreamland" at a Joni Mitchell tribute concert on the TNT network. When she had to cancel at the last minute, she was replaced by the feminist gospel group Sweet Honey in the Rock, who, at the event, criticized Joni's lyrics and accused her of racism.

Khan was aghast. "You know what? The thing I love about her is she sings the truth, with no holds barred. She doesn't care about the social crap. She cuts through all that, and that's what I love about her." Whether it was the lines about black babies covered in baking flour or the image of Tar Baby and the Great White Wonder, Joni represented her unconscious, filled with unsettling images.

As Joni puts it: "It's a long, long way from Canada."

Two years after Joni was booed by a room of black female prisoners in New Jersey, in December 1977, *Don Juan's Reckless Daughter* was released. Many people who first saw the album cover may not have realized that the image of a black man in full pimp regalia, captured by Norman Seeff's camera, was Joni herself. Joni's provocation—a white woman dressed as a black male boss pimp—comes with historical baggage, much of which was unknown to her. Blackface minstrelsy—white performers blacking up with burnt cork and singing "coon songs," the most famous example of which was Ernest Hogan's "All Coons Look Alike to Me"—was the dominant form of popular entertainment after the Civil War, all the way through the 1920s vaudeville era. White performers would perform in terrifying makeup and do imitations— sometimes grotesque, sometimes in homage—of the black performers doing a far superior version of songs in early jazz and blues, although there were also famous black minstrel performers, most notably Bert Williams and Johnny Hudgins. *The Jazz Singer* (1927), the first talkie, was a sentimental biopic for Al Jolson, torn between his Jewish family's expectation for him to be a cantor, and his passionate need to sing "Mammy" in blackface.

Joni, defending her own costume, also defended Jolson. "Al Jolson's not a Stepin Fetchit," Joni told me. "He's a Jew in blackface, so he's always getting the better end of the deal, kind of like Bugs Bunny. And I didn't see anything derogatory. But the prejudice was enormous.

When I did that, people thought it was a bro, and it wasn't stereotypical, it was individual. Why I got away with it . . . I got the greatest reviews for that record in black magazines. They saw the brother, they reviewed it, and they *got* it."

It's not clear how many black journalists even recognized Joni on the cover of the album or how many black magazines actually reviewed it. The black music journalist Greg Tate, who interviewed Joni for *Vibe* magazine in 1998 and wrote a poem, "How Black Is Joni Mitchell?" for Joni's honorary doctorate ceremony a few years later, would come out in passionate support for what he called her "stunt." Janet Maslin was the only journalist for a major publication, *Rolling Stone*, to criticize Joni's album cover. "The album offers what is, one can only hope, the ultimate in cute cover art," Maslin wrote. She is blunt in her attack: "Here and elsewhere, there seems to be the notion that blacks and Third World people have more rhythm, more fun and a secret, mischievous viewpoint that the author, dressed as a black man in one of the photos on the front jacket, presumes to share."

Maslin didn't approve, but she was one of the few journalists who actually noticed. Joni's costume was so convincing, most people did not realize it was *her*.

After Joni failed to reach a room full of black female prisoners because she, as Joan Baez said, "couldn't do black," she decided she'd one-up them all by *being* black. "So there came Halloween, and I was walking down Hollywood Boulevard," Joni recalled. "There were a lot of people out on the street wearing wigs and paint and masks, and I was thinking, 'What can I do for a costume?' Then a black guy walked by me with a New York diddybop kind of step, and he said in the most wonderful way, *Lookin' good, sister, lookin' gooood*. His spirit was infectious and I thought, 'I'll go as him.' I bought the makeup, the wig, the sideburns, I went into a sleazy menswear [store] and bought a sleazy hat and a sleazy suit, and that night I went to a Halloween party and nobody knew it was me, nobody."

When Joni was planning a memoir, she said that the opening would be "I was the only black man at the party," and her intent was to be a combination of pimp and artistic creation. She would dress up as this character from time to time and never got spotted, even by men who should have known. Sometimes she would call this character Art Nouveau; other times he would be Claude the Pimp. In a 1979 concert taped for Showtime, in the middle of "Furry Sings the Blues," on the line "everybody's fly," she turned into her pimp character. What was troubling was that her desire to be the black man on the street superseded the unsettling history. Art Nouveau/Claude the Pimp, as he appears on the cover of *Don Juan's Reckless Daughter*, is a dead ringer for Zip Coon, the minstrel character ridiculed for trying to dress the part of a gentleman. Zip Coon, like Jim Crow and Tambo, was a standard figure in minstrel shows. Zip Coon was the dandy, Tambo was the singing, dancing fool, and Jim Crow was ignorant and poor—a pretty accurate indicator for the intentions behind the Jim Crow laws. And yet Chaka Khan, who, as a teenager, had been a member of the militant Black Panther party, had no problem with the cover of the album for which she provided vocals. "I loved the cover of *Don Juan's Reckless Daughter*," she said unequivocally. "She's into color. She's a world of person, and she lived that, she sang that, she is that. I am, too. It's a beautiful thing. It's a way to go."

Joni debuted her costume at a 1976 Halloween party at the house of Peter Asher, the manager of James Taylor and Linda Ronstadt. A decade later, Asher would become Joni's manager as well. "She looked great," he recalled. "She had done a serious job of preparation. Nobody knew it, not even John David Souther." John David—known as J. D. Souther, who coauthored many Eagles hits and a few on his own—was, indeed, among the suckered guests, an especially impressive triumph considering that he was sleeping with her at the time. "Joan and I never saw each other exclusively," said Souther, decades later. "She really challenged my writing. Joan has a very sharp tongue when she wants to. She said, 'Well, John David, we're still waiting for your work to live up to your ego.'"

Maybe Joni should have been worried about how her alter ego would be perceived. But she wasn't. She never doubted that people—black and white—would "get it." And just as likely, she didn't care.

———

By the time Joni recorded *Don Juan's Reckless Daughter*, she was not only impersonating a black man but was in a serious relationship with one. Joni, at five feet six inches, was nearly a foot shorter than Don Alias, the mighty percussionist, someone she regarded as not only a swinging and soulful kit drummer but also a top-three auxiliary player— especially congas and bongos—in the world. Don Alias played auxiliary percussion on *Don Juan's Reckless Daughter* and would later play drums on her 1979 Shadows and Light tour. He came with an impressive résumé: He was in Nina Simone's trio and played on three Miles Davis albums, including *Bitches Brew*, where he played the trap set part on "Miles Runs the Voodoo Down," because he was the only one to get the slow, funky, swinging march feel Davis was looking for. Joni had loved Miles Davis's music since high school, and she would often cite his influence on her singing, especially on the title track of *Blue*. It was Joni's dream to play with Davis one day. Maybe Alias could help.

Between 1975 and 1981, Davis had retired from music. He was ensconced in his lair on West Seventy-seventh Street, doing any drugs he could get his hands on, and getting into as much group sex as he could get into, often as an observer, since the drugs had siphoned his libido.

Alias was usually possessive, but Miles was like a god to him. He delivered his woman to him. The rest was farce.

In 2015, nine years after Alias's death, Joni's encounter with Miles still amused her, sort of. Alias and Joni went to Davis's apartment. Joni had been given a small budget for a television special that never got made. She wanted Davis to appear as a guest, but, typically, he wanted the special's entire budget for himself, and this was in the midst of his six-year silent period. He hated the music business as much as Joni did. He said, as if offering a ransom note, that he wouldn't come out until someone paid him $1 million. "That was back in the days when a million dollars was a million dollars," Joni recalled. "I didn't blame him. I completely understood it, but he was killing himself in the meantime; he was so coked out. [Don brought Joni to Miles and] Miles kicked Don out of the room. And then he came on to me. And I thought, 'Oh, my God.' Don, with all his jealousy, didn't stay there to protect me. So I had to protect myself, which I can do pretty well. It was a funny scene, really. But I strayed into his web. That's all he was doing, escaping into sex and drugs in there. He had no respect for Don, but Don and everybody else admired Miles so much. He lunged towards me on the couch and I jumped up. And he flew off the couch with his hands around my ankle—and passed out. So I'm there with Miles clinging to my ankle, out cold. And I had to call for this crazy, jealous man, Don, and I was worried that he would accuse me of instigating it. He was insanely jealous. But anyway, we had to peel Miles off of my ankle, and he had a dead man's grip on it. It was a funny scene."

Maybe one day Miles would clean up and ask her to collaborate with him. There weren't many people she looked up to, but Miles Davis, at his best, was one of them. Sure, he could behave like a monster, but so could Picasso. Miles did stage a comeback with *The Man with the Horn*, but it was never the same. Joni knew that the great man had become considerably less great. Miles's final decade, for those who loved him at his peak, was just sad. "Miles at the end would play three notes and walk around, because his bands were so terrible and there was no inspiration," she said.

Joni couldn't get exactly what she wanted. But another opportunity came along, one that would give her an unexpected education, from another jazz giant.

24 ■ *MINGUS*

When *Don Juan's Reckless Daughter* achieved gold status—despite the fact that its singles failed to crack the Top 40—it seemed that Joni was that rara avis in pop music, an uncompromising artist who blissfully ignores commercial pressures, keeps evolving and experimenting in public, and still comes out ahead. Half a million copies of *Don Juan's Reckless Daughter* were sold—or at least shipped—in three months, and it entered the charts at an underwhelming but still respectable number twenty-five. The single "Off Night Backstreet," with backing vocals by Glenn Frey and J. D. Souther, who were making the charts elsewhere, did not register. Even if half a million record buyers were not necessarily hip to the audacity of Jaco or the subtlety of Wayne or a rhapsody that lasted more than sixteen minutes—nearly half of it taken up by a meandering orchestral suite occupying a side of an album (pushing it to become a double album, bumping the price up)—they were still invested in this woman who, even as she changed, took her sincerity with her. She was fleeing the mainstream, sure, but she wasn't fleeing her listeners, not yet.

The decade had begun with *Ladies of the Canyon*, an album that captured the zeitgeist and was loaded with hits, a triple whammy of "Big Yellow Taxi," "Woodstock," and "The Circle Game." It is a long way from there to the experiments and liberties of *Don Juan's Reckless Daughter*. But even though she was testing attention spans and baffling some critics, she held on to her audience, who were growing up, too. They, too, were having their sexual experiments, their spiritual quests, their broken families. Joni may have been writing for herself and her intimates, but her output in the '70s was, unintentionally, in sync with the decade's private and public life. Joni would later refer to the '80s as "The Lost Years." She would be told that she was out of sync with the time. Thank God, she thought. To be in sync with the '80s, she later wrote, "was to be degenerating both morally and artistically." She would have one more album and tour before she was done with her decade.

Among the listeners who were reacting to *Don Juan's Reckless Daughter*—the two records, the insatiable musical ambition, the black male costume on the cover—was the Italian record and film producer Daniele Senatore, who had produced a film, *Todo Modo* (1976), with a score by the legendary Charles Mingus, although none of Mingus's music ended up on-screen. (The score was entirely by Ennio Morricone.) The unused score represented a departure Mingus had been wanting to make since first teaching himself music theory—including the twelve-tone method of Arnold Schoenberg, which he had been studying since he was a teenager back in the 1930s, before Schoenberg was widely taught in school. But just as Mingus was continuing to move ahead, he was, suddenly and shockingly, diagnosed with ALS (amyotrophic lateral sclerosis, also known as Lou Gehrig's disease), a rapidly progressive degenerative motor neuron disease. Most people who get diagnosed with it die within a couple of years. (The quantum physicist

Stephen Hawking is an extremely prominent and rare exception.) The colossus of the upright bass—the loud, angry genius, the troublemaker—would be wheelchair-bound and struggling to speak.

Mingus was well known as one of the greatest bass players and bandleaders in jazz, but he wanted, above all, to be recognized as a great composer. He had played behind Louis Armstrong, Duke Ellington, and Charlie Parker, the three greatest figures in all of jazz history, and yet these gigs were but a footnote. His body of work was huge and wildly ambitious; he was a shambolic personality who produced music that packed a distinctive punch in more ways than one. He was known to fire and rehire musicians in a single set. He broke a stage light at the Village Vanguard that was never replaced. He punched the trombonist Jimmy Knepper in the mouth, breaking one of Knepper's teeth and ruining his embouchure—and attenuating his top octave—for several months. And yet Knepper kept working for Mingus anyway.

Joni knew where Mingus was coming from. "I hear too well, and I need purity of spirit," she told me. "It's the same thing with my master, Chögyam Trungpa. People would play music. He hated everything that they played. He told them to listen to me. I know why. It's the same reason Mingus listened to me, or Judy Garland, there's another one—pure. There's no guile in that music. There's no guile in Miles, even though he was a bad boy, offstage. He was pure as could be onstage. Mingus would punch players and say, 'You're falsifyin' your emotion!' Most people can't hear that. The phony note." Joni and Mingus were simpatico spirits.

Mingus could also be tender and sensitive, writing beautiful and complex love songs—"Celia" for his second wife, "Sue's Changes" for his fourth—that reflected his stormy, romantic, and all-too-human heart. Mingus's work is as demanding as it is pleasurable. Melody lines lead to unfamiliar places. Horns collide and work it out on the bandstand. Mingus took all that anger and sweetness and confusion and put it on his charts, indulging the brilliance of the multi-reedist Eric Dolphy and the pianist Don Pullen, two unorthodox virtuosi who played outside the laws of harmony, but in a way that fit into his own artfully constructed compositions, where chaos would come and go and come again. The most basic of jazz collections would be incomplete without at least a couple of these: *Pithecanthropus Erectus* (1956), *East Coasting* (1957), *Mingus Ah Um* (1959), *Mingus Dynasty* (1959), *The Black Saint and the Sinner Lady* (1963), *Mingus in Europe* (Volumes 1 & 2, 1964), *Let My Children Hear Music* (1972), *Changes One* (1974), and *Changes Two* (1975), among others. As he was nearing the end of his recording career, he was exploring the untrodden South American rhythms known as *cumbia*. He was still reaching for something new to the bitter end.

Mingus kept the past alive while looking to the future. His music is jam-packed with Dixieland, church shouting, Ellingtonia, bebop drive, and classical ambition. In a Mingus composition, many moments in jazz history are happening at once. Mingus manhandles that bass like no one else, and he makes the chaos sound intentional, artful, as passionate, violent, and vivid as Picasso's *Guernica*. Some of his ensembles were called the Mingus Workshop, and they were like group therapy, a wrestling match, or a think tank for improvisers, a place for instruments to come together, argue, and come together again. He looked deep within himself and once wrote a song called "All the Things You Could Be by Now If Sigmund Freud's Wife Was Your Mother."

In an idiom where even Duke Ellington, Charlie Parker, and Miles Davis sometimes took credit for songs they didn't write, or fully write, Mingus's accomplishments stand on their own. If his emotional volatility made it hard to organize his life—or maintain the kind of loyalty among band members that was part of Ellington's genius and Miles's aura—his compositions were his and his alone, with idiosyncratic touches like flamenco guitar, spoken-word rambles, and a cacophony that always made musical sense. There was no one like him. Mingus seemed larger than life—even larger than death. The final humiliation of such a terrible illness was a matter between him and the God he still wanted to write for. When Miles Davis and the rest went for fusion in the late '60s, he just kept writing for upright bass, acoustic piano, and brass, and had some great years before ALS did him in. In his final, terrible year of 1978, life was slipping from him each day, and he needed to do something to spread the word—maybe find a new audience for his records. Damn, he was fifty-five years old and not ready to check out. The concert stage was finally opening up for him! He was just getting ready for his renaissance.

Sue Graham Mingus, his indefatigable wife—who knew a thing or two about working the press when she edited the hip magazine *Changes*—was frantically looking for a final project. She wrote some lyrics for his songs, but they weren't good enough. The Philharmonic was booked. She needed something big right away. Daniele Senatore showed Sue and Charles the cover of *Don Juan's Reckless Daughter* and played it for them. Joni was clearly more than jazz curious, and was even using her record cover to explore her inner (and outer) black man. Could this be the woman to give Charles a fancy funeral? Could this be a way for Joni to get some musical education from a true master? They sent smoke signals in Joni's direction, and they wanted to give her an impression that Mingus, who had actually been unfamiliar with Joni's work, was a fan of "Paprika Plains," and admired how she was stretching out with Jaco Pastorius and other musicians not exactly on his radar. It hardly mattered. Not only was Joni summoned, she was importuned, but by the great man himself, a shrewd tactic on Sue's part.

Shortly after finding out that he was dying of ALS, Mingus invited Senatore over. "I want to talk to you about God," he said. Daniele said, "You've got the wrong guy," and suggested he read T. S. Eliot's *Four Quartets*. Reading *Four Quartets* is a sublime and distilled way of talking about God, in particular the God of Anglicanism, to which Eliot converted upon becoming a British subject in 1927—whether you believe in that God or not. *Four Quartets* is a devotional poem, but it is also apocalyptic, published in 1943, two years before the end of World War II. Although Eliot would live until 1965—and receive the Nobel Prize for Literature in 1948—*Four Quartets* would be his final major work of poetry. Mingus had a sense of eloquent farewell. "Burnt Norton," the first of the quartets and originally conceived as a stand-alone farewell to the medium, begins with these lines, "Time present and time past / Are both perhaps present in time future," and ends with

"Quick now, here, now, always— / Ridiculous the waste sad time / Stretching before and after." This was absurdity, this was keeping track of the clock, this was memory, and it was indisputably beautiful.

"Quick now, here, now, always": the poem is circular in its sense of time. The fire of cremation and the rose of fertility are one. Mingus, whose fecundity was fading fast, could dig this mixture of pastoral, eulogy, and ritual. He felt he could set it to music as a big send-off, the epitaph he had struggled to write on and off for decades. But he had to do it fast and make a little green while he was at it.

Joni, upon reading *Four Quartets*, was not inspired by it at all, and she was convinced that Mingus didn't even understand a lot of it. It is a good thing that she never told him this. Although Joni wrote poetic lyrics, her interest in poetry was very limited, mostly to poems she had memorized in high school, along with a little Leonard Cohen and what he recommended to her back in '67. "It certainly wasn't appropriate literature for a man who just found out that he was going to die," Joni told me, even though it actually seemed very apropos. "Mingus couldn't get anything nourishing out of it. And he didn't understand a lot of it. There was a lot of pseudo depth, a lot of tricky wordplay in it, but not a lot of meat. I always think poetry is kind of like cracking sunflowers with your nails to get the meat out. It's a lot of work for very little reward, in most cases. Even the hallowed ones among them. I didn't see that it had any kind of great pertinence to Charles's situation. But, still, the first project that he offered me was that he was going to get an Englishman with an Oxford or Eton accent, an upper-crusty accent to read passages from the *Four Quartets*. Then he wanted me to translate it into what he called 'the vernacular,' to make sense of it, if there was anything to glean from it. So that you could get something out of it so that you didn't have to crack this nugget with your fingernails, right? He likened it to tag-team preachers. Apparently, in some churches, you have a guy reading the 'thee, thou' text and another one putting it into street or bebop language. And he wanted me to play acoustic guitar. He was an acoustic man. He was a folkie in jazz. He didn't like electric jazz at all."

Joni knew almost nothing about Mingus—including his ability to comprehend T. S. Eliot. In fact, unlike Joni, Mingus loved poetry. His second wife, Celia Zaentz, recalled him wooing her with his own poems. He recorded part of an album with Langston Hughes and conscripted Allen Ginsberg to perform an ad hoc wedding ceremony with Sue Graham. He performed with the Beat poet Kenneth Patchen, and in 1972, wrote an unconventional string quartet (two violas and two cellos) as a setting for "The Clown," by the great New York School poet Frank O'Hara. A manuscript in the Charles Mingus Collection at the Library of Congress reveals a setting of "A Sane Revolution," a poem by D. H. Lawrence. And so forth.

John Guerin told her she would be crazy to give up this opportunity. He was also more than annoyed that it had landed in the lap of someone who knew so little about Mingus. She absolutely *had* to do this, he told her. Most musicians he knew would kill for this opportunity. She'd better learn fast.

Elliot Roberts and David Geffen, who had guided her career with so much freedom and so much care, thought it was finally time to intervene. They begged her not to take on this collaboration. Joni, you're going to lose your audience! Joni, you will be banned from the airwaves! And you will never recover!

When she first met Mingus, he was already in a wheelchair, facing the Hudson River. He had not yet lost his ability to provoke. "That song 'Paprika Plains,'" he told her. "The strings are out of tune." Mingus was testing Joni, but she adored him immediately and, of course, agreed with him about the strings on "Paprika Plains." She wished someone else had noticed. Illness had made Mingus vulnerable. He was sweet, but she saw the devil in him, too. Joni takes pride in her jive detector, and she knew that she was in the presence of the real thing.

When Joni read *Four Quartets*, she said she concluded that she'd rather set the King James Bible to music. The poem wasn't too daunting—she just didn't think it had enough meat on it. It reminded her of a quotation from Nietzsche she enjoyed repeating: "Poets muddy the water to make it seem deep." Anyway, wasn't she there for lyrics?

It was for the best that Joni didn't appreciate Eliot; she, not Eliot, was to be Mingus's scribe. Mingus figured this out pretty fast. It wasn't long until Mingus informed her that he had written seven pieces, titled "Joni I," "Joni II," all the way to "Joni VII." Mingus composed these melodies by singing weakly into a tape recorder; they were then set with chords by the arranger Sy Johnson. The melodies sound so peripatetic, it is a testimony to Joni's powers that she could find words for three of them. After all, it's not as if she had a background in doing such things. In the liner notes to the album, she compared turning these melodies into songs with lyrics to jumping into deep water, and it was not an exaggeration. Letting Jaco and Wayne riff behind you was one thing; this project was the biggest musical dare she had ever received, even bigger than "Paprika Plains." She was charged with taking Mingus's final melodies—with chords far more weird and obscure than anything Joni was accused of playing—and not only finding lyrics for them but words that would express the dying wishes of this larger-than-life genius.

"What's the first melody about?" Joni asked of "Joni I." She couldn't read music, so she was looking for a theme before she got a chance to hear it.

"Some things I'm gonna miss," he said.

Joni saw Mingus facing the Hudson River—looking north to the wilderness of the New Jersey Palisades and forward to construction of high-rises he knew he would never see completed—thinking of all the styles of music he wouldn't explore, all the musicians he wouldn't hire and fire, all the friends he'd miss, and, of course, all the beautiful lovers he would never get a chance to kiss. Mingus was entering a liminal space between life and death. ALS would make Mingus mourn himself, while watching others mourn for him.

The apartment on the forty-fourth floor of Manhattan Plaza had a spectacular view, but he felt like a hostage. The adventure was winding down. Joni took on his voice, his rage against the dying of the light. In his final summer, Mingus would be invited to a jazz performance at the Carter White House—the one where Dizzy and the onetime peanut farmer president shared a mic on "Salt Peanuts"—and, when everyone stood up for him, this guy who slapped the bass with as much force as anyone, and who could no longer play, was reduced to a quivering mess of tears. Joni, taken by the authentic and profound gravity of Mingus's condition, wrote an elegy. He knew that her voice would be narrating his music, his life. Blond Miss Thing would somehow become Mingus's spirit, and get his last melodies out to the world. He called her "Hillbilly" and "that skinny-ass folk singer." She adored him. He trusted her. After she had written some lyrics, she called him and asked, "How are you?"

"Oh, I'm dying," he said.

Joni had never put her voice or lyrics to someone else's music before, but this was an extraordinary figure in a dire circumstance. The idea of missing things was enough to fill a song. Sonny Rollins was making frequent visits, as were other musicians, including Dexter Gordon and Jack Walrath, who had played trumpet in some of Mingus's last ensembles, and who lived in the same building. Ornette Coleman stopped by, despite Mingus's backhanded compliment, back in 1959, that he was "playing wrong right." Even Jimmy Knepper, who got punched and severely injured onstage for "falsifyin' his emotion," called him in April 1978 on what would be Mingus's final birthday. Rivalries and alliances were all melting together on this farewell tour.

In addition to the seven melodies, Mingus instructed Joni to write lyrics for two melodies from his 1959 classic album *Mingus Ah Um*. One had the painterly title of "Self-Portrait in Three Colors," a composition that actually sounds closest to Joni's approach on *Mingus* to anything Mingus actually did. The song has an elaborate melody, with an impressionistic meeting of euphony and dissonance that would hit Joni's sweet spot. But what made it most like Joni's *Mingus* album is that it has no solos. It's like a classical piece for a jazz ensemble. Miles Davis's "Nefertiti," one of Joni's favorites, was also recorded this way, but only because the band made the spontaneous decision to keep repeating the melody, building up momentum with each turnaround. "Self-Portrait in Three Colors" was planned without solos, using subtle variations in tone in each verse. The three colors are the three verses. The first verse features a unison of the alto saxophonist John Handy with the tenor saxophonists Booker Ervin and Shafi Hadi; the second verse adds Jimmy Knepper on trombone; and on the third verse, Handy, Ervin, and Hadi break away from one another, then come back, Handy ending with a lingering, rhapsodic flourish. When Joni was at work on the album, she mentioned "Self-Portrait in Three Colors" among the album's projected contents. Even though the track was never finalized, the song would, consciously or not, provide a template for Joni's method and feeling. The balladic pace became fit for a dirge.

"Goodbye Pork Pie Hat," another ballad and perhaps Mingus's best-loved composition, was a requiem for Lester Young, the great tenor saxophonist, whose cool style would be, to Mingus's chagrin, imitated by an entire school known as "Cool Jazz." Even though Rahsaan Roland Kirk had already written lyrics for it (on his 1976 album *The Return of the 5000 Lb. Man*), Mingus believed that Joni could write better ones. He also told her to take John Handy's classic solo and make vocalese lyrics out of it. Joni initially balked.

"Why don't you get Jon Hendricks?" she asked. "He's the best bebop lyricist."

"I did," said Mingus. "Do you want to hear it?"

Mingus played it for Joni. "What do you think?" he asked.

"Oh, my God, it's maudlin," Joni said.

"Isn't it? The poor black guy this and the poor black guy that."

Now Joni had to outdo one of her few teenage heroes. And so she wandered all over Manhattan singing Handy's solo to herself, looking everywhere for inspiration. If you can believe in Magic Mind, you can think that the universe—or, in this case, Manhattan—is laid out with you in mind. Indeed, walking around Harlem, it seemed that she was given a sign. The song now had a structure. She just needed to know what to do with it. Mingus talked to Joni about Lester Young, who inspired the song. "This guy was the sweeeetest guy," Mingus told her. Mingus was lamenting a great who was gone, while Mingus himself was a great who was about to go, too. Joni wanted that lyric to contain both of them. The first verse was easy, but the rest of it was still a mystery. "HURRY UP PLEASE ITS TIME," wrote T. S. Eliot in *The Waste Land*. No doubt. She was dating Don Alias at this point, and they decided to get off the subway a block early. "And we came out near a manhole with steam rising all around us, and about two blocks ahead of us was a group of black guys—pimps, by the look of their hats—circled around, kind of leaning over into a circle," Joni recalled. "It was this little bar with a canopy that went out to the curb. In the center of them are two boys, maybe nine years old or younger, doing this robot-like dance, a modern dance, and one guy in the ring slaps his knees and says, 'Ahaaah, that looks like the end of tap dancing, for sure!' So we look up ahead, and in red script on the next bar down, in bright neon, it says 'Charlie's.' All of a sudden I get this vision, I look at that red script, I look at these two kids, and I think, 'The generations . . .' Here's two more kids coming up in the street—talented, drawing probably one of their first crowds, and it's . . . to me, it's like Charlie and Lester. That's enough magic for me, but the capper was when we looked up on the marquee that it was all taking place under. In big capital letters, it said 'PORK PIE HAT BAR.' All I had to do was rhyme it, and you had the last verse."

She walked right into the clue for the lyrics: a bar called Charlie's and a club called Pork Pie Hat Bar. It was just too perfect. How could Mingus be suffering such a cruel fate and Joni find inspiration laid out for her like that? Joni would have her moments grappling with fate later, though none so brutal as what Mingus was enduring. There was the story of Joni and Mingus and then there was the story of Mingus and Lester, which starts off the song, and, in a way, closes the circle, too.

A few years after the release of *Mingus*, Joni recalled a confrontation with Vic Garbarini, whom she described as a "pompous, stout, full-of-himself jazz writer," who thought she was out of her depth. He said that the word on the street was that she was pretentious. This was around the time that Rickie Lee Jones said that Joni wasn't a jazz singer, that she didn't walk on the jazz side of life. She compared Joni singing jazz to Barbra Streisand singing rock and roll. Rickie Lee Jones sang with a fake black accent. Wasn't that pretentious? Now Garbarini was accusing Joni of being pretentious.

"Okay, what am I pretending to be that I am not?"

Silence.

"Well, you do know what the word *pretentious* means, don't you?"

Silence.

"What's pretentious?"

Garbarini then quoted the lyric "The sweetest swinging music man had a Porky Pig hat on."

"You think that's pretentious? That's from Mingus. Because I'm his scribe. If he tells me, Lester Young had a Porky Pig hat on, that's colorful. I'm gonna take that down. What's pretentious about that?"

"That's not what it means," said Garbarini. "It's a derogatory term for porkpie hat."

Joni said, "You'd better take that up with the ghost of Charles Mingus. And besides, Porky Pig did wear a porkpie hat. What's pretentious about that? Look, here's the problem. You're gonna single me out as pretentious in a country where ninety-nine percent of all singers, no matter where they're from, sing with a fake black southern accent? The problem is probably that I'm the least pretentious and that's what's most pretentious about me." Boom.

Lester Young wore that Porky Pig hat back in his halcyon days with Count Basie in the 1930s, when he and Coleman Hawkins would play dueling tenors into the Kansas City night. When Mingus met Young, Mingus was in the same position that Joni was in twenty years later. Mingus was, like Joni in 1977, in his mid-thirties, with many years of triumphs and humiliations ahead of him; he was young and vital, and he saw this great man entering his final months, not quite making it to fifty. Young's wife on Long Island kicked him out, and so he spent his final months in a Manhattan apartment at the corner of Fifty-second Street and Broadway, not too far from where Mingus would be looking out into the Hudson. Mingus and Young watched a Cadillac they knew was owned by Stan Getz, a man Young might have called, in one of his coinages, half a motherfucker. "There's a guy who's driving a Cadillac on money from the way I play," said Young. Mingus's elegy is for Young's sound, ripped off, exploited, and misunderstood; what sounded cool was really Young's lyricism, his mellow tone (to use an Ellingtonism), and his impeccable command of space. When he and Billie Holiday recorded and performed together, she called him Mr. President and he called her Lady Day, and there was nothing cool about it. They approached ballads the way they were meant to be approached, waiting on the beat, sure, but brimming with warm bodies and vital souls. But Joni's lyrics merely mention Lester Young. They are really about how a black-and-tan fantasy became fate, how the New York streets were now safe for a black and white couple.

Lester Young had to suffer the indignities of being a man of greatness, one even elected Mr. President or Pres by Billie Holiday, who still had to sit at the back of the bus:

> *Black musician*
> *In those days they put him in an*
> *Underdog position*

The "underdog position" is a reference to Mingus's outlandish memoir *Beneath the Underdog*, which Joni was flipping through for quick inspiration. It might have also predicted the commercial trajectory for *Mingus*, which would enter the charts at number seventeen (phenomenal for a jazz-themed album), but fall fast.

This was new territory for Joni. Ever since she escaped the producer Paul Rothchild and bonded with her "more than an engineer" Henry Lewy, Joni hadn't needed to please anyone but herself. It was an honor to get the call from Mingus, sure, but he was demanding, challenging; if she deviated from a note he had written, he would upbraid her, and she wasn't used to being scolded by anyone, including a dying jazz god. How could Joni satisfy herself and honor a great man's dying wishes at the same time? "I didn't really know what the disease was going to do," Joni told me. "He was already in a wheelchair, and his speech was suffering. But it hadn't gone yet. I kind of live more for what's happening anyway, so I wasn't thinking in paranoid ways. As it came near the end, I didn't want him to die before I finished 'Goodbye Pork Pie Hat.' And I had a hell of a time getting that last verse until the magic happened. But he hated what I did."

But her wish to do him justice was superseded by her wish—her need—to do *herself* justice.

Finally, the record named for Mingus became a Joni Mitchell record. She would get to know him, study him, his personality, his memories, his sadness. But he would, in the end, become another one of her subjects. And even when she wanted listeners to imagine Mingus singing, she could only be assured with her own musicians playing the electric instruments Mingus abhorred. He would have appreciated a piano solo by, say, Don Pullen—his recent pianist of choice and a master of percussive dissonance and swing. On the other hand, Herbie Hancock on a Fender Rhodes, no matter how eloquent, would not have been a sound that pleased him. But then anyone familiar with Joni knew that she wouldn't be able to submit to Mingus's predilections anyway. The Fender Rhodes and fretless bass would have to be there. And three members of Weather Report—along with the head of the Headhunters—would be her band. It was not music Mingus approved of, but then he wasn't around to complain. So she went back to A&M studios in LA and cut it with Herbie Hancock, Wayne Shorter, Jaco Pastorius, and Peter Erskine. Mingus did, after all, hire Joni to write his epitaph.

People have wondered why the tempo on *Mingus* is so slow. In part, it was because of the elegiac nature of the material. This was certainly not consistent with Mingus's music, nor did it have the rhythmic variety of *Don Juan's Reckless Daughter*. The tempos of Weather Report ran at breakneck speeds. But the focus on *Mingus* would be the voice, lyrics, and melody. Anything as jam-packed as a Mingus session could be too distracting from getting the words out—or for giving enough space for Joni and her demands for audacity from Pastorius and minimalism from everyone else.

Similarly, many people in the jazz world have wondered why an album devoted (mostly) to Charles Mingus's music and featuring some of jazz's most stellar improvisers (even if they were not from Mingus's inner circle) had Herbie Hancock and Wayne Shorter discreetly riffing behind Joni, without any real solos. The album was less than forty minutes and certainly could have had room. But Erskine explained that maintaining those tempos was a challenge, and stretching the songs further just didn't feel right. Herbie and Wayne and Jaco could be heard taking solos on many records. This was a record guided by a voice.

Decades later, Herbie Hancock looked back on the album as the beginning of a friendship and satisfying collaborations to come. Hancock had been a child classical piano prodigy who played a movement of a Mozart piano concerto with Rafael Kubelík and the Chicago Symphony when he was eleven. His love for Ravel led him to embrace the jazz impressionism of Bill Evans. But at the same time, he loved rhythm and blues, and embraced both equally. He joined the Miles Davis Quintet at the age of twenty-three. He had already scored a hit when Mongo Santamaria covered his song "Watermelon Man." Herbie heard Miles whisper to him, "Take out the butter notes," when he really meant "bottom notes," but the point stuck. Herbie learned to do more with less, except when doing more with more was so powerful, he had to do that, too. Wayne Shorter was the dominant composer of the band, and they were kindred spirits, playing on each other's Blue Note dates while steering on Miles's second great ensemble.

They both became Nichiren Buddhists, and were both looking for something beyond jazz, beyond genre. It could include what was popular, but only if it fed the muse. By the '70s, they had both moved to Los Angeles. Shorter was playing with Weather Report, who were playing stadium shows with crowds that usually turned out for rock stars, and Hancock was having hugely successful albums with the Headhunters. Hancock and Shorter would periodically reunite for the VSOP (Very Special Occasion Project), which was the Miles band with Freddie Hubbard filling in for Miles. It was in this on-again, off-again moment—when they would dip in and out between fusion and traditional jazz—that they found themselves on the *Mingus* album. They were Miles people, not Mingus people, and Joni preferred it that way, since she was more of a Miles person, too. They were post-genre musicians and found themselves at home on a project where Joni was struggling with the musicians recommended by Mingus.

Joni and Herbie premiered "A Chair in the Sky" at the Bread and Roses Festival in Berkeley in the summer of 1978. "I love to play with Herbie," she told the audience afterward, and she did, even when he made it hard for her to find a space to come in. Even when it made her uneasy, she knew the results would be glorious. They both had Miles-shaped ambitions and compulsions to move forward, purists be damned, all the way to his Grammy-winning album *River: The Joni Letters*.

As Mingus deteriorated, Joni knew that he wouldn't live to hear this final album, but others would.

"You're playing a square note!" he would say when she was writing "Sweet Sucker Dance."

"What's square about a note?" Joni asked.

"Okay, motherfucker, you throw in your note with my note, and I'll throw in a grace note for God!"

Mingus's final months were spent on a wild-goose chase. The baritone saxophonist Gerry Mulligan recommended that Mingus be treated by a faith healer in Mexico named Pachita, and Mingus was so desperate, he followed the tip. Joni came along for the ride for ten days. Pachita conducted a ritual that purported to use Mingus's blood, but really did not. Mingus and Joni looked at each other when each realized she was a fake. They both had their jive detectors, even as his fuse was about to go out for good. They could communicate with each other, even when Mingus was nonverbal.

Don't blow my songs, he might have been thinking.

"It's my solo while you're away," she sang.

Mingus died on January 5, 1979 (along with, according to the album's liner notes, fifty-six beached whales). The album was released in June.

There are two songs on *Mingus* composed entirely by Joni—"The Wolf That Lives in Lindsey" and "God Must Be a Boogie Man," the last song written. Even though the lyrics and music are credited to Joni, the words are based on the first chapter of Mingus's memoir, *Beneath the Underdog*. In it, Mingus is trying to work out his dreams, his existential dilemmas, and his identity. "In other words, I am three," says the opening line. "One man stands forever in the middle, unconcerned, unmoved, watching, waiting to be allowed to express what he sees to the other two. The second man is like a frightened animal that attacks for fear of being attacked. There's an almost over-loving gentle person who lets people into the uttermost sacred temple of his being and he'll take insults and sign contracts without reading them and get talked down to working for cheap or nothing, and when he realizes what's been done to him he feels like killing and destroying everything around him including himself for being so stupid. But he can't—he goes back inside himself."

Considering Mingus's ambitions, his burdens, his history, his sensitivity, and his bathos, it should be considered a psychological miracle that he could pare all his necessary selves to merely three. In 1903, the great W.E.B. Du Bois wrote about the "double-consciousness" one feels as a minority in a majority culture:

It is a peculiar sensation, this double-consciousness, this sense of always looking at one's self through the eyes of others, of measuring one's soul by the tape of a world that looks on in amused contempt and pity. One ever feels his two-ness,—an American, a Negro; two souls, two thoughts, two unreconciled strivings; two warring ideals in one dark body, whose dogged strength alone keeps it from being torn asunder.

It was this double-consciousness that one can see most clearly in Joni's career. The desire to be "her own man" as a songwriter, a bandleader, and a studio producer. While at the same time, she is the woman looking for her next lover, the girl who went to every wedding in her small town, who admits that "love stimulated [my] illusions more than anything." Black cool can be a posture of strength against a mainstream society that refuses to allow you to live within the full range of your humanity. In those years after Rolling Thunder, after the Last Waltz, Joni in her own way was pushing back against the limitations of a society that didn't know quite what to do with her mix of creative muscle and distinctly feminine sensibility, to quote Du Bois, "those two warring ideals . . . whose dogged strength alone keeps it from being torn asunder."

25 ◼ NERVY BROAD

ouis Menand once floated a theory in *The New Yorker* that he called "the iron law of stardom." In it, he claimed that celebrity had a three-year limit and that "this law dictates that stardom cannot extend for a period greater than three years. There is no penalty for breaking this law, for the simple reason that it is unbreakable." Menand went on to explain that when we thought of celebrities who seemed to break this law, what we were witnessing was a celebrity who had enjoyed two three-year terms. The Beatles, he posited, had enjoyed one term as "lovable mop tops (1964–67)" and another term as "hippie artistes (1967–70)." Madonna, as another example, Menand offered, had "enjoyed three years (1985–88) as the downtown queen of sexual hip and then three years (1989–92) as an uptown version of the same thing."

One might argue that by the time Joni turned thirty-seven she had enjoyed two distinct turns on the celebrity merry-go-round. She'd been the girl who had embodied the vibrant rock scene of Laurel Canyon (1968–71) and then another turn as the grown-up goddess from *Court and Spark* to *Hejira* (1973–76). Joni hadn't done the expected and settled into the pop/rock/jazz synthesis of *Court and Spark* like Steven Spielberg making *Raiders of the Lost Ark* movies. She kept changing, and it was painful, surprising even, that her audience found it hard to follow. Menand wrote in his essay, "Stardom is the period of inevitability, the time when everything works in a way that makes you think it will work that way forever. The dial seems permanently tuned to the frequency at which the individual star is broadcasting. Stardom means that (if you are the star) that nothing you do can be asymmetrical with what people want . . . Stardom is the intersection of personality with history, a perfect congruence of the way the world happens to be and the way the star is. The world, however, moves on."

But after so many shifts in the industry, after the overdoses and the band breakups and the personal crack-ups, Joni had survived and was ready for another turn at the celebrity circle game. Joni was a good soldier for the *Mingus* album. She broke her eight-year ban on being interviewed by *Rolling Stone*—imposed since they ran their "Old Lady of the Year" diagram in 1971—and did two: a talk with Ben Sidran when the album was in process and Mingus was still alive, and, for a cover story (her second and, so far, her last), an interview with Cameron Crowe, barely out of his teens. He was so eager to please, he brought galleys to her house. She was, as usual, disappointed, but didn't show it. She also talked to *Down Beat* and the *Los Angeles Times* with Leonard Feather, the only major jazz critic to endorse the project without reservation; Larry Kart of the *Chicago Tribune*; Michael Watts for *Melody Maker*; and Bob Protzman for the *Charlotte Observer*, among many others. The publicity-shy Joni was suddenly opening up. She would do everything she could to prove Geffen and Roberts wrong, not only by talking to the press, but by launching her first full-scale tour since the debacle of her scuttled *Hissing of Summer Lawns* outing more than three years earlier. Her original plan was to use Weather Report as an opening act and backing band, just as she had done with the L.A. Express. The explanation for why this didn't happen came from Weather Report's keyboardist and co-leader (with Wayne Shorter), Joe Zawinul: "We ain't no fucking L.A. Express."

And so Joni, for her musical director, picked Pastorius, who, shortly after being given the assignment, missed rehearsals for weeks. Pat Metheny, Jaco's chosen guitarist and all of twenty-five, was suddenly given the musical director spot. Metheny had already used Jaco as a sideman for his 1976 album, *Bright Size Life*, and since then, the Jaco legend had grown exponentially, almost ready to explode. Metheny was a subtle player, a muted contrast to Jaco's rock-star-size virtuoso theatrics. Lyle Mays, a quiet musical partner of Metheny's, was given the keyboard spot. Michael Brecker got the position that Joni dearly wanted for Wayne Shorter. ("I wanted genius and settled for talent," she recalled.) Brecker was an excellent musician, but also overtly influenced by John Coltrane, whom, of course, Joni believed—without much consensus—to be overrated. (A greater consensus would call him overimitated.) When Pastorius eventually resurfaced for rehearsals he tried to fire Brecker, but Joni talked him out of it. Don Alias was given the drummer chair.

Joni told *The Washington Post* that although she still played songs like "Big Yellow Taxi" she was avoiding some of her older hits, especially "Both Sides, Now." She said of the song, "I've heard it too often in supermarkets and elevators. I guess my first reaction when I hear it is a rush of pride. It's getting universal—almost to the 'Happy Birthday' stage. But I'm also critical of it when I hear it. They've usually reduced it to the lowest denominator."

The band would be given a little room to solo, but not much. In addition to his few minutes of lead-in to "Hejira," Metheny had only one guitar solo. Mick Taylor or Ron Wood, as second guitarists, had many more chances to solo at a Stones concert. The muzzled musical director was a fan of *Hejira*, so they did many songs from that album, many more than from *Don Juan's Reckless Daughter* or even *Mingus*, which was the occasion for the tour's existence. The doo-wop group the Persuasions would be the opening act, and would also sing with Joni on "Shadows and Light" and the '50s standard "Why Do Fools Fall in Love?" Brecker got to play honest-to-God solos on two songs. The frustration Victor Feldman and Roger Kellaway had felt was palpable from some of these musicians, not used to toiling in the shadows. Lyle Mays didn't seem to mind hiding behind a pop star, but Metheny would later observe that procuring musicians of that caliber and then giving them such limited opportunities to blow was the equivalent of buying a Ferrari and driving it around the block.

Despite his complaints, Metheny loved listening to Joni sing and, like Larry Carlton and Robben Ford before him, used volume pedals to give subtle colorings to Joni's rhythm chucking. But, unlike Carlton or Ford, he didn't find that to be musically stimulating. Joni had her meeting with jazz, but she also didn't want to be upstaged, or perhaps uprooted, by long, virtuosic solos. Charles Mingus had famously called her a "nervy broad," and it was perhaps in how she led her bands that Joni showed her steeliness most. "Because of my wordiness, I am first responsible to my words," she explained later on. "So when I play with a band, I have to be the leader. Well, the words have to be the leader. And if there's any room for anyone to get in, well, good luck!"

The band, in other words, would still be an extension of her guitar, her voice, her songs. They would lend sophisticated musicianship, but not beyond pop-sized attention spans. A live double album, *Shadows and Light*, recorded at the Santa Barbara County Bowl in September 1979, would be released in September 1980, and a video of the concert would be made available in various formats and aired on cable television. It is the only commercially available footage of her performing with Jaco Pastorius, who was becoming even more unruly and uncontrollable than he had been before. Cocaine and bipolar disorder are a lethal combination. He would become lost to Joni and, eventually, to nearly everyone else. There were stories of him running naked through a fountain in Japan, and living in Washington Square Park after his landlord evicted him for filling his apartment with water and inviting people in to swim.

A decade of pushing, exploring, and risk taking would be coming to a close. And it turned out that Geffen and Roberts were right. The album didn't sell. It was the first of her '70s albums not to go gold, although it peaked at number seventeen and went silver, a huge accomplishment for such an experimental album. And they were also right that she would be exiled from the airwaves forever. *Je ne regrette rien!*

She would do it again no matter what, she will tell you. And yet the musical road she began to pursue would be rather different than the experimental *Mingus* album. When she was making it, she told *Melody Maker* that going back to rock and roll would be like going back to a metronome. But back to the metronome she went. She would spend the next decade following trends instead of setting them, inveighing against the '80s while using its commercial sounds, the aural equivalent of fluorescent lighting.

When David Geffen sold Asylum to Elektra, and debuted Geffen Records in 1980, it was clear that the era of Elektra/Asylum was over. His initial acquisitions included Joni, Elton John, and John Lennon. Unsurprisingly, Elliot Roberts pushed Joni to the label.

"I don't want to go there again. He's going to get bored and I know what's going to happen," Joni said.

"Joan, it's David," Geffen said. "It'll be like old times."

"So he gives me an advance," she told me. "It's not a great advance, but it's not a bad advance. Then he reneges on a quarter of it, which he says he needs to buy me out of a quarter with Elektra. And he said, 'Joan, you want me to make some money, don'tcha?' Disgusting, but I acquiesced . . . I wasn't aware of what he was doing, but he was damming up my incoming income until two hundred and twenty-five thousand dollars of it is paid off."

"I haven't seen a royalty check in twenty years," Joni would tell Brantley Bardin in a 1996 interview with *Details* magazine. "And at a certain point, Geffen dammed up my only income—which is my writer's income from my publishing company—so I had *no* money coming in. So I went to David Geffen and said, 'Let me go.' He said, 'Joan, you're not gonna find a better deal out there than this. I'll keep you here forever—I'll never drop you.' And I said, 'Slavery with tenure is not attractive to me.'"

Geffen bought Joni's contract for subsequent work, even as Elektra would have maintained ownership. He was essentially leveraging Joni for the buyout. This is standard industry practice—artists often complain about being in debt to their companies, even after they've made millions. At least Geffen expected recoupment on the $225,000 when he wrote the contract. What was unusual was that, according to Joni, Geffen mixed the revenue streams that would have usually been controlled by two different companies, not only through record sale royalties, but also through publishing royalties. Among the revenues from the publishing side were public performance rights from radio, mechanical productions, and so on. Usually, recoupment is from one or the other. This wasn't the act of a loving mentor; this was the act of a tycoon, building a business on the artists in his stable.

What Geffen was hoping for was another multiplatinum *Court and Spark*, for the '80s. But this would prove to be impossible. The commercial and artistic storm of *Court and Spark* belonged to an earlier time.

Joni was still hanging on to her relationship with Don Alias. In an interview with *The Washington Post*, Joni talked about Don. "We've talked about getting married," she said. "I don't know. Kids? I don't know about that either." Joni went on to say, "I'm really strong as far as child-bearing goes. But it's a difficult time to bring children in the world." One can only imagine how hard it must have been for her to give these interviews without thinking of her little girl, Kelly Dale, who would now be a teenager.

On February 5, 1981, when Joni was thirty-seven, she was inducted into the Canadian Hall of Fame by Prime Minister Pierre Trudeau. Joni's proud but racist parents came, begrudgingly, with her African American boyfriend. In her brief speech, where she thanked Henry Lewy as her "assistant in the recording studio," she had to think for a moment before remembering the name "Elliot Roberts," and she thanked her fans who had stuck with her through her experimental phase (and did this mean she was done experimenting?) and, especially, her close friends for making "this gauntlet called fame a—pleasant—and beautiful experience."

Joni realized that Trudeau was playing politics, saluting a girl from the prairies to broaden his support. "I was born in Alberta, but I left there when I was two and a half," Joni told me. "But he said I was

Alberta's. So he used me politically. So I thought he wanted to be my presenter because he liked my music, but it was just politics as usual." It was also "politics as usual" when she had to justify bringing Don Alias with her parents.

Myrtle McKee Anderson was scandalized. Meeting the prime minister with a black man! Heavens! "What would Trudeau say?" asked Joni's mother.

"Mother, he's a man of the world," Joni pleaded. "He deals with black leaders. He's a sophisticated man." Myrtle Anderson was still upset.

After the event, Joni, her parents, and Don Alias were seated at the end of a long table. Bill and Myrtle Anderson were visibly embarrassed. "They had to sit with this gorgeous black man, and we were down in the middle," Joni recalled. "Trudeau's on this side. There was also this very nice, handsome man, a good man, but he had gotten into a scandal. He had gotten a woman pregnant while he was married. And he did a very unusual thing for a politician. He took care of the woman and child, and he'd informed his wife about it, and women adored him because he didn't try to weasel out of it. So he got this huge women's vote for being a mensch. So I had him on one side of me and Trudeau on the other and a French singer-songwriter girl across the table."

As soon as they sat down, Trudeau said of Alias, "Good-looking guy."

"Yes, he's very handsome. But he's also the greatest conga player in the world. In a very unlucrative form, he's a master. Not just a pretty face."

The French singer-songwriter woman concurred, "Yes, Don Alias is fantastic."

On to politics. "You know," Trudeau said, "the trouble with Alberta is that it wants to be the east."

"The trouble with the east is that it wants to be New York," Joni replied.

Trudeau bristled and pulled back. There would be no more Christmas cards. That was the end of Joni's Pierre Trudeau relationship.

And soon after that came the end of her complicated four-year relationship with Don Alias. Even though he was willing to pimp her out to Miles Davis, his jealousy would brutally end the relationship.

"Don Alias was irrationally jealous and beat me up a couple of times," Joni recalled in 2015. "So, the first time, it was a long break. And then he went and appealed to all my friends. So I went back, and then he did it again, irrationally. He thought I was cheating on him. He invented it. Paranoia, and probably because he was on the road all the time and was probably cheating on me. I would say it was projection. He was very sweet, but you don't want to get beat up by a conga player—in the face. He's very strong and those hands are lethal weapons. He beat me up pretty badly."

The second time Alias beat Joni, she had gone out to dinner with John Guerin *with his permission*. They agreed to a time when Joni would come home. Anyone familiar with Joni's rococo conversation style would expect her to be late. She was. She rolled in after four a.m. and came home to a battering. The dinner was with a former lover, a longtime lover, a lover whose prowess Alias had been hearing about for a while. Alias must have known that Joni tried to maintain friendships with her exes, but he also knew how Joni had never quite let go of this one. She kept hiring Guerin for albums and forgave him for everything he put her through.

"I'm monogamous when I'm monogamous," Joni told me. "And it was with Don's permission. So I came home, he beat me up, then the next day, John, who was living with Pixie at that point, he went to work—and he's a studio musician, so his job depends on being on time—but our relationship was really deep and psychic. My housekeeper said we talked to each other in our sleep. My mother said that none of the men I chose suited me. It made me really mad, and I was coming down with double pneumonia at the time. I called her back and said, 'Let me explain to you these relationships you don't understand.' John Guerin and I were sleeping in Max's spare room, which had a twin bed. We were sleeping in a twin bed. And if you didn't wake yourself when you went over, you'd go over the edge. So I'm sleeping on the outer edge that night and, in my sleep, I'm rolling towards the edge. And in his sleep, John Guerin reached out his arm and pulled me in. In his sleep! There was a pause on the other end of the phone and my mother said, 'I see.'"

That extraordinary bonding carried Guerin for a long time. The next morning, on his way to work, he pulled up in front of the recording studio and thought, "Something's wrong with Joni." And he turned away—he would be late for the gig, a reckless move for a studio musician—and drove to the house. He still had a key. He came into the bedroom toward the canopy bed, and the curtains were pulled. He heard her moaning. At first, he thought she had a lover and he was reluctant to go any further, but he thought, "No, there's something wrong." He came and he saw that Joni was battered. Her face was black-and-blue. "Think of the intuition," Joni said.

The drummer boyfriend of the past came to comfort Joni, black and blue from the boyfriend of the present—soon to be of the past. Guerin was a philanderer, but he was always, to Joni, a lover. He loved women too much, but he really loved them. And seeing this woman he had loved—imperfectly, but deeply and passionately—in so much physical and emotional pain, inflicted by the guy who came after him, was overwhelming. All he could do was comfort her in the gentlest way possible. He was raised by women who taught him to love women, in his mischievous way. "John's mother was a wonderful woman with a great sense of humor. Handsome woman. She was an equestrian and she had great carriage," Joni recalled. "They were circus people. The grandmother was really carny and she played solitaire with a cigarette dangling out of her mouth and she had all kinds of little quips. John as a boy would come to her and say, 'Am I bad yet, Granny?' And she'd whisper, 'Yes, you're very bad, John.' They encouraged him."

And yet, in spite of it all, she still had fond memories of Alias, especially the music. "You can hear the love between Alias and I on 'The Wolf That Lives in Lindsey.' Those things are poignant and beautiful and valuable, and the fact that they don't go the distance, or that there are serious obstacles like battery, that's pretty serious. I couldn't live with him anymore." The third time Alias tried to beat Joni, they were in St. Martin and she outran him. "That's it!" she called out.

"You're not gonna get me again. You can't control yourself and I can't stay here."

"That's the only bad physical relationship," Joni recalled. "The other ones were bad psychologically. I can't say that any of them were a waste of time. For either one of us. There was a healthy trade-off. We made beautiful music and we learned things from one another. So I don't look back . . ."

John somehow knew Joni needed him. He could be very bad, but he could also be very good. He comforted her when she needed him. He couldn't be counted on to be faithful, but he could be counted on for other things. Joni would hire him for her next album. The '80s would be hard on Joni, and she was constantly on the defense against: engineers who bludgeoned her music; careless dentists; a tax law that applied only to a dozen people, which she would appeal twice and eventually win, after the lawyers got a big cut. The Board of Equalization found a vulnerable target in Joni. Because she was an independent contractor with no producer to hide behind, the state of California—about which she had sung so warmly and famously—was allowed to glom on to her income, because in essence, she was a somewhat independent entity making something for the record company for hire. These things were built into her contract by her lawyers and her management in order to protect her. Sometimes, history is a way of looking back and asking, How the hell did this happen?

Her polio symptoms would return, her soprano would disappear, and she would be pelted with ice on live television. And as much as she loved the man, she would not give Don Alias a third chance. It would also be a decade when, after 1982's *Wild Things Run Fast*, she would separate from her "more than an engineer" sonic twin, Henry Lewy. Maybe analog was over. Maybe pianos and acoustic guitars were a thing of the past. The '80s was a brave new world. "Hippie, Yippie, Yuppie," Joni described it. She permed her hair, wore bright, shiny colors and shoulder pads, and let the synths take over completely. Her alto—her natural range, according to her mother—became more shrill, more abrasive. People assumed this was from chain-smoking, even as she insisted it was from vocal nodes that she developed from rock and roll. Whatever the source, the proof is in the recording. Beginning with *Dog Eat Dog* (1985), her voice was so buried in a digital avalanche, it was hard to tell what was left of it. She could point fingers wherever she wanted, but after a decade of stretching out, she was contracting, getting the latest Fairlight to sound more techno than techno pop, as synthesizer saturated as Madonna, who worshipped Joni, and whom Joni compared to Nero. But before she completely succumbed to the '80s sound patches, she would make one more guitar-and-piano-based album, with one more private letter to make public.

Most decades don't officially begin in their first year. With the '50s it was the 1952 McCarthy hearings. With the '60s, it could be the March on Washington or the Kennedy assassination, both in 1963, or the Beatles' arrival in America in 1964. The '70s were defined, in some ways, as the winding down of the '60s, with the resignation of Richard Nixon, which happened as Joni was riding high with *Court and Spark* in 1974. But the '80s crashed down almost immediately, with the election of Ronald Reagan and the murder of John Lennon. Brutal times. Even though Joni personally encountered Lennon only at his most drunk and belligerent, she was still moved by his assassination to link him to Robert Kennedy and Martin Luther King in her 1985 song "Impossible Dreamer." And the dream of "Woodstock" was growing dimmer as the '80s unfolded. AIDS was discovered in 1981, and the discos and bathhouses emptied out. MTV debuted with a song by the Buggles called "Video Killed the Radio Star." The Buggles did not go on to become video stars, but

Michael Jackson, Duran Duran, the Police, and others became video stars of epic proportions.

Among '80s icons, Prince pledged fealty to Joni. *The Hissing of Summer Lawns* was not only his favorite Joni Mitchell album, but "the last album [he] loved all the way through." Joni was pleased to get this praise, but had difficulty hearing her influence on him. She thought he was one of the greatest performers she had ever seen—maybe even the greatest—and that he was a compelling hybrid of Sly Stone and, she supposed, herself. As he did with "Manic Monday" for the Bangles and "Nothing Compares 2 U" for Sinéad O'Connor, Prince wrote a song for Joni to sing—"Emotional Pump." The chorus was pure one-hundred-proof Prince: "You are my emotional pump / You make my body jump." There was no way Joni was going to sing that.

Peter Asher, who replaced Elliot Roberts as Joni's manager and was itching for his new client to make money, witnessed Prince giving Joni advice. "I remember Prince telling Joni how to have a hit," Asher recalled. "He was an obsessive Joni fan. They had a conversation where he couldn't understand why she couldn't have a hit single. He was telling her what she should do and how to have a commercial record. She had no interest in listening to what he said."

And yet the friendship endured, Prince's longtime band mate Wendy Melvoin would later recall. "For my twentieth birthday, Prince decided to throw a surprise party for me at a club called Tramps in Minneapolis. He even flew in my twin sister, Susannah. At one point during the party, he said, 'Do me a favor and sit down at this table and wait.' So I waited, and then in comes Prince and Joni Mitchell to sit with me, and she gave me three of her lithographs as a present. It was one of my most profound moments. Prince was a fan of Joni's, just like Lisa [Coleman] and I were, so to get to know her was incredible. I remember a time when we were in California, and Prince called me and said, 'Let's go out and have dinner at Joni's place in Malibu.' I just thought, Oh my god! The three of us get in the car and we played *Blue* on the drive to her place. We got there and opened the door and Joni was calling for her cat Puss-Puss in that beautiful voice of hers. The walls of her house were covered with her portraits of people like Miles Davis—it was amazing. So we're on the couch, having these incredibly deep conversations with Joni Mitchell, and Prince walks over to the piano and starts playing 'A Case of You.' Then Joni says, 'Oh wow! That's really pretty. What song are you playing?' We all yelled, 'It's your song!' Prince got such a kick out of that."

Nineteen eighty-two was the second year of MTV, and even though Reagan was in the White House, Thatcher was in 10 Downing Street, and Michael Jackson would saturate all media with *Thriller*, there was still enough of a hangover from the '70s for Joni to release an album that had some connection to her '70s self.

Wild Things Run Fast, released in October 1982, is never anyone's favorite Joni Mitchell album, even though some of her fans cherish some of its songs like protective parents. Even its cover painting, of Joni wearing a blazer and pants, leaning on a television, seems arbitrary. We don't imagine Joni leaning on a television. We imagine her running wild, howling with wolves that live in Lindsey. But it was bookended by two stone-cold masterpieces, one of which, "Chinese Café," was as revealing as she would ever be about a secret from her past. The other, "Love," would use words from the New Testament as a poetic inquiry about what love is and is not, a long way from a leotard-clad Olivia Newton John singing, in a 1982 number one single, "Let's Get Physical."

John Guerin would be on drums for his last Joni Mitchell session. (In addition to "Love," he would also play on "Chinese Café," "Ladies' Man," "Moon at the Window," "Be Cool," and "Man to Man.") And it would feature a new bass player, to replace a by now impossibly erratic Jaco.

"I was playing with John Guerin in a number of different things," Larry Klein, then a twenty-five-year-old bass player and engineer, re-called. "We played together in Victor Feldman's band. We were doing a lot of work together, actually, in the studio and club dates. In some respects, Jaco influenced my playing. I don't think you could be a bass player and not be influenced by him at that time. There was a great deal of imitation going on, of people glomming on to what he was doing, either trying to re-create it themselves or assimilate the most overt parts of what he was doing. One thing that I knew at a very young age is that it doesn't make sense to do that. That's a losing game."

To everything there is a season, Joni might have supposed. This young man was not the next Jaco Pastorius, but he gave her what she wanted. Around this time, she liked to say, she looked up to the heavens and said, "Look, I know I don't call. I don't write. But I just need a guy who's a good kisser and likes to play pinball." When Klein asked Joni if she wanted to play video games, she looked up and said, "Close enough." They were soon joined at the hip, emotionally and otherwise, and they married in a Buddhist ceremony on November 21, 1982. She was thirteen years older, and the marriage was the kind of thing a male celebrity would do without notice. She plucked a cute young thing from her band and then, because he had youth and claimed, somewhat prematurely, that he had engineering chops, gave him coproducer credit for the next albums she would make, ceding the independence that defined her in the '70s, when there was no producer credit at all.

Larry Klein said, "She had said to me, 'I need you to help me with my records.' I said, 'You seem to have done a good job on your own so far.' And she said, 'No, no. I want your help.' I know she was looking for something different. She always was, of course, and any vital artist is always looking for something new. That's how I came to produce these records with her. She very clearly insisted that she wanted and needed me to work on them. As young as I was at that time, I perceived that as probably a good idea, but a dangerous one. I didn't coproduce with her until we were married. Once we were married, I never took a salary, I never took any kind of advance or payment of any kind. I had some trepidation about the whole thing. I could see what could happen if she paid me to be in this role on the records. I thought it could cause problems at some point. What was naïve on my part—maybe romantically naive—was that we didn't tuck our assets away, so why should I ask her to pay me?"

After marrying Joni, Klein built up quite a résumé, playing bass with Robbie Robertson, Don Henley, Bob Dylan, Dianne Reeves, Bobby McFerrin, Neil Diamond, Tracy Chapman, Peter Gabriel, Warren Zevon, and Bryan Adams, among others. When Joni lost a Grammy in 1988 to Tracy Chapman, who was represented by Elliot Roberts, it was to a record that featured Klein.

"She had a huge influence on me when we met and started working together," Klein recalled. "I was working on one of her records when we met, and then we worked together for over fifteen years. For me, at twenty-four, I had never met a woman like this. There isn't really another woman like her on the planet. She was an incredible combination of things. For me, it very much was a learning experience, being in a relationship with her, whether it was working or in a personal relationship, because we were constantly discussing everything under the sun and she had absorbed an incredible amount of . . . everything. I'm a very curious person. It was an incredible environment for me to grow in every way. She was thirteen years older than me, and of course iconoclastic and idiosyncratic, an interesting thinker in every way."

Things began beautifully between Joni and Klein. It was only later that Klein realized that, amid such creativity, inspiration, and the full bloom of romantic love, as Joni sang on "Chinese Café," nothing lasts for long. "I think that the seed of the angry, narcissistic element of her personality was always there, but I think that it was a gradual process of that part of her growing, and the curious and joyful part gradually receding," Klein recalled in 2015. "When we first met she was just an incredibly stimulating, smart, of course incredibly talented, funny, and brilliant woman. I was so taken with her. I had never met a woman with a fraction of her intuitive intelligence in my life. I had grown up in the San Gabriel Valley, gone to music school, then had been on the road playing with my jazz heroes for about five years or so. In fact, I was still playing with Freddie Hubbard when I met her on the first sessions for *Wild Things Run Fast*. She was always thirsty for input on sessions, and I had developed some strong architectural ideas about music and arrangement, and I found her way of working to be a revelation."

Klein kept superb time, hit those harmonics, and knew, the longer he used it, how the studio worked. He was miles away from Jaco Pastorius, but then, it would have been hard to find anyone in Jaco's stratosphere, especially if she wanted someone dependable.

Wild Things Run Fast is the only album with the credit "Produced by Joni Mitchell," and it is the last of the decade not to be saturated by synthetic timbres. And her voice on the album is essentially the same as it was on Rolling Thunder, although that was on the cusp of changing. "How did you go bankrupt?" wrote Hemingway. "Two ways: gradually and then suddenly."

The sudden part would come soon. "I think that it is important to remember that *Wild Things* was recorded when she was thirty-eight years old," said Klein. "From the beginning of the time that we began working together, she smoked about four packs of cigarettes a day. What that amounts to is that she was literally smoking pretty much every waking moment. If you take what she says as the truth, she had been smoking since she was about nine years old. This kind of assault on the throat can only go on so long without really starting to show in the husk of the character of voice, the width of the vibrato, range, and intonation. Also, I do think that when you see this start showing up in singers who are living hard in one way or another, it does start piling on in somewhat of an exponential way once it starts becoming noticeable. She repeatedly tried to quit, but never successfully. One of the times that she tried, she was given an injection which was to, in effect, put the smoker into a sedated state for the first couple of days, which of course is the time when the withdrawal is most brutal. She had tried a number of times at home, but it had become quite evident that she became too ill-tempered and hostile towards anybody around her during the withdrawal, that I would end up saying, 'Here . . . please smoke!' I couldn't take being at the other end of these kinds of mood swings."

Klein volunteered to drive her out to Two Bunch Palms in Desert Hot Springs, so that "she could wake up from the anesthesia in a pleasant place where she didn't have access to cigarettes, and where I wasn't around as a focus of the negative effects of the withdrawal. I got her into her room, got everything set up, then drove back to LA."

After a couple of days he tried to call her, but couldn't get an answer. He began to worry, imagining that if she was having some kind of adverse effect from this injection, nobody would know. He drove back out to the desert. "When I got there, I discovered that she had borrowed someone's little Stingray bicycle to ride down to the local Thrifty's and get several packs of smokes," he told me. "Pretty funny. We both had a good laugh about it. I believe that we might have tried another scheme or two to try and get her off of tobacco, but I finally realized that on some very deep level, she actually would rather die than live without smoking."

Klein's devotion to Joni in these days was certainly a display of love, an emotion that has proved to be the complex theme she revisited, even when she thought she was through with it. A song called "Love" closes the album, but it actually began the sessions. The occasion was a film to be produced by Barry Levinson, whose breakthrough film, *Diner*, would be released in 1982, the same year as *Wild Things Run Fast*. Joni was among nine women to receive the following pitch from Levinson: "Write a 10-minute script on the subject of love, preferably from a sexual point of view. Whatever you write, I'll produce." The other women included Liv Ullmann, most notable for her performances in Ingmar Bergman films; the Irish novelist and playwright Edna O'Brien; and the *New Yorker* film critic Penelope Gilliatt (who tag-teamed with the far more influential Pauline Kael). Rebecca West, Gloria Steinem, and Jacqueline Kennedy Onassis all passed. Joni, more of a cineaste than a poetry reader, eagerly said yes. She was expected to write the soundtrack but instead wrote, directed, and starred in a film about Art Nouveau, her black male pimp character, who meets an old lover at a costume party. The project never got off the ground, but Joni's theme song for the project survived.

The lyrics for "Love" are adapted from 1 Corinthians 13. (As has been noted, Joni had become quite a Gideon reader in her days on the road.) St. Paul is speaking to the people of Corinth in the form of a letter, addressing both the spiritual and the material. Love is something in between.

Here is the King James Version, raw material for Joni to adapt:

1 Though I speak with the tongues of men and of angels, and have not charity, I am become as sounding brass, or a tinkling cymbal.

2 And though I have the gift of prophecy, and understand all mysteries, and all knowledge; and though I have all faith, so that I could remove mountains, and have not charity, I am nothing.

3 And though I bestow all my goods to feed the poor, and though I give my body to be burned, and have not charity, it profiteth me nothing.

4 Charity suffereth long, and is kind; charity envieth not; charity vaunteth not itself, is not puffed up,

5 Doth not behave itself unseemly, seeketh not her own, is not easily provoked, thinketh no evil;

6 Rejoiceth not in iniquity, but rejoiceth in the truth;

7 Beareth all things, believeth all things, hopeth all things, endureth all things.

8 Charity never faileth: but whether there be prophecies, they shall fail; whether there be tongues, they shall cease; whether there be knowledge, it shall vanish away.

9 For we know in part, and we prophesy in part.

10 But when that which is perfect is come, then that which is in part shall be done away.

11 When I was a child, I spake as a child, I understood as a child, I thought as a child: but when I became a man, I put away childish things.

12 For now we see through a glass, darkly; but then face to face: now I know in part; but then shall I know even as also I am known.

13 And now abideth faith, hope, charity, these three; but the greatest of these is charity.

Joni had to see beyond the archaisms and all the beareth, hopeth, and endureth-isms to create a song that would sound both ancient and contemporary, and also filled something passionate and vital. Joni creates one rhyming couplet in this prose poem:

> *Love suffers long*
> *Love is kind!*
> *Enduring all things*
> *Love has no evil in mind*

Wild Things Run Fast is extravagantly filled with love songs. Joni felt she was pilloried by critics who counted the number of times she said "the ell word." (Fifty-seven, went one count.) She was giddy, almost like a teenager, at the most cynical crossroads of the music industry. They had denied her entry in the past for being a social critic on *The Hissing of Summer Lawns*; for stretching out with jazz musicians on *Hejira, Don Juan's Reckless Daughter*, and *Mingus*; for sometimes eschewing her gift for melody to get the words out in the kind of speak-song heard on "Coyote," "Don Juan's Reckless Daughter," and elsewhere. But now that she was making something that had more resemblance to meat-and-potatoes rock and roll and straight-up conjugal bliss, they missed the ironic Joni, the lovelorn folk princess of *Blue*.

The fetish for hip was driving Joni up the wall, especially since, for the first time, she was trying, and trying hard. AOR, an acronym for album-oriented rock, was a big radio format, and songs with big, fat guitars were the sound of it circa '82—yet, for all these contortions, the songs of *Wild Things Run Fast* were not getting on the radio or MTV.

"I called up the president of the record company and said 'You'll be happy to hear my music is headed in a more rock and rollish manner,'" Joni said upon the album's release. "You'd think he would be delighted, but to his great credit he said, 'Oh no, don't do that: they'll know . . .'"

Was she still being punished for *Mingus*? Joni has written so many songs about love (which are not always love songs, per se) that, in 2013, she halted production on a ballet based on her songs called *Love* because she felt overwhelmed by the volume of material she had written on the matter. Fitting it in a single ballet seemed impossible. (It became a box set called *Love Has Many Faces*, released in 2014, and she removed Larry Klein's credit as coproducer on several tracks.)

Going back through Joni's catalogue, one finds a quality throughout that is elusive on the *Wild Things Run Fast* love songs (with the exception of "Love"): ambiguity. "Cactus Tree" is about accumulating love through experiencing many lovers; just one will not do, and, you know, there may be more. "My Old Man" is a straight-up love song for Graham Nash, but it is on the bridge about the "lonesome blues" that the chords get interesting, as they also do when she says they don't need no paper from the city hall. "Help Me" is melodically audacious, with a refrain about lovin' freedom more than lovin' (which is really the freedom to have more lovin'). "See You Sometime," like "Blue Motel Room," is about missing a lover (James Taylor for the former and John Guerin for the latter), knowing that there is a lack of fidelity on both sides. "A Strange Boy" is about an unworthy lover. "The Silky Veils of Ardor," which closes *Don Juan's Reckless Daughter*, is based on a traditional folk song, a cautionary tale about passion leading to pain and jealousy. Joni told what she believed many thought to be her cold truth on "Amelia": "Maybe I've never really loved, I guess that is the truth. I've spent my whole life in clouds at icy altitudes." This harsh imagery is especially powerful since it builds from the uncertainty of "Maybe."

This was the Joni Mitchell of our dreams, the one who came up from the darkness, skated over the river, and even if she had, indeed, lost her heart, had emerged to tell us the devastating tale while she was finding it yet again. Joni's love songs were often written at the tail end of a romance or on the uncertain quest of a new one. Or they even questioned love itself. Joni's audience responded to these songs because the emotions were as nuanced and eccentric as the chords accompanying them. It is a long way from there to *Wild Things Run Fast*'s "Yes I do, I love yah!" on the exuberant—maybe too exuberant—"Underneath the Streetlights." "Hot dog, darlin'," she sings unashamedly on "Solid Love," a song inspired by the ska crossover rhythms of the Police (if without the advertising-style repetitions that made their songs hits. Joni even wanted the Police to be her backing band for the album, but they couldn't fit it in around their blockbuster touring schedule).

A crucial aspect of a Joni Mitchell song is that it does not necessarily conform to expectations of what a Joni Mitchell song is. But the '80s were not the '70s, and it would be a more difficult environment for riding her changes. The Police began as punks who were so militant, Sting had to persuade his bandmates that they wouldn't lose their edge by having a song with a soppy girl's name. That girl was Roxanne, and Sting argued that if Elvis Costello could still have cred with a lovely song for another girl—Alison—then surely they could get away with it in a kind of punk tango.

Joni had more baggage than the Police. She had gone through more changes than pop stars usually got away with, and there was something about her angling for the mainstream that landed with a thud. Her love for Larry Klein was as sincere as it got, but peddling for the masses wasn't something she had tried to do before. Contrast with a decade earlier, in 1973, when she just heard the L.A. Express one night at the Baked Potato and found a musical cushion. But now it was the '80s. Everything would be different.

The decade may have seemed like the golden age of a certain kind of pop, but success in the '80s didn't come as easily as all those radio-friendly pop songs made it look, and for Joni, commercially, hits didn't come at all. She would record a total of four albums for Geffen Records—and she knew changes had to be made. She knew the albums were expensive to make. She could have recorded them with a lot less expense, and less of a need to recover costs. But success is as addictive as any drug. Once you've had a taste of it, it's hard to live without it, especially when you have people on your payroll, a lavish Bel-Air property to maintain, and a level of lifestyle that wasn't about to go back to that old Boho Dance. Joni's career moved with the culture—for a while. *The Hissing of Summer Lawns* was released in the year of Tom

Wolfe's "Me Generation." *Hejira* came out in the year of Gail Sheehy's bestselling *Passages*. *Don Juan's Reckless Daughter* was released in the year of *Annie Hall*. Joni was telling her listeners who and what they were, and as they were making their way through self-discovery and discursive relationships, Joni's personal expression was part of the larger conversation. But by 1982, those people were on second or third marriages, women were wearing shoulder pads and had become Yuppies, or middle-aged people trying to keep up with them. Some of them had even voted for Reagan. The critics were rewarding work that was edgy, cool, ironic. Vulnerability, emotionality, disclosure—these salient Joni qualities were dismissed as so '70s.

Wayne Shorter—who dodged jazz orthodoxies himself, not always to optimal effect—continued to be an empathic collaborator, and Victor Feldman, who complained all the way through his stint as keyboardist on the 1976 Hissing of Summer Lawns tour, continued his griping when he was playing vibes on "Moon at the Window." Feldman, author of the textbook *Musicians Guide to Chord Progressions*, could not tolerate this session. "I thought the words were bothering him because he's a family man and it was about people with the incapacity to love, and he had a very loving family," Joni recalled later. "I said, 'Are the words bothering you?' He said, 'I hate the harmony and the harmonic movement.' I had to stop and send him home. I said, 'You can't play on something that you hate!'"

The most extraordinary revelation on the album came from flawed, all-too-human Joni, making revelations that were entirely personal. "Chinese Café" has all the elements of an astonishing Joni Mitchell song, and the secret of her life was sung about in the open, daring her audience to find it. In contrast to the flowery language of "Little Green," so occluded in obscure, fairy-tale language, here she reaches out to Kelly Dale, who would now be eighteen, in a conversation with a Canadian friend named Carol, in the spirit of "Song for Sharon," imagining the road not taken all the way back to Saskatoon. Like Sharon Bell, Carol did the conventional thing: married with children, watching the little ones go off to college. Joni, at thirty-nine, is doing what would have been expected of her peer group twenty years earlier: finding a happy, stable marriage to a guy in his mid-twenties. Joni is watching Carol's daughter fly from the nest, remarking how "we look like our mothers now when we were those kids' age." It's the cycle of life, the forty-year-old version of the twenty-year-old boy's "Circle Game."

The song begins innocuously, "caught in the middle," with an old school friend, both "middle-class" and "middle-aged." (Joni despises being called the former, but it fits the purposes of the song.) Forty-year-olds who buy records surely remember when they were wild things, and for Joni, it was remembering the "birth of rock and roll days," when she could dance the night away without wondering what it meant.

Then, she doesn't even bury the lede. She leads with the revelation, eavesdropping on her own conversation. "Now your kids are coming up straight / And my child's a stranger / I bore her / But I could not raise her." There it is, on the table, the thing that, she later claimed, made her surrogate mother to the world when she couldn't be a real one. "Nothing lasts for long," she intones three times, building intensity with each repetition. The further we go into Joni's secrets, her pain, all that she had and all that she had given up, the song transitions to memories of youth, of dreaming on her dimes at the Chinese Café.

There was a real café. The CM Café was owned by Artie and Charlie Mack, two Asian men who allowed their customers to loiter and put another dime in the jukebox. The Chinese Café was a place for teenage Joni to smoke and listen to nasty rock and roll and swoony ballads, and the song, giving copyright where it's due, switches, like an associative jukebox, to the latter: the Righteous Brothers' "Unchained Melody." "Time goes by so slowly and time can do so much. / Are you still mine?" The way she sings it, this simple ballad sounds like it has more than twenty years' baggage. It's a shout-out to the past, to eighteen-year-old Kelly Dale, maybe even to herself. How much longer can I mother the world? Who am I suffering for? And where does the time go?

Joni would be a good soldier for *Wild Things Run Fast* and embark on her final long tour as a solo artist—from February 28, 1982, in Tokyo to July 30 at Red Rocks in Colorado. This was the longest tour she would ever do, and the strain of carrying an electric guitar showed in her face. She was as gorgeous as ever, but she had found a new limit and began pushing over it. She added Michael Landau, who, in stark contrast to the subtle timbres of Larry Carlton, Robben Ford, or Pat Metheny, busted in with an arena-sized rock and roll guitar, heavy, aggressive—really, in the pre–riot grrrl era, a cock-rock sound—that had never been associated with Joni Mitchell before. She thought he was better than Metheny, a shocking judgment to a jazzer. A new, focused hard rock groove gave new weight to chestnuts like "Song for Sharon."

Nostalgia would have been more remunerative, but Joni would never be a human jukebox, even as she trotted out the old hits with new sounds. "Mike Landau was and is a beautiful player," Klein told me. "She could be, I believe with some cause, critical of his sense of musical architecture. But we had a wonderful time playing with that band. A lot of great music every night. Beautiful and intuitive and painterly playing from everybody."

With Klein in the musical director role—one that had been Pastorius's and then Metheny's—the vibe would be a bass player who was also a loving spouse. "She wanted to record everything including sound checks, as improvised pieces were often making her want to write songs," Klein explained. The tour itself was idyllic. "We all loved each other's playing, Joan generally loved the way the band supported her. There were no hierarchical lines between crew and band; we all loved hanging together, laughing, drinking, and partying. A fair amount of drug intake for us all, but I have to say that we had a ball. The road becomes so insular and removed, and we had a year of all of us just traveling, playing her great songs, and enjoying each other. I was the de facto musical director, so when people would start overplaying, or things became problematic musically in any way, it was my job to work it out with the band. Joan hated confronting these things herself, as she, quite perceptively, thought that it would stiffen things up. We got along wonderfully during this time. Until later, we always got along in a wonderful way when we were working on records or touring. Seamless interaction. Always refining things. Our conversations about musical design would glide into philosophical discussions, then into other areas. A lot of laughter and mischievous smart jabbing at each other, and always a lot of music. She had a big personality, and was very opinionated, but was still capable of enjoying differences. I remember thinking during the Refuge tour that life doesn't get better than this."

When she did break out the dulcimer for "A Case of You," she had to transpose it down several keys. On the road, they were having too good a time to see that Joni was not being a devoted custodian to her own instrument. But her voice was starting to really show the wear and tear of the smoking. That, coupled with the endurance issues of touring—singing sometimes three days on and one day off, not getting much sleep, as her hours were by then completely turned around, making it very difficult for her to get up for flights, do sound checks— just started to really expose the lack of resilience that was there because of the smoking.

"It wasn't that she was singing too hard because of the band being too loud, as I was often the one who did her monitor mixes, and the band actually played quite softly onstage," Klein explained. "The fact that they did was responsible for the sound usually being outstanding in the house, aside from really unworkable basketball-arena-type places. She was just incorrigible when it came to taking care of herself on the road. Knowing that she had a tough time going to sleep every night, she still would drink cappuccino after the gigs, and of course was smoking from the moment that she woke up to the moment that she fell asleep."

All that toil and toll would lead to almost no money in the end. After the band and crew took home their checks, there was very little left.

Klein told me: "Joni was very naïve in the way that she approached money at that time. So was I! She never went to Elliot Roberts and said, 'How much will I net out of this tour?' Elliot of course didn't care much about that bottom line, as he took his cut off of the gross, like all managers. On the other hand, she was not able to survive the kind of work schedule that other singers could on the road. Part of this was because of the smoking at this point, but also because of her insomnia and inability to get a good night's sleep, then travel and play the same night. Every travel day off costs you on the road with a big crew and band."

Joni would not scale back her lifestyle, but money was something to worry about in the midst of living large, even more so after the tour was over. "I think that some of the financial setbacks that followed her not making money on the Refuge tour scarred her, and began a gradual process of embitterment that resulted in her becoming angry more and more of the time. I think that anger is poison, and these setbacks left her spending more and more time stuck in 'search for the guilty' mode."

He remembered well the ways in which Joni, who had once been the Queen of Rock and Roll, began to feel financially unmoored. "She was invested in real estate, and that was when everyone who had real estate took a beating," Klein told me. "She was repeatedly assured that she was still in good financial shape, but this didn't stop her from having 'Caine Mutiny' nights, where she would stay up all night trying to figure out who was against her, and what the next threat against her would be."

The California Board of Equalization singled her out for a retroactive tax during her peak years between 1971 and 1977, and since most of her work was done without a producer, there was no one to hide behind. She was, in effect, an independent contractor, and independence had its price. In addition, she suspected someone at Elliot Roberts's office had been pilfering her purse. She responded by leaving the agency, saying that Elliot was still a good friend, but that he was a manager in need of a manager. She signed with Peter Asher instead.

And then Dora, her housekeeper, accused her of beating her, said Klein. "It was settled out of court and the insurance company covered it. I always thought that she was making a lot of it up, but not all of it. I think Joan did physically attack her. According to Dora, she pretty much threw her around the room. The truth probably lies in between. You'd have to be like Hulk Hogan to do those things that Dora was claiming. Joan maintained that she kicked her in the shins. The housekeeper was small. She was short. Joan said that Dora planned it out and knew how to trigger her anger." Dora received $250,000.

"If you spend that much of the time angry," reflects Klein, "it eats away at your soul and makes you sick. This, and the smoking, just began to wear her health down. On one level she wouldn't hesitate to walk into an antique store and spend fifty thousand dollars on a lamp that she liked, but then she would be up all night angrily pacing the floor and hypothesizing irrationally about how her business managers were stealing from her, or how an innocuous comment from someone was really a veiled insult. All of this went along with a four-pack-a-day smoking habit and no reasonable sleep pattern. It just began to grind her down."

In the summer of 1985, while she was recording her next album, she was also nearly killed by a drunk teenager on the Pacific Coast Highway, totaling her car. When she went back to the scene of the crime weeks later, another car nearly ran her over. It was a time of bad omens, and an attempt to rage against the mainstream with the sounds of the mainstream.

Joni knew that her next album would be angry.

27 ▨ *DOG EAT DOG*

mid this turbulence, Joni would have to give up her precious creative freedom. For Joni's first eleven albums, she had the luxury of creating without any intervention from the suits. This was starting to change, as *Wild Things Run Fast*, despite all of Joni's efforts to reenter the mainstream, had peaked at twenty-five, even lower than *Mingus*'s peak at seventeen. The grueling nine-month tour, which barely broke even, also did not help matters, and, even worse, it marked the beginning of her post-polio syndrome. The filmed material from the tour, for the BBC and for her own *Refuge of the Roads* video, showed an unmistakable anguish in her face, with the electric guitar around her neck seeming like an albatross.

And she was angry. Very angry.

Melancholy, not anger, is an emotion more congenial to the Joni Mitchell canon. Of course, getting honest feelings across is always paramount, and if those feelings—in spite of a marriage that was still a good one—tended to be political, theological, and sociological complaints, then she had to go with her gut, as she always did. Before she fired him, Elliot Roberts, looking at the weak sales for *Wild Things Run Fast*, insisted that Joni hire a producer to acclimate her to the sounds of the mid '80s. Joni had escaped those knob twirlers ever since Paul Rothchild went on vacation and she and Henry Lewy finished *Clouds* on their own.

Larry Klein heard a convincing electronic cover of "The Jungle Line" by the synth wizard Thomas Dolby, who had scored an MTV hit with the playful and infectious dance record "She Blinded Me with Science." He was not only fluent in the new technology but was having fun with it. Maybe he could help translate Joni to the '80s and the '80s to Joni, because Joni was not having fun in the mid '80s. Joni had made it by being sincere, blunt, earnest, romantic; the '80s were ironic, ultra-hip, post-ironic. Paul Simon, a couple of years older than Joni, was hip to the new sensibility; "You Can Call Me Al" was impeccably clever stand-up wrapped in irony and Soweto rhythms. Joni's new songs were bereft of whimsy, and were an awkward fit with the new sounds.

Dolby's contract gave him a coproducer credit (with the engineer Mike Shipley, Larry Klein, and Joni herself), even though she thought of him as more of a synthesizer consultant. Klein had recently bought the latest Fairlight CMI (1985 retail price: £50,000, or approximately $100,000). He wanted to learn how to play with his expensive new toy. And so *Dog Eat Dog* was an album of its moment.

And what kind of moment was 1985? It was the year Tom Waits released *Rain Dogs*, an album of avant-garde Brechtian café music that wouldn't touch a Fairlight with a ten-foot pole. Sting, meanwhile, took a cue from the Joni Mitchell mid to late '70s playbook and recorded his first solo album, *The Dream of the Blue Turtles*, with the saxophonist Branford Marsalis's band; although it didn't match the dizzying success of the Police's *Synchronicity*, and he was accused of being very pretentious—a charge he became adept at surviving, especially as he darted in and out of the mainstream—the album still managed to hit number three on the UK album chart. Like Joni's *Shadows and Light* band, Marsalis was also fronting a group used to more solo space. But the money and exposure more than made up for it. Joni had no such luck. She was pilloried for working with jazz musicians while Sting was being praised for it.

Thomas Dolby regarded Joni as his hero. *Blue* was the first album he bought with his own money, and it was his dream to follow in the footsteps of her collaborations with Tom Scott and Jaco Pastorius. But this Joni was not the Joni of the '70s. The times had changed and so had she. "She felt that the guitar twang was not the right way to frame what she was feeling about the times," Dolby told me. "She needed to use the tools of the times to throw it back in their faces. I think that's why she was looking for somebody that could curate the technology for her. That was the principle behind it." The guitar twang was certainly front and center when she performed her new songs at the Farm Aid and Amnesty International benefits. Then again, people did not seem to be listening. Would the tools of the times do the trick for the album?

Many of Joni's contemporaries were facing this problem. Linda Ronstadt met failure when she tried to go New Wave, then collaborated with Nelson Riddle on a Great American Songbook album and the money rolled in. Paul Simon failed with *Hearts and Bones* before succeeding, counterintuitively, with *Graceland*. James Taylor and Jackson Browne had a couple of hits but otherwise vanished. Dylan found critical success with *Oh Mercy* (1989), but he would have to wait until the '90s for a full-on comeback. Like Dylan, the Rolling Stones, McCartney, and Harrison were too big to fail. Joni didn't fail, but her sales and her reviews were not good. An era would have to come to Joni Mitchell, not the other way around.

Yet forward was the only way to go. As the '70s had progressed, the level of musicianship kept getting deeper and more complex on Joni's albums. What made a hit with the L.A. Express brought her to a smaller but still devoted audience for *The Hissing of Summer Lawns*, *Hejira*, *Don Juan's Reckless Daughter*, and, to a lesser extent, *Mingus*. And while Jaco Pastorius's presence is missed on *Wild Things Run Fast*, the album, as commercial as it aspired to be, still had John Guerin's drums, Wayne Shorter's saxophone, and the inimitable, unfiltered presence of Joni. *Dog Eat Dog* would be different.

Wayne Shorter, no stranger to synthesizers, was still on board, but they were now on the synthetic side of the street. "We did a lot of talking from before the album started through the recording of the album, and it was clear to me that Joni was very angry about the times," Dolby recalled. "She was angry about far-right conservatism and the hypocrisy of evangelism. She was amazed by all the channels on the television where you could surf between them, going from one evangelist to another, which obviously inspired the Rod Steiger speeches on the album." With her own personal troubles and discontent with the way the world was changing, Joni was taking the '80s personally. "She was Joni against the world, really," said Dolby. "We had a little oasis in the studio for a few months, and I think she was searching for new ways to express this."

The album is bookended with a song about friendship, "Good Friends," about the Israeli sculptor and her SoHo landlord Nathan Joseph (with a vocal by the Doobie Brother Michael McDonald, whose voice was ubiquitous on '80s records), and a song about love, "Lucky Girl," which could have fit on an earlier album substituting John Guerin for the synth percussion. In between were harsh social critiques, created in deliberately unsettling timbres. It was the most expensive album Joni would ever make. Rather than let Thomas Dolby sequence on his own time, as he was willing to do, she wanted to be present for every moment of creation, as studio time went by at hundreds of dollars per hour. Even though Dolby was there as a collaborator, it was clear that she wanted to do things her way.

"It was her choice to bring me in," Dolby told me. "It's not like I was thrust on her by the record company. We went into it believing we could create something new and make two plus two equal five. That also reflects my memory of what it was like working with her. Part of the issue on musical terms is that when I arrange a song, I take a constructivist approach. I'll program a bass line, I might program a patch to play the chords. I'll program several sounds, which are designed to work together, and some of them may only be designed for a single line of melody or a few notes here and there, so I built this patchwork. Joni's style on the keyboard is a left-hand, right-hand style, with a rolling left hand and chords in the right hand, so if I'm programming a sound that might take twenty to thirty minutes, she'd come over and say, 'Oooooh, that sounds lovely, let me try that.' Then she'd sit down and play a piano part, using a sound that I designed to play three notes. And I'd say, 'I'm not sure that's really gonna work, because it's going to muddy up the sound that I'd been developing for several days.' And then she'd say, 'Wipe those, wipe those! Let's just put these over the top.' She is very impulsive like that. It was painful at the time. Looking back, it's quite comical, really."

Thirty years later, Joni looks back on *Dog Eat Dog* as a particularly frustrating experience. "What happened there was, suddenly, Klein, my bass-playing husband, appointed himself my producer," Joni said. "And then he appointed the engineer as a producer. Now, when you give a dwarf power, they get puffed up like you wouldn't believe. So I had three puffed-up dwarfs. Everything was divide and conquer with Klein. He busted up all of my relationships in his insecurity. When you have a tyrannical, insecure husband who is very young and you're trying to be a good wife, I questioned my own behavior.

"He insisted that we go from an eight-track machine with an ideal working relationship, an engineer who knew he was an engineer—and he was a great engineer, with no delusions to move up the corporate ladder; I called on him for things that had never been done before. We cut tape—I had to work in a very unorthodox way. I worked like a filmmaker, cutting tape and splicing. I gave him a gold-plated razor blade. After all those years, we were psychic. People would say, 'Do you know what she's talking about?' And Henry would grin and say, 'Yeah.' Look at that picture of Henry and I at that console. It was a beautiful relationship. It was a delightful relationship and Klein, I guess, was jealous of it.

"Klein broke up anything that was close to me. So I get into this studio and Thomas was standing right next to me. We had gone into the '80s and there was a new sound. I hated it. So did Henry. We called it 'sizzle and fry.' And we were determined to ride it through and keep a classical sound that wouldn't date. We both liked good mics, good musicians, and nothing too tricky. But Klein was young, and I learned the mechanics of hip when I was sixteen. I played around with it from twelve to sixteen. I manipulated fashions. I had a column, 'Fads and Fashions,' where I would start fashions and end them. By the time I was sixteen, I knew hip was a herd mentality. It's like saying, 'You've got those '70s plants.' What's '70s about a plant? That mentality is so sick and so rampant in America. People are so afraid not to be hip, so that's what a lot of the American marketplace is about—shallow, stupid people, keeping the economy going by being these frightened consumers. America works on that fear: It's in, it's out."

Joni Mitchell did not give up without a fight. And what a fight. And yet there is one song on *Dog Eat Dog* that somehow survived the production, where the sonic choices made sense with everything else, and that song is "Ethiopia." Nina Simone once saw Joni at the Beverly Center shopping mall. They had never met before, but Joni had respect for her and her work, particularly based on what Don Alias, who had been Simone's drummer, had told her. No matter how much Simone seemed to be losing her stability, she always, Alias maintained, treated her musicians with the utmost dignity. Simone spotted Joni after the release and the negative press of *Dog Eat Dog*. There she was, the great and notoriously hard to please Nina Simone, past her prime, but still. Simone lifted her arms like a Y, approached Joni, and said, "Joni Mitchell! Joni Mitchell! 'Ethiopia'!" Then she was gone.

She was on to something. It is a devastating song. Everyone is part of the problem and no one is part of the solution, especially well-meaning but ineffective celebrity charity jams. The song sounds like inconsolable grief by someone who knows she's part of the problem, too. "On and on, the human greed profanes," Joni sings in the first verse. We needed music to face ourselves in the face of a problem that was getting well-meaning media attention, but that we still didn't know how to solve. And Joni was crying to be heard. We are not exactly the world. We wish we were.

"Ethiopia" faces a complex human calamity with startling chords.

The song touched a nerve so deep, its structures confounded even Joni's most knowing and sympathetic listeners. Wayne Shorter, who had always gone the distance for Joni, was troubled by the chords. Joni recalls he told her that at the Berklee School of Music, they said that you weren't supposed to follow a suspended chord with another suspended chord. "What kinds of chords are these?" he asked. "These are not guitar chords. These are not piano chords." (Wayne Shorter, incidentally, has a music education degree from NYU and an honorary doctorate from the Berklee School, but did not actually *attend* the Berklee School.) All she could say was "This is a song about people starving to death. What is it supposed to sound like? 'Wake Up Little Susie'?"

Joni did not sing on "We Are the World" or at "Live Aid." She did sing on the Canadian famine relief song, "Tears Are Not Enough," but in truth she was skeptical that these events did any good beyond the posturing of the artists. And her response to the suffering of others was deeply personal. Being a penniless young Toronto folkie in 1964 is a long way from the Third World, but she had been a mother who felt she could not afford to raise her daughter. The helpless mother and her dying child—these are the images that linger longest, beginning with "Hot winds and hunger cries, Ethiopia / Flies in your babies' eyes, Ethiopia," and then describing a TV host "with a PR smile" who calls your baby "it." When Joni sings, "You suffer with such dignity," she is describing an unintentional performance by the starving and dying Ethiopians caught on video. Then she goes deeper, into the suffering itself. Joni was right to compose chords that would flummox even Wayne Shorter.

Joni could take the pain of losing her daughter and use it to imagine the pain of the mother watching her children die, while dying herself. "Ethiopia" is the sound of Joni inhabiting the voice of that mother, those children.

Thomas Dolby, before he realized the repellent effect he had on Joni, cherished his memories of her loaning him her blue '69 Mercedes convertible, of her stories of Greek caves, of Miles Davis falling asleep clinging to her ankles, and of piano shopping with her (when he tried, unsuccessfully, to get her to jam with him on her old songs). But he concluded from her interviews promoting the album that he wasn't her favorite person in the world. Which was putting it mildly. "Slimy little bugger," Joni called him forty years later.

Joni tells this story: At one point, Joni wanted Dolby to provide a click track—a synchronized track—of Marvin Gaye's "Trouble Man," just to use as a rhythmic basis for "Lucky Girl," the album's closing track. The results were not pretty.

"The lyrics of 'Trouble Man' are very honest and the form is very eccentric, but it's beautiful," Joni told me. "The form is very irregular, the architecture, the structure of the music. So I said, make me a click track in the same form as the 'Trouble Man' groove."

"I don't like it," sneered Dolby.

"I don't care whether you like it or not," Joni told him. "Just make me a click track to that tempo and that groove."

He stormed out in a huff. Two weeks later, he returned.

"I made you that track," he said. What he played her was, she recalled, "this corny-ass piece of music, with horns and everything."

"That's your composition," Joni said. "That's not what I asked you for. I asked you for a click track. Just give me that groove to play to and then I'm going to put drums in afterwards that are different."

The song they were arguing over, "Lucky Girl," was the only love song on the album. There was no love in the studio. Joni became so exasperated, she put Dolby on a beeper and told him, "If we need you, we'll call you."

They tried to get the rhythm track off his machine and the sounds were, to Joni's ears, hideous.

"Never mind," she said. "I'll block it out like a baby crying."

"I've been struggling to get this asshole to help, and he's refusing, and then he creates this whole piece of boring music that has no soul," Joni recalled. "So I played to it, but it was so abstract, and everyone was holding their ears. I played the piano to it, and when I was done, I yanked it out completely and started to rebuild it. Because it was so abstract, I couldn't tell which was the downbeat. So I took an upbeat as a downbeat, and I came to this really eccentric place, and when I came to program the drums, I had a problem, because it was moving on two and four, but on the four, I had built my own drum collection that I would use, including Jimmy Cliff on hand drums. Nothing worked. And it needed anchoring on four."

Shorter came in and the track was not finished. His brow knit up, he picked up his tenor, went out in the studio, and anchored the four beat with his horn. "Wayne's a genius. He went straight to the problem, he saw the problem right off the bat, he anchored it. All these drums had failed and what succeeded was just Wayne playing one note all the way through it on four. Then he picked up the soprano and played—total genius. Then the next thing I know, Thomas Dolby claims he wrote the song. Completely insane. There wasn't a note from his programming on it. All there was was the tempo, like I had asked. But what I had to go through were these crazy sounds. And I had a screaming match with him on the phone with his manager. It was like I had Tourette's. The audacity that he said that he cowrote that song. So he's a cheap little bastard. The only thing he contributed was when he said, 'Oh, I'm so excited' on 'Shiny Toys.' Other than that, we were just using his palette, which dates like crazy. I knew it would."

"How in the hell did I end up with three producers on the most unpleasant session of my whole career?" Joni thought. Suddenly there were three men, including her husband, telling her, "I don't like it." Joni, who had been so fiercely independent, was now arguing with a committee of men. Elliot Roberts hired these guys to coproduce. Now Roberts, who had been by her side for nearly twenty years, would be fired. "So now Elliot's gone and Henry's gone and Klein is just cleaning house," Joni recalled. "He tells me which friends I can keep."

Klein is, unsurprisingly, baffled by this account. "She contradicted herself. First, I was the bad guy, then Elliot was the bad guy. So I'm cleaning house and Elliot is gone, implying that I was the one who got rid of Elliot. So she was so unhappy with the situation that I had brought about with Thomas and Mike Shipley that she fired Elliot. Man, I tell you, that is really crazy stuff."

Elliot Roberts was replaced by Peter Asher; Joni says she never trusted him. Asher was part of the duo Peter and Gordon in the '60s and the brother of the actress Jane Asher, whom Paul McCartney was dating at the peak of Beatlemania. Peter and Gordon had hit singles with "World Without Love" and other Lennon-McCartney songs. Eventually, Asher went to the business side of music; he was the one who brought a fledgling and unknown James Taylor to the attention of McCartney and Apple Records.

In Joni's telling, Asher was curt with her; they were always fighting. He remembers it differently. "I disagree with her characterization of me, of course, but that's to be expected," Asher told me. "She didn't annoy me. I may be curt—I'm probably curt. I try to make the point succinctly. Elliot was the opposite of curt. Elliot would smoke a joint and ramble."

He thinks about it some more. Maybe, he says, Joni has a point. "I guess we were all doing lots of coke, including Joni. Cocaine was very much around in that era. It made us all a little extra curt. Maybe in my case it made me extra curt and it made Joni extra voluble."

Joni also believes that Asher had a conflict of interest because he also managed Linda Ronstadt and James Taylor, and Joni, in 2015, was convinced that she was bound to be on the losing end of that rivalry. When she left Elliot, she told me, "I was without management and it was all landing on Klein. I couldn't see a decent manager on the horizon, and Peter came up to me one day and said, 'I'm offering my services. Elliot says it's okay.' It was a stupid thing to do, because he was used to competing with Elliot, with James and Linda versus me and Neil Young. And he never lost that thing, so that he resented any successes of mine as being threatening to James, because they loved to pit James versus Carly and now they had me and James in the same stable. So when I put out *Dog Eat Dog*, James put out a competent album, but nothing spectacular. Elliot was afraid that the press would like *Dog Eat Dog* but not James's and it would invite unfavorable competition. So they liked James's album and they called *Dog Eat Dog* sophomoric, for being politically active at a time when 'Material Girl' was reigning and it was not a time for protest."

Here, Peter Asher draws the line. "Is Joni saying that *Dog Eat Dog* would eclipse James's album and get better press and then didn't, presumably through my efforts? That actually smacks of insanity. That's really mad. James and Linda versus Joni and Neil are chalk and cheese, particularly Linda's case. We had a career that was dependent on hit singles, not writing, a completely other kind of world. I never conceived of Linda and Joni as rivals or in the same business. It's distressing in the sense that I would only manage somebody without wishing them the utmost success. Why would anyone do that? I love Joni and think she's a genius. That's the only reason I worked with her. We worked very hard on *Dog Eat Dog*, getting it the best recognition and attention that we could. I'm not a shrink, but it reaches the point like the moon landings didn't happen or something like that. It's a completely alternate version of reality that doesn't even have a basis. It's distressing, it's worrying." Joni's anger was boiling, and about to boil over. She had already predicted, way back in "For the Roses," that it was only a matter of time before that wreath was going to be put around her neck and she'd be put out to pasture for good. Who would be around to watch over her now?

28 ■ EMERGENCY ROOMS

D espite the debacle of *Dog Eat Dog* and the financial strains, things seemed solid between Joni and Larry Klein. She felt that she had finally made a good marriage and continued to avoid writing personal songs about heartbreak. But this would change near the end of 1985, when Joni, surprisingly, became pregnant. A pregnancy at forty-two is delicate, and made even more parlous when the mother will not give up a four-pack-a-day habit, or drinking, or any other vice. Joni had a miscarriage that winter, and the fracture in her marriage with Klein would never entirely heal.

"He dragged me all over Europe, as sick as a dog, on his vacation," Joni told me. "Never a thought that his wife was pregnant and needed to go to a doctor. The baby died. I know the night: December eighteenth. We traveled and I miscarried on the twenty-eighth of January, 1986. And we ate in Italy and France. I was turning gray and green and he didn't even notice."

She remains fiercely bitter. "When I miscarried, he didn't comfort me, no arm around me. I was distraught, and in that state, rather than

being a comfort—and this was five days before he began his first le-
gitimate job as a producer—he just went out, stocked the fridge with
groceries, and got in his car, went to the airport. He had five days before it began: no comfort . . . Marriages break up when you lose a child,
let alone having a husband that behaved so badly. And his excuse was
that he didn't know how serious it was, and I was hemorrhaging. So
ten days later, I'm still bleeding, and my girlfriend said, 'You've got to
get to a doctor.' I said, 'I can't drive. I'm too weak.' She took me, and
then I had to go through D and C with a doctor who said, 'I can't
believe I'm doing this to Joni Mitchell!'"

The superfan doctor froze, she said. "I had to guide him through
it. This poor guy, I just said, 'Don't tremble. Come on. Be a professional.
Forget who I am. Let's just do this. We know it's painful. Be objective,
for Christ's sake. What kind of a doctor are you?'"

By 2015, Klein had gained some perspective on how the miscarriage was the beginning of the end of their marital happiness. But he
did not see her version of events as complete or entirely honest. "I have
to tell you the way that she portrays that situation . . . I certainly would
agree with certain things she says, but the story she tells is neither accurate nor full in the way that she relates it. What happened was that
she, to her amazement and mine, got pregnant. Then we were on a
press tour for something, and then she didn't know she had miscarried,
but she was already in the process of miscarrying. The sad part of this
whole thing is that, leading up to losing that child, which was a tragedy, of course, and it destroyed our entire world, she did not take care
of herself, and was not at all receptive to anyone else telling her to take
care of herself. And this happens. Still, it's a very sad, horrible thing.

"The position I was put in was that when this all came down, the
rest of the people who were involved in this Benjamin Orr record
were already at a residential studio in England getting set up and they
were waiting on me. And so I was in a really difficult situation. If
the same thing had happened to me now or any time after that, I
would've behaved differently. I would not have gone."

At the time, in a state of relative ignorance, Klein asked her for
advice. "This is a terribly difficult situation," Klein said to his recovering

wife. "What should I do? I'm holding everything up. Should I just tell them I can't come?"

"No, you can go," Joni said. He took this at face value, only to regret it later.

"Of course, after the fact, she said, 'Why did you listen to me?'" Klein recalled. "In retrospect, I shouldn't have listened to her. I should have stayed. I honestly did not know very much about this. I don't know how many times we talked it through and I thought we resolved it. Nevertheless, in her mind, I just sold her down the river. If you found a linchpin event that created the abandonment that would fuel her acrimony, the miscarriage was it. I told her, 'Listen, I didn't realize all the ramifications of a miscarriage. My mom had a number of them, but it was kept so hush-hush, I thought it was like a common cold.'

"I never knew all the emotional and psychological parts of the things that accompany something like that happening to a woman. I think you'd find a lot of men in my age group in the same boat. When I was growing up, we just didn't talk about miscarriage. Women would have them, and everything was kept away from the kids. So here, all these years later, I have to pick up books and find that she's reinventing history. All of a sudden, I'm the only bad guy in the plot, for having abandoned her, and that is very hurtful."

29 ■ SAVE THE BOMBS FOR LATER

omething good did come from Larry Klein taking the gig with Benjamin Orr. He ended up in Ashcombe House, Peter Gabriel's studio outside Bath in Somerset, played gratis on *So*, and then shared his new friends with Joni, who would sing with both of them on her next album. Because Klein didn't accept payment from Peter Gabriel, Gabriel invited Joni to record her next album at his studio, reciprocating Klein's good deed with another.

"When I went to England to produce Ben Orr's album with Mike Shipley, we were working at a studio in Somerset called the Wool Hall," Klein recalled. "It was just a little bit outside of Bath, in a very rural area that had a great music scene happening at that time. Peter Gabriel lived there, and had a studio built into a garage-type structure called Ashcombe House, the guys from Tears for Fears were up there and were part owners of the Wool Hall, Kate Bush, Peter Hamill, and a bunch of other interesting bands that were around at that time. Everybody would hop over to each other's studio and drop in, people would call each other to come play on things; it was a real catalytic place to be working. After I had been there for a while, Peter Gabriel, who at the time was trying to finish what was to become *So*, called me to come play bass on a few tracks over at his studio. I was already a big fan of Peter's music, so I was pretty thrilled to be asked. I went over, and the first track that he played me was 'Mercy Street.' Now, I had been a fan of Anne Sexton's poetry in my teens, so this song hit a very deep place inside me. I think that I was almost crying the first time that I heard the track. We finished working on what they had for me in a couple of days. I somehow felt awkward taking money for having played on his album. Now that I look back on it, I find it strange. I think that I had assimilated the noblesse oblige approach to these situations that was a part of how things worked between well-known artists when they were asked to sing or play on each other's albums."

On June 15, 1986, Joni Mitchell made a rare television appearance. The occasion was the Conspiracy of Hope benefit concert for Amnesty International. Joni was playing real good for free, and doing so for a good cause; she was also performing new songs that challenged the times she found herself in. Would a stadium audience—not to mention a fickle TV audience—get the picture? In an event for human rights, how humane would their treatment be of an artist they might have forgotten about—someone who headlined the first Greenpeace concert back in 1971, the year she recorded *Blue*? How charitable was this charity audience?

She came on at the Amnesty International concert unannounced, between Bryan Adams and U2, before a stadium crowd of about 150,000 rowdy ticket holders waiting for Pete Townshend, who couldn't show. Suddenly they were confronted by his replacement, Joni, singing a quiet rendition of a song that none of them knew. At forty-two, she looked stunning, and she delicately strummed, on acoustic guitar, a song from the all-electronic *Dog Eat Dog*. The noise of the crowd all but drowned her out.

For anyone listening, it was the closest one could come to imagining her in a folk club, singing this new song, "The Three Great Stimulants." Inspired by Nietzsche's take on (or takedown of) Wagner, this was Joni versus the pop '80s. "Only sick music makes money today," wrote Nietzsche. That was the 1880s. By the 1980s, Joni felt deeply, Nietzsche's prophecy had become fate. If Nietzsche was disgusted by Wagner, what would he have made of Hall and Oates, or Phil Collins? The sickness of the decade even plagued music that might have otherwise been good. The standards, in other words, were low, and the people were sheep.

The Police had reunited for the concert and the audience was with them, "sending out an S-O-S." Peter Gabriel (with Larry Klein on bass) got the crowd riled up with his impassioned performance of "Biko"—"oh-oh-oooooh," the crowd cried out for the slain South African activist. Bono did the thing that Bono does, making love to the camera, and everyone else, loving himself even more than he wants the audience to love him. Even Lou Reed, in spite of his misanthropic reputation, seemed, in his way, to agree with everyone else that Amnesty International was a good cause. He sang a classic Velvet Underground song about how someone's life could be saved by rock and roll, and it took on new significance. Someone in the third world could be saved by rock and roll, too. A month after the concert, Amnesty International reported 45,000 new members.

Joni could have come out and performed an anthemic "Woodstock" and had New Jersey begging for more. But she wasn't there to comfort them, or to love them. All by herself, she was there to perform an acoustic intervention. Joni was there to get her dark Nietzschean message out: We should not feel good about ourselves. We are decadent and far, far away from the garden. We may be far from combat, Joni is saying, but it is there, it is real, and we have become too weak and complacent to stop that rough beast. "No tanks have ever rumbled through these streets," she sang, her blond hair blowing in the summer breeze, looking like a Nordic goddess in a stadium of thugs. "And the drone of planes at night has never frightened me."

Just as she sang the word *frightened* she was suddenly pelted, on live TV, with enough ice to fill maybe a dozen Big Gulps. And it was even worse than it looked. It wasn't just ice cubes. "They hit a water glass and it shattered and it rooster-tailed up to eye level," Joni told me. "But they were throwing it at everybody and it just happened to hit something." When she continued, somewhat shaken up, with her line "I keep the hours and the company that I please," she added, in the middle—"*Not you!*" It was all too apropos that she concluded by repeating, "Oh, these brutal times!"

After the verses concluded, she let out a sound that she had not committed to record before *Dog Eat Dog*. It was not a sound of ecstasy or beautiful, tragic, yet mellifluous pain. It was an alarm of contempt blared from her chest cavity. She had to be careful with that falsetto, still there, but less supple. It would disappear for good by the end of the decade, and New Jersey didn't deserve it that night.

When the song was over, she went up to the mic and said, "Hey, save the bombs for later. I'm not that bad, you dig? Quit pitching shit up here!" Nobody seemed to be listening. These really were brutal times. Joni was not going to suck up to this crowd. What would be the point of that?

Later, she had a sense of humor about it. "Well, the thing is, that crowd was throwing stuff all day," she recalled. "It just happened that by the time I got out there, they'd had a lot of practice. Their aim was getting better." On the video, you can see Joni light up when she comprehends the absurdity of it all. These lyrics, she thought, are fucking perfect: "Will they shower you with flowers / Or will they shun ya / When your race is run?" Throw it! This is great theater!

Besides, she had been through worse.

Between August 26 and August 30, 1970, Ron and Ray Foulk staged a music festival almost a year after Woodstock: the Isle of Wight Festival. It was the festival's third consecutive year; the previous year, they featured Bob Dylan's first major performance since his motorcycle accident three years earlier. This would be an occasion to perform "Woodstock" for a crowd even bigger than the one she sang about but missed. Murray Lerner would document the concert for a film, and it would include Leonard Cohen, Joan Baez, the Who, Miles Davis, and, in their last filmed performance, the Doors.

In the aftermath of Woodstock, the Foulk brothers realized that they had to make the concert free. But as Joni was about to go on-stage, a Charles Manson look-alike, calling himself Yogi Joe—who had actually given Joni a yoga lesson—took the microphone to inform the crowd that, with the festival promoters lining their pockets, they were all going the way of Dylan's Desolation Row. He was removed from the stage by security, and Joni took the microphone to quiet the incensed crowd:

> Will you listen a minute? Now listen . . . A lot of people who get up here and sing . . . I know it's fun, you know, it's a lot of fun, it's fun for me. I get my feelings off through my music . . . but listen, it's like, last Sunday I went to a Hopi ceremonial dance in the desert and there were a lot of people there and there were tourists . . . and there were tourists who were acting like Indians and there were Indians who were getting into it like tourists . . . and . . . and . . . I think you're acting like tourists, man . . . *Give us some respect.*

The Hopi ceremonial dance she described included a bad peyote trip with James Taylor. And now this was a bad trip for real. She was facing six hundred thousand hecklers as she tried to perform the new "My Old Man." They thought because Joni was discouraging Yogi Joe from saying his thing—however incoherent—that she was one of them, the authoritarian festival establishment with their ticket charges, silencing the drugged-out hippie giving the peace symbol while being dragged away. And yet her rant also drew applause. By the time she delivered an ebullient "Big Yellow Taxi," she received a standing ovation from many of the same hippies who had been howling at her minutes earlier. "I just felt my heart go thump-thump-thump," she said after her set was over. This was a long way from stardust and golden. She knew how to tame this beast, but she never quite got over it.

And now, in East Rutherford, New Jersey, Joni was fondly recalling her debut at Carnegie Hall in 1969, when things could still be stardust and golden, and a banner reading "New York Loves You, Joni" was unfurled from the balcony. Despite the thugs in New Jersey, New York still did love her, and rallied to her side after her televised indignation. The next day, there was a radio station playing Joni's set. Joni and Klein were staying in the Varick Street loft she was still renting, and Nathan

Joseph came over and cranked it up, so that Joni could hear it through the wall. "They're playing your part in this performance!" he said. Victory, at least in Gotham.

That night, Joni and Klein went through town as celebrated martyrs. "And we went out on the town that night and New York was made aware," Joni told me. "We were walking through SoHo and Little Italy, and this guy comes out of an Italian restaurant and says, 'Joni! On behalf of New York, we are so sorry! What did they do to you? Come in! We'll make you a nice dinner!' And they made this gorgeous dinner with sweet lemons with icing sugar for dessert. We walked by this lesbian bar and these really butch lesbians came out and one of them said, 'We thought you were really great. Come in and we'll buy you a drink.' I survived it. It was okay. But I shouldn't have been put that high on the bill. Most of that audience probably didn't know who I was. When I saw it on video and I saw the moment where it hit, I thought, 'Don't throw me in the briar patch! I was born in the briar patch!'"

Rolling Stone called it the Worst Performance of the Year. Really? With all the sick music of 1986? They were apparently in agreement with the rabble in the pit. It's a shame that more people didn't hear the song performed that way, because it was the best it ever sounded.

Shortly before the concert, Joni was recording *Chalk Mark in a Rain Storm* at Peter Gabriel's studio in Bath, England. She was aware that this was not the same thing as sharing a studio with just any hit maker. Gabriel had been the lead singer of Genesis when they were an overtly and proudly noncommercial art rock band. He would perform in weird costumes that looked like amoebas or other things that could only be seen from Cold War–era microscopes in British state schools. They had a short, round drummer named Phil Collins. No one thought this guy would dominate the charts in the next decade, especially him. When Gabriel went solo, he found his way to the mainstream his own way, with less than obvious hits like "Shock the Monkey." MTV was weirdly perfect for him. When Joni was trying for a comeback, at forty-three, Gabriel, at thirty-five, was having his moment.

Henry Lewy was no longer working with Joni, and she cut the album with a third engineer, a trainee, someone who knew nothing except for how to turn on the console and make many, many mistakes. "I was only going to make a couple of demos, but then I got going on it," Joni recalled. At a certain point, Gabriel, who had been scheduled to play at the Amnesty International concert, asked Joni for advice. He had never played in a group show before, and this one would be on live TV. He sure came to the right person! Joni had never gotten over being crucified by half a million hippies at the Isle of Wight. She knew that Phil Collins, who had been the drummer for Genesis, had become a huge, shameless commercial pop star. She saw the potential for competition right away.

"Well," Joni said, "these group shows are a sea of egomaniacal behavior, from my perspective."

Then, Joni added, "They'll probably ask you to do an acoustic song."

"They did."

"Don't do it," Joni implored. "Take it from me. He who plays acoustic dies. That's my experience in those shows. You can't get enough volume to mask the roar of the crowd. They're not there for the music—they're there for the event. So you really need the camaraderie of the band and you need to be really loud. Second, bring in your own team, because they'll sabotage you. If someone gets competitive, which they frequently do, if you don't have your own team, they'll sabotage you. If they think you're going to be good, steal some thunder, or be the one that shines, they'll break your guitar. They'll come after you with a vengeance."

Peter Gabriel looked into Joni's eyes. They had just recorded a song of Joni's, "My Secret Place," in which they were finishing each other's sentences. Her raspy alto was in unison with his. They were almost the same person, and filmed a flirty video for it, even though they were both married to other people. Who was this person he thought he was getting to know so well? And what was with all this paranoia about music festivals? Didn't she write "Woodstock"?

"Your light is a puppet to cover your darkness," Gabriel said, shaken up. This made Joni furious.

"Oh, my God," Joni replied. "You're naïve! My light is my light and my darkness is my darkness. Neither one are present in this scenario. I'm just telling you. You asked me what it was like. I'm telling you the things that can go wrong. You're going out there to kick ass and you don't want Phil Collins to be the one that shines. You're not going out there without ambition. I know what you desire out of it, and I don't want to see you making mistakes. I don't go out there with that attitude, but I know it's all around me."

Joni's friendship with Gabriel and his wife would not last long. Pretty soon, he was saying things she considered to be stupid and petty. Plus, Joni felt snubbed by his wife at a restaurant. How disappointing! The truth, according to Larry Klein, was that "Joni spent too many evenings spewing her didactically nihilistic view of the world at him in the kitchen of the studio." But before all that, Joni went to the Amnesty show in LA, and she said to Gabriel, "It gives me great pleasure that you're on an exceptional tour. There's camaraderie, there doesn't seem to be abnormal competition. You're lucky. Forget what I said."

The songs were piling up again, and Joni began recording what eventually became *Chalk Mark in a Rain Storm* (1988). The synthesizers were still part of the soundscape (including, on one track, Thomas Dolby on "Fairlight Marimba"), but she was back to using a drummer—Manu Katché, from Peter Gabriel's band. It is a shame that she was not produced by Daniel Lanois, a huge fan of hers who was central to the successful sound on Gabriel's *So*, and also Dylan's *Oh Mercy* and his Grammy-winning *Time Out of Mind*. "She was always pretty dismissive of Lanois's talent," said Klein. "To my mind, she was not unproduceable, she was just unable to acknowledge that she needed anyone to make records, which she did. Hence Henry 'more than an engineer' Lewy was a producer on those records, and was given a royalty. She just couldn't bear to give him a producer's credit. She needed to conceive of herself as a completely self-sufficient entity."

Klein was in England, finishing his work on Ben Orr's album. "At a certain point I felt that Joni would be better off coming to join me,"

Klein said. "We found a house in the neighboring small town of Frome, and she came over. The travail of the previous period had triggered some writing for her, so while she was in Frome she set about finishing the first four songs that would become *Chalk Mark in a Rain Storm*."

Figuring that Gabriel owed him for his gratis contribution to *So*, Klein asked Gabriel if Joni could record in his studio. "He was in fact very happy to have us work in his studio, so work began on these tracks with Joni starting work during the afternoon, and I would come over after we would finish work in the evening at the Wool Hall. I ended up staying into the early morning hours over at Peter's studio. As much as it was a strain workwise, it was also invigorating having all this music gestating simultaneously. A really creatively charged atmosphere. Mike and I met with Robert Plant, who lived in Wales, not far from where we were, and I played him a couple of the sketches. There was one that he really liked, and he asked if he could try writing some lyrics for it towards his album. I was overjoyed, having been a big Led Zeppelin fan since my early teens. When Joan got to Frome I played her the pieces, and she loved three of them, including the one that Robert had claimed. I protested, saying that he had already claimed the track; how could I renege on having offered it to him. Joni insisted that I give all of them to her, saying that she had 'a wife's privilege' to take it back. I sheepishly called Robert, and he very generously agreed, saying that he would do it 'only because it was Joni Mitchell.' These three songs became 'Lakota,' 'Snakes and Ladders,' and 'The Tea Leaf Prophecy.'"

While she was in the midst of putting together a collection in the hope that she could replicate the success of Peter Gabriel, who had followed her advice so well when she couldn't, she appeared on the debut of a show to be hosted by Herbie Hancock called *Showtime Coast to Coast*, taped in New Orleans, on August 29, 1987. In a formula that would be replicated twenty years later for his Grammy-winning album *River: The Joni Letters*, Hancock, along with Wayne Shorter, would take two songs from *Hejira* and probe them for further jazz possibilities. They were joined by Bobby McFerrin, who still commanded respect among jazz musicians around the time that he released his Grammy-winning record "Don't Worry, Be Happy" (an accappella jam that was the very antithesis of a Joni Mitchell song).

"Furry Sings the Blues" would be loosened up; "Hejira" would be recast as a wild samba. Joni, smoking, chewing gum, was so nervous that, when she sang the "Hejira" line about "waving truce," she seemed to be attempting to wave the TV cameras away. And yet it was some of the finest music she had made in a very long time, at least since the standout tracks on *Wild Things Run Fast* five years earlier. Her voice was exquisite. Whatever huskiness was starting to build up only made the material deeper. She still had a soprano, and even if it was smoky, it was full of evocative and rich expression. Sarah Vaughan's voice dropped as she kept living and smoking, and it just fit into the trajectory of the great jazz singer she was until last call. It was as if the lessons Joni learned from Mingus—the man, not just the album—were coming to fruition. McFerrin, who seemed intrusive, was actually keeping Joni at ease. "Ooooh, I'm traveling in some vehicle . . ." she sang in her still stunning upper register. For just one late-night, early-morning session, Joni allowed herself to be heard without synthesizers, and with jazz masters, and we see the direction she could have taken if she had just kept her musical adventures of *Mingus* going.

At the Amnesty International debacle, the biggest audience responses came when she announced that she would, on "Number One," a track that would appear on *Chalk Mark in a Rain Storm*, be joined by Peter Gabriel's drummer and, as backup, Dolette McDonald. It was clear who was selling, and it must have been frustrating to be influencing people who were having the success that was eluding her. The song was a withering indictment of the dog race the music biz had become, and how the view looked from the sidelines. At Amnesty International, she threw these words at that audience: "Win and lose, win and lose / To the loser go the heartsick blues / To the victor goes to spoilin' / Honey, did you win or lose?" Winning and losing are for the bean counters at the record company. Beauty and truth are for the artist. Joni tried to dress this contempt with the rhythms and sounds that had worked for others.

She would stuff her album to the gills with celebrities. Do people buy albums for the guest stars? *Chalk Mark in a Rain Storm* would make the experiment. Don Henley, who was pushed aside for Lionel Richie on "You Dream Flat Tires"—because Richie's range offered more of a contrast—finally got his spot on "Lakota" and "Snakes and Ladders." (He made it clear he was ticked off by being pulled off.) Benjamin Orr of the Cars—whose solo record was, of course, produced by Klein—sang on "Number One" and "The Beat of Black Wings." Wendy and Lisa from Prince's band sang on "The Tea Leaf Prophecy." Billy Idol and Tom Petty both played characters fighting over Joni's character on "Dancin' Clown." Willie Nelson, the redheaded stranger himself, sang, effortlessly, a cowboy part on "Cool Water." All of these people, either as solo artists or as part of outfits, sold records. Could Joni cobble them together in a way that would get her in the black with Geffen?

Of all these appearances, the one that sounds the most like a genuine collaboration—not in composition, but in sound—was "My Secret Place" with Peter Gabriel. "My Secret Place," which opens the album, is, for Joni listeners, a relief after the synthetic assault of *Dog Eat Dog*. Instead of a programmed drum part, there is a real drummer, Manu Katché, a key player in the "World Beat" sound that brought Gabriel massive success in the '80s. Katché plays on the whole album, a welcome, living and breathing presence. "My Secret Place" even sounds like a Gabriel song. Rhythmically, it's not far off from "In Your Eyes"—the song John Cusack blares on a boom box to get his girlfriend back in Cameron Crowe's *Say Anything*—and lyrically, it's unlike anything Joni had done before. She sings in the first person but the narrator is clearly a fictional character, a woman born and raised in New York City, just getting used to Colorado. Joni's voice had become so smoky, she and Gabriel finish each other's sentences in the same range and timbre. It's a seduction song, showing a prospective lover a hiding place, a place where they can hide together if the planets align. The song ends with a question: "Why did you pick me / For the secret place?" Who is asking and who is answering? There was an accompanying black-and-white video of their flirtation, playful and evocative, perfectly capturing the song's mood. "Sledgehammer," a 1986 single from *So*, became the most played video in the history of MTV. "My Secret Place," for all its charms, was no contender.

Gabriel's studio happened to be a ridge away from the airstrip where U.S. troops were launching the 1986 air strike on Libya. The strike, in response to the Libyan bombing of a German disco, commenced on April 15. All told, there were forty Libyan casualties, along with two American airmen, whose plane was shot down. Shortly after, Joni recalled, "At night we could see the orange glow from the landing strip . . . During that period, all of our thinking turned to war . . ." The war inspired "The Beat of Black Wings," about a soldier, Killer Kyle, who felt he had vanished into the sediment, "a chalk mark in a rainstorm," an image that became the album's title. The song has notable fans, including Janet Jackson, who covered it, and Elvis Costello, who called it "beautiful but harrowing." The airstrike had transported Joni back to Fayetteville, North Carolina, 1967, where she met the soldier who would inspire the character of Killer Kyle. He had told this sweet young lady with her love songs that, from where he stood, there ain't no love. "I'm gonna tell you where love went," he'd growled. And he'd ended up sobbing in Joni's arms.

Like Joni, Killer Kyle lost a child, but unlike Joni, he lost a child for good. His girl had an abortion "without even grievin'." He had possibly, like many Vietnam vets, killed civilians. Killer Kyle feels useless, shrouded by the beat of black wings. He was trained to kill, but he wasn't prepared for the aftermath. Hope without an object cannot live, wrote Coleridge. Kyle lives without hope:

> *The old hate the young*
> *That's the whole heartless thing*
> *The old pick the wars*
> *We die in 'em*
> *To the beat of the beat of black wings*

Kyle was traumatized in an unwinnable war. This war had warped an entire generation. Following the release of Oliver Stone's Oscar-winning *Platoon* (1986), and anticipating Maya Lin's Vietnam memorial, it was a time to come to terms with America's greatest military failure. Unlike the David Crosby crowd she was running with, she, like Bob Hope, performed for soldiers. The war ruined many lives. Killer Kyle feels real because he was based on a real person. In the video for the song, Joni puts on makeup and plays him as a black man, the last time she did a variation on her Art Nouveau character. She really plays this guy as a drunk in an alley, a ruined man from a lousy war. Her performance as the character on record is some of the best acting she ever did.

For someone who captured the *Geist* in the *Zeit* of the '60s—who was mourning a cultural moment while it was still happening—1989 proved to be another pivotal year. The Berlin Wall would be torn down, and communism would, with the exception of Albania, disappear from the Eastern Bloc. Something new was afoot, and Joni Mitchell was tapped for an event where rock stars could perform at the site of the recently torn down Berlin Wall. The Cold War was finally over.

But the old battles continued.

In 1990, she appeared with Roger Waters, Sinéad O'Connor, Van Morrison, members of the Band, Cyndi Lauper, Bryan Adams, and the Scorpions, among others, to perform Pink Floyd's *The Wall* in Berlin. Waters, who wrote most of the album and was estranged from his bandmates, staged the production on his own, using the fall of the Berlin Wall to celebrate a new cultural moment. Joni sang on "Goodbye Blue Sky," a song she thought to be a dead ringer for the Rolling Stones' "Ruby Tuesday," but which also had an environmental message simpatico with hers. Probably because Joni was singing from the top of what used to be the Berlin Wall to accompaniment from the bottom, her singing was as unmusical as any she ever did in public. (It would be corrected for the video and the recording.) At the performance, she saw Thomas Dolby again for the last time, at her side on the finale, "The

Tide Is Turning," an uplifting anthem from a Waters solo album. Joni sang with her arm around O'Connor, who Joni thought was a "passionate little singer." It was time to pass the baton.

Except that, just as she warned Peter Gabriel about the Amnesty International concert, going backstage at an all-star rock and roll event is a minefield. "When I did *The Wall*, Thomas Dolby saw me and stuck his tongue out at me," Joni told me. "Cyndi Lauper said, 'My boyfriend made you tea. He didn't make me any.' The childish competitiveness, the lack of professionalism—I don't have a peer group. All of them, these spoiled children. It's not what I would have expected in an artistic community. I ran into Bryan Adams and he wanted his picture taken with me and then gave the camera to his girlfriend. He kept negating her, putting her down and ragging on his girlfriend. So his conduct was really bad. Then I went to the trailer camp. All of my trailer park experiences with other artists are very bad. So I went to Cyndi Lauper's to say hello and I didn't linger. Sinéad came out and she had bare feet and was looking at them. She was digging her feet in the ground, never looking at me. Everybody was so weird. And I went into the greenroom, and Garth Hudson was sitting there, and I walked over to say hello. We were doing a communal project! Was there an adult in the room? No. Not one single adult in the whole pack. Garth took one look at me, slid off the piano bench, and went in the other direction. Later, my daughter wanted to see a concert of his in Toronto, so I got her tickets and got her a backstage pass, and he says, 'Oh, I was always so in love with your mother.' And I went: Is that what it is? These seventh-grade boys? What is it? They frost me. I tried to say hi to people and I got nothing but very strange responses.

"And I was told that Roger wrote in his book that I was the only professional there. I didn't see anything but childishness all around me. When the press asked me in the end, 'Who was here that you wanted to meet?' And I said, 'Well, I would have liked to have met Picasso.' Because there was no one there that you could meet. They were all sullen children.'"

When Joni sang "Goodbye Blue Sky" atop a demolished Berlin Wall, a new cultural moment was coming. In a song called "Right Here,

Right Now," a band called Jesus Jones announced that a new time was coming, something different from the Woodstock generation. "Bob Dylan didn't have this to sing about," they sang. Dylan would have plenty of other things to sing about. What would Joni sing about? The Cold War was over, and so were the '80s. Good riddance to both. The music of the next decade would indeed be more sparse and acoustic. But, as Dylan put it, you can always come back, but you can't come back all the way. Joni's voice was now a smoky alto. The soprano would be gone for good, last heard in spots on *Chalk Mark in a Rain Storm*. Time and other thieves washed the past away. Something's lost but something's gained, sang Joni when she was just getting started. Or, as she put it when the '80s began: Nothing lasts for long.

30 ■ TURBULENCE

n the mid to late 1990s, though she would win an Album of the Year Grammy for *Turbulent Indigo*, Sweden's prestigious Polar Music Prize, and, after four years of eligibility, finally be inducted into the Rock and Roll Hall of Fame, it seemed to Joni that nothing she did, no matter how acclaimed, could compete with her earlier work. (Because the Rock Hall would not pay for her family's travel, $1,500 tickets to the event, and accommodations, she skipped the Cleveland ceremony.)

The day after she won the 1995 Album of the Year Grammy (with a second award for her artwork, a self-portrait in impressive imitation of Van Gogh's brushstrokes), she was declared yesterday's news. "I won a Grammy for *Turbulent Indigo* and the following day there was a newspaper article [about] singer-songwriters then and now, and I was in the 'then' column, *the day after winning the Grammy*," Joni said.

When Dylan was fifty and was declared to be finished, it turned out that his career would enter a vital late phase. What did it take for a broad in her fifties to get some respect in this racket?

The day before she began recording *Turbulent Indigo*, Joni and Larry Klein filed for divorce. "Last chance lost," she sang, "In the tyranny of a long goodbye." On Thanksgiving Day in 1992, Klein had reached his limit. He'd been battling with depression, and the level of anger and bitterness their marriage and home had come to hold was, he believed, killing him. He told Joni that they both would have to change the way they dealt with each other. According to Klein, Joni told him, "'I'm not going to be changing much at this point,' and that was it."

When she was introduced (by her mother) to Donald Freed, her next major love interest, he asked her how she was. "Undervalued," she said.

Joni had been feeling undervalued for a while. Even when she was honored, she often felt that the venerators weren't venerating her appropriately. Her anger and resentment began to bubble over, but unlike *Dog Eat Dog*, it presented itself in ways that her listeners found much more satisfying. Part of this was a return to acoustic guitar and piano-based music, but part of it was that, on the heels of a divorce, she was wearing her heart on her sleeve again, even as she was also a social critic. What came together so exquisitely on "Ethiopia" also crystallized on what became *Turbulent Indigo*. The sales spiked at around 311,000 copies—about 200,000 short of going gold, although it did attain gold status in Canada—but the critical consensus was that this was the return to form they had been waiting for (even if it had already returned on 1991's *Night Ride Home*). And then the Grammy that she had deserved for so long—the album of the year Grammy—finally came for this one.

Joni and Klein accepted the award arm in arm: Joni talked about making the album in a state of divorce, buying kittens to take off the bad vibes for the sake of the engineer, then let Klein have the floor, promising not to finish his sentences. Klein thanked her for "ten years of instruction in the arts." From the art of love to the arts of creativity, Klein got an instruction like no one else, if sometimes the punishments were severe. Klein lived from his mid-twenties to his mid-thirties with Joni.

Life had a way of going on. They managed to remain friends and musical collaborators, which would seem strange if Joni didn't have a tendency to continue working with ex-lovers. David Crosby became an ex-lover while they were working on *Song to a Seagull*. James Taylor played on *Blue* soon after their breakup, Graham Nash played harmonica on "You Turn Me On, I'm a Radio" a few years after their breakup, and John Guerin played drums with her on three albums past their stormy impasse. Joni and Klein even shared a limo with Donald Freed and Klein's girlfriend—a woman Joni called "the mistress"—to the Grammy Awards.

After Joni and Klein separated, Leonard Cohen came over and brought Joshu Sasaki Roshi, his longtime Rinzai Zen Buddhist teacher. Joni recalled, from her days of keeping him company, "Leonard's real problem was envy. He was the high prince of envy." Indeed, before Cohen found enlightenment and way before the eventual payday of "Hallelujah," the conquests of others could rankle him. And although he and Lou Reed crossed paths in the days of Max's Kansas City—Reed inducted Cohen into the Rock and Roll Hall of Fame in 2008—he could never get over the one who got away. "I didn't hear the Velvet Underground, but I was in love with Nico. I didn't like the fact that she was with all those guys in the Velvet Underground, sleeping with everybody but me! And that, incidentally, could describe a great deal of my activity, contrary to public opinion." As the years rolled by, Joni would hear Cohen lyrics like "First we take Manhattan, then we take Berlin," and think, "He's still singing about making conquests!" As someone who asked him for a reading list way back in 1967, Joni was haunted by hearing him sing, on his first album, "Are your lessons done?" Who would be learning and who would be teaching?

And yet, while Joni would always have complicated feelings about Cohen, she recognized that he had a great master and was a great disciple. "He had a great teacher and he worked hard. I wasn't a Buddhist when I was hanging out with him, but years later we hung out with Roshi, and Roshi and I laughed at the same things. We found the same things amusing, and Roshi decided he wanted to move in with me. I went, 'Great.' He was seventy at the time. And I never thought about it in any kind of man-woman way. I just thought he was a sweet little Buddhist monk. And he came by the house and I was going to show him that I had a spare room and he was welcome to it when he stayed in the city. Donald, the man I was dating at the time, was here, and Leonard, of course, was an old lover, and I treated him with respect. And suddenly he jumped up and said, 'Come on. Let's go. Roshi lonely! Roshi lonely!' And I didn't get it at first. It didn't take me long, though, and I thought, 'Holy shit!' I had been treating him with deference. It was so touching. It was so sweet. He became so human at that moment. Who knew? I thought, Oh, my God. My behavior to him *was* different than these two other guys. Too much respect.

"After Graham and I split up, he'd be sitting with Callie, his girlfriend who came after me and his wife, and he'd be joking around, kidding around with them, and then when he'd turn to me he'd give me too much respect. I thought, 'I know exactly what I did.' Graham couldn't kid around with me the way he could with his wife. Too much respect. Makes you lonely." Somehow, she felt a kinship with the septuagenarian Buddhist monk who jumped in her bed. Joni was lonely, too.

Night Ride Home (1991) brims with loneliness, an eternal cold that one can never come in from. One must have a mind of winter, wrote Wallace Stevens, and one must have a stoicism to survive when the love you are longing for is out of reach, or is exploiting and abusing you.

"Two Grey Rooms" began with a melody and chord setting so phenomenal, Jeremy Lubbock, an arranger on *Mingus*, fell madly in love with it and offered to arrange and record the strings at his own expense. That was in 1982, and Joni sang diphthongs over the track and called this thing of beauty "Speechless."

"This thing wants to be written in French," Joni thought, and her diphthongs did have a French feel, with echoes of Edith Piaf, whose recordings gave her goose bumps as a child. Luckily, she eventually came across an article about the German director Rainer Werner Fassbinder, legendary for films Joni would have seen at Manhattan's Film Forum in the '70s, when he, an erotic and emotional risk-taker like herself, was making brilliant, devastating films such as *In a Year of*

13 Moons, The Marriage of Maria Braun, and *Lili Thorleen* while she was renting her SoHo loft.

"I finally found a story to set to the fledgling melody," she said when the album was released. This story, according to the article, was "about a fellow who was part of Fassbinder's scene, homosexual, aristocrat, German who had had a lover in his youth whom he never got over and now in his forties he discovered the route by which this guy went to work. So he moved into these crummy rooms overlooking the street for the sole pleasure of seeing the man walk by in the morning and walk back in the evening." She added ten years to the man's age when he says, "I loved you thirty years ago," and this could have been to accommodate Joni's own age of forty-seven at the time of the album's release, or could even project a man in his fifties. Even the Joni of 1982 wouldn't have those textures that her voice would develop by the time she found the Fassbinder story. Like the method actor she was becoming, she inhabited this desperate and lonely ex-lover, obsessed with the past, who can live for nothing else.

"Things stick in my craw," Joni would say, and this thing certainly stuck in this man's craw. The two gray rooms could also be the mind itself, storing up those memories that are impossible to shake off. The thing that makes Joni an artist could easily be, in another person's life, something that would create obsessive, self-destructive behavior. For anyone looking for confession or autobiography, this wasn't it. She had the negative capability to inhabit this man's life, feel his longing, and belt out a melody that did not sound easy to sing. This aristocrat lived in an industrial dump just so he could watch his ex-lover walk back and forth from work. The song ends in a reverie for something self-destructive, yet poignant. It took another person's sorrow to build the edifice of "Two Grey Rooms." It would have made superb material for a Fassbinder film. (It might have if Fassbinder had not died at the age of thirty-seven of a drug overdose after making forty-one films.) There was even an ending: the aristocrat who lived to watch his ex-lover never approached him. There were seven years between the recording of the instrumental track and the version on *Night Ride Home.* The song needed those years. Joni grew into the character of that song. Her younger voice would have been a miscast role. It is a shame that Fassbinder did not live to hear "Two Grey Rooms."

There was no shortage of dark material from Joni's own experience. Of all her reveries of her prairie youth in central Canada, the song that is among the most vivid and the least nostalgic is "Cherokee Louise." When Joni performed the song at the Gene Autry Museum of Western Heritage, vamping on the A minor riff in a near shuffle, she did not exactly tell the story of the song, but she led into it, evocatively hinting, and only hinting, at what the song is really about: "This is another song that takes place on another bridge in Saskatoon, this time the Broadway Bridge . . . I had a best girlfriend when I moved from North Battleford, Saskatchewan, to Saskatoon, which was the closest thing we had to a big city up there. The Paris of the North! The City of Bridges! And the Broadway Bridge was a big concrete-span bridge. And the boys did their youth rites there. You had to crawl across it on your belly from one side to the other. And the river was wide, like the Mississippi, so it took some daring. I had a girlfriend who got misunderstood in the community, basically because of her genetics. She was an Indian kid in a foster home. This is her story."

Joni's voice drips with condescension when she announces little, provincial Saskatoon as the "Paris of the North." The bridge that Joni sings about has nothing to do with the Seine and everything to do with that misunderstood girlfriend. Those boys doing their slimy rites of passage, they are nowhere in this song. We have patches of memory in Louise, of swinging in the breeze one year, and then of her hiding from her predatory foster dad the next. Throughout this harrowing tale, Wayne Shorter is not only an accompanist, he is the Greek chorus, reacting, as we do, to this poor girl, misunderstood by local racists, without a stable home, and stuck with a foster dad who forces her to give him fellatio. There is no transition between childhood play and this sudden, unwanted, and horrifying introduction to adult sexuality. One day they're putting pennies on the rails and jumping around like fools. The next, Louise's foster dad "opens up a zipper / And he yanks her to her knees." Innocence and the violation of it clash violently in this story.

In 2013, Saskatoon was planning to honor Joni on her seventieth birthday, but plans were scuttled when Joni said—loudly and publicly—that her hometown was as racist as the Deep South. (She had no problem accepting a Lifetime Achievement Award from it in 1993, perhaps because her parents were still alive.) That element of Louise's pain—a Native American "misunderstood" by the yokels—is in Joni's introduction to the song from 1995, but is only hinted at in the lyrics. Joni wants to make this misunderstood young woman understood, and by the time the song is through, it is impossible to miss.

Back in late April 1992, a little over a year after the release of *Night Ride Home*, Los Angeles, in an event evoking Watts of 1965, exploded in riots after the LAPD was found not guilty in the beating of Rodney King. Even though King expressed his hope that everyone get along, it was clear that everyone would not. In a few days in South Central, at least sixty-three people were killed and two thousand were injured. None of this touched Bel-Air, but Joni, who had lived in Detroit during the 1967 riots, was attuned to a time and city where, as she put it, "everyone hates everyone." That phrase is from "Sex Kills," the second song on *Turbulent Indigo*. It is Joni at her most dystopic. It is the Janus-like opposite of "Sisotowbell Lane" or "California." Joni no longer wanted Oscar Wilde's map with Utopia on it, because she no longer thought it was possible. She felt the apocalypse coming. Things were already bad; she was sure, like a seer, that they would become even worse. She remembered pulling up behind a Cadillac belonging to the rapper Just-Ice, and she saw JUST ICE on his license place. She had never thought of justice that way. What is justice anyway? Is it just ice? Is it cold as ice? Is justice "just as" things should be? It was hard to believe.

There is no justice in "Sex Kills." Indian chiefs see the balance is undone. Gas leaks, oil spills, rapists haunt public swimming pools, little kids pack guns to school, and, in the closest thing this song has to levity, "Lawyers haven't been this popular since Robespierre slaughtered half of France." That's funny for a second, but this whole song is so dark, it builds up to this: sex sells everything and sex kills. It's a long way from the garden, a long way from loving the one you're with. Literally, sex means AIDS, which, in the pre-protease-inhibitor days of 1992, killed. But sex also kills emotionally. And in a marriage beginning to fray, sex no longer offers a sense of comfort. Now it can not only wound you, given an unfaithful partner, it can actually kill. One comes in from the cold only to find, even in Sunny California, just ice.

Joni went on a media campaign singing this song from west (on Jay Leno in 1995, her first American television appearance since *The Johnny Cash Show* in 1970) to east (on *David Letterman*). "Sex Kills" did not have a pleasing message, yet she got this platform to spread it, whether it was a colossal bummer or not. "Sex Kills" railed against many, many things. Joni saw the degradation of the human spirit—and, in this case, the human body—for what it was, and if it was a contrast to the sweet homage of "California," it was also a sequel to "Down to You," where easy pleasure is followed by a trouble that leaves too slow (and a night that covers you like a fig leaf, with trouble already lurking in the garden).

But Joni does more than moralize on *Turbulent Indigo*. She also says what art is and what it is not, which, for Joni, is everything. One of her most haunting melodies accompanied some of her vindictive lyrics on "Not to Blame." In September 1992, Joni's ex-boyfriend Jackson Browne was all over the tabloids. Although no charges were pressed, the actress Daryl Hannah claimed that Browne beat her badly enough to put her in a hospital, a charge that was supported by Hannah's uncle, the cinematographer Haskell Wexler. There was violence of some kind—allegedly in both directions—during Joni's relationship with Browne, and this song finds her carrying a grudge twenty years later.

> *Your charitable acts*
> *Seemed out of place*
> *With the beauty*
> *With your fist marks on her face*

The reference to "charitable acts" fits Jackson Browne's appearances at No Nukes and Farm Aid and the Amnesty International concerts (Joni appeared at all three); Browne also cofounded the groups Musicians United for Safe Energy (MUSE), Nukefree.org, and the Success Through the Arts Foundation, which serves the same kids in South Central LA who were directly affected by the riots Joni sang about on "Sex Kills."

Lest there be any question who she is singing about, in the third verse, she returns to his wife Phyllis Major's suicide. Joni alluded to it on "Song for Sharon" on *Hejira* ("A woman I knew just drowned herself . . ."). Now she went at it—and Browne—with a double-barreled shotgun. "I heard your baby say when he was only three / "Daddy, let's get some girls, one for you and one for me."" Ethan Zane Browne was indeed nearly three years old when his mother committed suicide.

"It was abusive to employ that image of my son as somebody who treated his mother's death lightheartedly," Browne said a few years after the release of *Turbulent Indigo*. "I mean, he was a three-year-old baby, you know. This is inexcusable."

In the midst of the violent and personal attack—all of it about a man who did her wrong twenty years earlier—the song is wrapped in a haunting and lyrical melody, where beauty and truth still prevail in the end. On her media blitz for the album, Joni was repeatedly asked if the song was about Browne. She never confirmed it, but she never exactly denied it, either, sometimes saying it's a song that is generally about spousal abuse, sometimes—in a classic songwriter dodge— saying the character is a "composite," one that, even by omission, could include Browne. (Browne never denied that he wrote "Fountain of Sorrow" for Joni.) But if Joni was inveighing generally against wife beaters, why cover an obscure '80s-era James Brown song, "How Do You Stop," elsewhere on the album? Of course, no one questions the greatness of the Godfather of Soul, but his version of this obscure song was recorded in 1986, during the same period when he was known to be beating his wife. Besides, Joni also loves Miles Davis and Picasso, despite their own histories of spousal abuse. "Most of my heroes are monsters, unfortunately, and they are men," she said in 1992. "If you separate their personalities from their art, Miles Davis and Picasso have always been my major heroes."

There is a finality to ending your album with the book of Job—

"The Sire of Sorrow (Job's Sad Song)." What else is there to say? Man is the sire of sorrow, and even if that is the end of the story, is there any redemption before last call?

In 1994, Joni appeared on the Canadian TV show *Intimate and Interactive*, which capitalized on the still-new technology of e-mail, along with faxes and a live audience mostly composed of young people. Joni, who won Canada's Gemini Award for her performance, appeared in khaki overalls, with an acoustic guitar in hand, and sang several songs, beguiling the host, Denise Donlon, who told her, "I had no idea you were so funny." And even though there was an irony about Joni's rogue inspiration, there was absolutely nothing funny about the songs she'd come to play. At fifty, it was as if she had gone back to the coffee-house days, telling meandering yet compelling stories about where the songs came from. And she told the story behind "The Magdalene Laundries" in what seemed like forensic detail:

"I live in British Columbia as much as I possibly can. Because I'm absent sometimes, I have a man named Hans who, he and his family caretakes my place. So Hans, sucking on his pipe, said to me one day, 'You know, Joni, you're basically a cheerful person, but you write these melancholy songs,' he said. 'It seems to me that you should write more in the daylight. You're always writing at night.' So I sat out in the sun on a rock and I tuned my guitar to the sound of that day, because I play in open tunings . . . So I tuned to the crows and the seagulls and the sonic references available. And it was a fairly cheerful chord progression. It was a little melancholy, because beauty has a little. I intended to write quite a cheery lyric to it, but I went to the supermarket to get my groceries, and standing in the line between the *Enquirer* and the *Star* was the *Vancouver Sun*. I had never bought a paper in my life. What possessed me, I don't know. But I picked this paper up and I never got past the first page.

"To the left hand of the page was a story out of Ireland. The Sisters of Our Lady of Charity outside of Dublin, which was a nunnery, had sold eleven and a half acres to realtors. The realtors, in plowing this land for development, unearthed over a hundred bodies in unmarked graves, thus opening up a scandal that had rocked Dublin from, they said, 1800 to 1970 [when] these laundries were closed. Basically, the

Magdalene Laundries, which stood outside of every major Irish town and maybe some minor ones, . . . took as slave labor fallen women. Fallen women were classified as the obvious, I guess—prostitutes, unmarried mothers, frequently impregnated by their parish priest, their father, their brother. But the worst of all was that an unmarried woman in her late twenties, if the men of the village were looking at her, she could be deemed a Jezebel by the parishioners and even her own family, for her indecisiveness in choosing a mate, and incarcerated for life, or at least until somebody managed to get her out . . . 'Dickensian conditions' was the way it was described. Well, there went my cheerful song."

Here was a Joni Mitchell song that Joan Baez singled out for admiration, the kind of protest song that Joni normally avoided. But this was indeed a horrifying morality tale, with corrupt priests, heartless nuns (who reminded her of ones she knew in the polio ward), and a hypocritical Catholic Church.

Of all the categories of fallen women, Joni leads the song as a woman condemned not for anything she did, but simply because of the reaction she got:

> *I was an unmarried girl*
> *I'd just turned twenty-seven*
> *When they sent me to the sisters*
> *For the way men looked at me*

When Joni was an unmarried girl of twenty-seven, she was recording *Blue*. And when she was pregnant at twenty-one, she felt a shame comparable to those martyred laundresses, even if she didn't have to pay their terrible price. Just as "Ethiopia" came from an empathy with women who couldn't afford to feed their babies, "The Magdalene Laundries" was both not an autobiographical song and one that dovetailed with a secret in her life that would soon become not such a secret at all.

In song, Joni had reached out to the daughter she gave up a couple of times. In "Little Green," hidden in flowery language that no music

critic could get beyond. In "Banquet": "Some watch their kids grow."
Ten years later, even more explicitly in "Chinese Café": "My child's a
stranger / I bore her but I could not raise her."

By 1995, after the tabloids had finally revealed Joni's search for her
daughter, she confirmed the story without evasion. Her parents, who
were the main reason she kept her daughter a secret all those years,
were in their eighties and could handle it. And so, in the pages of the
April 1995 issue of *Vogue*, she said, bluntly, "I had a child, and I was
broke, literally penniless . . . And I met Chuck Mitchell, and he said
he would take us on. I was kind of railroaded . . . we were never suit-
able. I went down the aisle saying, 'I can get out of this.'" Boom. Joni
Mitchell's giant secret was now officially out. It was harder for a public
figure to have privacy by 1995, and by then, Joni didn't fight the beast.
On this matter, she and the media were on the same search.

Around the same time, thirty-one-year-old Kilauren Gibb, a single
mother and runway model from Toronto who reminded people of a
young Joni Mitchell and who eventually would remind Joni of a young
version of her mother, and Wally Breese, founder of jonimitchell.com,
connected on the Internet, a venue that Joni actively avoided. But before any of that happened, Joni had another album to make.

31 ■ SEE YOU AT THE MOVIES

Joni's hatred for the music business had reached a tipping point. And yet the superb young jazz drummer Brian Blade reminded her why she loved music. All of Joni's musical eccentricities that flummoxed her critics and typical musicians were things that Blade embraced and played right back to her. Blade came into Joni's life just when she was ready to throw in the towel. A Gen X native of Shreveport, Louisiana, Blade grew up as an admirer of Joni's music. Just as the master drummer Tony Williams grew up memorizing every rimshot and cymbal ride played by Philly Joe Jones on Miles Davis records, Blade, from adolescence onward, grew up in awe of Joni's records, starting with *Hejira*. Blade was first gaining prominence in the mid '90s as the drummer for the tenor saxophone player Joshua Redman, who caught the final wave of major label interest in jazz, when executives were still trying to spot the next Wynton Marsalis. The handsome and charismatic Redman—he was the son of the free jazz saxophonist Dewey Redman, and a Harvard graduate who turned down Yale Law School—led a quartet including some of the most dynamic and exciting jazz musicians to emerge in the '90s, including the pianist Brad Mehldau and the bassist Christian McBride, both exemplars on their instruments. This was a band of stars before they became stars, and it was clear at the time that every accompanist was no mere sideman.

Like Tony Williams in his prime, Blade's attack on his instrument was sensitive to everything around him, so nuanced, rhythmically and emotionally, his attunement was microtonal. Like Wayne Shorter, who employed him in his quartet beginning in 2000, Blade knew exactly when to shine and when to fade—and everything in between. His approach to drums was anything but rudimentary. He'd heat things up with sticks, cool them off with brushes, and rumble in the mysterium on mallets. Like Russ Kunkel, he was as intimate as a heartbeat, but with many more variations. Blade was, like Joni's beloved Miles Davis, a master of space and minimalism. And like Joni, Blade understood the cinematic element of musicianship. As Shorter would say before he brought Blade and the rest of the band onstage, "See you at the movies."

Joni had gotten a jazz education from drummer boyfriends before, first from John Guerin and then from Don Alias. Now she was hearing herself reflected back in just the right ways, by someone she started talking to when he was a twenty-three-year-old wunderkind. "Kid," she would tell him when they first started playing together, "you're dotting my i's and crossing my t's." To be Joni's dot and cross felt like a miracle for Blade, but before her music was revived, Joni was convinced that the muse had deserted her and that she would finally quit this crazy scene. (And when the muse went out of music, Joni would say, all that was left was the "ick.")

Joni had been introduced to Blade by the producer Daniel Lanois, and they had been talking on the phone on and off since 1993. Joni invited Blade to what she said would be her swan song at the New Orleans Jazz and Heritage Festival on May 6, 1995. Joni had listened to Blade on recordings but had never played with him before. She hadn't even met him in person.

"I'm coming down to play the jazz festival," she told him. "Come in and wing it with me." Blade was amazed that Joni would give him such trust. And he was equally crestfallen that he had already committed to play with Joshua Redman that night. Looking back on it, he felt that he realized he was being tested. Would he commit to his principles or follow his dream? "One thing I learned from my heroes in New Orleans was that if you give your word, you can't take it back just because something seemingly better—or something that you desire more—comes along," Blade recalled. "I learned it the hard way. I realize in hindsight, it was the right thing to do, as much as it hurt."

Joni could hear that this was a young simpatico spirit. "Now, Brian Blade is another breed," Joni said in 2015, when what she liked was getting whittled down. "There's a young jazzer who loves all things jazz but also loves acoustic guitar and words. He's a new breed. Before, they were very apartheid. Jazz had its own box. Mingus was an acoustic man and was very limited in what he could like. I'm very limited in what I can like. At this time: not much. I hear too well, and I need purity of spirit."

She found that purity of spirit in Blade. Their first gig together was an American Way benefit organized by Gary Trudeau and Norman Lear. The next was a gig at Fez, in the basement beneath the Time Café in the NoHo section of Manhattan, an event where the Pretenders' lead singer, Chrissie Hynde, had to be restrained from showing her love a bit too exuberantly.

"That's a real singer up there!" she hollered, as Carly Simon tried to rein her in.

What was really up with Chrissie Hynde? Sure she loved Joni, but why did she have to climb all over her to prove it? Just the night before, it happened that Joni was backstage with Hynde and her manager, Tony Secunda. "She's in a really bad mood," said Secunda. "I'm just gonna warn you." And Hynde was indeed storming around the dressing room. The Pretenders had just played LA and she was complaining about her fans. "I didn't get into this business to have girls throwing themselves at me!" she groused. And just one night later, Hynde came to Joni's gig at Fez and got blasted around Natalie Merchant and other young female singer-songwriters.

Joni was appalled by Hynde's behavior. "Chrissie was sitting close to Carly Simon. And she just got drunker and drunker and yelled,

'YOU ROCK, JONI!'" Joni recalled. "And this was a small room, so Carly told her to be quiet, and was shushing her, and she started insulting Carly, so Carly had to leave, and she left a note of apology. And then Chrissie came backstage and was literally climbing my body. And just the night before, she was complaining about all these women throwing themselves at her. It was so bizarre, the contrast."

Being loved so intensely by someone who was so intensely loved herself was, while a bit odd, also flattering. Joni was about to turn fifty-two, and she suddenly felt that maybe she wasn't quite ready to pack it in. She would throw obscurities from her catalogue to Blade— "Moon at the Window" or "The Three Great Stimulants"—just to see what he would do with them. Even the least canonical Joni Mitchell song still held vitality for Blade, who was clearly more than willing to go the distance with her. The Blade-Mitchell duo did television, including *CBS This Morning* ("A morning gig for Joni," Blade recalled. "Not the wisest thing in the book. But she was a trouper.") and Jay Leno, where they performed the new song "Love Puts on a New Face." For Blade, every new song by Joni was a lifeline.

"I call Brian my youngest, because when he was a kid he was just so open, and saying, 'Listen to this, Joni,'" Joni told me, when her own musical enthusiasm was contracting. "And he just loved everything. Now he's getting narrower because when you get older you become more discerning. Also, you need something to feed you so you keep growing. It's harder to get. That's why Miles at the end would play three notes and walk around, because his bands were so terrible and there was no inspiration."

Joni did not want to become like that. Blade helped her feel young just a little longer. Their infrequent trips to the studio became more frequent, until they had enough songs for *Taming the Tiger*. Some of the songs Joni performed live with Blade ended up without drums, in the spirit of *Hejira*, where Guerin's drums came and went. Wayne Shorter is on hand for six tracks, Blade for five. Larry Klein's bass is present for only three tracks, with Joni playing other bass parts on synthesizer. (By 1997, synthesizers had improved substantially since the *Dog Eat Dog* era, with fake sounding less fake.) At fifty-four, she was still in love, still filled with rage, still looking into the soul of her own sadness, still playful, still wanting to dance. She hated on the music business—no shock there. And yet she was still offering intimacy and musical curveballs. The question of whether she was at the top of her game seemed irrelevant. For listeners in 1998, this Joni Mitchell was the only one they were going to get. Her soprano was not ever coming back, but her alto was a rugged and resilient instrument, good for a sultry memory of being a bad girl ("Harlem in Havana"), mourning and melancholia ("Man from Mars," rescued from Allison Anders's film *Grace of My Heart*), a genuine pissed-off rocker that opened with "Kiss my ass!" ("Lead Balloon"), the I Hate the Music Biz song for which she had been preparing her listeners in interviews ("Taming the Tiger"), and shaming everyone involved in the U.S. military rape scandal on Okinawa ("No Apologies," which rhymes with "outraged Japanese"). There were no epic songs on the scale of "The Sire of Sorrow" or "Come in from the Cold"; none even made it to five minutes. One song, "The Crazy Cries of Love," which used her then boyfriend Donald Freed's name in the first person, began with, "It was a dark and stormy night" as a response to the bad writing competition, the Bulwer-Lytton Fiction Contest. (The song was never submitted.)

It was while she was finishing *Taming the Tiger* that Joni would finally be reunited with her daughter, Kilauren Gibb. Some have remarked that they could detect a change in tone in Joni's voice on those final vocal tracks. Many believe that "Stay in Touch" was a song Joni wrote for Kilauren. Susan Lacy's *American Masters* documentary of Joni used the song, with Mark Isham's emotive muted trumpet, to accompany material about the reunion. Even if "Stay in Touch" was intended that way, though, the song had its roots in a different era, when she and Donald Freed were throwing the I Ching the night they met. That night, they each threw change, and Joni took notes:

> *This is really something*
> *People will be envious*
> *But our roles aren't clear*
> *So we mustn't rush*

Taming the Tiger, released September 29, 1998, would be Joni's last collection of original songs for ten years. It would sell an anemic 133,000 CDs, fewer than half of *Turbulent Indigo*. Joni seemed to see this coming, especially on the vitriolic title track. But it would be, gratifyingly, backed by a tour. The last time out, on the 1983 Refuge of the Roads tour, had nearly wrecked her—barely breaking even, exhausting Joni's voice and, with her post-polio flaring up, her back. But in 1998, she toured with her old friend Bob Dylan, whose album *Time Out of Mind* would win him his first Album of the Year Grammy and usher in an era of rebirth in many ways. By teaming up with him, along with Van Morrison, Joni did not have to worry about carrying on a tour operation completely on her own. She would be with Dylan, who had been on some version of his Never Ending Tour since 1988, and who was at home on the road.

Joni wasn't. The exposure to air-conditioning and other irritants would ravage her immune system. And there were days on the road when she was so exhausted she could barely move. "Walk!" she would say in her head, and one foot went forward. And with every step she had to command the automatic function for walking. One night in San Jose, she was so sick with the flu that she spent the whole day in a steam cabinet, just trying to get the gunk out of her so she could go on. Every time she hit a high note, she thought she would pass out from all the congestion in her head. By the time she went onstage, she was delirious. She warned, "Just so you know, I might fall to the ground at any minute." Always the high-wire artist.

But two things kept her going: the pleasure of working with Brian Blade, and her Roland VG-8 digital guitar processor, which allowed her to program all of her tunings and that also had the crucial benefit, with all her post-polio back problems, of being much lighter around her neck. Suddenly, the guitar wasn't such an albatross. It wasn't a perfect solution. The Roland VG-8 sounded like a computerized approximation of a guitar with a head cold, a rhythm instrument with a digital tinge. Still, it was necessary for keeping Joni in the game. To the people who missed the sound of her on acoustic guitar, she said, "Go sit on a tack!" Pushing on those frets was becoming an ordeal. In her fragile state, it was a miracle she could make music at all in 1998.

At this point, Joni's most devoted fans, who had lived through the synthesized wilderness of *Dog Eat Dog*, were ready to tolerate this new electronic timbre, knowing that such matters seemed superficial compared with going the distance with this artist. Many would go to the concert out of loyalty to their favorite periods of Joni, usually from the '70s. Some of them would also be Dylan people or Van Morrison people. Bruce Springsteen took his mother to one of those concerts. He writes movingly in his memoir, *Born to Run*, about how the concert inspired him to regroup the E Street Band and get back out on the road.

In the *Chicago Tribune*, Greg Kot gushed, "With Larry Klein sliding around the rhythm on bass, and Brian Blade dancing with brushes on the trap kit, Mitchell's exquisite guitar voicings guided her band. The quintet conjured lush tones at even the quietest volumes, with Greg Leisz's pedal steel drifting like a desert tumbleweed on Mitchell's luminous 'Amelia.'"

"I'm not used to arenas," Joni said. "And my music was bouncing off the walls. That had happened to me before in 1976, and there was no way that I could sing when it's bouncing around like that. I was just hearing echoes of myself. So I turned down and turned down some more. It was still slapping back. I turned down till I hit the sweet spot and it stopped slapping, right?"

Joni, in other words, did what seemed impossible. She turned the music down until it could be heard. "Only a woman would turn down," thought Joni. Big, loud, and fast: that's the masculine aesthetic. "Those shows are always too loud."

"So, Dylan got very upset about this because I'd gotten the good review. And he fired Fast Eddie, who's a great soundman. Before we went out on tour, I went to a show of Bob's, and you couldn't hear the words. It was illegible. It was a mushy sound." Fast Eddie—a.k.a. Ed Wynn—was known to be among the best in the business. He had been Joni's soundman on the Refuge tour in 1983, back when she could afford him. Wynn and the drummer Vinnie Colaiuta moved on to bigger and better-paying gigs after that tour. Joni knew what Wynn could do then and what he could do again. Joni was a tough critic of sound, and Wynn met her standards.

Joni spoke to Elliot Mintz, Dylan's media consultant at the time.

"Look," Joni said, "he's got this new stuff and I can't hear the words. Can't you get Eddie to dig him out?"

"No, that's the way Bob likes it. He likes to be an enigma."

"Eddie was my soundman," Joni said. "And I couldn't afford him after everyone else took him. There's nothing wrong with Eddie. He's a great soundman. But Bob fires him! And he hires a new soundman like it was Eddie's fault that I got a good review. No! I turned down. You saw *This Is Spinal Tap*, where the amps go up to eleven! That's all it was: common sense. It's the same with sus chords. Only a woman could have discovered harmony that was never used before in the history of harmonic movement."

Larry Klein agrees with Joni's take on this. "The version of things that I heard was that when the Chicago review came out praising the sound on our portion and denigrating Bob's sound, that he reacted by firing Ed," Klein recalled. "The reason that our sound was better was that we played very quietly onstage. That enables the house soundman to have a fighting chance at doing something legible in a big basketball arena. If the band plays loud onstage, it's over."

This was a tour where Joni's (as she called him) "magnificent ex-husband" played bass, and where her boyfriend was along for the ride. The two men got along well enough. Keeping cool—especially in the midst of frail health and wounded egos—was the order of the day. "We had managed to split up while staying on good terms," Klein recalled. "But she was in a relationship with Don Freed, who was an unusual guy—albeit being a very unusual situation, touring with her, with the ex-husband on board. He used to sit around with earphones on, humming to himself. I guess that was how he dealt with conversation with Joan, which was increasingly becoming like witnessing a monologue."

Off the road, Joni had a life to get back to like never before. Suddenly, Joni, a woman of heart and mind with no child to raise, had a daughter—grandchildren, even. Her life, she thought, was complete. The songwriting began shortly after she gave birth in 1965, and each song was somehow a message to her daughter, or to the world in which she was growing up. Now that she had her daughter back, she had the ultimate excuse to bolt from music. She held on to this reasoning for about ten years, including in a 2005 interview with the cultural critic Camille Paglia, who began the interview stating, "I'm interested in your creative process." Paglia had included Joni in a collection called *Break, Blow, Burn*, an anthology of what she considered to be the forty-three greatest poems in English, beginning with a Shakespeare sonnet and ending with "Woodstock."

Paglia called herself a "pro-sex feminist," even as her writings were often calculated to offend normative feminists, especially in a *New York Times* op-ed called "Madonna: Finally a Real Feminist." Joni once compared Madonna to Nero, and yet she and Madonna had common ground: tough, independent women who did not identify with conventional feminists. But the creative process was not something Joni could talk about in the present tense; her songwriting had been on sabbatical for a while. Toward the end of the interview, Joni explained why she wrote and why she wasn't writing. "I don't write at all anymore," Joni told Paglia. "I quit everything in '97 when my daughter came back. Music was something I did to deal with the tremendous disturbance of losing her. It began when she disappeared and ended when she returned. I was probably deeply disturbed emotionally for those thirty-three years that I had no child to raise, though I put on a brave face. Instead, I mothered the world and looked at the world in which my child was roaming from the point of view of a sociologist. And everything I worried about then has turned out to be true."

This was an enormous claim, one that she was certainly feeling at the time. While the theme of suppressed motherhood came out implicitly in "Ethiopia" or explicitly in "Little Green" or "Chinese Café," she was now making the more radical claim that every pain or conflict in every song was from the suppressed sorrow of giving up her daughter. It would be reductive to view all of her work only from this perspective, but then this was the Joni who rushed into a relationship with a troubled young woman with all the intensity of a love affair, which, in a way, it was. But Joni's love affairs either ended badly, or at their most benign, simply ended. And this love affair would have its ups and downs. By the time that the songwriting did come back for *Shine* (2007), it would be for an album that had no love songs. By then, the bloom of the reunion had wilted for a while. The first tussles were resolved, but Joni's attempt to offer parenting advice to her daughter was angrily rebuffed. Joni resolved never to give advice without solicitation. But things kept going south. Joni decided that Kilauren was a "damaged" person, someone who would never forgive Joni for abandoning her. When Joni asked a friend to introduce her daughter to people at the Viper Room, the friend came back with the conclusion that Kilauren was "a far cry from Joni" and was "a barroom bitch—someone who hangs around bars and starts mouthing off."

Did Joni expect a kid who was not troubled? Did she think that, just as they looked alike, they would be alike? Like Kilauren, Joni was a rebel, someone who would not fit in any institutional setting. But Joni was a genius, whose greatness presented itself early. "I sang 'Urge for Going,' my second song, on television shortly after I gave birth to Kilauren," Joni recalled. By the time she was twenty-two, she was already developing an idiosyncratic approach to guitar playing and had written "Urge for Going" and "The Circle Game"; at twenty-three, she had written "Both Sides, Now." When they were reunited, Kilauren, at thirty-three, had dropped out of various schools (including stints as a nonmatriculated student at Harvard and the University of Toronto). She was living on student loans and studying desktop publishing at George Brown College in Toronto. Her only professional experience was as a model with the Elite agency for ten years. She had two children with two different fathers, and brought a host of emotional problems into Joni's life.

One problem that loomed increasingly large was her resentment toward her birth mother for giving her up. She was not convinced by the argument that Joni had been penniless and that Kilauren would have been better off. In many ways she had been better off with the well-meaning upper-middle-class family who adopted her. And Joni had no career to speak of on February 19, 1965. Until she met Chuck Mitchell the next month, she could not even afford a union card. Her songwriting, which became her first and most lasting source of income, began later that year, and if she hadn't given up her daughter, the songwriting might not have come at all—at least according to Joni's reasoning in several interviews.

Over the years, Joni adjusted to an on-again, off-again relationship with Kilauren. She did bring her onstage at the Luminato Festival in 2013 when everyone in the program sang "Woodstock." "The first two weeks with Kilauren were very pleasant, but after that, she was hostile," Joni said in 2015. The disappointments and bitterness were still present in 2015. According to Tony Simon, Kilauren was not listed as Joni's official next of kin when she needed a medical proxy, and, when she was summoned to her mother, lying in a hospital bed installed in her Bel-Air home, she claimed to have no money for the plane ticket from Toronto.

Still, the relationship gave Joni something she had long been missing, to be able to see her parents in her daughter's children. Joni may have left the provinces of Canada as quickly as she could, yet she carried them with her, made music out of their beauty, and brought their beauty to the world. She told me, "Marlin, my grandson, can think for himself. He's a thinker. Even at five, he'd listen to stuff and then he'd look at me to see what I thought, and then he'd come up with his own conclusions. He's very sweet and smarter than you would know. He's gotten very quiet as an adult—he's a good listener. He takes in what you're saying and he laughs. He's like my dad in that way. My dad was like that. He had a very unusual mind, and I do, too. I think it's like an Oriental mind."

Joni was equally proud of her granddaughter. "Daisy's an A student," she told me. "She's an honor student. She's learning ukulele, and I asked her if she could play something and she said, 'Oh, no. I'm only in my second year.' Second year? I had mastered it in six months. Marlin has a different mentality. I think it's the Sami blood. Norwegians don't have the extremely high cheekbones as a rule. But the place I come from, which is close to the border where the Sami run—the Sami have them. To my father's horror, I know we have Sami blood."

The difficulties with her daughter were worth it for the grandchildren. As for the songwriting, now that she had Kilauren back, she wasn't sure if it would ever return. And so Joni rounded out her recording contract by channeling the writing of others, and then recasting her earlier material; the arranger Vince Mendoza would conduct and write the charts for *Both Sides Now* (2000) and *Travelogue* (2002).

Suddenly, without an instrument other than her voice—and without any new songs—she would, without a fight, now relinquish the writing and orchestration to others. Near the end of Billie Holiday's short life, Lady Day would record *Lady in Satin* with a battle-scarred voice matched, devastatingly, with Ray Ellis's lush orchestra. It would be Holiday's final completed album, and the roughness of her instrument only made the heartache she sang about even more profound. Lady Day was only forty-two when she recorded it, but she sounded like she had lived many lifetimes. By the time Joni was in her fifties, she was closer in intonation and range to late-period Billie Holiday. And even though Vince Mendoza's charts were carefully chosen for a comfortable range, what was revealed was just as bare-bones as *Lady in Satin*.

Joni had been honest in all of her work, whether it was in an effortless multi-octave instrument or whether, as the years and cigarette butts accumulated, that range narrowed to a spot that was still sweet, even when it was bitter. Joni first worked with Mendoza on Kyle Eastwood's *From Here to There* (1998), where she first tried out her take on Marvin Gaye's "Trouble Man," and what was breathy in the studio became more percussive and precise the more times she sang it on the road in every performance she gave that year. "Trouble Man" dates back to 1972, the year of *For the Roses*, when Joni had not yet channeled her inner black man. The line "I feel the kind of protection that's all around me" was changed to "I see the kind of pretension that's all around me," and that, of course, is what the jive detector is for.

Joni often referred to her collaboration with Charles Mingus as a musical education, and yet the albums that immediately followed *Mingus*—especially the electronic din of *Dog Eat Dog*—did not reveal any obvious fruits. But by the time Joni appeared on Herbie Hancock's *Gershwin's World* (1998)—singing "Summertime" and "The Man I Love"—it was clear that her phrasing and overall conception had far surpassed her *Court and Spark* cover of "Twisted" or even the ambitious hybrid experiments of *Mingus*. By then, Hancock told Joni that she was the best jazz singer alive. Joni later complained about Ira Gershwin's limitations as a lyricist—"Shame on you, Ira Gershwin," she said, referring to the phrase "And so all else above"—but there was no doubt that George Gershwin's melodies were the perfect vehicle for Joni to show off her new jazz chops, which became more sultry with age. She was no longer the ingénue who had done her homework. She sounded like experience itself.

It was Mr. Kratzmann back in seventh grade who not only circled her clichés, but told her that if she could paint with colors she could paint with words. Now that she wasn't bringing new material to the table, interpretation was all, and her word painting, along with her method acting, became even more acutely attuned. Wayne Shorter, who shares Joni's pictorial approach, was on hand, and Vince Mendoza's arrangements and conducting were in consultation with Larry Klein, all with this idea that she would reveal herself anew with someone else's material, or her own songs from an earlier self.

As Joni seemed to be concluding her recording career, what began as the minimalism of the first few records turned into the kind of maximalist orchestras that David Crosby rightly kept off *Song to a Seagull*, which then set the minimal tone for *Clouds*, *Ladies of the Canyon*, and *Blue*. At that point, Joni's voice could cover three octaves, containing such a near orchestral range that an actual orchestra would have been redundant. But it was not Sinatra listeners they were aiming for, not yet. By the time she was in her fifties, she was ready to sing her variations on "It Was a Very Good Year," looking back with tenderness, with sorrow, a bit of wistfulness, and more than a little melodrama. Everyone involved with *Both Sides Now* knew that including Bill Carey and Carl Fischer's "You've Changed," which had been covered by many legends, including Nat King Cole, Sarah Vaughan, and even Marvin Gaye, would invite comparison with Billie Holiday's Sturm und Drang version from *Lady in Satin*, an album that beautifully exploited the aesthetic possibilities of an eviscerated larynx with strings.

The two versions seem similar, but are in fact a study in contrast.

Holiday was out of range and out of breath. Joni was in a comfortable range, letting the song, and not just the pathos of the singer, tell the story. "There's a theory that you need to be wrecked when you read the lyric to 'You've Changed,' but there's another read to it when you're not wrecked," Vince Mendoza recalled. "Realizing that the person you loved is not the person you thought they were could have a tragic read or just a different kind of read than that, and the orchestra in that piece was the tragedy. The approach to writing that was transfigured ninths and Schoenberg and post-Romantic orchestral approach and not as an orchestra playing behind a jazz standard. Joni's approach to singing it was much smoother. She didn't need to be tragic. She just let the words do the talking. I totally resonate with her theory about the singer getting into character. And in every chart I work on, I have to get into character to figure out what I want the lyric to mean. The idea of it was tragedy. But she didn't need to impart that with her voice."

The performance that made the largest impact from *Both Sides Now* was the near-millennial reading of the title track, a reminder of how many new meanings had been accumulated from the many lives Joni had been living since she wrote that song and, a few months later, sang it to Judy Collins on the phone in that auspicious middle-of-the-night encounter. Joni had finally, in many ways, earned the right to sing her song. In the '70s, she heard Mabel Mercer sing it—when Mercer was in her seventies—and went backstage and, without introducing herself as the author, told Mercer that it takes an older woman to bring the song across. Mercer was offended, and Joni, still in her tender years, learned that a woman is never an older woman. And yet when her time came to redo the song with the gravity of accumulated years, Joni, for theatrical purposes, decided that sometimes a woman is an older woman after all. If wisdom was the prize for the indignities of aging, she would take it and run with it. As Joni was vamping it up in the studio, the orchestra, which included members of the London Symphony Orchestra, were in tears, and Mendoza was having trouble holding it together, too.

"There are so many layers to what happened on 'Both Sides, Now,'" Mendoza recalled. "The woman who wrote it didn't really know the gravity of the lyric until many years later, as an older woman reading it. Also, the same person who sung it was singing it again. The song itself—the melody is so beautiful. That totally scared the hell out of me when we were doing it, because I grew up with that song. I didn't know how I could do it justice without ruining it, and then adding an orchestra to the cast of characters might bring it into another world that we didn't want it to be in, so I'm happy that it worked out well. At the sessions, you could tell from the first line that she read that she sang that this would be the one. It's funny when you're on the other end of that pathos. When you're a twenty-three-year-old singing about being older, you still know that you're just twenty-three. All of her younger lyrics were wise beyond her years. My recollection of the sessions is that she seemed like she was quite delighted with the way that the voice and the orchestra came together, and there were certain things about the lyric that came out as a result of the orchestration. I don't remember her getting emotional about it. I remember seeing a little smile. She was delighted. I never saw her getting emotional about it. I do remember that the musicians were in tears."

Joni knew exactly what she was doing and the effect she was getting. The arranger and the musicians were losing it, but Joni was smiling. She had them exactly where she wanted them. She knew she had achieved spectacular theater just by getting older and going back to a song people thought they knew. The song was more than three decades old, and even though it was among her most covered songs—by hundreds of artists representing a cross section of genres, from Dolly Parton and Frank Sinatra to Doris Day and Dizzy Gillespie, all the way to *American Idol*.

Joni was sure that, in 1967, she couldn't possibly adequately cover the subject of fantasy and reality in a short pop song. But by the time she was in her mid-fifties, she had lived it, and her nicotine-stained mezzo sounded as weary as the words she rasped. Her voice might have lost clarity, range, and dexterity, but it had gained a new emphasis, and Wayne Shorter's soprano filigrees at the end—playing in the range that twenty-three-year-old Joni could reach—embodied the song's refrain that "something's lost, but something's gained." The folk waif in the pastel miniskirt was long gone. Joni gasped for breath between phrases, but the struggle was a crucial part of the performance. The lyrics were familiar, but the delivery was startling. When she was a girl, clouds were like "ice cream castles in the air." "Now," Joni at fifty-five growled with phlegmatic wisdom, "they only block the sun / They rain and snow on everyone." She takes her time between the words: "So many things . . . I . . . could have done . . . but clouds got in my way." When the London Symphony Orchestra members broke decorum and cried, perhaps they were lamenting the multi-octave voice gone, a pristine and mellifluous instrument decimated. Maybe they were crying because for the first time, they were hearing what the song was really about. It took all these years for Joni to finally sound like she had looked at life from both sides, now. "It was quite amazing to see an English orchestra get that emotional," recalled Klein.

Joni did a brief tour—twelve dates in 2000. She was surrounded by superb musicians, including Herbie Hancock on piano and Wallace Roney on trumpet. Mendoza was on hand for conducting the orchestras, which were different in every city. A constant presence was Roney, who had been recommended by Wayne Shorter. Roney had the ultimate Cinderella moment of jazz trumpeters when an ailing Miles Davis, who was attempting to play the parts he had mastered with the arranger Gil Evans, was too weak to step up to them again when he was paired with Quincy Jones for a Montreux performance in 1991. Miles Davis never looked back and never asked for help. Now he was doing both and Roney, at the age of thirty-one—the age of Miles at his summit—was able to fill in what was needed with superb musicianship. He had gotten to know Shorter when he was plucked to play Miles Davis's parts when Shorter, Herbie Hancock, Ron Carter, and Tony Williams reunited as the Tribute to Miles band in 1992. Eight years later, he found himself as the only featured soloist on a tour with Joni and orchestras. "I was standing right next to Joni every night," Roney recalled. "I didn't travel with the orchestra. I traveled with her and the band. She traveled with us but in her own car. She was cool, you know? The music she had been playing all along was jazz, even if it was in a folk-rock form. She was always an improvisational artist. When she had a chance to draw on her jazz influences—Miles and Billie Holiday—she went for it."

The tour lasted less than a month, from the Greek Theatre in Los Angeles on May 12 to the Blockbuster–Sony Music Entertainment Centre in Camden, New Jersey, on June 2. If anyone speculated whether this would be Joni's final tour, Roney had no idea. Onstage, he took in the meaning of her words and intonations. He was certainly there to be original. "I remember we did 'Comes Love,' that was the first thing I did with her," Roney recalled. "Mark Isham, the trumpet player before me, would do Harry 'Sweets' Edison's opening every night. I felt that was a bit Hollywood. I knew 'Sweets' Edison. He was one of my mentors. I would never do that. I played it as though I was in the moment that Sweets was in when he came up with it. Joni had no problems with that. Every night was in the spirit of what this music is—in the spirit of the moment." He already knew the standards on her set list—"You're My Thrill," "At Last," "Comes Love," and so on. "Trouble Man" came out easily. Since he was her star soloist—the saxophonist Bob Sheppard emerged from the ensemble for one saxophone solo—they were in their own dressing room. The perennial topic was Miles: his beautiful music and his bad behavior. Joni spoke of Don Alias in the present tense, as if their romance hadn't ended nearly twenty years earlier.

This brief tour was such rough going for Joni, healthwise, it was not a surprise that it would be her last. "I was very ill and I had to stay separate from people to save my energy," Joni told me. "I was in isolation to get through that tour. I was lucky I didn't fall down. The disease was coming on, and I didn't know what it was yet. We were picking up orchestras in every town with shitty horn sections. We needed a lead trumpet player, because horn sections were so shabby. We kidnapped Wallace in Boston. The only thing we carried was a drummer, bass, and saxophone, and we carried a first violin, and in every city we picked up an orchestra. LA wasn't bad and New York wasn't bad. They've got big musician pools in those towns. Florida was pretty bad, Atlanta had a good horn section although the strings sucked, although I heard them on a classical station and they were better. Detroit was horrendously bad. But Boston had this great trumpet player. We kidnapped him because we needed a good leader for the brass section in these other towns because we still had Detroit, Chicago, and Philadelphia to go."

By then, Joni was slipping more of her own songbook into the mix, including a bombastic "For the Roses," a Beethovenian "Judgement of the Moon and Stars," and a cooled-off version of "Be Cool," a gem buried in the middle of *Wild Things Run Fast*. Even though she no longer had a guitar to tune, as she did with her folk audiences, she told many rambling stories, including, in an introduction to "Judgement of the Moon and Stars"—a song that had already been introduced many times since she started performing it in 1972—and came up with an anecdote that fit her current disgust with the music business: Beethoven put a little melody into a music box made by the inventor of the metronome—she called him "Metronomio." It was a smash hit all over Europe, she said, and Beethoven had to live with the idea that he would be most remembered for the biggest piece of shit he ever wrote. Joni did not have that problem.

She was most remembered for her younger work, which is always a frustration when one is no longer younger. These performances naturally led to *Travelogue*, a project that would fulfill her contractual obligation while also revisiting her young work as a woman who was, despite what she'd learned from her encounter with Mabel Mercer, an older woman—and what she had left was certainly aged, filtered not just through American Spirits but decades of experience. She thought some of those songs were miscast for an ingénue. And she wasn't going to do this on the cheap, either. Gone were the days of acoustic guitar and a couple of mics. She was now accompanied by a seventy-piece orchestra including some of the same London Symphony Orchestra members from the *Both Sides Now* sessions. But crucial to the project was her collaborations with jazz musicians who had become a part of her musical family, especially Brian Blade, Wayne Shorter, and Herbie Hancock. "Jazz musicians use standard tunes as vehicles for improvisation," recalled Mendoza. "The lyrics are not as important as the changes and the rhythm behind it, and what that implies for the rest of the improvisation. A songwriter reprising a song like that needs to retain whatever that song needs. A fresh version of it retains a certain meaning of the lyric. I don't think that Herbie, Wayne, and Brian even cared what the original versions were. They were interested in the moment that you create right then." And, like Joni, Mendoza found that recasting material in an exquisitely worn voice was like a form of Method acting; Joni was a natural. Mendoza said it was "like working with Robert De Niro."

The good news was that Mendoza won a Grammy for his arrangement of "Woodstock." The bad news was that the album, which cost around $300,000 to record, sold around 72,000 copies, by far her lowest sales figure. Joni blamed it on having got what she saw as a demotion to Nonesuch, what she called Warner Bros.' "boutique label"—a label that had, at one time or another, the Kronos Quartet, the MacArthur-winning experimental artists Don Byron and John Zorn, along with more commercial fare by the Black Keys and Natalie Merchant. Joni was not impressed. She simply saw it as a downgrade. Her only publicity would be an interview with *W* magazine, in which she stated, to James Reginato, "I'm quitting after this, because the business has made itself so repugnant to me." (She later added, "Don't make me sound too dissy.")

Her contractual obligation was fulfilled. She had no songs in her, certainly no more energy for the road. She would surface to promote a series of collections of her least popular work—from the 1980s and '90s, with nothing new but cover art—in an effort to shift the conversation. Mostly she was painting, living her life, dodging health disasters, from post-polio to symptoms of Morgellons syndrome, a condition that the medical establishment doesn't recognize, or it is dismissed as psychosomatic, but to its sufferers, including Joni, it feels indisputably real. "I have this weird, incurable disease that seems like it's from outer space," she told the *Los Angeles Times*. "Garbo and Dietrich hid away just because people became so upset watching them age, but this is worse.

Fibers in a variety of colors protrude out of my skin like mushrooms after a rainstorm: they cannot be forensically identified as animal, vegetable or mineral. Morgellons is a slow, unpredictable killer—a terrorist disease: it will blow up one of your organs, leaving you in bed for a year. But I have a tremendous will to live: I've been through another pandemic—I'm a polio survivor, so I know how conservative the medical body can be. In America, the Morgellons is always diagnosed as 'delusion of parasites,' and they send you to a psychiatrist. I'm actually trying to get out of the music business to battle for Morgellons sufferers to receive the credibility that's owed to them."

In 2007, she skipped the Grammy Awards when Herbie Hancock won for *River: The Joni Letters*. She loved glamour, she loved accolades, but no amount of makeup could cover up what she was doing to her face—picking at it, peeling back layer upon layer. She became convinced that the disease was not only causing damage to her skin, but was eating away at her brain, as well. Doctors responded by prescribing antibiotics, but they were no help at all. Just as Joni left hints about her unwanted pregnancy and adoption in "Little Green" and "Chinese Café," she also sang, in "The Sire of Sorrow (Job's Sad Song)" of "pompous physicians" and "nights without sleep and festering flesh."

She began to be regarded as a recluse, even as she still gave interviews here and there, and even as she took most of her meals in public and would chat people up when she felt like it. It would be another four years until the muse would return one last time.

32 ▨ CURTAIN CALL

When the songs did come back, in 2006, it was because of a combination of gratitude and incipient doom, and the two were deeply connected. Love, Joni's most enduring and most complicated subject, was nowhere to be found, at least not the romantic kind. She had love of the earth, and she had found pastoral inspiration on her British Columbia property, but it was also in danger of being yet another paradise paved away. She had love for her grandson, whose precocious words "bad dreams are good in the great plan" would inspire what goodness she could find with plundered ecosystems and a war in Iraq waged on lies and deceit. She was more outspoken against the Iraq War than the Vietnam War, and everything she was creating was either implicitly or explicitly protest art in various media. And so, after ten years of drought, the songs came pouring out, mostly, as she put it, of environmental and theological complaint.

One, an instrumental piece in the tradition of Mahler's *Das Lied von der Erde*, The Song of the Earth, called "One Week Last Summer," would win a 2007 Grammy for best instrumental piece. And the title track of the album on which it appeared was called *Shine*. *Shine* calls on the illumination of everything: the polluters and the polluted, the church and its heretics, civilization and its discontents. Like Dylan's 1964 "Chimes of Freedom," in which hiding from a rainstorm brings together a coalition as broad as a song could handle, Joni alludes to the gospel standard "This Little Light of Mine," while calling for the shining of a light that nothing can escape.

> *Shine on good humor*
> *Shine on good will*
> *Shine on lousy leadership*
> *Licensed to kill*

Joni shines her light where it is needed most: dying soldiers, mental patients, "Dickens, Rembrandt, and Beethoven"—her peer group—even the "asshole passing on the right." High and low, from the inspired to the broken, and everyone in between, Joni lights it all up.

That light—is it just poetic illumination, or is this some sort of search party? In the midst of this nearly eight-minute epic, all sublimely rumbling with the ride cymbals and soft rim shots of the ever virtuosic Brian Blade, the song has a bigger heart than the singer, or really all of us. To shine does not mean to forgive. It could mean that if we can view the world, even at its most wretched, with all delivered luminescence, our all-too-human and battered hearts could open up a little more.

Joni piles up image after image centered on a single theme, just as she did so many years before on "Both Sides, Now." This is a song, she said, "that could have had a million verses. So what are the pertinent things to shine on at this time? It starts, 'Shine on Wall Street and Vegas / Place your bets.' I have written about sixty different verses and rhyming couplets to this thing and I've kept twelve. 'Shine on the dazzling darkness that restores in deep sleep / Shine on what we throw away and what we keep.' Are they the best ones? I don't know. I could write sixty a week. What are the twelve most important things to illuminate? It's overwhelming."

When Joni got her inspiration back, it flowed so extravagantly, it seemed like the well would never go dry again. And just as the song-writing had been reawakened (her ten years of silence was longer than the Beatles' entire recording career) the French Canadian choreographer Jean Grand-Maître, who had no way of knowing that Joni was writing songs again, wrote to her to invite her to participate in a project in a medium that had always fascinated her.

"Please forgive my somewhat imperfect English as I am a native of Quebec and I am still brushing up on this new language," wrote Grand-Maître. "Next year will be Alberta Ballet's 40th Anniversary Season and as Artistic Director, I would be enthused by the possibility of choreographing a ballet to your brilliant and profoundly moving music.

"I would really love to fly to Los Angeles," he went on, "and meet you personally for a very short moment." That "very short moment" turned into a marathon chat into the wee small hours. Dance, since girlhood, had been a major passion of Joni's, and writing for dance was a natural outlet for her. After defeating polio, the teenage Joni danced the night away as often as she could back in Saskatoon, even adding an extra night on Wednesdays because she couldn't wait for the week-ends. "I want to wreck my stockings in some jukebox dive," she sang on "All I Want," the song that opens *Blue*, an album known more for introspection than dancing.

Joni felt affection for Grand-Maître from the beginning and found him to be soulful. But she did not like his initial idea—a retrospective called "Dancing Joni," revolving around a blond Australian ballerina who would be dancing events imagined from Joni's life. Joni said yes to a ballet, but nixed the concept. In addition to writing songs that ended up on *Shine*, she was also embarking on a new art project after her flat-screen television malfunctioned and turned everything green. Her television was transmitting an uncanny commentary of the times, with Busby Berkeley musicals, CNN, the History Channel, and Iraq War footage drenched in the same tint of green. And so a photo installation, called *Green Flag Song*, was being prepared for exhibits in LA and New York.

Some of the artwork was also used for the ballet, which was renamed *The Fiddle and the Drum*, after her antiwar acappella ballad from *Clouds*, back in 1969. The song made no references to Vietnam or any other topical subject, and so would be as relevant to the War on Terror as it was to the Cold War. In the midst of an imperiled environment and a war that was losing support the more the facts came in, this new work would be a way to get Joni's new (and least appreciated) music alive on the stage with beautiful young dancers who would represent the pulse and passion of the music. And with an emphasis on underappreciated songs from the 1980s and '90s—rhythmically charged and better for dance than her earlier work—she would also be calling attention to her most neglected work. But Grand-Maître's choreography and Joni's music would roar out a warning. "It's a red alert about the situation the world is in now," she said. "We're wasting our time on this fairy-tale war, when the real war is with God's creation. Nobody's fighting for God's creation."

It was a big gamble for Grand-Maître. Not only had he alienated some of his sponsors in oil-rich Calgary, but, while Joni had taken over the project conceptually—integrating it with her art show, changing the songs and the theme—she had no involvement with the dance itself, and no one knew how she would react. There was a two a.m. celebratory dinner planned if she was happy, and a plan B if she wasn't. The dancers, who were trained to peak at performance, were deliberately holding back through the rehearsals. In the darkness, Joni could be seen by Grand-Maître, taking notes, and, when she felt like it, gyrating to the rhythms of her own music. This was as close to the stage as she was going to get—so near and so far.

"I never really explained to her what I was choreographing physically, but rather how I was staging it," Grand-Maître recalled. "Like when Mary Magdalene appeared on a screen during 'Sex Kills' or when Killer Kyle in 'Beat of Black Wings' transforms from innocence to aggressive behavior. I told her I wanted to create that in a dance performance. She loved that." This was similar to the trust that she put in Brian Blade, when they were to perform together without any rehearsal. "Come in and wing it with me," she had said. But this was a completely new medium. This was uncharted territory.

Joni was elated. This was the Joni who was determined to prove the doctor wrong at the iron lung. She would walk in time for Christmas. She would not sink. Lovers would come and go, popularity would wax and wane, celebrity would offer perks and punishments. She would dance the night away at the Saskatoon sock hops, at Studio 54, even in a private movement at the Calgary Performing Arts Centre. These bodies onstage were young and vital. Her music would find a new purpose. She would find a new collaborator. Before the world fell apart, her music would be getting a new lifeline. Nietzsche wrote that he could only believe in a god who could dance. That night, Joni certainly believed in the dance itself. She had a new record to promote, and a new art exhibit.

"I'm working three shifts," Joni said at the time. "I'm doing the work of four twenty-year-olds. Between the art show and the ballet and the new album, I've never worked so hard in my life." At sixty-three, Joni was still in the midst of creation. Her muse hadn't deserted her after all. The *Fiddle and the Drum* ballet went on at Calgary's Southern Alberta Jubilee Auditorium on February 8, 2007, while outside the Canadian prairie got pounded with snow. Journalists murmured excitedly and photographers lugged their cameras from vans. But Joni was not quite ready. She hadn't performed since 2000, and this was a surprising reentry into the spotlight. She had been fussing with her outfit and her hair, knowing the cameras would be flashing, that her unlifted sixty-three-year-old face would be compared with images of her younger self. "Do I have to look good?" she had asked as she checked herself out in the mirror the morning before the dress rehearsal.

She had settled on a fatigue-green A-line dress in ripped gauze, cinched at the waist with a macramé belt with a pouch attached, an effect that was simultaneously glam and earthy. At the last moment, she added a green beret, a gift from Graham Nash for her sixtieth birthday, perhaps a nod to the ballet's antiwar sentiment and color scheme. Despite this uncertainty, when she made her way to the stage, it was obvious that she belonged nowhere else. Her face was alight, her body alive to the music. The lights dimmed, and, if you looked closely from the right sight lines, you could see her reacting to the dancers. After a decade of silence, the new songs of theological and environmental complaint were now coming out. Two of them were getting their world premiere at the ballet. Grand-Maître swept Joni onstage for the curtain call, and the crowd in Calgary went berserk. The dancers all did their stage bow in unison, and even though Joni had practiced it in dress rehearsal, she just couldn't bow with the chorus. She was taking a bow all by herself. The crowd cheered for more.

33 ■ JUST LIKE THIS TRAIN

On March 31, 2015, Joni was discovered unconscious in her kitchen. She had been lying there for three days before she was found. A call was made to 911: she had suffered serious brain trauma from an aneurysm. She was rushed to the hospital, had emergency brain surgery, and was put in an ICU. (Joni, while conscious, was against Western medicine, but her treatment at this point was determined by the state of California.) Leslie Morris, a onetime manager of Crosby, Stills, Nash & Young, was named her medical conservator. Her prospects, according to every expert, were not good. Eventually, she was moved back to her home in Bel-Air. She might have had a laugh if she knew that the doctors and nurses attending to her came from the David Geffen School of Medicine. (Some things never end!) After a while, she started talking, and then started asking for cigarettes. She was told that if she could walk out on her own, she could do whatever she wanted.

After she had begun talking but not walking, Larry Klein, who was among those pushed away by her in the months before the aneurysm, came by and showed her their wedding pictures. She identified nearly every person in them. He wondered if she remembered how they had left things, but thought it best to not bring it up. (As with many survivors of brain trauma, her long-term memory was better than her short-term memory.) They held hands and spoke sweetly to each other. Joni's friend the neuroscientist and musician Daniel Levitin was making regular visits. He was bringing in CDs for her to listen to, music he knew she loved. But listening to recordings lying in the dark just wasn't doing it for her. She needed something more.

She decided to see the jazz pianist Chick Corea at Catalina Bar and Grill in Hollywood; they had worked together on one of the *Mingus* sessions. Herbie Hancock came along. Although she was beginning to get her walking function back through physical therapy, it was still weak, and there were too many hazards in the dark nightclub, so she was pushed through in a wheelchair. Sometimes it is marvelous to listen to your favorite music in the dark, but there are times, if you can, when you just have to get out of bed. When she was ten, she prayed to the Christmas tree: *Give me back my legs and I'll make it up to you.* At seventy-three, when the odds were stacked again, Joni came back yet again. The pictures went viral.

Joni was wearing a black cape over a black-and-orange dress. Hancock looked thrilled. Joni looked defiant. They were holding hands, but she didn't seem to be holding on for dear life. She seemed relaxed, even serene. She was planning to go to more shows. Herbie and Wayne Shorter were playing the Hollywood Bowl the following week. (Chick was playing the Blue Note in New York, and she considered going. Traveling would be easier now that no one was letting her smoke.) She was working intensely with physical therapists. One of them danced with her, and she smiled. She was getting herself back more day by day. And the piano was waiting for her to play it, guitars were waiting to be strummed, new chords, maybe even new words would come. Larry Klein had given her music apps for her iPad. A new canvas was waiting to be filled.

After the show, she hung out with Herbie and Chick and they talked for about an hour. At one point, she was in the middle of talking and her voice trailed off. She was spacing out like this sometimes, and it was hard to tell what was going on when she did it. "Did you lose your train of thought?" she was asked. There was nowhere to go but forward. So many years ago, the words she wrote as a young woman, sung at so many summer camps and quoted in so many high school yearbooks, were truer than ever. We're captive on the carousel of time. We can't return, we can only look behind from where we came.

What was coming next? Would there be another painting? Another song? Would she ever sing again? *The seasons, they go 'round and 'round. I really don't know life at all. All romantics meet the same fate. Help me, I think I'm falling. I'm always running behind the time, just like this train. Each of us so deep and superficial from the cradle to the stone. Nothing lasts for long. She says she's leaving, but she don't go. This time you went too far.*

"Joni? Did you lose your train of thought?"

"Yes," she finally said. "Yes. But that's not such a bad thing for a writer to do."

NOTES

The story of Joni Mitchell is one that has been shaped by many people—those whose music I've listened to and those who have been generous enough to share their memories and observations with me. To tell the life of any person, especially a complex and multifaceted one, is to accumulate other stories and other lives. I am grateful to everyone whose influences have surfaced, both implicitly and explicitly, in *Reckless Daughter*. Much of this book was informed by interviews conducted between 2007 and 2017 with the following people: Joni Mitchell, Sharon Bell Veer, Jeanine Hollingshead, Sharolyn Dickson, Lorrie Wood, Tony Simon, John Uren, Chuck Mitchell, Nick Jennings, Murray McLauchlan, Buffy Sainte-Marie, Jonathan Rosenbaum, Leonard Cohen, Judy Collins, David Crosby, Graham Nash, Dick Cavett, Ron Stone, Russ Kunkel, Annie Ross, Boyd Elder, Joan Baez, Kinky Friedman, Ronee Blakley, Garth Hudson, J. D. Souther, Larry Carlton, Max Bennett, Robben Ford, Miles Greer, Chaka Khan, Wayne Shorter, Herbie Hancock, Mike Gibbs, Peter Erskine, Sy Johnson, Bob Mintzer, Nathan Joseph, Rafi Zabor, Sue Mingus, Larry Klein, Thomas Dolby, Peter Asher, Greg Leisz, Brian Blade, Vince Mendoza, Wallace Roney, Sue McNamara, Simon Montgomery, and Daniel Levitin. Quotations in the text that do not come from these interviews are detailed in the notes that follow.

PREFACE

This chapter draws on interviews with Joni Mitchell conducted in the years 2007 and 2015.

1. ALL THINGS CONSIDERED, I'D RATHER BE DANCING

This chapter draws on interviews with Joni Mitchell, Sharon Bell Veer, Jeanine Hollingshead, Sharolyn Dickson, Robben Ford, and Tony Simon conducted in the years 2012–2015.

9 *"There were only two stores in town"*: Malka Marom, *Joni Mitchell: In Her Own Words* (Toronto: ECW Press, 2014), 3.

9 *"The Hit Parade was one hour a day"*: Cameron Crowe, "Joni Mitchell Defends Herself," *Rolling Stone*, July 26, 1979.

9 *"I was anti-intellectual"*: Joni Mitchell, "Joe Smith Interviews Joni," transcript posted on JoniMitchell.com, November 3, 1986.

10 *"I don't know how to sell out"*: Ibid.

12 *"Don't worry, I'm not going to sing"*: "A Tribute by Margaret Atwood," Canadian Songwriters Hall of Fame, YouTube video, posted on JoniMitchell.com, January 28, 2007.

13 *"Joan should pay attention"*: James Brooke, "For Joni Mitchell, Artist, Singing Was Not Enough," *New York Times*, August 22, 2000.

13 *"He and I went to some pretty far-out movies"*: Marom, *Joni Mitchell*, 9.

13 *"And that piece of music thrilled me"*: Ibid.

14 *"I wrote this ambitious"*: Michael Small, "She's Looked at Life from Up and Down, So Joni Mitchell Has New Ways to Write About Both Sides Now," *People*, December 16, 1985.

15 *"You have to learn to paint"*: Warwick McFayden, "The Teacher and the Debt," *The Age*, December 15, 2002.

15 *"If you can paint with a brush"*: Joni Mitchell, *Woman of Heart and Mind*, directed by Susan Lacy, CBC, 2003.

15 *"[Joni] wrote well"*: McFayden, "The Teacher and the Debt."

16 *"his constant creativity, his restlessness"*: Joni Mitchell, *The Charlie Rose Show*, PBS, November 15, 2007.

16 *"The way I saw the educational system"*: Crowe, "Joni Mitchell Defends Herself."

16 *"The fishbowl is a world diverse"*: Timothy White, *Rock Lives* (New York: Holt, 1991). Posted on JoniMitchell.com as "Joni in Conversation with Timothy White, March 17, 1988."

17 *"I felt sorry for celebrities with talent"*: Elio Iannacci, "The Interview: Joni Mitchell," *Maclean's*, November 22, 2014.

17 *"I lived in the tail end of"*: Marom, *Joni Mitchell*, 2.

17 *"My poetry is urbanized and Americanized"*: Susan Gordon Lydon, "In Her House, Love," *New York Times*, April 20, 1969.

2. LET THE WIND CARRY ME: LESSONS IN WOMANHOOD

This chapter draws on interviews with Joni Mitchell, Sharon Bell Veer, Jeanine Hollingshead, Sharolyn Dickinson, Lorrie Wood, and Tony Simon conducted in the years 2012–2015.

19–20 *"It was the day before I was paralyzed . . . Christmas was nearing"*: Joni Mitchell, "'Pamela Wallin Live' Interview," CBC TV, February 19, 1996.

20 *"The loneliness that many polio"*: Daniel J. Wilson, *Living with Polio: The Epidemic and Its Survivors* (Chicago: University of Chicago Press, 2007), 126.

21 *"Somewhere all the cells said"*: Mitchell, "'Pamela Wallin Live' Interview."

22 *"I celebrated my legs"*: Ibid.

22 *"There . . . came a stage"*: Cameron Crowe, "Joni Mitchell Defends Herself," *Rolling Stone*, July 26, 1979.

23 *"I lied to her once"*: Malka Marom, *Joni Mitchell: In Her Own Words* (Toronto: ECW Press, 2014), 10–11.

23 *"My identity, since it wasn't"*: Crowe, "Joni Mitchell Defends Herself."

24 *"rock and roll went through a really dumb"*: Ibid.

24 *"When I wanted a guitar"*: Marom, *Joni Mitchell*, 14–15.

25 *"the most original person I knew"*: Ibid., 15.

25 *"I had a column in the school paper"*: Ibid., 14.

27 *"Each of Mitchell's songs"*: Loriane Alterman, "Songs for the New Woman," *New York Times*, February 11, 1973.

3. WILL YOU STILL LOVE ME TOMORROW?

This chapter draws on interviews with Joni Mitchell, Sharon Bell Veer, Jeanine Hollingshead, Sharolyn Dickson, Lorrie Wood, Tony Simon, and John Uren conducted in the years 2012–2015.

30 *"I sing my sorrow"*: Deirdre Kelly, "I Sing My Sorrow and I Paint My Joy," *Globe and Mail*, June 8, 2000.

30 *"I couldn't do what I first"*: David Fricke, "Guitar Gods," *Rolling Stone*, April 1, 1999.

30 *"I didn't have the patience"*: "Introducing Joni Mitchell," *Rolling Stone*, May 17, 1969.

32 *"That [pregnancy out of wedlock] was a terrible thing"*: Joni Mitchell, "'Pamela Wallin Live' Interview," CBC TV, February 19, 1996.

4. A COMMON MODERN-DAY FAIRY TALE

This chapter draws on interviews with Joni Mitchell, Chuck Mitchell, David Crosby, Joan Baez, and Murray McLauchlan conducted in the years 2012–2015.

34 *"couldn't get in"*: Malka Marom, *Joni Mitchell: In Her Own Words* (Toronto: ECW Press, 2014), 18–19.

34 *"it was the attic room"*: Sheila Weller, *Girls Like Us: Carole King, Joni Mitchell, Carly Simon—and the Journey of a Generation* (New York: Atria Books, 2008), 10.

34 *"She wore long gowns"*: Ibid., 147.

36 *"get the baby out of hock"*: Ibid., 209.

36 *"prairie girl [from a] rube place"*: Ibid., 212.

36 *"We lived in the black neighborhood"*: Marom, *Joni Mitchell*, 21.

37 *"By day, newlywed Joni"*: Weller, *Girls Like Us*, 213.

37 *"We have this issue, Chuck"*: Ibid., 215.

37 *"Mother left Canada"*: Ibid., 216.

41 *"the pretty, 'poetic' lyric"*: Timothy Crouse, "Joni Mitchell: Blue," *Rolling Stone*, August 5, 1971.

43 *"As my work began to mature"*: Joni Mitchell, *Woman of Heart and Mind*, directed by Susan Lacy, CBC, 2003.

43 *"Every bit of trouble"*: Ibid.

5. DON'T GIVE YOURSELF AWAY

This chapter draws on interviews with Joni Mitchell and Judy Collins conducted in the years 2008, 2013, 2015, and 2017.

44 *"I was reading Saul Bellow's* Henderson the Rain King*"*: Robert Hilburn, "Both Sides, Later," *Los Angeles Times*, December 8, 1996.

44 *"We are the first generation"*: Saul Bellow, *Henderson the Rain King* (1959; reprint, New York: Penguin Books, 2012), 280.

46 *"I loved the beautiful melodies"*: Joni Mitchell, *Woman of Heart and Mind*, directed by Susan Lacy, CBC, 2003.

50 *"Joni invented everything about her music"*: James Taylor, ibid.

51 *"A short time ago, a friend"*: "Footnotes to Both Sides, Now: Joni in Conversation with Gene Shay, 'Folklore Program,' March 12, 1967," JoniMitchell .com.

6. THE WORD MAN: LEONARD COHEN

This chapter draws on interviews with Joni Mitchell, Leonard Cohen, and Judy Collins conducted in the years 2007, 2013, 2015, and 2017.

54 *"boudoir poet"*: Robert Enright, "Words and Pictures: The Arts of Joni Mitchell," *Border Crossings*, February 2001.

56 *"Master Poet. Master Painter"*: Leonard Cohen, "A Few Lines for Joni," written for the Luminato Festival, Toronto, 2013.

57 *"My lyrics are influenced by Leonard"*: Karl Dallas, "Joni, the Seagull from Saskatoon," *Melody Maker*, September 28, 1968.

58 *"Joni is incredibly innovative"*: Ian Popple, "Honouring Joni," *McGill Reporter*, October 28, 2009.

62 *"Leonard got mad at me"*: Malka Marom, *Joni Mitchell: In Her Own Words* (Toronto: ECW Press, 2014), 38.

63 *"stone Cohenite"*: Larry Sloman, *On the Road with Bob Dylan* (New York: Three Rivers Press, 1978), 383.

7. EXPERIENCED

This chapter draws on interviews with Joni Mitchell and David Crosby conducted in the years 2007, 2009, 2013, and 2015.

66 *"When she first came out"*: Elliot Roberts, *Woman of Heart and Mind*, directed by Susan Lacy, CBC, 2003.

66 *"I started at a time when folk clubs"*: "Introducing Joni Mitchell," *Rolling Stone*, May 17, 1969.

66 *"Elliot pitched being my manager"*: Barney Hoskyns, "Lady of the Canyon," *Guardian*, October 16, 2005.

66 *"The role model was Bob Dylan"*: Sheila Weller, *Girls Like Us: Carole King, Joni Mitchell, Carly Simon—and the Journey of a Generation* (New York: Atria Books, 2008), 248.

66 *"sort of snooping"*: Malka Marom, *Joni Mitchell: In Her Own Words* (Toronto: ECW Press, 2014), 34.

67 *"He really could do nothing for me"*: Ibid., 110.

67 *"the position that I had"*: Ibid., 110–12.

68 *"rainy fall night"*: Weller, *Girls Like Us*, 244.

74 *"I'm starting to get my own vocal styling"*: Joni Mitchell, *Woman of Heart and Mind*, directed by Susan Lacy, CBC, 2003.

74 *"Just who—and what—is Joni Mitchell"*: "Introducing Joni Mitchell."

77 *"I hadn't recorded it well enough"*: Wally Breese, "A Conversation with David Crosby," JoniMitchell.com, March 15, 1997.

79 *"It's about a night in any city"*: "Footnotes to Night in the City: Joni Introduced the Song This Way on November 15, 1966, at the Wisdom Tooth," JoniMitchell.com.

82 *"Arrived in Ottawa"*: "Oh What a Night! Joni and Jimi Come Together," *Ottawa Citizen*, October 24, 1998.

82 *"We heard of this great girl singer"*: Mitch Mitchell, *Jimi Hendrix: Inside the Experience* (New York: Harmony, 1990), 132.

84 *"I'm too hung up about what's going on"*: Karl Dallas, "Joni, the Seagull from Saskatoon," *Melody Maker*, September 28, 1968.

85 *"I think she had more understanding"*: David Crosby, *Woman of Heart and Mind*.

8. *CLOUDS*

This chapter draws on interviews with Joni Mitchell, Larry Klein, and Dave Douglas conducted in the years 2013 and 2015.

89 *"It's good to be exposed to politics"*: "Introducing Joni Mitchell," *Rolling Stone*, May 17, 1969.

91 *"Henry, I can't go through this"*: Joni Mitchell, "Joni Mitchell in Conversation with Barney Hoskins," unpublished, September 14, 1994, JoniMitchell.com.

92 *"I found that all the producers were men"*: Timothy White, "Joni Mitchell—A Portrait of the Artist," *Billboard*, December 9, 1995.

93 *"I wrote ['Chelsea Morning'] in Philadelphia"*: Robert Hilburn, "Both Sides, Later," *Los Angeles Times*, December 8, 1996.

96 *"Joni wrote 'That Song About the Midway'"*: Judy Collins, *Sweet Judy Blue Eyes: My Life in Music* (New York: Crown, 2011), 218.

97 *"I guess people identify with songs"*: Mark Bego, *Joni Mitchell* (Latham, MD: Taylor Trade, 2005), 48.

9. OUR HOUSE

This chapter draws on interviews with Joni Mitchell, David Crosby, and Dick Cavett conducted in the years 2007, 2009, 2013, and 2015.

102 *"I was their first racehorse"*: Robert Hilburn, "Out of the Canyon," *Los Angeles Times*, February 24, 1991.

102 *"It was the time everyone was coming"*: Elliot Roberts, *Woman of Heart and Mind*, directed by Susan Lacy, CBC, 2003.

103 *"Joni took this really potent, popular image"*: Bill Flanagan, ibid.

103 *"I can only liken it to Vienna"*: Graham Nash, ibid.

104 *"The sun had just left the western sky"*: Graham Nash, *Wild Tales* (New York: Crown, 2013), 2.

105 *"There really was an ethic"*: Elliot Roberts, *Woman of Heart and Mind*.

105 *"She's the only one who can sing"*: Susan Gordon Lydon, "In Her House, Love," *New York Times*, April 20, 1969.

105 *"Watching her was the most interesting process"*: Graham Nash, *Woman of Heart and Mind*.

106 *"was built in the 1930s"*: Nash, *Wild Tales*, 131.

106 *"perched on an English church chair"*: "Introducing Joni Mitchell," *Rolling Stone*, May 17, 1969.

106 *"It's a long way from Saskatoon"*: Joni Mitchell, *Woman of Heart and Mind*.

106 *"the audience at Carnegie Hall"*: Graham Nash, ibid.

107 *"picked up a copy of* The New York Times*"*: David Geffen, ibid.

107 *"The boys weren't going to"*: Joni Mitchell, ibid.

108 *"The deprivation of not"*: Dave Zimmer, *Crosby, Stills & Nash: The Biography* (New York: Da Capo Press, 1984), 101–102.

108 *"They showed up raving about it"*: "Joni Mitchell Remembers the Time She Never Got to Woodstock," MTV website, August 14, 1998, as posted on JoniMitchell.com.

110 *"So I stayed home in New York"*: Joni Mitchell, *Woman of Heart and Mind*.

111 *"By the time we got back"*: Graham Nash, ibid.

111 *"She contributed more to people's understanding"*: David Crosby, ibid.

112 *"My relationship with Graham"*: Cameron Crowe, "Joni Mitchell Defends Herself," *Rolling Stone*, July 26, 1979.

112 *"I don't know whether you know"*: Graham Nash, interview by Terry Gross, "Graham Nash Has Wild Tales to Spare," *Fresh Air*, December 25, 2013. Transcript on NPR.org.

112 *"It was an intense time"*: Graham Nash, *Woman of Heart and Mind*.

113 *"Graham and I have been"*: Joni Mitchell, ibid.

10. *LADIES OF THE CANYON*

This chapter draws on interviews with Joni Mitchell and David Crosby conducted in the years 2007, 2009, and 2015.

114 *"perhaps the first entry"*: Don Heckman, "Ladies of the Canyon," *New York Times*, April 5, 1970.

115 *"Sometimes a best friend"*: "Footnotes to Conversation: Joni's Introduction to the Song on October 12, 1967, at the Second Fret in Philadelphia," JoniMitchell.com.

116 *"old rambling folky lyrics"*: Jim Beebe, "Joni Mitchell Has Matured," *Toronto Daily Star*, July 4, 1970.

116 *"Joni Mitchell is better able"*: Geoffrey Cannon, "Heart's Spokesman," *Guardian*, April 28, 1970.

117 *"In 1968 we all stood"*: Annie Burden, "Thoughts on the Song 'Ladies of the Canyon' and the Time," JoniMitchell.com, May 4, 2008.

117 *"My husband, Gary, worked"*: Ibid.

118 *"in gratitude I made her"*: Trina Robbins, "Trina Talks About the Song 'Ladies of the Canyon,'" JoniMitchell.com, April 19, 2008.

118 *"That is the core of the beast"*: Estrella Berosini, "Estrella Talks About the Song 'Ladies of the Canyon,'" JoniMitchell.com, March 25, 2008.

119 *"Hotels are rising on every hand"*: William W. Yates, "Waikiki Beach Has Tidal Wave of New Visitors," *Chicago Tribune*, January 10, 1960.

120 *"I have been hopelessly in love"*: Heckman, "Ladies of the Canyon."

11. SAND

This chapter draws on interviews with Joni Mitchell, David Crosby, and Ronee Blakley conducted in the years 2007, 2009, 2013, and 2015.

122 *"I had sworn my heart to Graham"*: Joni Mitchell, *Woman of Heart and Mind*, directed by Susan Lacy, CBC, 2003.

122 *"If you hold sand too tightly"*: Graham Nash, *Wild Tales* (New York: Crown, 2013), 185.

123 *"Joni met us just outside of Panama"*: Ibid., 182.

125 *"I can't describe what Joan's room"*: Ibid., 140.

126 *"Free love—now we know"*: "A Day in the Garden," *Entertainment Weekly Online*, August 18, 1998.

12. *BLUE*

This chapter draws on interviews with Joni Mitchell and Russ Kunkel conducted in the years 2007, 2013, and 2015.

127 *"He wasn't very well known"*: Mark Bego, *Joni Mitchell* (Latham, MD: Taylor Trade, 2005), 84.

129 *"A constant stream of singers"*: Carole King, *A Natural Woman* (New York: Grand Central, 2012), 209.

130 *"Studio C had a reddish wood Steinway"*: Ibid.

131 *"the luxury of being able"*: Malka Marom, "Self-Portrait of a Superstar," *Maclean's*, June 1974.

132 *"By the time of my fourth album"*: Cameron Crowe, "Joni Mitchell Defends Herself," *Rolling Stone*, July 26, 1979.

132 *"I lost my daughter"*: Malka Marom, *Joni Mitchell: In Her Own Words* (Toronto: ECW Press, 2014), 56–57.

136 *"My individual psychological descent"*: Joni Mitchell, *Woman of Heart and Mind*, directed by Susan Lacy, CBC, 2003.

137 *"It's taking personal responsibility for the failure"*: Joni Mitchell, interview by Renee Montagne, "The Music Midnight Makes: In Conversation with Joni Mitchell," NPR's *Morning Edition*, December 9, 2014, transcript on NPR.org.

138 *"It is a song I've grieved to"*: Eric R. Danton, "Beth Orton Covers Joni Mitchell's 'River' for Holiday Playlist (Exclusive Premiere)," *Wall Street Journal*, November 5, 2014.

138 *"It's such a beautiful thing"*: J. Freedom Du Lac, "How a 'Thoroughly Depressing' Joni Mitchell Song Became a Christmas Classic," *Washington Post*, December 7, 2016.

138 *"near perfection of her arrangements"*: Peter Reilly, "Joni Mitchell Sings Her Blues," *Stereo Review*, October 1971.

139 *"I suspect this will be the most disliked"*: Don Heckman, "Pop: Jim Morrison at the End, Joni at a Crossroads," *New York Times*, August 8, 1971.

13. BETWEEN BREAKDOWN AND BREAKTHROUGH

This chapter draws on an interview with Leonard Cohen conducted in 2015.

140 *"Love does not begin and end"*: David Leeming, *James Baldwin: A Biography* (New York: Arcade, 2015), 2.

143 *"private letters that were published"*: Michael Watts, "Joni Mitchell: The Public Life of a Private Property," *Sunday Times of London*, April 17, 1983.

143 *"Otherwise," she said in 2013*: Joni Mitchell, interview by Jon Pareles, *New York Times* TimesTalks, YouTube video, recorded at the Luminato Festival, June 16, 2013.

143 *"I was demanding of myself"*: Joni Mitchell, *A Woman of Heart and Mind*, directed by Susan Lacy, CBC, 2003.

143 *"some of the most beautiful"*: Timothy Crouse, "Joni Mitchell: Blue," *Rolling Stone*, August 5, 1971.

145 *"The club thing was kind of fun"*: Joni Mitchell, *Woman of Heart and Mind*.

145 *"Tours are like bullfighting"*: Jack Hafferkamp, "Ladies and Gents, Leonard Cohen," *Rolling Stone*, February 4, 1971.

147 *"there's good wine in every generation"*: Michelle Mercer, *Will You Take Me As I Am: Joni Mitchell's Blue Period* (New York: Free Press, 2009), 104.

148 *"At that period of my life"*: Cameron Crowe, "Joni Mitchell Defends Herself," *Rolling Stone*, July 26, 1979.

149 *"A restless woman travels"*: "Critics' Choices; Albums as Mileposts in a Musical Century," *New York Times*, January 3, 2000.

149 *"You have to have a certain grab-ability"*: Joni Mitchell, "Joe Smith Interviews Joni," November 3, 1986, JoniMitchell.com.

14. THE SUNSHINE COAST

This chapter draws on interviews with Joni Mitchell, Tony Simon, and Leonard Cohen conducted in the years 2007, 2013, and 2015.

150 *"a little stone house like a monastery"*: Richard Ouzounian, "Joni Mitchell Opens Up to the Star After Years Away from Spotlight," *Toronto Star*, June 11, 2013.

151 *"She could transform a shack"*: Graham Nash, *Wild Tales* (New York: Crown, 2013), 131.

152 *"I bought every psychology book"*: Ouzounian, "Joni Mitchell Opens Up."

153 *"It was all about his struggles"*: Ibid.

154 *"This is a song about Beethoven"*: "Judgement of the Moon and Stars," YouTube video, from a performance recorded on May 19, 1972.

15. *FOR THE ROSES*

This chapter draws on interviews with Joni Mitchell and Russ Kunkel conducted in the years 2013 and 2015.

156 *"It comes from the expression"*: "Footnotes to 'For the Roses': Joni's Introduction to the Song at Carnegie Hall on February 23, 1972," JoniMitchell.com.

157 *"I was their first racehorse"*: Robert Hilburn, "Out of the Canyon," *Los Angeles Times*, February 24, 1991.

157 *"I'm a little in awe of cities"*: Hubert Saal, "The Girls—Letting Go," *Newsweek*, July 14, 1969.

157 *"came to stay with David Geffen"*: Joni Mitchell, *Woman of Heart and Mind*, directed by Susan Lacy, CBC, 2003.

157 *"We were roommates"*: Mark Bego, *Joni Mitchell* (Latham, MD: Taylor Trade, 2005), 107–108.

158 *"At a time when so many"*: Robert Hilburn, "Joni Mitchell's New For The Roses," *Los Angeles Times*, November 21, 1972.

160 *"Joan, how would you like to see"*: Cameron Crowe, "Joni Mitchell Defends Herself," *Rolling Stone*, July 26, 1979.

160 *"unique feeling that one gets"*: Stephen Davis, "Joni Mitchell: For the Roses," *Rolling Stone*, January 4, 1973.

161 *"Her voice has a far greater range"*: Don Heckman, "Concert Is Given by Joni Mitchell," *New York Times*, February 25, 1972.

162 *"For all its individuality, the rock-music"*: Hubert Saal, "The Girls—Letting Go," *Newsweek*, July 14, 1969.

162 *The* Newsweek *article echoed the still-new idea*: Carol Hansich, "The Personal Is the Political," February 1969, CarolHanisch.org.

163 *"Love's tension is Joni Mitchell's medium"*: Davis, "Joni Mitchell: For the Roses."

163 *"I kept on telling Joni"*: David Geffen, *Woman of Heart and Mind*.

16. STAR-CROSSED

This chapter draws on interviews with Joni Mitchell, Larry Klein, and Judy Collins conducted in the years 2015 and 2017.

170 *"If I have to feel lonely"*: Malka Marom, *Joni Mitchell: In Her Own Words* (Toronto: ECW Press, 2014), 64.

17. *COURT AND SPARK*: SOMETHING STRANGE HAPPENED

This chapter draws on interviews with Joni Mitchell, Russ Kunkel, Max Bennett, Larry Carlton, and Annie Ross conducted in the years 2013, 2014, and 2015.

176 *"On first listening, Joni Mitchell's"*: Jon Landau, "Joni Mitchell: Court and Spark," *Rolling Stone*, February 28, 1974.

178 *"The significance of such a quantifiably"*: Sean Nelson, *Joni Mitchell's Court and Spark* (New York: Continuum, 2007), 16–17.

179 *"I always kept my goals very short"*: Malka Marom, "Self-Portrait of a Superstar," *Maclean's*, June 1974.

180 *the premiere issue of* People *magazine*: "The Press: People's Premiere," *Time*, March 14, 1974.

180 *"citing Bob Dylan as an example"*: Peter Lyle, "Why Do So Many Escape Mitchell's Web?" *Guardian*, September 12, 2007.

182 *"The music business has always been"*: Joni Mitchell, interview by Brian Stewart, "Interview," *CBC Magazine*, February 11, 2000.

183 *"about as modest as Mussolini"*: Cameron Crowe, "Joni Mitchell Defends Herself," *Rolling Stone*, July 26, 1979.

184 *"What came first? The music or the misery?"*: Nick Hornby, *High Fidelity* (New York: Riverhead Books, 1996), 24.

188 *"That's the music that I play"*: Cameron Crowe, "The Durable Led Zeppelin," *Rolling Stone*, March 13, 1975.

188 *"Later Jimmy was aglow"*: Stephen Davis, *Hammer of the Gods: The Led Zeppelin Saga* (New York: William Morrow, 1985), 246.

188 *"Prince attended one of my concerts in Minnesota"*: Ethan Brown, "Influences: Joni Mitchell," *New York*, May 9, 2005.

189 *"Before Prozac, there was you"*: *Globe and Mail*, October 1994.

18. *MILES OF AISLES*

This chapter draws on interviews with Joni Mitchell, Robben Ford, and Max Bennett conducted in the years 2013–2015.

191 *"I felt like having come through"*: Barbara Gail Rowes, "Joni Mitchell's Search for Satisfaction," *Circus*, June 1974.

19. THE QUEEN OF QUEENS

This chapter draws on interviews with Joni Mitchell, Robben Ford, Max Bennett, Joan Baez, Kinky Friedman, and Boyd Elder conducted in the years 2013–2015.

205 *"There's nothin' down here"*: Sam Shepard, *True West* (New York: Samuel French, 1981), 58–59.

205 *"Her word maneuverings tend to verge"*: Sam Shepard, *The Rolling Thunder Logbook* (New York: Viking Press, 1977), 122.

206 *"How could I compete with her?"*: Chris O'Dell, *Miss O'Dell: My Hard Days and Long Nights with The Beatles, The Stones, Bob Dylan, Eric Clapton, and the Women They Loved* (New York: Simon & Schuster, 2009), 328.

207 *"We came here to give you love"*: Les Ledbetter, "Knocking on Hurricane's Door," *Rolling Stone*, January 15, 1976.

209 *"I had talked to Hurricane on the phone . . . Fine"*: Phil Sutcliffe, "Joni Mitchell," *Q Magazine*, May 1988.

20. *HEJIRA* AND THE ART OF LOSING

This chapter draws on interviews with Joni Mitchell and Max Bennett conducted in the years 2013–2015.

219 *"Hejira presents the Queen of El Lay more explicitly"*: Perry Meisel, "An End to Innocence: How Joni Mitchell Fails," *The Village Voice*, January 1977.

21. CRAZY WISDOM

This chapter draws on interviews with Joni Mitchell, Robben Ford, and Sharon Bell Veer conducted in the years 2013 and 2015.

225 *"I was introduced to Buddhism"*: Malka Marom, *Joni Mitchell: In Her Own Words* (Toronto: ECW Press, 2014), 193.

226 *"When I asked Trungpa Rinpoche"*: Pema Chödrön, "Unconditionally Steadfast," *Tricycle*, Fall 1999.

231 *"I don't know if it's the best"*: Joni Mitchell, interview by Jon Pareles, *New York Times* TimesTalks, YouTube video, recorded at the Luminato Festival, June 16, 2013.

232 *"He had this wide, fat swath"*: Joni Mitchell, "The Life and Death of Jaco Pastorius," *Musician*, December 1987.

233 *They became lovers in a noncommittal way*: Bill Milkowski, *Jaco: The Extraordinary and Tragic Life of Jaco Pastorius*, rev. ed. (New York: Backbeat Books, 2006), 95.

241 *"It was a relief"*: Doug Fischer, "The Trouble She's Seen," *Ottawa Citizen*, October 8, 2006.

22. MIRRORED BALL

This chapter draws on interviews with Joni Mitchell, Garth Hudson, and Michael Gibbs conducted in the years 2007, 2014, and 2015.

245 *"The road has taken"*: Robbie Robertson, *The Last Waltz*, directed by Martin Scorsese, United Artists, 1978.

251 *"Five days a week I used to go up there"*: Bert Cartwright, "The Mysterious Norman Raeben," the Wayback Internet Archive.

23. *DON JUAN'S RECKLESS DAUGHTER*

This chapter draws on interviews with Joni Mitchell, Chaka Khan, and Wallace Roney conducted in the years 2007, 2009, 2013, 2014, and 2015.

257 *"The album offers what is"*: Janet Maslin, "Joni Mitchell: Don Juan's Reckless Daughter," *Rolling Stone*, March 9, 1978.

257 *"So there came Halloween"*: Phil Sutcliffe, "Joni Mitchell," *Q Magazine*, May 1988.

24. *MINGUS*

This chapter draws on interviews with Joni Mitchell, Sue Mingus, and Rafi Zabor conducted in the years 2007, 2013, 2014, and 2015.

262 *"was to be degenerating"*: Mark Bego, *Joni Mitchell* (Latham, MD: Taylor Trade, 2005), 193.

270 *"This guy was the sweeeetest guy"*: Vic Garbarini, "Joni Mitchell Is a Nervy Broad," *Musician*, January 1983.

270 *"And we came out near a manhole"*: Garbarini, "Joni Mitchell Is a Nervy Broad."

272 *"There's a guy who's driving a Cadillac"*: Gene Santoro, *Myself When I Am Real: The Life and Music of Charles Mingus* (New York: Oxford University Press, 2001), 152.

277 *"In other words, I am three"*: Charles Mingus, *Beneath the Underdog* (New York: Knopf, 1971), 1.

25. NERVY BROAD

This chapter draws on interviews with Joni Mitchell conducted in 2015.

279 *Louis Menand once floated a theory*: Louis Menand, "The Iron Law of Stardom," *The New Yorker*, March 24, 1997.

280 *"We ain't no fucking L.A. Express"*: Dave Blackburn, "A Conversation with Alex Acuna," JoniMitchell.com, December 4, 2013.

281 *"I've heard it too often in supermarkets and elevators"*: Carla Hall, "The New Joni Mitchell: The Songbird of Woodstock Soars into Jazz," *Washington Post*, August 25, 1979.

282 *Charles Mingus had famously called her a "nervy broad"*: Vic Garbarini, "Joni Mitchell Is a Nervy Broad," *Musician*, January 1983.

282 *"Because of my wordiness"*: John Ephland, "Alternate Tunings," *Down Beat*, December 1996.

283 *"I haven't seen a royalty check in twenty years"*: Brantley Bardin, "Joni Mitchell Q and A," *Details*, July 1996.

284 *"We've talked about getting married"*: Hall, "The New Joni Mitchell."

284 *"this gauntlet called fame"*: Joni Mitchell, "Canadian Music Hall of Fame Award," YouTube video, recorded February 5, 1981.

26. *WILD THINGS RUN FAST*

This chapter draws on interviews with Joni Mitchell and Larry Klein conducted in the year 2015.

291 *"For my twentieth birthday"*: Carla Hall, "The New Joni Mitchell: The Songbird of Woodstock Soars into Jazz," *Washington Post*, August 25, 1979.

298 *"I called up the president"*: Mick Brown, "Happy Talkin' Joni," *Guardian*, April 22, 1983.

301 *"I thought the words were bothering him"*: John Ephland, "Alternate Tunings," *Down Beat*, December 1996.

27. *DOG EAT DOG*

This chapter draws on interviews with Joni Mitchell, Larry Klein, Thomas Dolby, and Peter Asher conducted in the years 2007, 2013, and 2015.

28. EMERGENCY ROOMS

This chapter draws on interviews with Joni Mitchell, Larry Klein, and Peter Asher conducted in the years 2013 and 2015.

29. SAVE THE BOMBS FOR LATER

This chapter draws on interviews with Joni Mitchell, Larry Klein, and Thomas Dolby conducted in the years 2013 and 2015.

324 *"Well, the thing is"*: David Wild, "A Conversation with Joni Mitchell," *Rolling Stone*, May 30, 1991.

325 *"Will you listen a minute?"*: "Joni Mitchell Scolding Audience at Isle of Wight Festival 1970," YouTube video, posted by "Senor Silencio," May 8, 2016.

332 *"At night we could see"*: Craig MacInnis, "Joni Mitchell Fields the Silliest Questions with Humor," *Toronto Star*, March 23, 1988.

30. TURBULENCE

This chapter draws on interviews with Joni Mitchell and Larry Klein conducted in the years 2014 and 2015.

336 *"I won a Grammy"*: Mary Aikins, "Heart of a Prairie Girl," *Reader's Digest*, July 2005.

340 *"I finally found a story"*: Wally Breese, "Biography: 1990–1995 Return to Roots," JoniMitchell.com, January 1998.

341 *"This is another song that takes place"*: "Cherokee Louise," YouTube video, recorded on January 26, 1995.

344 *"It was abusive to employ"*: Al Brumley, "Feud Takes a Public Turn," *Dallas Morning News*, September 24, 1997.

344 *"Most of my heroes are monsters"*: David Wild, "Q&A: Joni Mitchell," *Rolling Stone*, October 15, 1992.

345 *"I live in British Columbia"*: Joni Mitchell, "Interview—Intimate & Interactive," YouTube video, from MuchMusic, *Intimate and Interactive*, September 23, 1994.

347 *"I had a child"*: Charles Gandee, "Triumph of the Will," *Vogue*, April 1995.

31. SEE YOU AT THE MOVIES

This chapter draws on interviews with Joni Mitchell, Larry Klein, Brian Blade, Wallace Roney, and Vince Mendoza conducted in the years 2013–2015.

354 *"With Larry Klein sliding around"*: Greg Kot, "Rock Review, Joni Mitchell at United Center," *Chicago Tribune*, October 26, 1998.

356 *"I'm interested in your creative process"*: Camille Paglia, "The Trailblazer Interview," *Interview Magazine*, August 2005.

363 *"It was quite amazing"*: Mark Bego, *Joni Mitchell* (Latham, MD: Taylor Trade, 2005), 300.

366 *"I'm quitting after this"*: James Reginato, "The Diva's Last Stand," *W*, December 2002.

366 *"I have this weird, incurable disease"*: Matt Diehl, "It's a Joni Mitchell Concert, Sans Joni," *Los Angeles Times*, April 22, 2010.

32. CURTAIN CALL

This chapter draws on interviews with Joni Mitchell conducted in the years 2007 and 2015.

ACKNOWLEDGMENTS

I must begin by thanking Joni Mitchell, for her music, for her impact on my thinking and feeling, for inspiring my writing and my teaching, for instructing me on the human heart and suspended chords and so much more, and for talking to me with such candor and revelation for so many hours, conversations that I will take with me for the rest of my days. We had several interviews in 2007 and several more in 2015, and she revealed more and more of herself every time. I told her once that, long before I met her, she was my teacher. She always will be.

I am very grateful to my agent, Chris Calhoun, my impassioned advocate and dear friend. His rock-solid belief in the book and in me was crucial to making it a reality all the way through.

Deepest gratitude for my editor, Sarah Crichton, for her support of this book, her patience, her vision, and her impeccably high standards. Being locked in with her during the editing process put me against the wall and made me be better than what I thought was my best, over and over again. She gave me an education in the written word that I will take with me as long as I move that blinking cursor across the screen. I owe her everything.

I am also thankful to Kate Sanford and Rob Sternitzky at FSG; John McGhee (copyeditor); Rebecca Caine and Chandra Wohleber (proofreaders); and Robert Guinsler at Sterling Lord Literistic for helping the book at crucial junctures and in essential ways.

To Amy Leal, my magnificent ex-wife, for her beauty and truth. She gave me the deepest love and support when the book was hatched and underway, and she offered her inimitable literary and spiritual wisdom on the pages she read. I am in awe of her devotion to our son, Julian, who I hope will grow up to read these pages and love music.

I am grateful to everyone who read this book in manuscript form and offered their suggestions and improvements. Jaya Chatterjee took exceptional care of the manuscript and its author. I am also deeply grateful to the late Charis Conn, Jamie Malanowski, and especially Veronica Chambers, for her resourcefulness and superb literary instincts. Thank you to the supersmart Julia Mead for her assiduous fact-checking. For writerly advice and assistance and friendship, I thank David Hajdu.

Syracuse University gave me extremely generous time to write when they named me the Dean's Fellow in the Humanities from fall 2013 through spring 2015. I am especially grateful for the support of Nancy Cantor, Eric Spina, George Langford, Gerry Greenberg, Karin Ruhlandt, Kal Alston, Harvey Teres, Silvio Torres-Saillant, Brooks Haxton, and Ken Frieden. Syracuse has given me academic freedom, which includes teaching students about Joni—a joy beyond measure.

Other friends helped me make it through. I am especially grateful to Jeff Cass-van, John Matteson, Matthew Gasda, Krin Gabbard, Aram Veeser, Keri Walsh, Joe Hooper, Fred Kaufman, Adam Shatz, Ansel Elkins, Severin Garanzuay, Tony Torn, Lee Ann Brown, Nick Mills, Elon Green, Adam Bradley, and Salima Yacoubi-Soussane. Jessica Firger and George Hodgman were very helpful in the beginning. Sheila Weller did a huge favor for me near the end. I am thankful to Idil Mese and everyone else who helps keep my music going. And to Monica Lawty, who introduced me to Joni's music when I was fifteen, and who is a wonderful source of laughter and being for real.

I am especially grateful to my friend Bob Faggen for appointing me as the Gould Faculty Fellow in the Humanities at Claremont McKenna College, where I taught my first Joni Mitchell class, which included a field trip to Laurel Canyon. Bob also facilitated an unforgettable evening with Leonard Cohen, whose insights I was honored to record for this book.

Les Irvin, webmaster of jonimitchell.com, has been extraordinary in referring me to the right people to get me the information I needed when I needed it. I also talked to Tony Simon many times, and he was also enormously helpful in referring me to Joni's friends from back home. Larry Klein went above and beyond, and I learned so much from our conversations and exchanges. I am also very grateful for conversations with Sharon Bell Veer, Jeanine Hollingshead, Sharolyn Dickinson, Lorrie Wood, John Uren, Nick Jennings, Murray McLauchlan, Buffy St. Marie, Leonard Cohen, Judy Collins, David Crosby, Dick Cavett, Ron Stone, Russ Kunkel, Annie Ross, Boyd Elder, Joan Baez, Kinky Friedman, Ronee Blakely, Garth Hudson, J. D. Souther,

Larry Carlton, Max Bennett, Robben Ford, Chaka Khan, Wayne Shorter, Herbie Hancock, Mike Gibbs, Peter Erskine, Sy Johnson, Nathan Joseph, Rafi Zabor, Sue Mingus, Donald Fagen, Thomas Dolby, Peter Asher, Greg Leisz, Brian Blade, Vince Mendoza, Wallace Roney, Sue McNamara, Simon Montgomery, Lee Mergner, Sam Stone, and Daniel Levitin.

I am very happy to dedicate this book to my parents, Martin and Connie Yaffe, who supported me in my lifelong quest to discover the music and spread the word. They met in Toronto, where my father played five-string banjo with Ian and Sylvia in the same clubs where Joni got her start a year later. They moved on to another life and raised me. This book is for the part of my father who sang "Last Night I Had the Strangest Dream" and the part of my mother who is still a gypsy dancer.

INDEX

A

A&M Records, 129, 207, 247, 250, 274
Abstract Expressionism, 29
Academy Awards, 4
Acuña, Alejandro, 255
Adams, Bryan, 294, 322, 333, 334
Adderley, David, 78
Adler, Lou, 130
AIDS, 290, 343
Airto, 255
Alberta Ballet, xii, 370–73
Alberta College of Art and Design,
   28–30
albums, Mitchell's: *Blue*, xi, 4, 41, 128,
   129–49, 158, 161, 163, 174, 196, 197,
   199, 219, 220, 259, 291, 298, 322,
   338, 346, 360, 370; *Both Sides Now*,
   359–66; *Chalk Mark in a Rainstorm*,
5, 326–32, 335; *Clouds*, 77, 86–101,
162, 308, 360, 371; *Court and Spark*,
135, 138, 171–89, 197, 207, 220, 223,
279, 280, 290, 360; *Dog Eat Dog*, xv,
289, 307–18, 322, 324, 331, 337, 351,
354, 359; *Don Juan's Reckless Daughter*,
187, 253–62, 265, 274, 281, 299, 301,
309; *For the Roses*, 27, 152, 153,
156–64, 167, 171, 173, 174, 194, 359;
Hejira, xv, 32, 217, 219–24, 228–42,
245, 279, 281, 299, 301, 309, 329,
344, 348, 351; *The Hissing of Summer
Lawns*, 87, 92, 194–98, 210–17, 229,
234, 255, 280, 291, 300–301, 309;
Ladies of the Canyon, 113, 114–21,
122, 262, 360; *Miles of Aisles*, 187,
190, 193; *Mingus*, 87, 267–78,
280–83, 299, 309, 330, 339; *Night
Ride Home*, 255, 337, 339–42;

albums, Mitchell's (*cont.*)
  Shadows and Light, 232, 282, 308;
  Shine, xii, 357, 369, 370; *Song to a*
  Seagull, 14, 70–81, 90, 98, 188, 244,
  338, 360; *Taming the Tiger*, 351–53;
  Travelogue, 227, 359, 365; *Turbulent*
  Indigo, 336–37, 342–45, 353; *Wild*
  Things Run Fast, xvi, 288, 292–302,
  307, 309, 330, 365. *See also* covers,
  album; *specific albums and songs*
Ali, Muhammad, 209
Alias, Don, xii, 243, 252, 259–60, 284,
  349, 364; Mitchell and, 243, 259–60,
  270–71, 281, 284–88
Allen, Woody, 109, 169
"All I Want," 130–31, 133–35, 136, 239,
  370
Alpert, Herb, 129
Altman, Robert, 152, 183
Amchitka, 127
"Amelia," 223, 230, 239–40, 299, 354
American Idol, 362
American Masters documentary, 15, 352
American Way benefit, 350
Amnesty International concert, 309,
  322–26, 327, 330, 334, 343
Amsterdam, 167
Andersen, Eric, 237–38
Anderson, Kelly Dale. *See* Gibb,
  Kilauren
Anderson, Leroy, 25
Anderson, Myrtle McKee, 3–8, 342;
  relationship with daughter Joni, 5–8,
  17, 20–26, 34, 38, 107, 125, 132, 141,
  285, 286, 337, 347, 358
Anderson, Roberta Joan. *See* Mitchell,
  Joni
Anderson, William, 3, 5–8, 25, 95, 342;
  relationship with daughter Joni, 6–8,
  20, 25, 26, 34, 107, 125, 285, 347, 358

Annie Hall (movie), 301
antiwar movement, 99–101, 117, 332,
  333
AOR, 298
Apple Records, 316
Armatrading, Joan, 129
Armstrong, Louis, 263
Armstrong, Peter, 13
"Arrangement, The," 115
Ashcombe House, 321
Asher, Peter, 258, 291; as Mitchell's
  manager, 258, 291, 305, 316–17
astrology, 10–11, 83, 99, 109, 207, 213
Asylum Records, 152, 163, 181, 283;
  Mitchell on, 152, 163–64, 187
Atwood, Margaret, 12, 18

B

Bacharach, Burt, 58, 129
Badrena, Manolo, 255
Baez, Joan, 30, 38, 47, 52, 64, 67, 75,
  93, 129, 200, 324; "Dida," 207–208;
  Dylan and, 80, 200–205; Mitchell
  and, 38–39, 200, 203–209, 257, 346;
  on Rolling Thunder Revue tour,
  200–209
Baker, Chet, 173
Baldwin, James, 140
"Ballerina Valerie," 76–77
ballet, xii, xiv, 13, 101, 299; *The Fiddle*
  and the Drum, xii, 101, 370–73
Band, The, 67, 90, 202, 222, 244–46,
  333; *Last Waltz* concert, 244–46;
  Music from Big Pink, 244; "The Shape
  I'm In," 246; "Tears of Rage," 246
Bangles, "Manic Monday," 291
"Banquet," 347
"Barangrill," 193

Bardin, Brantley, 283

Basie, Count, 173, 272

bass, 221–22; fretless, 222, 274; Larry Klein on, 292–94, 321–23, 351, 354, 355; Charles Mingus on, 263; Pastorius on, 221–22, 230, 232–34

BBC, 89, 128, 152, 180, 307

Beach Boys, *Pet Sounds*, 142

Beatles, 74, 115, 149, 234, 279, 290, 316; "Hey Jude," 248; *Sgt. Pepper*, 70, 71, 73, 141; "Tomorrow Never Knows," 241

"Beat of Black Wings, The," 331, 332–33, 371

Beats, 226, 267

Beatty, Warren, 60, 165, 166, 168–69; Mitchell and, 168–69, 170, 183

Beck, Jeff, 28, 81

"Be Cool," 292, 365

Beethoven, Ludwig van, 152–55, 365; *Eroica* Symphony, 248; Ninth Symphony, 248

Bell, Sharon, 7, 12–13, 17, 20, 23, 32, 33, 235–39, 301

Bellow, Saul, *Henderson the Rain King*, 44, 51

Bennett, Max, 174–75, 191, 192–93, 212, 217, 222–23, 230, 232

Bergman, Ingmar, 133, 240, 296

Berklee School of Music, 313

Berlin, Irving, "White Christmas," 136

Berliner, Jay, 142

Berlin Wall, fall of, 333–35

Bernstein, Joel, 160, 228–29

Berosini, Estrella, 116, 118

Berry, Chuck, 9

Beyoncé, 159; *Lemonade*, 76

Bible, 11, 202, 203, 239, 267, 292, 296–97, 344–45

Big Sur festival, 133

"Big Yellow Taxi," 3, 4, 9, 41, 76, 114, 115, 119–20, 262, 281, 325; Dylan cover of, 119; environmentalism and, 119–20

Billboard charts, 66, 90, 164, 178, 193

Bishop, Elizabeth, 218

Björk, 159

"Black Crow," 230, 240–41, 243

black culture, and Mitchell, 207, 209, 231, 256–60, 265, 271–72, 277–78, 284–85, 296, 333, 359

Blade, Brian, 348–53, 365, 369, 371; Mitchell and, 348–54

Blakey, Art, 254

Blakley, Ronee, 152

Bleecker Street, 40, 93–94, 199

Bloomfield, Mike, 47

"Blue," 139, 143, 145–46, 185

Blue, xi, 4, 41, 128, 129–49, 158, 161, 163, 174, 196, 197, 199, 219, 220, 259, 291, 298, 322, 338, 346, 360, 370; cover art, 130; dulcimer on, 133–34, 135, 147; emotional vulnerability of, 131–44, 148–49; influence of, 140–49; recorded in Studio C, 129–30; reviews, 138–39, 143–44, 148–49; sales, 138, 141; songs, 130–39, 143–48; success of, 138–49. *See also specific songs*

Blue, David, 207

"Blue Boy," 115

"Blue Motel Room," 230, 299

Blue Note, 254, 275, 375

blues music, 176, 231–32, 256

"Boho Dance, The," xv, 29, 159

Bonnie and Clyde (movie), 168

Bono, 323

"Born to Take the Highway," 39

"Both Sides, Now," 4, 32, 44–51, 57, 59, 64, 69, 73, 87, 90, 94, 101, 144, 194,

"Both Sides, Now" (*cont.*)
198, 210, 223, 247, 281, 357, 369;
Both Sides Now version, 361–63;
Clouds version, 90, 94, 101, 105;
Collins cover of, 47–50, 64, 90, 94,
101, 105, 361; repeated trope in, 45;
song structure, 45–46; success of,
47–50; tuning, 50–51
Both Sides Now, 359–66; reviews, 366;
sales, 366; songs, 359–63; tour,
363–65. *See also specific songs*
Bowie, David, 4, 200, 282
Brand, Oscar, 39
Brando, Marlon, 109, 133, 141
Bread and Roses festival, 217, 276
Brecht, Bertolt, 38, 308
Brecker, Michael, 221, 281
Breese, Wally, 347
British Columbia, Mitchell in, 150–56,
158, 159, 160, 163, 170, 240, 243,
345, 368
Brown, James, 173, 234, 344
Brown, Ray, 233
Browne, Beatrice, 167
Browne, Ethan Zane, 344
Browne, Jackson, 50, 117, 167–68, 309,
343; "Fountain of Sorrow," 344;
marriage to Phyllis Major, 236–38,
344; Mitchell and, 167–68, 169, 171,
236–38, 343–45; "Not to Blame" and,
343–44
Bruce, Jack, 222
Buddhism, xiv, 54, 99, 131, 147, 275;
Mitchell and, 225–28, 236, 241–42,
293, 338–39; Tibetan, 225–26; Zen,
54, 63, 99
Buffalo Springfield, 79, 104
Buggles, "Video Killed the Radio Star,"
290–91
Burden, Annie, 116, 117

Burden, Gary, 117
Burundi drums, 288
Bush, Kate, 321
Byrds, 68, 102
Byron, Don, 366

C

cabaret, 38
"Cactus Tree," 80–81, 88, 98, 183, 299
Cafe Au Go Go, 40, 57, 93
Calgary, 28–33, 370–73
"California," 136, 139, 146–47, 342, 343
California, 32, 116, 146–47, 157; Board
of Equalization, 288, 305; Laurel
Canyon scene, 102–13, 116–18, 136;
Mitchell moves to, 70, 73, 102–103
Camus, Albert, 54, 55, 234–35;
Notebooks, 1935–1951, 234
Canada, 3–18, 20, 65, 79, 81–83, 89, 95,
98, 107, 116, 150–56, 157, 231, 244,
248, 284–85, 370–73; Gemini Award,
345; Mitchell's childhood in, 3–18,
19–27, 91, 140–41, 235–36, 341–42,
358, 372; Sunshine Coast, 150–56,
158, 159, 160, 163, 170, 240, 243;
Toronto music scene, 33–35, 66–67, 73
Canadian Broadcasting Corporation
(CBC), 19
Canadian Songwriters Hall of Fame, 3,
12, 284–85
Cannon, Geoffrey, 116
Capote, Truman, 109
"Carey," 132, 134, 136
Carlton, Larry, 175–76, 181, 184, 191,
197, 230, 240, 303
Carnegie Hall, 106–107, 145, 251;
Mitchell's debut at, 106–107, 325; 1972
Mitchell performance, 156–57, 161

"Car on a Hill," 180–81, 197

Carr, Emily, 152

Carson, Rachel, 119–20; *Silent Spring*, 119–20

Carter, Jimmy, 268

Carter, Ron, 250, 363

Carter, Ruben "Hurricane," 198–99, 207, 209

"Case of You, A," 62–63, 136, 147–48, 160, 172, 292, 304

Cash, Johnny, 138, 343

Castaneda, Carlos, 206; *Teachings of Don Juan*, 206

Cavett, Dick, 107, 109; Mitchell on TV show of, 107–11

CBS This Morning, 351

Chalk Mark in a Rainstorm, 5, 326–32, 335; songs, 328–32. *See also specific songs*

Changes magazine, 265

Chapman, Tracy, 294

Charles, Ray, 9, 128

Charlotte Observer, 280

Chelsea Hotel, 93

"Chelsea Morning," 50, 56, 73, 87, 90, 93–94

Cher, 157, 171

"Cherokee Louise," 341–42

Chicago, 84, 365

Chicago Tribune, 280, 354, 355

Child ballads, 30, 32

"Chinese Café," 292, 294, 301–302, 347, 356, 367

Chisholm, Shirley, 157

Chödrön, Pema, 226–27

Christianity, 11, 202, 203, 239, 267, 292, 296–97, 344–46

Christie, Julie, 183

Cicalo, Hank, 130

cigarettes, xii, 158, 208, 214, 289, 295–96, 304–306, 318, 374, 375

"Circle Game, The," 3–4, 50, 59, 73, 90, 114–15, 144, 262, 302, 357; *Ladies of the Canyon* version, 114–15, 119, 120

Circus magazine, 191

civil rights movement, 88, 290

Clapton, Eric, xvi, 69, 78, 81, 117, 136, 244

Clash, 244

classical music, 13, 152–55, 177, 238, 248, 249, 275

Cliff, Jimmy, 315; "Vietnam," 100

Clinton, Chelsea, 94

Clouds, 77, 86–101, 162, 308, 360, 371; cover painting, 86–87; production, 91–93; songs, 90, 93–101. *See also specific songs*

cocaine, 204, 208, 218–24, 228, 229, 239–42, 282, 303, 316

Coconut Grove, Miami, 68–70, 71, 97

Cohen, Leonard, xiv, 4, 47, 49, 53–63, 72, 74, 86, 93, 96–97, 103, 116, 170, 182, 234, 236, 324; "Bird on the Wire," 60–61; Buddhism and, 99, 147; "Don't Go Home with Your Hard-On," 74; "Joan of Arc," 59–60; "Master Song," xiv; Mitchell and, 53–63, 97–98, 143, 145, 147–48, 151, 167, 199, 266, 338–39; at Newport, 52–53, 54; "So Long, Marianne," 74; *Songs of Leonard Cohen*, 53, 54, 56, 72; "Suzanne," 55, 56

Colaiuta, Vinnie, 354

Cold War, end of, 333–35

Cole, Nat King, 360

Coleman, Lisa, 291, 331

Coleman, Ornette, 269

Collins, Judy, 30, 47–50, 53, 55, 74, 75, 78; "Both Sides, Now" cover, 47–50, 64, 90, 94, 101, 105, 361; *In My Life*,

Collins, Judy (*cont.*)
55; Mitchell and, 47–50, 52–53, 96, 115; *Wildflowers*, 47, 48, 55
Collins, Phil, 323, 326, 327, 328
color, 8, 40–41, 57, 58, 94, 144
Coltrane, John, xiii, 81, 142, 172, 222, 254, 281
Columbia Records, 72, 249
"Come in from the Cold," 352
comics, 117–18
Considine, Tom, 130
"Conversation," 115–16
"Cool Water," 331
Corea, Chick, 375
Costello, Elvis, 196, 300, 332
Cotton, Elizabeth, 30
"Court and Spark," 176–78
Court and Spark, 135, 138, 171–89, 197, 207, 220, 223, 279, 280, 290, 360; influence on other musicians, 187–89; L.A. Express and, 172–76, 183, 184; reviews, 176; sales, 178–79, 193, 284; songs, 176–89; success of, 178–79, 187–89, 193–95, 210, 284; tour, 190–93; vocal style, 176, 177. *See also specific songs*
covers, album, 86–87, 336, 366; *Blue*, 130; *Clouds*, 86–87; *Don Juan's Reckless Daughter*, 256–58; *For the Roses*, 160, 228; *Hejira*, 228–29; *The Hissing of Summer Lawns*, 87; *Ladies of the Canyon*, 113, 117; *Mingus*, 87; *Wild Things Run Fast*, 292. *See also specific albums*
cowbell, 114
"Coyote," 204, 206, 207, 210, 220, 228, 229, 230, 232, 245, 298
"Crazy Cries of Love, The," 352
Cream, 222
Crete, 122, 132

Crosby, David, 43, 50, 68–73, 96–97, 104–105, 117, 123–24, 188, 333, 338; "Almost Cut My Hair," 99–100; drug use, 148; Mitchell and, 68–73, 92, 97–98, 111, 124–25, 144, 183, 360; as *Song to a Seagull* producer, 71–81, 97; Woodstock and, 107–12
Crosby, Stills & Nash, 104–105, 124, 133, 134, 158, 246; "Our House," 112–13, 124; "You Don't Have to Cry," 104
Crosby, Stills, Nash & Young, 107, 117; Woodstock and, 107–12; "Woodstock" cover, 111, 244
Crouse, Timothy, 41, 143
Crow, Sheryl, 178
Crowe, Cameron, 112, 132, 280, 331
Crusaders, 175
cumbia, 264
Curie, Marie, 10–11, 55, 120

D

"Dancin' Clown," 331
Danko, Rick, 222, 246
Darin, Bobby, 17
David Letterman, 343
Davis, Angela, 157
Davis, Miles, xiii, 24–25, 81, 84, 86, 98, 155, 172–74, 192, 199, 234, 253, 254, 263, 264, 275, 286, 292, 324, 344, 348, 349, 351; *Bitches Brew*, 173, 174, 259; drug use, 259–60; *Kind of Blue*, 111, 249; *The Man with the Horn*, 260; Mitchell and, 259–60, 275; "Nefertiti," 269; *Seven Steps to Heaven*, 192
Davis, Richard, 142

Davis, Stephen, *Hammer of the Gods: The Led Zeppelin Saga*, 188

"Dawntreader, The," 96–97

Dawson, Pic, 117

Day, Doris, 362

"Day After Day," 31–32, 39

Debussy, Claude, xiii, 100, 177, 180, 199, 249; "Clair de Lune," 177

Dee, Sandra, 17

De Niro, Robert, 200

Depression, Calgary, 30–31

Details magazine, 283

Detroit, 36–38, 342, 365; 1960s music scene, 37–39

Diamond, Neil, 244, 294

Dickens, Charles, 159

Dickinson, Emily, 130

Dickson, Sharolyn, 14–15

Diddley, Bo, 95, 115

Diltz, Henry, 117

Diner (movie), 296

"Dr. Junk, the Dentist Man," 96, 98

Dog Eat Dog, xv, 289, 307–18, 322, 324, 331, 337, 351, 354, 359; production, 308–15; reviews, 316–17; songs, 310–15. *See also specific songs*

Dolby, Thomas, 308–15, 328, 333–34; as *Dog Eat Dog* producer, 308–15; "She Blinded Me with Science," 308

Dolphy, Eric, 263

"Don Juan's Reckless Daughter," 206, 210, 223, 229, 255, 298

Don Juan's Reckless Daughter, 187, 253–62, 265, 274, 281, 299, 301, 309; cover art and controversy, 256–58; reviews, 257, 261–62, 298; sales, 261; songs, 253–56; success of, 261–62. *See also specific songs*

Donlon, Denise, 345

Donovan, 65; "Season of the Witch," 76

"Don't Interrupt the Sorrow," 196, 205, 207, 255

Dont Look Back (documentary), 80, 196

Doors, 91, 92, 117, 324

Dora (housekeeper), 305–306

Douglas, Dave, 98; *Moving Portrait*, 98; "Roses Blue" cover, 98

Down Beat, 233, 280

"Down to You," 184–86, 220, 343; performance of, 185–86

"Dreamland," 255–56

drugs, 70, 71, 123, 128–29, 131, 142, 144, 148, 157, 201, 203, 208, 245–46; Mitchell's use of, 131, 204, 208, 218–24, 228, 229, 239–42, 303, 316

drums, 114, 115, 172, 259, 315; Blade on, 348–53; on *Blue*, 134, 135, 136; on *Court and Spark*, 174; Guerin on, 172–74, 223; on *Ladies of the Canyon*, 114–15

Dublin, 345

Du Bois, W.E.B., 277, 278

dulcimer, 133–34, 304; on *Blue*, 133–34, 135, 147

Duran Duran, 291

Dylan, Bob, xiv, 4, 47, 52, 64, 66, 67, 74, 80, 86–88, 93, 96, 99, 103, 119, 149, 157, 162, 180, 182, 196, 236, 244, 246, 294, 309, 324, 325, 335, 336, 369; Baez and, 80, 200–205; *Blonde on Blonde*, 199, 200; *Blood on the Tracks*, xiv, 142, 199, 200–201; "Blowin' in the Wind," 72, 99–100; bootlegs, 200–201; *Bringing It All Back Home*, 74, 199; "Chimes of Freedom," 369; debut album of, 72; *Desire*, xiv, 172, 201; "Don't Think Twice, It's All Right," 96; *The Freewheelin' Bob Dylan*, 72; *Gates of Eden*, 80; "A Hard Rain's A-Gonna

Dylan, Bob (*cont.*)
Fall," 72, 76; *Highway 61 Revisited*, 199; "Hurricane," 199; "It Ain't Me, Babe," 96; "It's All Over Now, Baby Blue," 42; "It's Alright, Ma (I'm Only Bleeding)," 80; "Like a Rolling Stone," 46–47, 248; "Masters of War," 72, 99; "Mr. Tambourine Man," xiv, 36, 37, 68, 127–28; Mitchell and, 187–88, 198–212, 251, 353–55; *Modern Times*, xiv; 1965 UK tour, 80; *Oh Mercy*, 309, 328; "One More Cup of Coffee," 251; as a painter, 251; "Positively 4th Street," xiv, 46, 96; religious conversion, 202; Rolling Thunder Revue tour, 63, 198–209, 210, 243; "Sara," 199; as songwriter, 46–47, 97, 100, 142, 187, 199; *Street Legal*, 217; "Tangled Up in Blue," 142, 199; *Time Out of Mind*, 328, 353
Dylan, Sara, 199, 202, 251

E

Eagles, 211, 258
Earhart, Amelia, 220, 239
Eastwood, Kyle, *From Here to There*, 359
Edison, Harry, "Centerpiece," 212
"Edith and the Kingpin," 197
Elder, Boyd, 211
Elektra Records, 48, 50, 283
Eliot, T. S., 55, 265; *Four Quartets*, 265–68; *The Waste Land*, 270
Ellington, Duke, xiii, 16, 25, 86, 100, 172, 199, 263, 264
Elliot, Cass, 69, 78, 117, 136
Elliott, Ramblin' Jack, 199
Ellis, Ray, 359

Eno, Brian, 72
environmentalism, 114, 119–20, 127, 333, 368
Erskine, Peter, 274, 275
Ertegun, Ahmet, 182
Ervin, Booker, 269, 270
"Ethiopia," 312–13, 346, 356
Evans, Gil, 363
Everly Brothers, 9
Evers, Medgar, 88

F

"Fairlight Marimba," 328
Farm Aid, 309, 343
Farrow, Mia, 180
Fassbinder, Rainer Werner, 339–41
Fayetteville, North Carolina, 94–95, 332
Feather, Leonard, 280
Feldman, Victor, 173, 192, 281, 292, 301
Feliciano, José, 195
feminism, 117, 118, 158, 356
Fender Rhodes, 274
Fez, New York City, 350–51
"Fiddle and the Drum, The," 100–101, 371
Fiddle and the Drum, The (ballet), xii, 101, 370–73
Fiedler, Bernie, 66–67
First Nation, 150
"Fishbowl, The," 16–17
Fitzgerald, Ella, 52, 174
Fitzgerald, F. Scott, *The Great Gatsby*, 231
Flanagan, Bill, 103
folk music, 49, 52, 66, 172, 174; decline of, 66, 94, 179; Mitchell's beginnings in, 30–43, 66–68, 85, 93, 114; Newport Festival, 52–54. *See also specific musicians*

Ford, Gayle, 214–16, 225, 227, 229

Ford, Robben, 14, 175, 191–92, 214, 221, 225, 229, 303

"For Free," 114, 190

"For the Roses," 153, 156–57, 158–59, 197, 365

For the Roses, 27, 152, 153, 156–64, 167, 171, 173, 174, 194, 359; cover art, 160, 228; reviews, 161, 163; sales, 163; songs, 153–55, 156–64; vocal quality, 158, 161. *See also specific songs*

Fort Macleod, Alberta, 3

Foulk, Ron and Ray, 324

Frampton, Peter, 129, 193

Freed, Donald, 337, 338, 339, 352, 355

"Free Man in Paris," 4, 181–82

Freud, Sigmund, 152, 166, 196, 204, 219

Frey, Glenn, 261

Friedman, Kinky, 209, 211

"Furry Sings the Blues," 90, 212, 229, 230, 231–32, 246, 258, 330

G

Gabriel, Peter, 294, 321–22, 326–29; "Biko," 323; "In Your Eyes," 331; "Mercy Street," 322; Mitchell and, 326–32; "Sledgehammer," 332; *So*, 321, 322, 328, 332

Gaga, Lady, 188

"Gallery, The," 98

Gandalf, 37–38, 56

Garbarini, Vic, 271–72

Garland, Judy, 263

Gaslight, New York City, 38–39

Gaslight South, Miami, 97

Gaye, Marvin, 314, 360; "Trouble Man," 314, 359, 364; "What's Going On," 142, 157

Geffen, David, 65, 70, 102, 107, 152, 181–82; *Free Man in Paris* and, 181–82; Mitchell and, 70, 102, 157, 163–64, 166, 171, 181–82, 187, 191, 193, 195, 267, 280, 282–84, 317, 331

Geffen Records, 283–84, 300

Genesis, 326, 327

Gershwin, George, 360

Gershwin, Ira, 360

Getz, Stan, 173, 174, 272

Gibb, Kilauren, 33, 334, 347, 355–59; birth of, 35; given up for adoption by Mitchell, 35–37, 40–41, 43, 132, 154, 158, 194, 284, 301–302, 313, 346–47, 352; as "Little Green," 40–41, 143, 346–47, 356; relationship with Mitchell, 352, 355–59; secret messages in Mitchell's songs for, 40–41, 143, 301–302, 346–47, 352, 356

Gibbs, Michael, 249–50

Gilbert, Ronnie, 49

Gillespie, Dizzy, 52, 174, 249, 268, 362

Gilliatt, Penelope, 296

Ginsberg, Allen, 74, 200, 201, 226, 267

Girls (TV show), 4

"God Must Be a Boogie Man," 276–77

Goffin, Gerry, 58, 148

"Goodbye Pork Pie Hat," 270–72, 273

"Good Friends," xv, 310

Gordon, Dexter, 269

Gorson, Arthur, 65

Gould, Glenn, 249

Grammy Awards, 3, 49, 220, 294, 353, 366, 367, 368; for *Clouds*, 93; for Collins's "Both Sides, Now," 49–50, 64, 101; for *Turbulent Indigo*, 336, 337

Grand-Maître, Jean, xii, 100, 370–73

Grateful Dead, 102

Gray, Wardell, "Twisted," 186

Great Album theory, 141–42

Great Britain, 28, 89, 319, 321, 326, 328–29

Greece, 122, 130, 132, 133, 146

Green, Debbie, 237

Green Flag Song, 370

Greenpeace, 127, 322

Grogan, Emmett, 215–17

Grossman, Albert, 64–65

Grotjahn, Martin, 166, 168–70

Guardian, The, 116

Guerin, John, 172–76, 181, 204, 239, 252, 309, 338, 349, 351; Mitchell and, 172–76, 191, 193, 195, 196, 200, 210–16, 219, 223, 234, 235, 267, 286–88, 292, 299

guitar, 24, 30, 33, 81, 235, 289, 337; "Cotton Picking," 30; Hendrix and, 81; Mitchell's style of, 39–43, 59, 133, 135, 165, 172, 175–76, 191–92, 235, 247, 266, 303, 309, 312–13, 353–54; tunings, xvi, 39, 49, 50–51, 59, 86, 147, 172, 191–92, 237, 353

Guthrie, Woody, 119

H

Hackman, Don, 161

Hadi, Shafi, 279, 280

Haggard, Merle, 71

Half Beat, Toronto, 33, 66

Hamill, Peter, 321

Hamilton, George, IV, 39

Hammond, John, 53, 72, 182

Hancock, Herbie, 144, 173, 221, 254, 274, 363, 365; *Gershwin's World*, 359–60; Mitchell and, 274–76, 329–30, 359–60, 375; *River: The Joni Letters*, 276, 329, 367

Handy, John, 269, 270

Handy, W. C., 231

Hanisch, Carol, "The Personal Is Political," 162–63

Hannah, Daryl, 343

"Harlem in Havana," 352

harmonica, 246

harmony, 4, 46, 50, 58, 101, 104, 128, 143, 162, 172, 175, 192, 208, 230, 264, 301; Crosby, Stills & Nash, 104–105, 246; *Last Waltz* concert, 246

Harris, Emmylou, 245

Harrison, George, 309

Harrison, Noel, 59

"Harry's House," 195–96, 212

Hawaii, 118–20

Hawkins, Coleman, 272

Headhunters, 274

Heckman, Don, 120, 139

"Hejira," 230, 234–35, 281, 330

Hejira, xv, 32, 217, 219–24, 228–42, 245, 279, 281, 299, 301, 309, 329, 344, 348, 351; cover art, 228–29; reviews, 219, 298; songs, 229–42. *See also specific songs*

Helm, Levon, 244, 245

"Help Me," 3, 178–79, 298; as Top 10 single, 178

Hemingway, Ernest, 295

Hendricks, Jon, 96, 186, 212, 270

Hendrix, Jimi, 71, 72, 81–84, 110, 136, 173, 223, 245; *Are You Experienced*, 72; Mitchell and, 81–84; songs of, 81

Henley, Don, 294, 331

Hilburn, Robert, 102

"Hissing of Summer Lawns, The," 195, 255

Hissing of Summer Lawns, The, 87, 92,
    194–98, 210–17, 229, 234, 255, 280,
    291, 300–301, 309; cover art, 87;
    reviews, 218–19, 298; sales, 210;
    songs, 195–98; tour, 198, 202,
    210–17, 219, 220, 221, 225, 255, 301.
    See also specific songs
Hit Parade, The, 9
Hodges, Johnny, 16, 172, 253
Holiday, Billie, 52, 86, 173, 174, 199,
    273, 359–61; *Lady in Satin,* 359, 360
Holland, Milt, 114, 115
Hollies, 104
Holly, Buddy, 245
Hollywood, 104, 129; collapse of studio
    system, 166; of early-mid 1970s,
    157–58, 165–70; Hays production
    code, 166; parties, 168, 180, 200–
    201, 209
Horn, Trevor, 180
Hornby, Nick, *High Fidelity,* 184
Hubbard, Freddie, 275, 294
Hudgins, Johnny, 256
Hudson, Garth, 244, 245, 334
Hughes, Langston, 267
Hynde, Chrissie, 350–51

I

Ian, Janis, 49
Ian and Sylvia, 49
Idol, Billy, 331
"I Don't Know Where I Stand," 96
"I Had a King," 41–43, 188
"Impossible Dreamer," 290
Internet, 347
Intimate and Interactive (TV show), 345
Iraq War, 368
Ireland, 345–46

Isham, Mark, 352, 364
Isle of Wight festival, 324–25, 327
"I Think I Understand," 94, 99–100
"It Was a Very Good Year," 360–61

J

Jackson, Janet, 137, 332; "Got 'til It's
    Gone," 137
Jackson, Michael, 291; *Thriller,* 149, 292
James, Harry, 25
Japan, 302
jazz, xiii, 4, 52, 81, 96, 99, 111, 142,
    154, 172–75, 186, 192, 221–22, 250,
    253–54, 256, 259–60, 263–64, 309,
    330, 348–50, 360–65; fusion,
    253–60, 264, 275; Mingus–Mitchell
    collaboration, 262–78; rock music
    crossover, 172–76, 192, 280, 308–309;
    West Coast, 173. *See also specific
    musicians*
Jazz Singer, The (movie), 256
Jefferson Airplane, 102, 109, 110
"Jericho," 187, 255
Jesus Jones, "Right Here, Right Now,"
    334–35
John, Elton, 283
Johnny Cash Show, The, 343
Johnson, Sy, 268
Jolson, Al, 256
Jones, John Paul, 222
Jones, Philly Joe, 348
Jones, Quincy, 129, 363
Jones, Rickie Lee, 271
Joplin, Janis, 65, 74, 245
Joseph, Nathan, 184, 243, 310, 325–26
Judaism, 147
"Judgement of the Moon and Stars,"
    153–55, 365

Jung, Carl, 152, 196
"Jungle Line, The," 288, 308
"Just Like This Train," 172, 184

K

Kael, Pauline, 296
Kart, Larry, 280
Katché, Manu, 328, 331
Kay, Connie, 142
Keaton, Diane, 168
Kellaway, Roger, 192, 281
Kennedy, John F., 68, 290
Kennedy, Robert F., 100, 117, 290
Kent State massacre, 89
Kerouac, Jack, 201
Khan, Chaka, 255–56; Mitchell and, 255–56, 258
King, Carole, 58, 66, 129, 148, 158, 200; "I Feel the Earth Move," 130; Mitchell and, 168, 170; *A Natural Woman*, 129; *Tapestry*, 129, 130
King, Martin Luther, Jr., 87, 88, 117, 290
King, Rodney, 342
Kingston Trio, 24
Kinks, 73; *The Kinks Are the Village Green Preservation Society*, 73, 142
Kipling, Rudyard, 14; "If," xiii; *Kim*, 14
Kirk, Rahsaan Roland, 270
Klein, Larry, 92, 167, 292–96, 360, 363, 374–75; on bass, 292–94, 321–22, 351, 354, 355; divorce from Mitchell, 337–38, 355; marriage to Mitchell, 293–98, 307–308, 311, 318–21, 328–29, 337, 375; as Mitchell's producer and musical director, 303, 311–12, 315, 319

Klonitsky, Marsha, 147
Knepper, Jimmy, 263, 269, 270
Kooper, Al, 46–47, 200; Mitchell and, 46–48
Kot, Greg, 354
Kratzmann, Arthur, 14–15, 31, 360
Kristofferson, Kris, 61, 131, 141
Kronos Quartet, 366
Kunkel, Leah, 136
Kunkel, Russ, 134, 135, 164, 216, 349; Mitchell and, 135–36, 174
Kusturica, Emir, xiv

L

Lacy, Susan, 15, 352
"Ladies' Man," xvi, 292
"Ladies of the Canyon," 116–18
Ladies of the Canyon, 113, 114–21, 122, 262, 360; cover art, 113, 117; reviews, 116, 120–21; sales, 114, 115; songs, 114–21, 122; success of, 114. *See also specific songs*
L.A. Express, 172–76, 183, 210, 216, 219, 280, 300, 309; Mitchell and, 172–76, 183, 184, 191–93, 210, 216, 219
"Lakota," 329, 331
Lambert, Dave, 96, 186
Lambert, Hendricks, and Ross, 96, 186, 212; *Sing a Song of Basie*, 96
Landau, Jon, 176
Landau, Michael, 303
Langhorne, Bruce, 37
Lanois, Daniel, 328, 349
"Last Time I Saw Richard, The," 133, 134
Last Waltz concert, 90, 217, 220, 244–46; film, 90, 232, 244, 245
Lauper, Cyndi, 333, 334

Laurel Canyon, 59, 70; Mitchell in, 70, 73, 94, 102–107, 112–13, 116–18, 136, 146, 279

Lawrence, D. H., 267

"Lead Balloon," 352

Lear, Norman, 350

Led Zeppelin, 188, 222, 329; "Going to California," 188

Lee, Peggy, "Fever," 174

Leisz, Greg, 354

Lennon, John, 28, 99, 103, 169–70, 195, 241, 283; "Give Peace a Chance," 99; murder of, 290

Lennox, Annie, 159

Leno, Jay, 343, 351

Lerner, Murray, 324

Let's Sing Out (TV show), 39–40

"Let the Wind Carry Me," 26

Leventhal, Harold, 49

Levinson, Barry, 296

Levitin, Daniel, 375

Lewis, Furry, 231–32

Lewy, Henry, 77, 91–92, 130, 196, 207, 247, 273, 311, 326, 328; as Mitchell's producer, 91–92, 247–50, 288, 308, 315

Library of Congress, 267; Charles Mingus Collection, 267; National Recording Registry, 161

Libya, 332

Lightfoot, Gordon, 67, 158

"Little Green," 40–41, 143, 301, 346–47, 356, 367

"Live Aid," 313

Lloyd Webber, Andrew, *Jesus Christ Superstar*, 191

Logie, Anne, 25

London, 89, 93, 167, 185–86

London Symphony Orchestra, 185–86, 361, 363, 365

Lookofsky, Harry, 250

Lookout Mountain house, 102–107, 112–13, 116–18, 146, 279

Lorca, Federico García, 54, 62

Los Angeles, 69, 102–103, 127, 275, 342, 344, 364; of early-mid 1970s, 157–58, 165–76, 190; Laurel Canyon scene, 102–13, 116–18, 136; Mitchell moves to, 70, 73, 102–103; music scene, 69, 157–58, 172–76; parties, 168, 180, 200–201, 209; studio musicians, 173–76

Los Angeles Times, 158, 280, 366

"Love," 292, 296–98, 299

Love, Courtney, 65

Love Has Many Faces, 299

"Love or Money," 187

"Love Puts on a New Face," 351

Lowell, Robert, 128

LSD, 71, 131, 142

Lubbock, Jeremy, 339

"Lucky Girl," 309, 314–15

Luell, David, 210

Luminato Festival, 231, 358

Lydon, Susan Gordon, 105

Lynn, Loretta, "Coal Miner's Daughter," 158

M

Maclean's, 179

MacMath, Brad, 31, 32

Madison Square Garden, 198, 208–209

Madonna, 159, 279, 289, 316, 356

"Magdalene Laundries, The," 345–46

Maidstone, Saskatchewan, 12, 32, 235

Major, Phyllis, 236–38, 344

Malibu, 70, 209, 245, 291

Mama Cass. *See* Elliot, Cass

Mamas and the Papas, 91

Mandolin Brothers, 235

"Man from Mars," 352

Mann, Aimee, "Nothing Is Good Enough," 182

"Man to Man," 292

Manuel, Richard, 246

"Marcie," 57–58, 62

Mariposa Folk Festival, 34

Marom, Malka, 34, 37, 179, 225

Marsalis, Branford, 308

Marsalis, Wynton, 348

Martin, George, 91, 172

Maslin, Janet, 257

Matisse, Henri, 16

Mays, Lyle, 281

McBride, Christian, 349

McCabe & Mrs. Miller (movie), 183

McCarthyism, 290

McCartney, Paul, 103, 141, 309, 316

McDonald, Dolette, 330

McDonald, Michael, 310

McFerrin, Bobby, 294, 330; "Don't Worry, Be Happy," 330

McGuinn, Roger, 68, 199

McKitrick, Frankie, 13

McLean Hospital, Belmont, Massachusetts, 128

Mehldau, Brad, 98, 349; "Roses Blue" cover, 98–99

Meisel, Perry, 219

melody, 4, 39, 46, 105–106, 162, 206, 234; "Both Sides, Now," 45–46; Mingus and, 268

Melody Maker, 84, 280, 283

Melvoin, Wendy, 291–92, 331

Memphis, 231–32

Menand, Louis, 279, 280

Mendes, Sergio, 129

Mendoza, Vince, 359–66

Mercer, Mabel, 361, 365

Merchant, Natalie, 350, 366

Metheny, Pat, 175, 281–82; *Bright Size Life*, 281; Mitchell and, 281–82, 303

Method acting, 141, 340

Miami, 68–70, 71, 98

"Michael from Mountains," 48, 69, 90

Midnight Special (TV show), 151

Miles of Aisles, 190–93, 255; album, 187, 190, 193; tour, 175, 185–86, 187, 190–93, 214; venues, 190–91, 192

Mingus, 87, 267–78, 280–83, 299, 309, 330, 339; on charts, 273, 282, 307; cover art, 87; reviews, 280, 281, 298; songs, 270–72, 276–77; tempos, 274–75; tour, 280–82; weak sales, 282. *See also specific songs*

Mingus, Charles, 142, 221, 250, 262–78, 280, 282, 350; ALS of, 262–69, 276; *Beneath the Underdog*, 273, 277; catalogue of, 264; death of, 276; *Mingus Ah Um*, 264, 269–70; Mitchell collaboration, 262–78, 359; "Self-Portrait in Three Colors," 269–70

Mingus, Sue Graham, 263, 265, 267

Mingus Workshop, 264

Minimalism, 29

Minneapolis, 291

Minnelli, Liza, 129

Mintz, Elliot, 355

Misfits, The (movie), 170

"Mr. Blue," 76

Mitchell, Chuck, 36–43, 54, 68, 90, 167, 357; divorce from Joni, 42–43; marriage and duo with Joni, 36–43, 44, 113, 132, 248, 347

Mitchell, Joni, xi–xvi; aging of, 158, 220, 288–89, 304–309, 335, 361, 366; Alias and, 243, 259–60, 270–71, 281,

284–88; at Amnesty International concert, 322–26, 330; at art school, 28–30; on Asylum, 152, 163–64, 187; Baez and, 38–39, 200, 203–209, 257, 346; as bandleader, 213–17, 282; Beatty and, 168–69, 170, 183; beauty of, xv, 54, 56–57, 59, 61, 87, 103–104, 110, 160, 198, 303; Bel-Air home, 168, 193, 200–201, 221, 243, 247, 300, 358, 374; birth of, 3–4; birth of her daughter, 35; bitterness and anger of, 15, 50, 98, 167, 236–38, 294, 305–18, 337; black culture and, 207, 209, 231, 256–60, 265, 271–72, 277–78, 284–85, 296, 333, 359; Blade and, 348–54; brain aneurysm of, 374–76; breakup with Nash, 122–26; in British Columbia, 150–60, 163, 170, 240, 243, 345, 368; Jackson Browne and, 167–68, 169, 171, 236–38, 343–45; Buddhism and, 225–28, 236, 241–42, 293, 338–39; Carnegie Hall debut, 106–107, 325; on Cavett show, 107–11; childhood in Canada, 3–18, 19–27, 91, 140–41, 235–36, 341–42, 358, 372; as cigarette smoker, xii, 158, 208, 214, 289, 295–96, 304–306, 318, 374, 375; clothes of, 23, 25, 40, 53, 57, 107, 118, 160, 215, 219, 228–29, 288, 345, 372, 375; Cohen and, 53–63, 97–98, 143, 145, 147–48, 151, 167, 199, 266, 338–39; Judy Collins and, 47–50, 52–53, 97, 115; Crosby and, 68–73, 92, 97–98, 111, 124–25, 144, 183, 360; daughter given up for adoption by, 35, 36, 37, 40–41, 43, 132, 154, 158, 194, 284, 301–302, 313, 346–47, 352; Miles Davis and, 259–60, 275; divorce from Klein, 337–38, 355;

divorce from Mitchell, 42–43; domesticity of, 37, 65, 103–107, 112–13, 117–18, 124, 151; domestic violence and, 286–88, 305–306, 343–44; dreams of, 6–7, 248; drug use by, 131, 204, 208, 218–24, 228, 229, 239–42, 303, 316; Dylan and, 187–88, 198–212, 251, 353–55; early influences on, 13–14, 24–25, 30–33, 57–58, 199; early writing of, 14–17; education of, 9–10, 13–16, 24, 28–30, 240; emotional vulnerability of *Blue* sessions, 131–44, 148–49; as exile, 89; fans of, 136, 163, 179, 187–89, 219–20, 280, 284, 291, 326, 351, 354; first album of, 14, 70–81; folksinger beginnings of, 30–43, 66–68, 85, 93, 114; Gabriel and, 326–32; Geffen and, 70, 102, 157, 163–64, 166, 171, 181–82, 187, 191, 193, 195, 267, 280, 282–84, 317, 331; on Geffen Records, 283–84, 300; Grammys of, 93, 336, 337, 368; as a grandmother, 355, 357–59, 368; Guerin and, 172–76, 191, 193, 195, 196, 200, 210–16, 219, 223, 234, 235, 267, 286–88, 292, 299; guitar style, 39–43, 59, 133, 135, 165, 172, 175–76, 191–92, 235, 247, 266, 303, 309, 312–13, 353–54; Hancock and, 274–76, 329–30, 359–60, 375; hatred for music business, 159, 182, 259, 283, 348, 352, 366; Hendrix and, 81–84; independence of, 22, 32, 40, 43, 97, 184, 277, 293, 305, 315; influence on other musicians of, 140–49, 187–89, 199–201, 291; insomnia of, 304–306, 367; at Isle of Wight, 324–25, 327; jazz-pop and, 172–76, 192, 280, 309; L.A. Express and, 172–76, 183, 184,

Mitchell, Joni (*cont.*)
191–93, 210, 216, 219; last public
performance and interview, 230–31;
Last Waltz concert, 244–46;
laughter of, 9, 77; in Laurel Canyon,
70, 73, 94, 102–107, 112–13,
116–18, 136, 146, 279; marriage to
Klein, 293–98, 307–308, 311,
318–21, 328–29, 337, 375; marriage
to Mitchell, 36–43, 44, 113, 132,
248, 347; Miles of Aisles tour,
190–93; Mingus collaboration,
262–78, 359; miscarriage of,
318–20; as a model, 29; money
troubles, 283–84, 288, 300,
304–306; Morgellons syndrome,
124, 366–67; move to Los Angeles,
70, 73, 102–103; move to New York,
38–43; Graham Nash and, 103–13,
114, 122–26, 127, 137, 143, 144,
146, 151, 298, 339; nature and,
17–18, 150–52, 159, 160; at
Newport, 49, 53, 54, 97; 1980s
and, 262, 283–84, 288–92, 298,
300–306, 308–11, 322–23, 333, 335;
originality of, 25–26, 39, 50, 59,
111, 160–62, 176; as a painter, 13,
16, 28–30, 60–61, 86–87, 112, 144,
243, 251, 336, 366; Pastorius and,
221–22, 229–34, 249, 250, 255,
280–81, 282; in performance,
39–43, 49–51, 67–68, 76, 89, 93, 95,
106–107, 127–28, 145, 156, 161, 167,
185–87, 190–93, 198–217, 229–32,
244–46, 258, 280–82, 302–304,
322–26, 333–35, 341, 345, 349–50,
353–55, 372–73; pimp character of,
257–58, 296; polio of, 19–22, 30,
154, 172, 219, 288, 307, 370, 372;
politics and, 84–85, 87–89, 99–101,

140, 192, 207–209, 256–58, 332–33,
342–46, 368; post-polio syndrome
of, 307, 353, 366–67; pregnancy of,
31–35, 346; Prince and, 179, 188,
291–92; as "Queen of El Lay," 144,
148, 185, 219; relationship with
daughter Kilauren, 352, 355–59;
relationship with her father, 6–8,
20, 25, 26, 34, 107, 125, 285, 347,
358; relationship with her mother,
5–8, 17, 20–26, 34, 38, 107, 125,
132, 141, 285, 286, 337, 347, 358; on
Reprise, 70–76, 90, 163; resilience
of, 21–22, 43, 148; as rising star,
49–50, 64–85; on Rolling Thunder
Revue tour, 198–209, 210, 220, 229;
sexism and, 73–74, 92–93, 120,
143–44, 148, 162–63, 182, 237, 309,
336; Shepard and, 204–207, 232;
shoplifting incident, 22, 25; as
skater, 228–29; as songwriter,
31–32, 39–51, 57–58, 64, 66, 69,
76–81, 93–101, 105–11, 114–21,
130–39, 143–49, 153–64, 176–89,
195–98, 206, 223, 229–42, 247–56,
292–302, 310–15, 328–32, 352,
355–59, 368–70, 375; success and
fame of, 138–49, 156–57, 160,
178–79, 187–95, 279–80, 300;
suppressed motherhood theme,
40–41, 143, 301–302, 312–13,
346–47, 356; tax problems, 288,
305; James Taylor and, 127–30, 138,
143, 144, 145, 147, 148, 159, 166–67,
169, 299, 325; travels of, 122,
132–33, 167, 220–21, 234–35,
240–42; as truth-teller, 54, 132–33,
137, 138, 161, 195, 236, 256, 258,
276, 323; virginity and, 31, 73; voice
of, 30–31, 50, 74, 79–80, 93, 111,

116, 121, 148, 154, 158, 161, 176, 177, 198, 208, 212, 220, 222, 288–89, 294, 304, 324, 327, 330, 335, 340, 352, 359–66; at *The Wall* concert, 333–35; Woodstock missed by, 107–11, 176; Neil Young and, 89–90, 245–46, 248. *See also specific songs and albums*

Mitchell, Mitch, 82–84; *Jimi Hendrix: Inside the Experience*, 82–83

Modern Jazz Quartet, 142

"Molly McGee," 5

Monk, Thelonious, 81

Monkees, 68

Monroe, Marilyn, 170

"Moon at the Window," 292, 301, 313, 351

Morgellons syndrome, 124, 366–67

"Morning Morgantown," 107, 114

Morricone, Ennio, 262

Morris, Leslie, 374

Morrison, Van, 244, 333; *Astral Weeks*, 142

Motown, 142

movies, 13, 90, 141, 165–70, 232, 240, 244, 245, 256, 296; collapse of studio system, 166; Fassbinder, 339–41; of 1970s, 165–70. *See also specific movies*

Mozart, Wolfgang Amadeus, 153

Ms. magazine, 158

MTV, 290–91, 292, 298, 308, 326, 332

MTV News, 108

Mulligan, Gerry, 173, 276

Murray, Albert, *Stomping the Blues*, 130

Myers, Vali, 76

"My Old Man," 127, 135, 143, 144, 298, 325

"My Secret Place," 327, 331–32

N

Nadien, David, 250

Nash, Graham, xii, 103–13, 196, 211, 338, 372; Mitchell and, 103–13, 114, 122–26, 127, 137, 143, 144, 146, 151, 298, 339; "Our House," 112–13, 124; *Wild Tales*, 123–24, 125

Nash, Larry, 192

Nassau Coliseum, 216

National Women's Liberation Conference, 117

Naylor, David, xvi

Nelson, Sean, 178

Nelson, Willie, 331

Neuwirth, Bob, 196

Newman, Randy, 71, 115

New Orleans, 329, 349

New Orleans Jazz and Heritage Festival, 349–50

Newport Folk Festival, 49, 52–53, 54, 97

Newport Jazz Festival, 52

Newsweek, 162; "The Girls—Letting Go," 162

Newton John, Olivia, "Let's Get Physical," 292

New Wave, 309

New York City, 38, 70, 73, 157, 173, 190, 205, 215, 243, 270, 325–26; Carnegie Hall debut, 106–107, 325; Chelsea, 93–94; Mitchell moves to, 38–43; 1960s music scene, 38–43, 57, 64, 93–94, 116, 202

New Yorker, The, 279

New York magazine, 188

New York Times, The, xii, xv, 17, 27, 107, 181, 356; on Mitchell, 105, 114, 120, 139, 149, 161, 231

Nicholson, Jack, 168, 169

Nico, 59–60, 72, 338
Nietzsche, Friedrich, xiii, 15, 27, 152, 160, 193, 267, 322–23, 372
"Night in the City," 73, 79–80, 114
Night Ride Home, 255, 337, 339–42; songs, 339–42. *See also specific songs*
Nirvana, 149
Nixon, Richard M., 88, 100, 117, 192, 290
"No Apologies," 352
Nonesuch, 366
No Nukes, 343
North Battleford, Saskatchewan, 12–14, 341
"Not to Blame," 238, 343–45
NPR, 137
"Number One," 330–31
Nyro, Laura, 87

O

Obama, Barack H., 119
O'Brien, Edna, 296
Ochs, Phil, 65, 129
O'Connor, Sinéad, 333, 334; "Nothing Compares 2 U," 291
O'Dell, Chris, 205–206
"Off Night Backstreet," 261
O'Hara, Frank, 267
Onassis, Jacqueline Kennedy, 296
"One Week Last Summer," 368
On the Waterfront (movie), 141
open tunings, xvi, 39, 86, 147, 172, 191–92, 237
Ornot, Martin, 34
Orr, Benjamin, 319, 321, 328, 331
Orton, Beth, 138

Ostin, Mo, 71
Ottawa, 81–84, 98

P

Page, Jimmy, 81, 188
Paglia, Camille, 356; *Break, Blow, Burn*, 356
Painting with Words and Music concert, 15
Panama, 123, 124–25
"Paprika Plains," 247–52, 253, 254, 265, 267, 268
Pareles, Jon, 231
Paris, 76, 146, 181–82, 215
Parker, Charlie, 81, 174, 222, 223, 253, 263, 264
Parks, Van Dyke, 71
Parrish, Maxfield, 103
Parsons, Gram, 65
Parton, Dolly, 362
Pastorius, Jaco, 142, 221–22, 225, 252, 253, 254, 261, 265, 268, 274, 275, 292, 293, 296, 303, 309; on bass, 221–22, 230, 232–34; drug use and bipolar disorder of, 282; on *Hejira*, 229–34, 240; Mitchell and, 221–22, 229–34, 249, 250, 255, 280–81, 282; "Portrait of Tracy," 221, 222, 229, 233, 234
Patchen, Kenneth, 267
Paxton, Tom, 49
Payne, Freda, "Bring the Boys Home," 100
Pennebaker, D. A., 80
People magazine, 131, 180, 207
"People's Parties," 180
Persuasions, 281
Peter and Gordon, 316
Peterson, Oscar, 52, 233

Petty, Tom, 331
Philadelphia, 41, 58, 87, 94, 115, 212,
    365
photography, 112, 130, 160, 228, 370
Piaf, Edith, 42, 86, 100, 195, 197, 199,
    339
piano, 59, 79, 81, 91, 95, 110, 111, 154,
    166, 247, 275, 289, 310–11, 337; on
    Blue, 130, 134; on *Ladies of the
    Canyon*, 114–15; in Lookout
    Mountain house, 103, 112–13; on
    "Paprika Plains," 247–51; Studio C,
    130, 134; on "Woodstock," 111
Picasso, Pablo, 16, 86, 144, 155, 260,
    344; *Blue Nude*, 144; *Guernica*, 264
Plant, Robert, 188, 329
Plath, Sylvia, 128
Police, 291, 300; *Synchronicity*, 308
polio, 19–22, 30, 154, 172, 219, 288,
    307, 370, 372; vaccine, 20
pop music, 142–43, 184, 223, 300, 323;
    jazz crossover, 172–76, 192, 280,
    308–309
Powell, Bud, 81
Presley, Elvis, 9, 119, 245
Prestige Records, 186
Pretenders, 350
Prince, 4, 179, 188, 196, 331; "The Ballad
    of Dorothy Parker," 179; "Emotional
    Pump," 291; Mitchell and, 179, 188,
    291–92
Pro Tools, 251
Protzman, Bob, 280
psychology, 152, 166, 168–70, 196;
    Martin Grotjahn and, 166–70
Public Enemy, 149
publishing royalties, 284
Puente, Tito, *Dance Mania*, 149
Pullen, Don, 263, 274
Pynchon, Thomas, *Gravity's Rainbow*, 88

Q

Q-Tip, 137
Quaid, Dennis, 209
Queen Mary, 251

R

Rachmaninoff, Sergei, 100, 199, 238,
    249; "Rhapsody on a Theme of
    Paganini," 13; "The Story of Three
    Loves," 238
racism, 82–83, 256–58, 342
radio, 3, 9, 25, 66, 244, 284, 290,
    325–36; AOR format, 298
Raditz, Cary, 132, 143, 146
Raeben, Norman, 251
Ramones, 149, 244
rap music, 137
Reagan, Ronald W., 290, 292, 301
Record World, 70
Redding, Otis, 245
Redman, Dewey, 348
Redman, Joshua, 348
Reds (movie), 168
Reed, Lou, 323, 338
Reeves, Dianne, 294
"Refuge of the Roads," 227, 230,
    241–42
Refuge of the Roads tour, 302–304,
    307, 353, 354
reggae, 100
Reginato, James, 366
Reilly, Peter, 138
Rembrandt van Rijn, 86
Renaldo and Clara (movie), 201
repeated trope, 45
Reprise, 70–76, 83; Mitchell on, 70–76,
    90, 163

Rhode Island School of Design (RISD), 28

rhythm and blues, 275

Richards, Keith, 28

Richie, Lionel, 331

Riddle, Nelson, 309

Righteous Brothers, "Unchained Melody," 302

Rilke, Rainer Maria, 54, 63

"River," 136–38, 143, 146

Rivkin, Josh, 48

Robbins, Trina, 116, 117–18

Roberts, Elliot, 65, 68, 87, 102, 105, 157, 294; as Mitchell's manager, 65–66, 71, 160, 163, 200, 214, 216, 267, 280, 283, 291, 304, 305, 308, 315–16

Robertson, Robbie, 67, 81, 181, 244–46, 294; *Last Waltz* concert, 244–46

Rock and Roll Hall of Fame, Mitchell inducted into, 3, 336, 338

rock music, 28, 154, 245; AOR, 298; jazz crossover, 172–76, 192, 280, 308, 309. *See also specific musicians*

Roland VG-8 digital guitar processor, 353–54

Rolling Stone, 22, 30, 41, 68, 74, 145, 146; on Mitchell, 74–76, 89, 106, 132, 143, 144, 148, 160, 163, 176, 185, 203, 209, 219, 257, 280, 326; "Queen of El Lay" label for Mitchell, 144, 148, 185, 219

Rolling Stones, 182, 222, 281, 309, 333

Rolling Thunder Revue tour, 63, 196, 198–209, 210, 220, 226, 229, 243, 255, 295

Rollins, Sonny, 81, 254, 269

Roney, Wallace, 363, 364

Ronstadt, Linda, 258, 309, 316–17

"Roses Blue," 98–99

Roshi, Joshu Sasaki, 338–39

Ross, Annie, 96, 186–87

Roth, Philip, 136

Rothchild, Paul, 91–93, 273, 308; as *Clouds* producer, 91–93

Royal Albert Hall, London, 186

royalties, 49, 284; publishing, 284; record sale, 284

Rufus, 255; "Something Good," 255

Rush, Tom, 37, 39, 49, 65, 120

S

Sainte-Marie, Buffy, 49, 65–66, 88–89, 120

Salk, Jonas, 20

Sam and Dave, 221

"Same Situation," 170, 177, 182–84

Sample, Joe, 174, 191

San Francisco, 117, 190, 244

Santa Barbara County Bowl, 282

Santamaria, Mongo, "Watermelon Man," 275

Saskatoon, Saskatchewan, 8, 14–18, 19–27, 28, 29, 65, 106, 125, 140, 151, 157, 206, 235, 248, 301, 341–42, 370

Save the Whales benefit, 217

saxophone, 253–54; Shorter on, 253–54

Say Anything (movie), 331

Scandinavia, 6

Scenes from a Marriage (movie), 240

Schoenberg, Arnold, 262, 361

Schubert, Franz, 4

Schumann, Robert, 154

Scorpions, 333

Scorsese, Martin, 90, 244, 245; *The Last Waltz* and, 90, 244–46

Scott, Tom, 173–76, 184, 191, 210, 309

Sechelt, 150

Second Fret, Philadelphia, 41, 115

Secunda, Tony, 350

Seeff, Norman, 228, 256

Seeger, Pete, 30, 49

"See You Sometime," 299

segregation, 83

Senatore, Daniele, 262, 265

sexism, 73–74, 92–93, 120, 143–44, 148, 162–63, 182, 237, 309, 336

"Sex Kills," 342–43, 344, 371

Sexton, Anne, 322

"Shadows and Light," 245, 281

Shadows and Light, 232, 282, 308; tour, 175, 259, 282

Shakespeare, William, 62; *Julius Caesar*, 62, 147; *Romeo and Juliet*, 98

Shangri-la studio, 245

Sheehy, Gail, *Passages*, 301

Shepard, Sam, 200, 201, 204–206, 207; Mitchell and, 204–207, 232; *Rolling Thunder Logbook*, 205; *True West*, 204–205

Sheppard, Bob, 364

"Shine," 369

Shine, xii, 357, 369, 370

"Shiny Toys," 315

Shipley, Mike, 308, 315, 321

Shorter, Wayne, 98, 142, 173, 174, 221, 252, 253–54, 261, 268, 274–75, 280, 281, 301, 309–10, 329, 349, 351, 360, 362, 363, 365, 375; Mitchell and, 253–54, 274, 275, 313, 315, 341; as songwriter, 254

Showtime, 258, 282, 329

Showtime Coast to Coast, 329–30

Sidran, Ben, 280

"Silky Veils of Ardor, The," 299

Sill, Judee, 181

Simon, Carly, 316, 350, 351; "You're So Vain" 165

Simon, Paul, 88, 103, 309; *Graceland*, 309; *Hearts and Bones*, 309; "You Can Call Me Al," 308

Simon, Tony, 7, 8, 21, 23, 70, 151, 358

Simon and Garfunkel, 71; *Bookends*, 73, 74, 142; "Sounds of Silence," 71; *Wednesday Morning, 3 A.M.*, 72

Simone, Nina, 259, 312

Sinatra, Frank, 149, 360, 362

Siquomb, 56, 65

"Sire of Sorrow (Job's Sad Song), The," xiv, 344–45, 352, 367

"Sisotowbell Lane," 342

ska, 300

Slick, Grace, 109

Sloman, Larry, "Ratso," 203

Sly and the Family Stone, 173, 291

Smith, Huston, 241

Smith, Patti, 205, 244; *Horses*, 205

"Snakes and Ladders," 329, 331

"Solid Love," 300

"Song for Sharon," 32, 60, 120, 223, 230, 235–39, 241, 248, 301, 303, 344

"Song to a Seagull," 89

Song to a Seagull, 14, 70–81, 90, 98, 188, 244, 338, 360; advertising, 73; David Crosby as producer of, 71–81, 97; remixing, 78; reviews, 74–76; sales, 87; songs, 72–73, 76–81; sound quality, 77–78. *See also specific songs*

Souther, J. D., 258, 261; Mitchell and, 258

Spector, Phil, 91

Spectrum, Philadelphia, 212

Spielberg, Steven, 280

Springsteen, Bruce, 176, 354; *Born to Run*, 354

Squamish, 150

Staples, Mavis, 245

"Stay in Touch," 352

Steely Dan: "Kid Charlemagne," 230; *The Royal Scam*, 230

Steinem, Gloria, 296

Stereo Review, 138

Stevens, Cat, 129

Stevens, Wallace, 80, 339

Stills, Stephen, 79, 104–105; guitar style, 133, 134; "Love the One You're With," 144; Woodstock and, 107, 109, 110

Sting, 300, 308, 309; *The Dream of the Blue Turtles*, 308

Stipe, Michael, 28

Stone, Ron, 113

Stoner, Rob, 172

St. Paul's Hospital, Saskatoon, 19–20

"Strange Boy, A," 221, 230, 299

Stravinsky, Igor, *The Rite of Spring*, 234

Streisand, Barbra, 96, 271

Studio City, 173–74

Sullivan, J.W.N., *Beethoven: His Spiritual Development*, 152

Summer of Love, 125–26

Sunset Boulevard, 103, 129

Sunset Sound, Los Angeles, 79, 129

Sunset Strip, 73

Sunshine Coast, 150–56, 158, 159, 160, 163, 170, 240, 243

"Sweet Bird," 197–98, 223

Sweet Honey in the Rock, 256

"Sweet Sucker Dance," 276

synthesizers, 245, 288, 289, 295, 308, 309, 310, 328, 351, 354

T

Talking Heads, 28, 244

"Talk to Me," 202–203, 210, 229, 234, 255

"Taming the Tiger," 159, 352

Taming the Tiger, 351–53; songs, 352; tour, 353–55; weak sales, 353. *See also specific songs*

Tate, Greg, 257

Taylor, James, 50, 115, 127–30, 157, 158, 258, 309, 316–17, 338; drug use of, 128–29, 143, 145, 148, 166; "Fire and Rain," 128; Mitchell and, 127–30, 138, 143–48, 159, 166–67, 169, 299, 325; *Mud Slide Slim and the Blue Horizon*, 128; "River" cover, 138; "You Can Close Your Eyes," 128

Taylor, Mick, 281

"Tea Leaf Prophecy, The," 6, 25, 329, 331

television, 39–40, 107, 151, 179, 288, 343, 345, 351, 370; *American Masters* documentary, 15, 352; Amnesty International Concert, 322–26; Canadian, 345; Mitchell on Cavett show, 107–10; Mitchell's early performances on, 39–40; MTV, 290–92, 298, 332; *Showtime Coast to Coast*, 329–30. *See also specific shows*

"That Song About the Midway," 48, 96–98

30th Street Studio, New York City, 249

"This Little Light of Mine," 369

Thoreau, Henry David, 151

"Three Great Stimulants, The," 322–24, 351

Tibetan Book of the Dead, The, 241

"Tin Angel," 91, 93, 94

TNT, Mitchell tribute concert on, 255–56

Todo Mondo (movie), 262

Tokyo, 302

Tolkien, J.R.R., 37, 94; *The Lord of the Rings*, 56, 99

Tork, Peter, 68, 70

Toronto, 33, 34–35, 65, 79, 190, 231; music scene, 33–35, 66–67, 73

Toronto Star, 116, 153
Townshend, Pete, 28, 81, 322
Travelogue, 227, 359, 365
Troubadour, Los Angeles, 127
"Trouble Child," xii, 170, 223
Trudeau, Gary, 350
Trudeau, Pierre, 100, 109, 284–85
Trungpa Rinpoche, Chögyam, 225–28, 233, 236, 240, 241–42, 263
tunings, guitar, xvi, 39, 49, 50–51, 59, 86, 147, 172, 191–92, 237, 353; open, xvi, 39, 86, 147, 172, 191–92, 237; standard, 39
Turbulent Indigo, 336–37, 342–45, 353; Grammy for, 336, 337; reviews, 337, 344; sales, 337; songs, 342–45. *See also specific songs*
"Twisted," 186–87, 360
"Two Grey Rooms," 255, 339–41

U

ukulele, 12, 24, 30, 33, 358
Ullmann, Liv, 296
"Underneath the Streetlights," 300
Universal Ampitheatre, 190–91
University of Maryland, College Park, 216–17, 220
Uren, John, 30, 31
"Urge for Going," 39, 50, 62, 73, 241, 357
U2, 88, 322, 323

V

Vadim, Roger, 237
van Gogh, Vincent, 86, 153, 155, 160, 195, 336
Vanguard Records, 64, 71

Van Ronk, Dave, 40, 48, 105
vaudeville, 256
Vaughan, Sarah, 330, 360
Velvet Underground, 72, 323, 338; *Velvet Underground & Nico*, 72
Ventura Boulevard, 112
Verve, 96
Vibe, 257
videos, music, 290–91, 332, 333
Vietnam War, 89, 95, 99–101, 117, 158, 332, 333, 368
Village Vanguard, New York City, 263
Village Voice, The, 205, 219
Vogue, 74, 146, 347
VSOP, 275

W

Waits, Tom, *Rain Dogs*, 308
Wallace, David Foster, 128
The Wall concert, 333–35
Wall Street Journal, The, 138
Walrath, Jack, 269
Warhol, Andy, 93, 117; *Chelsea Girls*, 93; Factory, 93
Washington Post, The, 138, 281, 284
Watergate scandal, 158, 192
Waters, Muddy, 244
Waters, Roger, 333, 334
Watts, Michael, 280
Way It Is, The (TV show), 140
"We Are the World," 313
Weather Report, 174, 253–54, 274, 280
Weavers, 49
Weill, Kurt, 38
Wein, George, 49, 52
Weinstock, Bob, 186
Weller, Sheila, *Girls Like Us*, 37
West, Rebecca, 296

Wexler, Hannah, 343

White Swan, Leicester, 93

Who, 324

Wickham, Andy, 71

Wild Things Run Fast, xvi, 288, 292–302, 307, 309, 330, 365; cover art, 292; reviews, 298; songs, 292, 296–302; tour, 302–304, 307; vocal quality, 295; weak sales, 308. *See also specific songs*

William Morris talent agency, 65

Williams, Bert, 256

Williams, Hank, 245

Williams, Robin, 200

Williams, Tennessee, *Sweet Bird of Youth*, 198

Williams, Tony, 348, 349, 363

Williamson, Sonny Boy, 244

"Willy," 114, 122

Wilson, Brian, 142

Wilson, Daniel J., *Polio*, 20–21

Wilson, Tom, 47

Winnipeg, Manitoba, 89

Winterland, San Francisco, 244

"Wizard of Is, The," 56

W magazine, 366

Wolfe, Tom, 300–301; *The Painted Word*, 29

"Wolf That Lives in Lindsey, The," 276–77, 287

"Woman of Heart and Mind," 161

Wonder, Stevie, 109, 142, 255; *Innervisions*, 142

Wood, Lorrie, 25, 29, 31, 35

Wood, Ron, 281

"Woodstock," 3, 108–109, 111, 114, 115, 119, 137, 244, 262, 290, 323, 324, 356; on *Both Sides Now*, 366; CSNY's cover of, 111, 244

Woodstock (film), 245

Woodstock festival, 88, 107–11, 176, 190, 201, 324

Woolf, Virginia, 232

"World Beat" sound, 331

World War II, 9, 265

Wyman, Bill, 222

Wynn, Ed, 354–55

Y

Yamaha CS80 synthesizer, 245

Yarrow, Peter, 49

Yogi Joe, 324–25

"You Dream Flat Tires," 331

Young, Lester, 173, 270–73

Young, Neil, 20, 79, 89–90, 94, 110, 115, 192, 221, 316–17; drug use of, 145, 246; "Helpless," 90, 245, 246; *Last Waltz* concert, 244, 245, 246; Mitchell and, 89–90, 245–46, 248; "Ohio," 89; polio of, 20; "Sugar Mountain," 90

"You Turn Me On, I'm a Radio," 90, 161, 164, 338

"You've Changed," 360–61

Yuppies, 301

Z

Zaentz, Celia, 263, 267

Zawinul, Joe, 280

Zen Buddhism, 54, 63, 99

Zevon, Warren, 294

Zorn, John, 366

A Note About the Author

David Yaffe was born in Dallas, Texas, in 1973. He is a professor of humanities at Syracuse University and a 2012 winner of the Roger Shattuck Prize in Criticism. His writings have appeared in many publications, including *The Nation*, *Harper's Magazine*, *The New York Times*, *Slate*, *New York*, *The Village Voice*, *The Daily Beast*, and *Bookforum*. He is the author of *Bob Dylan: Like a Complete Unknown* and *Fascinating Rhythm*.